T0354292

THE AMERICAN POET

Weedpatch Gazette
For 1999

Samuel D. G. Heath, Ph. D.

iUniverse, Inc.
New York Bloomington

The American Poet
Weedpatch Gazette For 1999

Copyright © 2009 Samuel D. G. Heath, Ph. D.

iUniverse books may be ordered through booksellers or by contacting:

iUniverse
1663 Liberty Drive
Bloomington, IN 47403
www.iuniverse.com
1-800-Authors (1-800-288-4677)

ISBN: 978-1-4401-4915-3 (pbk)
ISBN: 978-1-4401-4916-0 (ebk)

Printed in the United States of America

iUniverse rev. date: 12/22/2009

CONTENTS

CHAPTER ONE

The good news is that for 1998 the stamp displaying Sylvester and Tweety was the big seller at the post offices. There still has to be hope for America. And Jesse Ventura who ran on a Reform Party ticket as the new Governor of Minnesota! Take that, you professional politicians! Jesse beat out both the Republican and Democrat professionals. America needed that breath of fresh air on the political front. At least we can understand what Ventura says.

California, on the other hand, gets Democrat Gray Davis. As if we didn't have enough to deal with having two Democratic Senators, Dianne Feinstein and Barbara Boxer. Too bad the weather gets so cold in Minnesota, otherwise.... Oh, well.

Davis says he is going to make education in California the priority of his administration. God knows it needs to become the priority! But, as usual, unlike a real human being like Jesse of Minnesota, politician Davis was long on generalities and abysmally short (virtually non-existent) on specifics. Politics as usual.

It was recently so cold complaining didn't work; which reminds me of a recent discovery of mine that I passed on to the head of the Department of Geriatrics at Weedpatch University, Doctor Pudley B. Tredlop, Jr., M.D.

We know married men live much longer than unmarried men do. I have discovered the answer to the mystery of this. I know why. Married men have a wife to complain to; and about.

Of course this doesn't minimize two other most important factors: the eating habits of bachelors vs. married men, and ... oh, you know.

Speaking of the cold, I came home from Modesto where I spent Christmas with my children and grandchildren to find the pipe from my well to the pressure tank had ruptured from the ten-degree temperature. Not good. But then I thought of last February when I was flooded and laid in bed that first night trying to keep warm while the freezing, muddy water swirled around me and through the house, hoping it wouldn't rise any further and soak the bed, and that put things in perspective.

It also helped keep things in perspective that Christmas two years ago I was stranded in Tahoe for three weeks due to the snow and flooding we had in California back then. And so many are suffering from such violent weather in other parts of the country right now that I have little room to complain.

Besides, I'm better prepared if the creek rises this year. The kids gave me some winter pajamas for Christmas that are really the cat's ... Blew that line. No way is Furrina getting these pajamas. How about the cat's meow?

I do have to put in a plug for my daughter Karen and son-in-law John. I'm really proud of them. They own and operate Black Ives Rottweilers. Karen is a superb animal trainer and takes a lot of first place ribbons at dog shows. She recently placed two of her dogs on a plane to an influential lawyer in South Africa. Karen also supplies the dogs to Police agencies and just placed one with the Redwood City PD. If you are interested, the e-mail address is: blkives47@aol.com.

While the holidays showed some promise of being a week from hell with no end in sight when even your hair hurts, there were the good parts like visiting the kids and the new pajamas. And the kids also gave me some Starbucks coffee. Boy! That's real coffee! A few cups of that and even my hair stopped hurting. But I have a good well, when it's not frozen, and the pure, unpolluted water makes good coffee. At least it doesn't taste like it's been filtered through old socks and bicycle sprockets.

The good things of the holidays helped offset the drive north. I was in the middle lane of the freeway when four big rigs that were racing boxed me in. I was doing the speed limit of 70 and one rig nearly clipped my rear bumper as it passed me in the far-left lane doing at least 90. That was when my hair started hurting.

Speaking of hair- and headaches, how many of you have watched the Tylenol Theater on TV? Now why do I find it an incongruity that the manufacturers of a headache remedy are promoting a TV show? It reminded me of a commercial that says buying a RV should be fun. But that's the American Way. Going thousands of dollars into debt should be fun. I still find it an obscenity, however, when I see those commercials touting Casinos and losing money at slot machines as *All the fun and gaming excitement you can stand!* I've decided that the rest of the world has made up its mind about America on the basis of our commercials. God help America!

How many of you got the same laugh I did at the public service announcement about how to reduce stress during the holiday season? Make a to-do list, plan a realistic budget, and enjoy friends and family. Who makes up this stuff? They just can't be real Americans.

But, of course, the readers of TAP are a breed apart. You intelligent and special people never eat something called Mystery Burrito Surprise and you don't wear suede shoes or boots while driving if you have a leaking master cylinder.

Now with all due humility, self-effacing that I am and freely sacrificing the slightest iota of pride or ego, I admit I have been wrong once or twice in my life. You cannot reasonably ask or expect more of any normal man than for him to admit to more than that. With that needful caveat, I have to say that there is nothing wrong, strange, or immoral about my putting socks in my oven that are not thoroughly dry after laundering.

Say, speaking of socks in the oven (as though there was some connection) how about those octuplets. I know that at least a part of me is a born skeptic because about the same time I learned cootie catchers didn't really work and babies didn't come from the stork or K-Mart, it seemed odd to me as young as I was that people could blame both God and science for some really stupid choices. But, then, maybe I'd read just one too many MAD magazines.

When I first heard of the octuplets, I immediately thought of Clinton, especially since we are now learning about the paternity suit brought against him by a black mother who claims Clinton paid her for sex. As one tabloid put it, Clinton has a thirteen-year-old child by this woman that couldn't get past the janitor at the White House. There may be a Massa, mint julep, and plantation mind-set to the Prexy after all in spite of the fact that I've never seen him in a white suit or carrying a whip (but the cigar is there). One has to wonder what Clinton thought of the film Mandingo? At the time of my writing about this, Jesse Jackson has not responded to this latest news of Clinton's expression of compassion for black folks as well as twenty-one year old interns.

With all the dirt being found in his background, that (the whip) may be another facet of the President's sexual orientation yet to be brought to light- Clinton in leather? Who knows? Hillary? But if so, it would be something that might bring forth more True Confessions from Representatives and Senators. Hoo Boy! The mind reels! And Clinton as a deadbeat dad facing thirteen years back child support payments and alimony? Whew!

But in respect to the octuplets, you go to a doctor and tell him you want treatment for infertility; science to the rescue. So you litter like a pig or dog because of science gone haywire and then tell people it's because God wanted it that way? So what if the resulting babies cost the taxpayers millions and some of the babies die while many of the survivors will have medical complications the rest of their lives. It's a blessing! Praise God! Dumb and dumber. And I don't really think God needs this kind of credit or press. In cases like this I'm far more inclined to give the Devil credit.

I am far more inclined to give the Devil credit for many of the things some people say they believe, and say, are of God. Too many of these people remind me of those who still believe babies come from the stork or K-Mart. Or believe octuplets are a blessing of God.

But regarding my skepticism it never made sense, for example, that God would start over again with Noah when He must have known, according to

3

the doctrine of omniscience; that violence would just start all over again with Noah's son Ham.

On a more cheerful note and further good news is my encouraging a George Bush/Elizabeth Dole ticket for the presidential election of Y2K. Why is this good news? Because it proves how far I have come from my former position as a certified, card-carrying, redneck, fundamentalist conservative and chauvinist; and if there is hope for me, there is hope for anyone!

Still, as I shared with Governor Bush who, by the way, is the first Governor of Texas to be elected to back-to-back terms of office, I remain too conservative for liberals and too liberal for conservatives. But this gives both sides the right to vent their spleens in my direction. It's a relatively harmless hobby and I'm happy to give them something to do when they are not making life miserable for others.

Another plus to this is the hobby it gives me in answering some of my detractors, kind of like unraveling a can of nightcrawlers. It's quiet and absorbing work. There are worse occupations. Still, detractors should always keep in mind the old adage that if I'm wrong and won't admit it, that's my problem. If I'm right and you won't accept it, that's yours.

What did George Wallace and Eldridge Cleaver have in common? Both were born into, and raised in, racial hatred. What else did they share in common? They changed their minds. Wallace became more politically liberal and Cleaver more politically conservative toward the end of their lives. As human beings they eventually met on middle ground, and as with me, this gave the far left and right an excuse to abuse both men.

Henry Adams said: "Politics, as a practice, has always been the systematic organization of hatreds." Had it not been for the time frame, I think Adams would have included religion in the statement. But only a poet or a child would point to Santa as another direction for humanity:

SANTA

Two American figures of great stature and familiar to most, Benjamin Franklin and Samuel Clemens, speculated whether humanity was a species deserving of survival. Franklin's opinion was formed from having dealt with so much of the evil that men do. Clemens, while fully as aware as Franklin of such, was further motivated to such an opinion by the tragedies of life.

And few men experienced so much tragedy in their personal lives as Clemens did. Yet this great gift of humor existed in the man side by side with the on-going tragedies that dogged this greatest of writers.

It takes a sense of great personal tragedy, a cup of grief drunk deeply to its foulest dregs to say as Clemens did, that death is the only truly pure and unalloyed gift of God to humanity.

Like Clemens, I have never suffered, been allowed or permitted a lacuna, a hiatus in my life, nor have I ever discovered the waters of Lethe, that sea of forgetfulness, no matter how diligently sought in those times of the psychosis of grief.

People like Lincoln, Clemens, and me aren't gifted with the ability to find surcease from sorrow in a lachrymose melancholia. We may live with the resulting grief of tragedies, but our eyes remain dry and our hearts leaden within us once the object of joy and happiness is cruelly removed from our lives. But the duty and responsibility of living remains. And a real man or woman will do their duty regardless of tragedy just as Lincoln and Clemens.

Like these two greatly worthy men, I considered my children my angels. Our children are truly representative of what we believe of goodness and innocence. Yet to love a child is to expose yourself to all the potential pain and grief of the suffering and death, or even the betrayal of the one loved.

Two of the most endearing qualities of a child are trust and imagination. They will believe in magic, they thrill to stories of fairies and enchanted lands. Christmas, Santa Claus, the Easter Bunny, stories of birds and animals, these are the domain of childhood.

We don't forsake these things in adulthood. We continue to want our Merlins, Camelots and enchanted glades. As parents, we enjoy making things like Santa and his elves and reindeer real to our children. All too quickly, we grow up and learn of the fantasies of childhood but the intent of parents in wanting their children exposed to the myths is the innocence of goodness.

Santa is the ultimate angel to a child. There isn't the slightest trace of evil connected to Santa; he could never do anything wrong or anything to hurt a child. Santa believes in children, in the innocence of childhood.

Our desire, as adults, to believe in angels follows the same pattern. We grow up and have to leave the myth of Santa, but we desperately want to continue to hold on to what he represents.

The history of Santa Claus is interesting. He is generally thought to derive from Saint Nicholas, the bishop of Myra about the end of the 4th or beginning of the 5th century. But no written document attests of this.

Legends surround the bishop who became the patron saint of children and sailors. These legends and devotion to the saint penetrated into every part of the world.

Early Protestant Dutch settlers in what was to become New York replaced St. Nicholas (Sinter Claes in Dutch) with Santa Claus. The change to Father Christmas began in Germany and extended into other countries through the Reformed Churches.

No other saint of the church has the popularity of St. Nicholas when it comes to children. And no other made the transition through the Reformation to acceptability in Protestantism; though not, of course, in the tradition of Catholicism.

The emphasis of Santa relating to children is the basis of his enduring popularity. He personifies the love of children and the best of childhood as no other figure, historical or mythological.

Yes, Virginia, there is a Santa Claus. Who will forget these words to a little girl written by Francis Church for the New York Sun in 1897?

His concluding words to little Virginia:

"Alas! How dreary would be the world if there were no Santa Claus. It would be as dreary as if there were no Virginias. There would be no childlike faith then, no poetry, no romance, to make tolerable this existence...the eternal light with which childhood fills the world would be extinguished... The most real things in the world are those that neither children or men can see. Did you ever see fairies dancing on the lawn? Of course not, but that's no proof that they are not there. Nobody can conceive or imagine all the wonders there are unseen and unseeable in the world. Thank God! He lives, and he lives forever. A thousand years from now, Virginia, nay, ten times ten thousand years from now, he will continue to make glad the heart of childhood."

Do I believe in Santa Claus? Of course! I couldn't be a poet otherwise; I would lose the best part of the man that makes me so, the child within.

The Christmas season with the distinctive music and decorations, the buying of gifts, the celebration of the hope of peace on earth is something none of us would like to see disappear.

Singing Jingle Bells, Santa Claus is Coming to Town and reading 'Twas the Night Before Christmas celebrate the season. Children write letters to Santa and hang stockings with care and we watch A Christmas Carol, It's a Wonderful Life and Miracle on 34th Street.

We have added the Grinch to the story of Scrooge, there is now A Charlie Brown Christmas, Frosty the Snowman, The Little Drummer Boy, Rudolph and so many more with all the innocence, charm and fantasy of childhood.

The story of the North Pole, Santa's home and the workshop of elves, the magic of Santa's being able to visit every home with a child in a single night, going down chimneys, his Ho, Ho, Ho, children leaving cookies and milk for him and, very important, Santa knows if you have been bad or good, naughty or nice.

Believing in Santa is as natural to a child as faith and prayer. George Beverly Shea sings a beautiful song: "If I Could Pray as a Child Again." How many of us, as adults, haven't wished for this?

Childhood is of so very short duration, such a short time in which to teach and encourage children in the things that will prepare them for adulthood. The whole concept of Santa is one of the things that will do this. We know that all too soon our children will face the denouement of Santa. But the lesson of goodness and the memory of the magic and innocence of childhood, like the healing power of a mother's kiss, should remain.

The non-Christian world recognizes the jolly old elf, separating him from sectarian religious beliefs. And unlike the cruel religious wars of Christianity, Judaism and Islam, none have ever been fought over Santa Claus.

To my Christian friends I would say Santa is not the enemy of Christ. Quite the contrary. Santa epitomizes the very essence of the Gospel. This past Christmas, a store displayed Santa hanging on a cross. Many people were outraged but the storeowner said he was only trying to make people aware of how commercialized the season had become.

The philosophical aspect of this revolves around the substitution of Santa for Christ. People would yawn over a crucifix, but Santa? Perhaps, I say to myself, this may be the result of the virtually non-controversial universality of the goodness of Santa versus an image that separates people and one that has been steeped in controversy and bloodshed for nearly two thousand years and is still on going?

Some of you will remember a song, Green Christmas, by Stan Frieberg years ago that satirized the season. Many radio stations would not play it. Frieberg was only following Charles Dickens' A Christmas Carol, which made the name Scrooge a household word. But many religious people reviled Dickens because the emphasis of the story, as with Frieberg's song, was on the spirit of human goodness rather than Christ. The larger view of an entire humanity to which the Gospel makes a universal appeal is lost to such people.

It isn't surprising then, that these people make Santa the enemy of Christ. It would be interesting, indeed, to know the thoughts of that early Bishop of Myra about this turn of events. But, of course, Santa turned out to be an expression of goodness, hope and belief that transcends all sectarianism chiefly because he is the champion of children and childhood.

Children, I say, are the basis upon which the peoples of the world can come together and coalesce for the common good of humanity. Once they are made the proper priority of humanity.

Far be it from me, as Rhett told Scarlett, to disabuse of the religious instruction of childhood, but it is far past time that humanity grew out of and overcame sectarian hatreds. Santa represents what the attitude of all adults should be toward children and childhood devoid of any evil.

To repeat, because it bears repeating:

Henry Adams said: Politics, as a practice, has always been the systematic organization of hatreds. Had it not been for the time frame, I think Adams would have included religion in the statement.

But only a poet or a child would point to Santa as another direction for humanity.

***

If anyone doubts my statement that America deserves a president like Clinton, the recent Gallup poll showing him the most admired man by Americans should be proof enough. The Pope came in second in the poll. Hillary came in first among the most admired women.

But to the shame of America, we not only deserve Bill and Hillary; this also means there are seemingly so few men and women for Americans to admire. At least so few to whom the media pays any attention. Hyping good people doesn't sell newspapers and Nice doesn't make Film at Eleven.

Clinton's supporters would have us believe everybody lies, cheats, and steals. To a degree, it would be fair to say that no one is perfect. But this isn't the same as saying everybody is so utterly and arrogantly selfish that their behavior is the norm.

The homosexual lobby would have people believe their behavior is normal. The facts are otherwise. Homosexuals comprise from one to two percent of the population. That is medical and behavioral scientific fact. The homosexual propaganda would have people believe perverts are closer to ten percent.

But even at the higher figure, which is nothing but pervert propaganda, such behavior could never be construed as normal in any sense of the word. That too is a fact.

But Clinton and his cohorts would have Americans believe the President is normal in his multiple perversions. Consider what this means if it were true. A mad man running the asylum would be an apt analogy; an admittedly perverse and even dangerous situation.

America now faces the fact of The United States of Europe and the Euro. As the world becomes an increasingly Global Village, we need Statesmen and women, not politicians. The world is becoming far too dangerous for politicians to be running it.

But if the best America can do is a Clinton, just what are our prospects of making the world a better and safer place? Granted thoroughgoing cynicism would have us believe we can't do better. But we can! We can make children the priority of the world and overcome this cynicism!

I believe it to be a delusion that humanity has to be led and dictated to by nothing but economics. Our soul, Emerson's Over Soul, our higher nature, knows better. When we hear the laughter of a child, when we take time to look at the stars, we know better. The historical problem has always been how to do better.

The Amendment holds promise of a New Way, a New Path, for humanity, one that has never been tried. I believe the idea of the Amendment has come just in time and could prove the first step in the right direction for the salvation of humanity; a new path away from number 92 of the periodic table, among other things. But to even try this New Way, we must remove ourselves from the hyper-cynical delusion that such a thing cannot be done.

And it is self-delusion to believe such a thing is not possible. But to know how self-deluded a person can truly be, just look at Clinton and his statements about how he says he thinks history will regard him. And this asinine arrogance in spite of this past Christmas when some cigar makers were making a bundle off him! And did you happen to see the Clinton wristwatch on a shopping channel? It has a picture of the Prexy with a Pinocchio nose that grows longer with each passing hour; quite clever, actually. I'm sure it will become a collector's item.

Well, Bill, as I warned you long ago, this is how history will actually remember you. And your part in the Iraq debacle will always be remembered with you as Commander-in-Heat. If Clinton really believes history will treat him kindly, America is truly at risk from the decisions such a greatly deluded man may make in the months ahead! We begin the New Year with a surfeit of issues awaiting resolution. More Junkyard Politics, I'm certain, will follow those of last year.

I write quite a bit about virtue and good, civilized manners. After all, somebody ought to. If we take it as a given, as per Confucius, Socrates, Emerson, Thoreau, and so many others, that if a nation has virtuous leaders, those governed by such leaders will be virtuous, there is cause for genuine alarm here in America!

Still, there were rays of hope during the congressional hearings like J.C. Watts, Jr. of Oklahoma. There was Democratic Senator Robert Byrd's comment that Clinton was guilty of the most egregious display of unforgivable arrogance. And Jay Dickey of Arkansas had the courage to echo my own words and point out the fact that support of Clinton spoke more of the lack of character in the American people than such a lack in the President. To echo something else I keep saying: We get the kind of leadership we actively support. Ergo, America asked for and deserves Clinton.

While 1998 will stand historically as the most shameful year in America for the office of the President, it wasn't the most shameful year for our political leadership overall. That distinction belongs to the one following the Civil War and is not likely to be surpassed since it encompassed all three branches of the federal government in a shamelessly concerted effort, largely successful, to abrogate the Constitution and punish and plunder a defenseless South. These wounds to our nation and our Constitution have yet to be healed.

While there is no minimizing the damage Clinton has done to the office of the President of the United States, neither is there any minimizing the damage done to our country by the federal government, all three branches, during the Tragic Era from which we have never fully recovered, an era precipitated by the murder of one of the greatest men in the world who ever lived, President Abraham Lincoln.

The moral authority to lead? As we watch and listen to people like Jesse Jackson, personal integrity and morality isn't supposed to be a factor when it comes to the leadership of America, the world's only Superpower. But it is my position that such an office demands a leader of unimpeachable personal moral integrity. For me, that is empirical and pragmatic logic for one single, and basic, reason: How can America lead other nations with the stench of moral hypocrisy attaching to us?

It does no good for the enemies of America, and by extension, the rest of the world, to try to trivialize our present difficulty through attempts to make Clinton's lies and actions of only personal significance. At the best, this is plainly stupid. In fact, it is hypocrisy and flies in the face of logic. To deny the logic is to embrace a prejudice. If the polls are right, it is a prejudice that attempts to excuse the lack of morality of a large portion of Americans, not to mention so many in other nations.

It occurred to me that the selfishness of so many Americans evidenced by the divorce rate and hatred of children reflects the polls that favor Clinton as a proper leader for America. It would be naive at best to think his popularity is based on the Dow and NASDAQ in light of the fact that the rich have been getting richer and the poor, poorer under his administration.

On the contrary, it may be to the shame of America that Clinton is representative of the lack of real character in a majority of Americans. Few seem to think the marriage vows are an oath before God and men. Most treat the marriage vows like a quaint anachronism, a mere formality at best.

If to Americans the vow, the oath, of faithfulness to a marriage partner is of no consequence, how easy it is to excuse such betrayal of oaths by Clinton, to both his wife and America as a mechanism of self-justification and self-righteousness on the part of those who do evil.

While speculating on the polls that give Clinton such popularity by Americans (they must be ignoring people like me), I've come to the conclusion that the divorce rate has something to do with this.

Most people get married. And, in most cases, they make vows (take an oath) to each other in the sight of God and witnesses. Well, the marriage oath doesn't seem to carry much weight in America. And if you are going to excuse yourself for lying and betraying the marriage oath, maybe it makes it all right to you to excuse Clinton. Especially since many claims and accusations made during divorce hearings properly belong in the category of perjury.

I conclude, therefore, that since so many Americans are guilty of infidelity and perjury, they salve their consciences by excusing Clinton. And by extension, hope for the enlarging and ever greater excusing of such lack of moral character on their part by his continuing as President. This doesn't exclude those who give Clinton such high approval on the basis of a steady economy and not wanting to rock the boat. On the contrary, such a reason to discount morality falls into the same category: Selfishness! As to character assassination, this presumes character is there to begin with. In this, Clinton is a mockery. It may have taken Lincoln's observing a slave auction for him to say: "If slavery is not wrong, then nothing is wrong!" But that doesn't mean Lincoln hadn't held this view before he saw that auction. He certainly did.

But we know Lincoln would have left the issue alone for the sake of preserving the Union without war, knowing as he did, that the peculiar institution of slavery in America was doomed in any event and was, in fact, in the process of dying a natural death by economics; and how many times seeming morality is ruled by economics.

Circumstances. How often they alone dictate history. The difference between reality and fiction is that fiction must make sense and dare not be as strange as truth. Poetry must deal with the truth. But from the earliest works of poetic epic such as the Iliad and Odyssey, poetic imagery, whether by raphsodes, or written once the Phoenicians had delivered an alphabet and Semitic peoples were perfecting theirs, cannot be perfunctory and is often used to emphasize, and make memorable, essential truths.

A sunrise is always remarkable yet is most often taken for granted. But to greet Aurora in the sense that those like Thoreau use the phrase is not the same as Hi there, sun! The difference is in trying to find the words that make that first utterance of *Mommy* or *Daddy* from a little one poetry, and trying to find the words that express the feeling in your heart when you hear a child's first real laughter. The very attempt is like trying to hold a sunbeam or rainbow in your hands. But for those who feel the reality of these things, for those who recognize the eternal and priceless value in such love and beauty, the poverty of words doesn't lessen the joy of the heart.

Thoreau's Walden is not poetry though there is much that is poetic about it; this because Thoreau had the heart of a poet and considered himself a poet above anything else. As a classicist, Thoreau's attempts at classic poetry leave me unimpressed. But I well understand his heart's need for the attempt, particularly in light of his time. And his classical training served him well in the philosophical and poetic power he brought to descriptions of ordinary things, ordinary events, and of nature. His little book, Walden, far more than his attempts at classic poetry, defined his real poetic genius.

I never tire of Thoreau because he is a poet speaking to a poet. And I love his sense of humor. At his own cost, he had a thousand copies of his Week printed most of which never sold. But he would tell people his personal library contained nearly nine hundred volumes, over seven hundred of which he had written himself. We are close friends as a result.

A newspaper publisher I know well was in a real quandary when I submitted my article about the death of a friend and drunk, Nelson, some time ago. A typical column or article runs about 250 words. My article would run a full half page in the newspaper. I had made a note to the editor with the submission that he should feel free to cut and edit to make it suit the needs of the paper. It never entered my mind that the editor would print the whole column.

When this editor and publisher called me he said he wanted to run the piece in its entirety, that he wouldn't consider cutting any of it or changing a single word. I've never had an editor tell me this. It's an editor's job to cut and edit, not run a lengthy article full-length straight from the writer's pen (or processor).

It was some time after our conversation and reflecting on the peculiar reaction of the editor that I realized the piece about Nelson was poetry. It had flowed so naturally from my mind and heart and I was so close to my friend I hadn't seen it as such. In fact, I had written it the very same day of Nelson's death. Something written under such emotional stress had to be flawed. That was my thinking. However, there it was; an ordinary story told in an extraordinary way, the very essence of poetry. An ordinary story, even an extraordinary one, told in an ordinary way is good journalism, but it isn't poetry.

But neither did Lincoln see his Gettysburg Address as poetry. He really believed his words would be soon forgotten. The death of a single individual by suicide or the deaths of thousands on a battlefield, while tragedies are ordinary stories. But they can be made extraordinary through the magic of words.

The murder of a child is too often treated as an ordinary event and reported in an ordinary way. It is the duty of the poet to make the murder of a child extraordinary. It is the duty of society to see that justice is done. But it often takes the poet to move society to do justice.

Recently six children perished in a fire. A grandmother was supposed to be watching over them while their mother was in the hospital having another baby. No man or father was mentioned. This has become an ordinary event in

America. Only a poet is going to make such things so extraordinary that the people will rise up to confront this kind of tragedy inflicted on children.

I favor sterilization of child molesters, I favor forced birth control for men and women who won't take responsibility for children and continue to force taxpayers to foot the bill for their irresponsibility. But politicians won't confront this issue, especially politicians who are so sensitive to the howls of Racism and Discrimination that would be hurled in their direction in cases like this.

By the mechanism of the universities and their products the politicians and judges catering to the lowest common denominator, America has become an ignorant, illiterate, and too often irresponsible, nation. I am often reminded of a Bloom County episode where Opus decides he is going to stop watching TV, go to the library and check out books and start reading. Once at the library, he looks at all those thousands of books and the last panel of the strip shows him in front of his TV munching out and watching Gilligan's Island.

No doubt about it, working for and earning a real education is a daunting process requiring a lot of self-discipline and accepting a lot of personal responsibility. Just think; the Vatican Library alone contains some ten million books and manuscripts. There is a great deal of knowledge awaiting a serious student.

As a consequence of the dumbing down of America, if you ask someone to describe poetry they will probably reply with something to the effect of sentimentalism and gauzy, ethereal scenes painted in smarmy words contained in a book covered with soft satin and adorned with pastel tints and lace. There will probably be butterflies, flowers, and angels involved in the motif. A book, in short, of no significance meant only to while away an idle hour for ladies or gentlemen of delicate sensibilities, a book designed as an ornament for a gracious home to be ostentatiously displayed for the benefit of visitors.

While there is an honored place for the poetry that extols virtue and beauty, awe and wonder of God's creation and the softer and gentler things of love and romance, tyrants and despots don't persecute and murder poets for such things. They persecute and murder them for some of their ideas which are better represented by a book with iron binding held together with rivets, the words graved on steel sheets instead of paper and a picture of the Grim Reaper, pointing an accusing skeletal, rapier-nailed finger toward the tyrant, while with another he is pointing toward maimed and slaughtered and starving children, adorns the cover.

In a message of such power, extraordinary in its brevity as well as its words, Lincoln made the battlefield tragedy of Gettysburg real in an extraordinary way. He made the deaths of those thousands profoundly significant and count for something far beyond the obvious, far beyond the ordinary. That is poetry.

Thoreau labored over Walden Pond. He spent years refining it. The finished book turned out to be a masterpiece of enduring literature that continues to be read by millions.

I first read the small book forty years ago. I bought a fifty-cent paperback. I still have it. It has been a constant companion; well worn and filled with underlining. But after a few years, I stopped the underlining realizing that I had begun to read the book as a letter from a friend. No, more than that. When I read it now, it is a conversation with a friend.

I suppose one of the losses to this present generation which I feel very keenly has to be so many not knowing what I am talking about, to have a book as such a close companion, to come to know books and those who wrote them as friends. Like good music, the encouraging of children to read good books is the responsibility of the leadership of a culture, from the parents on up. The failure of a society to properly value children can easily be seen by the failure to encourage these things in children.

Like all friends, Henry and I have our points of disagreement. He can be pompous and egotistical at times and I always chaff at this. But his very humanity matches my own and I'm sure he recognizes the same faults in me that I see in him.

I may wonder at, but never abuse, those who fail to find my friend Henry as admirable and charming as I do. But when it comes to the evil and ravenous machinery of government, Henry has no peer in exposing it. His treatise Civil Disobedience stands alone.

It has always been a source of gratitude on my part to have met Henry when I was so young. And then to get to know him so very well over these past forty years, to, in a sense, grow with him. I can't help but wish everyone could be so fortunate.

Because we are so close, his little book is kept on my nightstand and hardly a night goes by that we don't share something in conversation. My own wilderness experience as a boy living on a mining claim in the Sequoia National Forest gives me insights to what Thoreau discovered while living at Walden Pond. His experiment in simplicity in living was thrust upon me by circumstances.

But I have always been very grateful for the experience. Few my age can speak with authority about such a life pared to the bare essentials. And in spite of the hardships imposed by such an environment and lifestyle, how I have wished all children could have the opportunity of having a forest with a wild river and trout stream as their playground.

Some have wondered that I have never replaced the little 50-cent, badly worn and scotch-taped copy of Walden with handsome, leather bound, gilded and annotated edition. But Henry has proven a dear and close friend. Doing so would somehow lessen the value of his letter to me. Besides, I don't reverence Henry; he was subject to many of the same human weaknesses and frailties as I. Consequently, I love him as a friend, I do not deify him. Quite the contrary; we have often criticized each other and told each other on too many occasions that one or the other is wrong.

But I never fail to profit from my conversations with Henry. The following will give the reader a good understanding of why this is the case:

There is never an instant's truce between virtue and vice. Goodness is the only investment that never fails... Many an irksome noise, go a long way off, is heard as music, a proud, sweet satire on the meanness of our lives... We are conscious of an animal within us, which awakens in proportion as our higher nature slumbers. It is reptile, sensual, and perhaps cannot be wholly expelled; like the worms, which, even in life and health, occupy our bodies. Possibly we may withdraw from it, but never change its nature...we may be well, yet not pure.

Philosophers, even those whose major claim is literary like Shakespeare, have long known the truth of Thoreau's words. But it takes the poet/philosopher to put such truths in words that stick with you.

The verisimilitude of the disputed Homeric and Shakespearean authorship's does not detract from the genius of the works. But there has never been any doubt of Walt Kelly's authorship or genius.

Walt Kelly popularized via Pogo: "We have met the enemy and he is us."

If Walt (or so many like Thoreau or Clemens) were alive today, what a field day he would be having with our present politicos. The recent congressional hearings would tax the genius of Gary Larson. Can you imagine one of his Far Side cartoons depicting that recent segment of human behavior?

Speaking of the Far Side, I recently received a call from Jerry Falwell's organization. The caller asked if I were willing to listen to a recorded message of Falwell's regarding the impeachment of Clinton. I told the caller I had written extensively on the subject but wasn't interested in anything Jerry had to say until he showed the courtesy, and the courage, to respond to my proposed Amendment for children. After all, fair is fair. I still haven't heard from Jerry.

Generation X is well named if we take the X as standing for X-rated. I wonder that the song titled Smut by Tom Lehrer isn't played more often. Maybe generation X isn't aware of it or perhaps its biting satire is more than they want to hear.

12-29-98 C-SPAN2. I watched and listened to Doctor Clovis Maksoud, former Arab League Ambassador to the United Nations, pointing out the abysmal ignorance of Middle Eastern nations on the part of the West. And I was reminded of the cause of the war with Japan for this very same reason. But I learned many years ago that the first casualty of war is the truth.

It occurred to me that one of the characters in my novel is wrestling with what we are facing. Permit me to introduce Doctor Clement Mathison with a part of his soliloquy from a chapter of the book:

A bridge is needed, a bridge between the poet-philosopher and the scientist. But I know men will die building such a bridge, just as that French philosopher Saint-Exupery pointed out. The fanatics of religion and politics will fight against such a thing.

The images of war suddenly flooded his mind, the carnage of the battlefield with the mangled, bloody bodies of so many men, women, and children during this most recent attempt at world dictatorship.

And to what purpose?

Clement suddenly wanted to shake his fist in the face of God himself, if God there be!

Where was truth to be found in such things; must the seeking for truth always result in the carnage of a battlefield strewn with broken and maimed, bloody bodies? Why must truth and justice be bought with cannon and rifle, sword and bayonet?

And does an honest search for truth and justice always require the sacrifice of those innocent who don't even know why they are being maimed and killed? Must some bloodthirsty deity representing itself as truth demand continual human sacrifice to appease its hatred and anger toward humanity and the human failure to meet divine expectations? Insanity!

Bloody religion! Bloody politics! Bloody humanity! Confound it, why do I let such things, such questions plague me!

***

If it is true that the arms manufacturers and suppliers are the ones that should be targeted, rather than nations like Iraq, as Jules Verne and so many others since have pointed out, and most recently Clovis Maksoud of the Arab League, and UNICEF, why isn't this being done? And we can reasonably ask why our nation supplied China with technology to advance its program for making nuclear weapons with long-range capability?

Just before WWII more than one adult I heard as a child was deploring the shipping of scrap iron to Japan with the words: This stuff is going to be used to make bombs to drop on us!

But now we have progressed? To nuclear bombs. Number 92 looms large on the world's horizon. But how to accomplish Emerson's and Napoleon's bloodless revolution, how to make the heritage of our children as Thoreau hoped the spade and the plow rather than the sword and the musket?

Virtue comes from the top down. Parents are supposed to be virtuous for the sake of their children, to teach their children to love virtue. Leaders are supposed to be virtuous for the sake of those led or governed in order for civilization to advance.

But advances in love and compassion have not matched our advances in science and technology. As a result, I wouldn't say humanity has advanced in wisdom since true wisdom grows from love and compassion.

I ask myself whether my generation had the best that civilization had to offer? For example, the great musicals were the last time poets worked in America. But their success was predicated on a culture that was still capable of believing in love and romance, a culture that was still capable of making Santa and fairy tales real to children; in brief, a culture that had not given in to hedonistic cynicism.

My fear is that we may have indeed experienced the best in my generation and that it may not be recovered, that the present cynicism may lead to number 92. As Michio Kaku and others have so well pointed out, other civilizations in other worlds, if they existed, may have done themselves in at this stage of knowledge.

I would add that our advances in knowledge without an accompanying advancement of love and compassion make the threat quite real. Those ancient poets often dwelled on heroes made larger than life. The singers or raphsodes who would extol the virtues of battles fought evidenced much knowledge of human nature but failed to bring a balance to heroics necessitated by war, and virtue attendant on peace.

Both the Greek and the Semitic literatures are replete with blood but where is the wisdom exemplified by a love of peace? Much talk and little achievement; in the words of Thoreau: Talk of heaven! Ye disgrace earth!

And this has been the history of the human race; and of religion, politics, and governments in general.

It is small wonder to me that so many of the Jews of Jesus' time were so Hellenistic, so attracted to the Greek culture, poetry, and philosophy. Both Semites and Greeks had developed writing and poetry to a high art. But that art, as evidenced by the literature, had been too often corrupted to the glorification of war and discrimination! So much for the wisdom of these ancients- which only goes to prove that a practice or belief of thousands of years' duration is no guarantee of its being wise or even right.

Unless, by my reckoning, America can be returned to the ideals of our Founding Fathers and democracy that so inspired de Tocqueville, we have every right to fear that number 92 is our fate rather than growing in wisdom. But it is my contention that the proposed Amendment can accomplish a turning away from war and a turning toward wisdom.

It is my further contention that Lincoln accomplished his part by the Emancipation Proclamation leading to the Thirteenth Amendment. It now remains for us to do our part by the passage of the proposed Amendment, the Emancipation Proclamation for children!

The freeing of slaves and enfranchising women followed the Grand Experiment in Democracy and Human Rights for which De Tocqueville praised America. I believe America must follow these historic acts by the proposed Amendment for the sake of our future, our children, who are not yet represented by our foundational charter of government, our Constitution. However, for this to happen humankind must choose the path of wisdom and turn away from the demons that still haunt and plague us throughout the world; demons that make us fearful of the reorganization of civilization where children are the priority of humanity. But children, all children, must become the world's priority. And America has the responsibility for taking the first step in making this a reality!

I am grateful for and proud of those who speak to issues like the banning of land mines. This is an appeal to humanitarianism that speaks well for all of us who support such efforts. But such things miss the real target, which is coming together on the basis of valuing children throughout the world.

As to the demons that still haunt and threaten, it is well known that the mind is able to shorten or prolong life. Most of us are familiar with stories of witch doctors and shamans in ignorant cultures that are successful in casting spells, even causing death, by the power of suggestion.

It has been a long time since Peter's shadow or Paul's hanky or apron healed people miraculously. Have advances in science put such myths to rest? The technology of science made it possible for people to put their hands on a radio for healing. Following the radio evangelists, we got the TV evangelists. Some progress. Still, there is the power of the mind to make physiological and psychological changes in people who are real and alien abductees can always point to Elijah, Jesus, and Muhammad for confirmation.

Legitimate medical doctors often face the dilemma of whether to tell patients bad news knowing how powerfully the mind can react to it. In many cases, the patient will go into a deep depression and shorten his life as a consequence.

Much of neurotic, even psychotic, behavior is learned; if you believe in something strongly enough, it can have both psychological and physiological results. The power of suggestion, the placebo effect, is well authenticated. Virtual miracles, so-called, are the product of the mind whether for good or ill. Our problem, scientifically, is of not fully understanding brain function. And not having a known terminus, we really have no idea of how far we have come or how far there is to go in such understanding.

A recent book, "The Hand", deals with the importance of our hands to brain function. The premise of the book is that much of the brain's learning has to do with our hands. And that makes sense. My own experience, especially in the trades and teaching shop classes, evidenced much of this premise. It explains why the best of writing, composition of words and music, painting and sculpture, even mathematics, are the result of genius combining hands and mind. It also explains why most people find their hands active while speaking. The hands are actively involved in all these things in an attempt to realize abstractions.

Research in particle physics will, undoubtedly, give us many of the needed answers to brain function, capability, and for things that presently fall into the category of Psi and religion. Of course, once many of these answers are known, shows like the X-Files and others will become passe. Not to mention a whole lot of unctuous and vacuous TV evangelists and those of their ilk who will be out of a job and may be forced into comparatively honest work like purse snatching and burglary.

A few people have asked whether Clinton really believes he told the truth. Due to his supremely overweening arrogance, I don't believe so. But I have to admit that is a possibility. The mind is perfectly capable of self-delusion, even conviction concerning fantasy. It may be that Jimmy Swaggart in his salad days really believed by anointing his old car with oil and praying over it that God gave it a needed valve job. Hearing the audible voice of God and of angels is understandable in cases of delusion and self-induced hysteria like those of Swaggart.

Clinton wouldn't be the first in history by any means that believed he was divinely anointed of God and was a chosen vessel irrespective of vile behavior. But in the President's case, I still think he is just a small-minded shyster lawyer who carried the Ol' Boy Politics of Arkansas into the White House and is still a pig's ear trying to pass as a silk purse. The problem seems to be too many people willing to accept a pig's ear and not willing to set their sights higher.

Admittedly, were it not for my children and grandchildren, I'm not that certain I would care all that much. But I care about their future; I care deeply about the kind of America in which they have to live, the kind of future they will have. And like most parents, I want them to have it even better than I had.

But we are not presently on a track that promises a better America. And that concerns me deeply. I am altogether too convinced that de Tocqueville was right. And if so, what is my part in making America better, especially better for the sake of my children and all children. To me, that is a reasonable question all citizens should be asking themselves.

I believe the Amendment will get America on the right track since, among other things it is so far removed from our present position and direction of selfishly hedonistic cynicism.

California's newly elected Governor says he will make education the priority of the state. But we've heard this before from many politicians. Talking about caring for children always plays well to the electorate. But what politician has ever delivered on this? None. All we get is the typical lip service to carry a vote.

Good guys finish last. Does this mean the good has to become more violent, cunning, and devious than the evil? Stephen King's "Needful Things" has the Devil giving people what they want. For a price. A take-off from Goethe's Faust, the story does point out an essential fact of human nature: The constant battle we wage against selfishness.

Children and family were intended of God, I believe, to teach us unselfishness, to teach the needed lesson of sacrificial love. The story of Jesus was intended to make this point, albeit the point has been lost in religion. Children do not vitiate the need for remonstration. Train up a child means incorporating discipline with love.

If we have evolved into a society that acts like it hates children, this means we as a society, not just individually, have left off the responsibility to train children properly. But no one wastes their time on something they consider to be of little or no value.

The kaleidoscope is a marvelous device. As a child, I was entranced by it. As I grew a little older, I became entranced and fascinated by the study of fractals, of the symmetry in nature as exemplified by the patterns of colors in butterfly wings in which I delighted as a child, the symmetry to be found in all of nature.

And what normal man isn't entranced by the symmetry to be found in the physical attributes of a beautiful woman? Without such beauty of symmetry, there would be no poets extolling her beauty.

Now that same study which began with things like a child's toy is making it possible for us to entertain the idea of teleportation and star travel. But we should never forget this started with things like the kaleidoscope and the patterns in butterfly wings. And the physical attributes of a beautiful woman.

Studies in particle physics are well on the way to proving that we do, indeed, live in a sea of consciousness, that Psi, the paranormal, will be understood through the efforts of such research and the hopes of men like Sir Arthur Conan Doyle will be realized.

A frequency of sound that can produce heat and light is a realized fact in sonoluminescence. Who is to say that a frequency may not yet be found that would enable those passed on to communicate with us? Entrancing idea; it certainly entranced Doyle.

The ancient poet/historians were composers of music. Singing and music were spoken, and later, written, without instrumental accompaniment. Instruments to accompany words were a later invention. We still retain some knowledge of this in our language. *Her words were music to my ear,* or *My heart sang,* for example. The melody and harmony of Nature's Universal Lyre so popular with poets is another.

Writing is of comparatively recent invention. Not until about the eighth century BC did it really come into vogue, as we understand writing. But at its inception, it was not considered of much worth and oral communication in keeping traditions and stories alive were still preferred up until about the sixth century BC

It is no wonder, given oral communication and the lack of any real understanding of science that the ancients failed to pass on much of substantive value and so much of mythology and superstition was kept alive and given broad credence. However, it takes a written language of a high degree of sophistication to pass useful knowledge from one generation to another.

But without science, much of the earliest writing was given to perpetuating myths and superstitions. So much so that even the dawn of the age of science did not dispel many of these myths and superstitions. And many, such as astrology, still are given credence today.

In this, one thing has not changed: No man also having drunk old wine straitway desireth new: for he saith, The old is better (by the way, if you try to find this verse in an old Scofield Reference Bible using its abbreviated concordance, you won't find the word wine; an interesting commentary on Scofield's religious prejudice and religious prejudice in general. But you won't find the words piss and pisseth in his concordance either though mentioned seven times in the Old Testament).

As I wrote previously, the reorganization of the institutions of a society, of a civilization, is a fearful undertaking to most. But there have been things along the path of history like the invention of writing that has done this. The invention of movable type, the printing press, did this. And there have been the books like Newton's "Principia" and "Uncle Tom's Cabin" that have changed (more properly, re-directed) history.

In short, we have come a long way in a very brief time compared to the thousands of years past. But in our journey we have not, to repeat myself again, made any substantial progress in the wisdom that comes from an advance in love and compassion. We have made astounding progress in knowledge, but not in the wisdom to use that knowledge for the best purposes.

In the beginning when the Amendment first suggested itself as a New Way, a New Path for humanity, I had already spent years considering the problem of just why the human race seemed doomed to repeating the mistakes of the past, the repeating cycle of history?

Back to the problem of that Old Wine and the fearfulness of trying a New Way. That is a legitimate fear. But what is the alternative? I asked myself; potentially, number 92. Logically, we cannot put the genie back in the bottle. Nor can we hope to avoid number 92 as long as people continue to murder one another in the name of God or politics.

We could stick our heads in the sand and try to ignore Michio Kaku's reasoned statement that he believed no other civilizations in other worlds, if they existed, had made it past the atomic energy stage. Given the ready availability of such to destroy our world together with so much religious and political hatred inflicting humanity, Kaku's dispassionate logic must be taken into account.

I know what I consider my own logic is not infallible. As I've said many times, I have come to question the wisdom of others because I have learned to question my own. But what I consider logical is that if a problem persists, if it seems to defy a solution, the approach to an answer must be wrong.

We have a problem of historic dimension that has persistently defied solution. The peoples of the world can't seem to get along together. Real education, real knowledge, holds promise of understanding the problem, of being able to properly state it, which is half of the solution. But the other half of the solution, logic dictates, must come from wisdom. And wisdom dictates that love and compassion must become the norm in order to avoid number 92, Armageddon!

I hate bullies. I especially hate the preeminent and cowardly bully; the child molester. The solution that must come from the wisdom exercising itself from love and compassion must originate with removing the bullies of children from our civilization. That is the logical starting point. But this must be done by law because it cannot be done in any other way. That too, is logical.

Tragically for humankind, having equal recourse to law is laughable. We do, in fact, have a civilization that in too many ways is one in which real justice is made to bow to how much justice you can afford. Ok, that is a reality. But it is a reality that is historically flawed, one that has succeeded only because real wisdom has not been the operative conditioning of the human race. A New Way, New Wine, is desperately needed.

The proposed Amendment offers a start on that New Way, the New Wine, which is preeminently logical. To protect the innocence of childhood, to protect the future of the human race, to guarantee a child shall not be molested, is a very good start.

But it would be naive in the extreme to think that such a thing can be done without the force of law. And to be just, that law must have a universality of application. This is why my appeal has been to a U.S. Constitutional Amendment, to emancipate children from the bullying and cowardly cruelty of the molester, something no nation in history has ever incorporated in its foundational charter of government.

In spite of all the arguments I have heard against it over the past two years, I am ever more convinced that America must lead the world in this fashion in order to solve the historic problem of the inability of the peoples of the world getting along together. The basis of the solution must be prioritizing children, the future of America, the future of the world. This, to me, is fundamentally logical. On behalf of the Amendment, I have written extensively about the enormity of the impact of molestation in history and in America, which cannot be overemphasized.

Science does not have an answer to the mindless primitive that dogs humankind in men still thinking of females as prey. Deep in that primitive is the hunter who excuses himself for preying even on children. What science cannot do, what conscience will not do, the law was designed to do. It is law, just law, which we must call on to overcome that mindless primitive hunter who sees only the prey, not another human being.

What would be the opinion of the American people if Chelsea said her father had molested her as a child? Impossible? Given his track record of abuse of others, who could consider it unthinkable of a man like Clinton? But the point is not to tar Clinton with that brush. The point is that most molestations go unreported. And like little JonBenet, where is justice to be found for these little victims when great power and wealth are used to pervert justice?

That mindless primitive is something that needs to be overcome. He is the thing of nightmares for humanity. And only just law, the Amendment, will beat him. As Thoreau pointed out, "We are conscious of an animal within us, which awakens in proportion as our higher nature slumbers. It is reptile, sensual, and perhaps cannot be wholly expelled; like the worms, which, even in life and health, occupy our bodies. Possibly we may withdraw from it, but never change its nature...we may be well, yet not pure."

The question Americans face is whether we really want to subdue the reptilian primitive, whether we really want our higher nature to awake and overcome? Or are we become such lovers of war, so selfish and self-indulgent that we are incapable of making children our priority? God help us if so! Should that be the case, most certainly number 92, Armageddon, is our future and earth will be only a burned out ember, a fitting tombstone for the primitive who finally overcame the attempt at a successful civilization.

The mythologies of various cultures acknowledge the primitive, the beast, creation and the origin of evil, the fallen Adam, etc. Doctrines of sin, paradise lost, the need of a messiah, these are all attempts to deal with the problem. I go into some depth of the subject in my "Hey, God!" book.

There is a wealth of material on the subject but it has yet to be systematized. And no so-called systematic theology or philosophy has yet proved satisfactory. Not surprising since women, fully one-half of humankind, have always been excluded from the discussion.

CHAPTER TWO

Clinton is a perjurer and has done all he can to obstruct justice and disgrace the White House. Philadelphia leaders and police lie about crime in the city, even having crimes erased or their severity changed to a lesser degree, thereby skewing FBI crime statistics. And Philly isn't alone in this by any means. Utah bribes the International Olympic Committee and members of the Committee demand bribes. Is nothing sacred? And just recently, a friend's cat died. Yessir, '99 is off to a roaring start! As the fellow said, "Cheer up, things could be worse." So I cheered up and sure enough, things got worse.

How about those souvenir pens with which the Senators signed in that had United States Senator spelled Untied States Senator? As serendipitous and sardonically, even sarcastically, ironic the error, the pens were probably made in Taiwan or Puerto Rico. I would gladly accord the error being made purposely. But given the low estate of education in this country together with the increasing reliance on spellchecker programs, it probably was unintentional and the pens may well have been made in the U.S.

I actually did a little taxidermy while living on the mining claim as a boy. And I did a pretty fair job of it if I do say so myself. The first projects were a snake and a chicken. They proved to be really difficult and very uncooperative so I asked grandad about the proper procedure in preparation for stuffing the critters. Grandad knew all about such things.

Having plenty of snakes and chickens in attendance around the claim, getting them was easy enough. But I was having a problem trying to carry out grandad's instructions. When I asked grandad about this, he quickly determined the root of the trouble. They were supposed to be dead before trying to skin and stuff them. Don't take anything for granted. Dumb and dumber will always be there. For example, plucking or stuffing a live chicken will always prove a formidable task.

Who but us members of the National Rifle Association would know the phrase the whole nine yards originated from the length of ammo belts used by WWI machine guns mounted on aircraft? And now you know. A lot of people think the phrase has to do with football, which doesn't even make sense.

I recently asked Doctor Fritz Krautmacher, the head of Weedpatch University's Political Science Department, what his thoughts were about the impeachment hearings. Forgetting himself, he answered in German, forgetting also that it is my second language. His remarks were a little stern. I'll soften them a bit by eliminating the words scum, dirtbags, worms, tax-fattened hyenas, etc. In short he said it gave him a lot of material for his classes and we could be expecting suitcase nuclear devices being brought to us by terrorists any day now. Fritz has always been one of those people of sunny disposition who delights in putting the best face on things.

And speaking of education, it was while I was a teacher at David Starr Jordan High School in Watts in South Central L.A. that the principal Jay Settle was honored by community leaders with a plaque naming him an Honorary Negro. I can see Clinton being honored in a similar fashion. Surely Jesse Jackson has thought about this.

But as I considered the subject, it occurred to me that no one would have thought to present Martin Luther King, Jr. a plaque naming him an Honorary Caucasian. Jesse Jackson? Not hardly! Now why this double standard? The folks in Watts really believed they were doing something nice for Mr. Settle; they were genuinely trying to show their appreciation for the job he was doing in the War Zone of Watts.

Why would it seem demeaning, patronizing, or condescending to present such a plaque to King or Jackson but not the obverse in the case of Jay Settle, a white man? This is a very profound and extremely complex and disturbing question once you get past the whimsy of it.

Jordan went through two Caucasian principals while I was there before the L.A. City Schools finally wised up and appointed a Negro as a principal. This made it rough on me as a white teacher in an all black school because the black principal made it clear to me that he didn't want any white teachers.

Well, what can you do? Discrimination based on prejudice is an ugly thing no matter how practiced, by whom, or for what reasons. I'm reminded of the time Jesse Helms thanked the KKK for not endorsing him. And I don't think I'm in any danger of being made an honorary homosexual.

I put out my flag on Martin Luther King Day to honor the courage and ideals of those who fought for their rights as American Citizens. In other words, I honor courage and ideals in this case, not a man. I still consider it an affront to God to call any man reverend. I didn't allow this when I was a preacher. Reverence belongs to God alone.

In spite of the despicable actions of Clinton, as an American I honor the office, not the man. And I still pray the Senate will get this man out of office. If not, I fear irreparable harm may be done to the office of President. So much so, that it will be impossible to honor the office, let alone the man!

A lot of Negro folks showed enormous courage, including Dr. King, in confronting the injustices that were designed to keep colored people as second class citizens. And it wasn't only colored people being jailed, hurt, and even murdered during this sorry episode of the Civil Rights Movement. There were some equally courageous white people who laid it on the line as well.

One of the things I truly admired about the message of Dr. King was that of non-violence. He recognized, as did Ghandi, Thoreau's message of Civil Disobedience in confronting the injustice of evil laws and evil authorities.

But I have deeply rooted feelings about those who betray the love and trust of a marriage partner. This is why I have not written men like Representatives Hyde or Livingston to congratulate them on the job they have done in Congress. Their words are good but will always ring hollow to me when they have betrayed their mates. Such men and women have nothing to say to me of any moral consideration.

Regardless my personal feelings about some parts of The Civil Rights Movement and some of those involved; the fact is that I hate bullies with a perfect and passionate hatred! And without question, black people were being bullied. I have always found the abuse of authority to be hatefully despicable. This is the reason I hate the child molester so much. This is why I despise Clinton.

There are those who decried forced integration of the schools. Who will forget George Wallace in this respect at this time in history? Sadly, people don't read anymore so I will refer to the film "Separate But Equal" starring Sidney Poitier and Burt Lancaster.

The film did an excellent job of presenting the problem America faced at this time and how it was addressed in the Supreme Court. America went through a real social upheaval as a consequence. But the Separate But Equal argument didn't hold up when confronted by the facts. And in spite of the abuse of power by the Federal Government in enforcing the Supreme Court's decision, by force of law a grave injustice directed at blacks was confronted.

I have given this era of American history much thought because of the Amendment. What people will not do for the sake of conscience, what they will not do simply because it is the right thing to do, the only redress is the law.

Our pledge is One Nation, under God, with liberty and justice for all. The troubling thing about our pledge, as with the Declaration of Independence, is that it continues to be an embarrassing conceit to America. But as de Tocqueville rightly observed, Americans, more than any other people in history, have tried to rise above this conceit and remove it from an abstraction to a reality and we often invoke our ancestors to this end. And well we should; it was these ancestors that gave us a nation conceived in the ideal of personal liberty beyond that of any nation in history.

But the Civil War was not, in my opinion, the end of America's War for Independence. As long as children suffer, as long as the Pledge of Allegiance and the Declaration of Independence remain embarrassing conceits, there is still another war to be fought on American soil. And it may be the seed of America's demise as a nation may have been planted in slavery.

However, it is my most fervent prayer that this final conflict will be fought without cannon and musket by We the People in the arena of the courts and legislatures for the sake of the rights and protection of children on the basis of: *If perversion is not wrong, then nothing is wrong!* Only then will America have the right to any claim of being a moral nation with liberty and justice for all!

The equal protection guaranteed by the fourteenth Amendment was written specifically for Negroes at the time. But when have we seen equal protection for blacks, the poor, or for children under this Amendment? Let alone realized the ideal expressed in our Pledge of Allegiance?

Thurgood Marshall had to argue before the Supreme Court that segregated schools did not meet the guarantee of equal protection by the Constitution. And he won. But not before the Supreme Court had held for segregated schools in seven previous cases.

The forcing of social views and social change by fiat of court decisions is often repugnant. But often needed as well because what will not be done by conscience, the law must do. It is very easy to be humanitarian in the abstract, but how very difficult because it is simply right. We all know how difficult it would be to feed ourselves in the abstract. You would soon starve. It was well said of one Supreme Court Justice that he was a great humanitarian philosophically, but he just didn't like people.

I am a very vocal presenter of facts. But I struggle with facts that seem to contravene my opinion or prejudice. It is easy to pay lip service to a concern for children in the abstract. The reality is quite something else. When it comes to human behavior much is learned of people by observation. But I know reality is not dependent on human observation but on those stubborn things called facts.

It is a wonderful thing to find yourself unintimidated by the truth, because the truth is too often a most uncomfortable thing. But this should turn our thoughts to what it is that makes the truth uncomfortable.

Those who argued against desegregation were not all evil by any means. They asked for time in order that circumstances would prevail for needed changes. As Lincoln knew slavery would die a natural death given time, so the opponents of desegregation argued the same point.

But a flash point in history, ignited by Uncle Tom's Cabin, and fomented by the selfishness of a few, caused the Civil War. The selfishness of others, especially Carpetbaggers and Scoundrels, created the Jim Crow South following the war.

Is the point of facing and confronting prejudice to be justice, liberty, and equality for all? I was told by a powerful man of influence in DC when I first proposed the Amendment that it was very timely. And I agreed. I agreed because I strongly believe the world is running out of time. It has now been two years since I proposed the Amendment to the President, Governors, and Senators. In light of current events, my fear is that we may be running out of time.

Thirty years ago, I taught in a Concentration Camp called Watts in South Central Los Angeles. Have things gotten any better for the people in that Camp since the Watts Riots? Not hardly. But why not? I believe it is because such areas have no political significance or influence.

The Amendment must become politically important, just as slavery and segregation had to reach such a point. But do we have time for it to become so? I had no illusions from the very beginning that educating people to the need of the Amendment would prove to be a very time-consuming task. And so it is proving to be. It took time for me to be convinced of the need.

In light of the thousands of years of history that clearly declare nations have acted without wisdom, that they have consistently followed a wrong path invariably leading to conflict, this New Way via the Amendment is... I was about to say a daunting challenge. But that would trivialize it. It is a challenge beyond words!

Our Declaration of Independence states that all men are created equal. But we know the poor, women, and Negroes were not the intention of that statement. Still the ideal of equality is clearly set forth in our Declaration of Independence, our Constitution and all its articles, and our Pledge of Allegiance. It should be borne in mind at all times that our Constitution and its articles are law throughout. In spite of this, I have had some ignorantly say to me that the Constitution should not be a mechanism to make laws!

Libertarians may howl but if someone with terminal body odor insists on sitting next to me in a restaurant, why should I be the one forced to move? Why should I be forced to move to get away from a bad neighbor? Why should I be the one to live in fear if I am called on as a witness by the court to give testimony against someone who has committed a crime?

No, my good libertarian friends, where positive action is missing because of a lack of conscience, either personal or social, the only redress is law or anarchy; thus the absolute need of the Amendment as the place to start, a law which begins to address the abuses through lack of conscience towards the most innocent of American citizens, our children.

Equal Protection? Thurgood Marshall argued this point successfully in the cause of Negro children being given the same educational rights as white children. But where is the Thurgood Marshall who will stand up for all children regardless of color to argue equal protection in the cause of a lawfully protected, innocent childhood free of the most vicious form of all slavery and discrimination with its attendant prejudice, bigotry, bullying, cowardly, and conscienceless abuse, the slavery of molestation?

As Thurgood Marshall stood making his plea for the rights to equality on behalf of Negro children before the Supreme Court he was surely thinking to himself: If not now, when? As I plead the case for the Amendment knowing the perilous circumstances everyone in the world is facing, I have to ask myself: If not now, when? But unlike Marshall, I have to think as well in terms of portending Armageddon!

Referring to my Mad Man Hypothesis as per Dostoevsky, Tolstoy, and Harper Lee, the Amendment must, by force of law, do the right thing for children since conscience will not. And once made law, people will wonder, as they did in the case of the Supreme Court's decision on Separate But Equal, at their former insanity and lack of conscience. But this has to do with genuine morality; something which is, as with true education, sadly, even tragically, so lacking in America today.

Clinton will not only be remembered by history for his immorality, for his dishonoring the office of President, as a cowardly bully and the butt of dirty jokes, but for his disastrous foreign policy (the utter lack thereof, that is). Donald Devine of the American Conservative Union rightly points out that Clinton's despicable actions in the sullying of the office of President leading to making America a laughingstock to other nations (a very dangerous position in itself as I have pointed out) has over-shadowed the real story of a new Tripartite agreement between Russia, China, and India that is of greatly disturbing potential.

This cannot help but call to mind the Tripartite agreement of the Axis powers of WWII. While the leadership of America seems bent on involving us ever more deeply in Iraq and Bosnia at a cost of billions with no end in sight, this serves the propaganda machines and the cohesion of Russia, China, and India.

I believe Devine is right in saying that Clinton may well be remembered for placing America in the direst of perils because of disastrous foreign policy rather than Monica and peculiar definitions of sex. That is, if a man who has proven himself so stupid in not being able to keep his pants zipped in the Oval Office is really so clever and cunning that he can invite terrorism and manipulate world affairs to bring about a nuclear confrontation. If his actions are born of supremely selfish and egotistical arrogance rather than stupidity alone, America has much to fear from such a man.

I early on warned that a man without conscience but with great power and authority is a most dangerous man; especially a man with Clinton's selfish arrogance and utter disregard for his actions and the impact of those actions on individuals and America. I do not believe any man is more capable than Clinton of a scorched earth policy to satisfy his narcissistic egocentrism.

God forbid Clinton should take this tack! If he does, there may well not be a future for the world or any left to write of his part in history! My own position has become increasingly one of wanting the man out of office because of the danger he poses to America and the rest of the world rather than his inability to control his baser instincts.

It is of more than passing interest that Clinton could make such an asinine statement that there are no foreign missiles pointed at the U.S. any longer! Why would he tell such an outrageous lie? And why isn't the problem of huge amounts of weapons grade nuclear material disappearing from Russia an issue? A scorched earth scenario on Clinton's part becomes an increasing possibility in the light of such facts. I can only hope and pray that someone in Congress is minding the store.

As the readers of TAP know I am encouraging a Bush/Dole ticket for Y2K. This because I believe we need a woman like Elizabeth Dole in the White House. But the country won't elect a woman President. At least not yet. One of the reasons for this is because while the country would go for Elizabeth Dole or Hillary Clinton for Vice President, women won't vote for a woman President. Why not? Women don't trust women.

I explore this interesting phenomenon in my Birds book. Not to belabor the point, one of the reasons for this is the fact that women steal the boyfriends and husbands of other women. And it didn't help the position of women or the churches when those two old fat and ugly lesbians were recently united in a holy ceremony of togetherness with the sanction of a church while a congregation of perverts cheered them on with all possible religious trappings and fervor. God didn't need this kind of press.

It was refreshing to hear Jack Anderson's recent presentation to the National Press Club. It was refreshing to hear a lucid recitation of the facts of the Clinton impeachment and how desperately America needs moral integrity in its Presidents. When I was a child, loving grandparents and a great-grandmother taught me three things in addition to The Golden Rule that have always stuck with me: If it's wrong, don't do it. If it's not true, don't say it. If it's not yours, don't take it.

Echoing one of my own points concerning Clinton's place in history, Anderson said the President's place is assured as the butt of dirty jokes. Few would disagree that of all who made presentations to the Senate of the case against Clinton, none surpassed Lindsey Graham of South Carolina. In fact, I was so impressed by his thoroughgoing honesty and sincerity in his presentation that I wrote him a personal letter of thanks and gratitude. In my letter to Representative Graham I mentioned that he must have been raised with the same principles that I had been.

But in spite of good men like Lindsey Graham in Congress, America still lacks wisdom. Virtually every nation throughout history has suffered the same lack and has fallen as a result of this deficiency. To bring such a horrendous accusation against America and other nations, past and present, presumes I know what wisdom is and many do not. Now that, my friends, is a truly mind-boggling degree of presumptuousness! Unless I'm right. And you will be the judge of that.

Let me begin by stating the obvious: Knowledge may be power but it is not wisdom. If people had acted with wisdom, there would have been no need to address the issue of segregated schools. The same quality of education and facilities would have been given Negro children.

But the Supreme Court itself had held that Separate But Equal was Constitutional. Only when faced with the facts of irreparable harm being done for decades to Negro children, American citizens, was the Court finally willing to admit it had to change from its previous position.

Had Lincoln not been murdered and had the North acted with wisdom after the Civil War, there would have been no Jim Crow laws to confront. Had the South acted with wisdom and been willing to give up slavery, there would never have been a Civil War. Had the Southern plantation owners acted with wisdom and heeded the acknowledged wisest man in the country, Benjamin Franklin, slavery would have been abolished by the Constitution and there would never have been a John C. Calhoun later arguing that slavery was the natural order of the human race! Had England never embraced slavery and the earliest settlers of the Colonies acted with wisdom, slavery would never have been introduced into America. Had the great civilizations like those of Egypt, Greece, and Rome acted with wisdom in ages past, slavery would never have been countenanced. The very idea, an idea totally abhorrent, repugnant, anathema, and antithetical to wisdom, that a person can own another human being as a piece of property, has a very long and ignoble history. But it is a damning fact of history that as much as anything else is proof of a lack of wisdom throughout the history of humankind. That is if you believe wisdom derives from love and compassion.

The brevity of the example I have given concerning the historical lack of wisdom on the part of humankind evidenced by slavery should not trivialize the point or the importance of the issue. Just as the similar case of the degrading of the value of women and children, another historical fact of the lack of wisdom on the part of the rulers of history, men, should never be trivialized.

No, I most certainly do not mean to trivialize by brevity. The subjects are worthy of a thousand, lengthy volumes. I only treat the subjects here as the briefest introduction of an apologetic for an equation that is based on wisdom deriving from love and compassion, that my position that humankind has lacked wisdom throughout history is a valid one.

The years devoted to learning led me to the conclusion that if a problem persisted and defied solution, the approach to an answer must be wrong. If peace has been so elusive throughout history, there had to be something wrong with the approach to an answer. But what was that thing?

Many philosophies and religions teach it is an innate flaw in human nature, the Fallen Man, Sin, etc. But if I was right in determining that women have been excluded or made subordinate throughout history in the philosophies, religions, and governments of nations, that men have purposely kept women subordinate, that men make wars, not women, here was a substantial part of the problem. And please don't try to beg the facts or quote exceptions to the rule as though that made the rule any less than the facts. That is only pseudo-intellectualism at best.

This exclusion of women led me to write my book: "Women: The Missing Half of Humankind!" In the writing of the book, I was able to put many of my thoughts and learning into focus on the problem. This in turn led me to consider another aspect of the problem. No nation in history had ever made children its priority. What if America should do so?

The two facts of the exclusion of half of humankind in the decision-making processes of men and the lack of prioritizing children led to the Amendment as a place to start in finding a solution to the problem of the constant conflict between people and nations.

I have had to face many bullies in my life. I have had to face the ugliness of discrimination and prejudice against me many times in my life. I have had to face those who thought that the killing of a man or the burning of his home, the taking of all his possessions, would mean the end, the death, of an idea! And this, I believe, as much as anything else, proves my point that humanity has always suffered a lack of wisdom. And still does so.

It wasn't Thoreau's ego speaking when he wrote that his elders had not contributed anything of wisdom to his own. He was saying the same thing I have said; that the supposed and vaunted wisdom of the past has not made any progress in making people more loving and compassionate.

But my friend Henry missed the boat concerning wisdom. He never addressed the fact that none of those he admired, not even those of Eastern philosophies, had missed the same boat. None of the wise men with their philosophies or holy scriptures of the past had ever admitted wisdom was impossible as long as women were continually excluded from the Great

Conversation, as long as children were never made the priority of philosophers or the works and scriptures of nations. To this extent, even the greatest of poets have been delinquent.

In the last issue of TAP when I made the comment that while we have made remarkable, literally astoundingly near miraculous, advances in knowledge this has not been matched by a commensurate advancement in love and compassion, I simply echoed Thoreau's own thoughts. Henry, though, wrote better than he knew in this respect since he never married and never had children.

As I also pointed out, knowledge has given us the ability to state the problem that is half the solution. But as I also said, the other half must come from wisdom. And wisdom grows in proportion to advancing in love and compassion. And this is why humanity still gropes, fumbles, and stumbles for an answer to the historic problem of the inability of the peoples of the world getting along together. Knowledge has given us the power to bring about Armageddon, to destroy the earth. But only wisdom will prevent this happening.

It is my contention that the Amendment, through prioritizing children for the first time in history, is a good start, a logical start, to solving the problem. Logical knowledge dictates that no nation that fails to cherish its children can possibly survive. Nor does it deserve to. But this is empirical and logical knowledge, not wisdom.

So I offer for your consideration Heath's Equation:

Knowledge + Wisdom = Peace

If, as I maintain, wisdom derives from love and compassion, I believe my equation is correct. This obviously presumes that perfect love is fully knowledgeable of evil, that whatever the origin of evil, it has had a domino effect throughout all of history. Thus, the lack of wisdom has repeatedly doomed humanity to making the same mistakes over and over again, the cycle of evil, which is the cycle of history that continues to dog humanity.

Knowledge is derived from learning. But can people learn wisdom? I believe they can. Once the abuses of slavery and the denying of equal rights under the law were addressed, people could look back and realize that they had learned a degree of wisdom throughout the processes that confronted these evils.

Wisdom has people in fact, cherishing their young. And there is such a thing as learning to love and hate. I believe God intended children to teach us to love and through such love, to hate evil. The proposed Amendment is based on real, logical and empirical knowledge. But only wisdom combined with knowledge will enact the Amendment and make it operative in people's lives.

As with the need of law in the case of redressing the shameful abuse of black Americans, and following this, the realization of a former lack of conscience, so the Amendment will begin with law and be followed in the same manner with an awareness of the lack of conscience toward our treatment of children. In short, the Mad Man Hypothesis will have worked once more. But in the case of the Amendment, it may prove the salvation of all humanity by our finally learning wisdom!

But raising the awareness of the need of the Amendment is the most daunting of any task ever undertaken for the saving of the world. It requires, first and foremost a sensitivity to the problem, which few actually possess. But, of course, it was this very lack of sensitivity that necessitated the Civil Rights Movement resulting in the force of law being brought to bear on the problem. The Amendment, as law, is necessitated for the very same reason.

I have many a curious conversation with myself. I have many arguments with myself and sometimes I lose the argument. Being compelled on my present course of the Amendment, I become very fatigued. It is tiring to have to deal with such profoundly complex issues as the Amendment brings to light, issues I would far rather have someone else deal with. I really am a sensitive man; I bleed when I'm cut just like you do. I'm hurt when people say bad things about me and I really would far rather go along in order to get along.

But it seems that as a well-qualified mad man, I just can't let it alone. The idea is there and won't go away. And I find myself constantly discovering more and more vindication for the idea, that the Amendment is needed if the world is ever to know peace. Speaking of sensitivity, and attempting to get away from such a profoundly complex and personally fatiguing issue as the Amendment for a moment and find a few moments' surcease from a troubled mind, I often escape into music and humor.

Those who know me know of my love of opera and the music of the great musicals. But it is often a difficult task to fit the music to my mood. For example, my mood the other day led me to listening to some of the following great classics evocative of a by-gone era when the finer tastes, sensibilities, and civilized manners prevailed:

A'Feudin' and A'Fightin', I'm a Lonely Little Petunia in an Onion Patch, Melancholy Baby, Too Fat Polka, I Never See Maggie Alone, and Pistol Packin' Mama. And one of my all-time favorites, Cocktails For Two by Spike Jones and his City Slickers (I still can't find The Dooky Bird Song and I've misplaced Cigareets 'n' Whusky, 'n' Wile, Wile Wimmin). Ah, the things people don't know they are missing due to their being culturally deprived (this is the humor in case you missed it).

Few men of creative genius were as gifted in artistic versatility as Noel Coward who was knighted in 1970. A playwright and composer, his plays and some of his songs like I'll See You Again, Room With a View, Someday I'll Find You, and others remain among my favorites. I even like Mad About the Boy in spite of the fact that I know Coward didn't write it with a woman singing it in mind.

Most know of Coward's Blithe Spirit, which remains popular. And his film Brief Encounter, taken from his play Still Life, never fails to bring a lump to my throat and a catch in my breast when I watch it. Coward was an accomplished actor and singer as well as playwright and composer. Many of us know of his triumph on stage in Las Vegas. None of us will forget his animated performance of Mad Dogs and Englishmen. Most English actors and actresses of note who went on to fame started in Noel Coward plays and films. The time would fail to mention those who owed their start and future success to Coward.

But the man possessed of such artistic genius once said the thing that bothered him most was not having children. He said he felt this was a void in his life, that having given himself to so many experiences of life, he often wondered if this was not something that left a vital gap?

Perhaps this is why Coward, who placed such emphasis on laughter and romance, was a lonely man who could write so sensitively and passionately of romance but couldn't speak of it. No one could ever draw him into a conversation on the subject except in the most superficial way. Still, one only has to watch "Brief Encounter", one only has to listen to the best of his romantic compositions, to know this was a man of deeply sensitive romanticism.

His "In Which We Serve", however, showed his longing to be heroic; a reaction to his last name? Perhaps. But most likely, as with not having children, he knew in his heart that he really was a coward. As such, and not having a family and children, he died alone with no one who could really help him die.

I have mentioned Noel Coward for a couple of reasons; first, to pay my respect to his creative genius. The second is more complicated. Recently, I had a column in the paper in which I said that it is insane for parents to be forced to submit their children to a homosexual teacher in the classroom. As the Founding Fathers had taken great pains to prevent a State Religion, so they would have taken equally great pains to prevent children being exposed to perversion. But such a thing as we face in America today would have been virtually impossible for the Founding Fathers to have foreseen. So low has America sunk into the cesspool of immorality.

An acquaintance of mine, Ward, took vehement exception to my column. Ward only visits the Valley occasionally but he gets the local paper to stay informed since his elderly father lives here. Ward is a very gifted man artistically and prominent among Hollywood personalities. He rubs shoulders with, and is in demand by, people like Spielberg and others of equal fame.

Whenever Ward and I get together, he always expresses his consternation over my living in the Valley where there is such a dearth of culture. He knows I suffer from the lack of intellectual and artistic stimulation to be found in places like L.A. and San Francisco. He also worries about my living alone in such seclusion.

It isn't an easy question to answer. My travels and years of living in places like L.A. and San Francisco are constant reminders of what I am missing in my life. As to living alone, better that than with the wrong woman. Both for her sake and mine. I've learned at least this much in my dotage.

But being an intimate of the Hollywood crowd, it wasn't surprising that Ward would take vehement exception to my column. He had just returned from a shoot in the Caribbean and was regaling me with the story when he suddenly asked: "Sam, how can you be such a sensitive artist, have such an educated background and be so intellectually gifted yet have this bias concerning homosexuality?"

Ward's praise wasn't flattery; I knew that and appreciated it. But his question reminded me of Noel Coward. Like Coward, Ward didn't have children and he was a part of a society and industry, which has been thoroughly infiltrated and propagandized by homosexuals. His own mind-set, his own bias, prevented his understanding what he called bias on my part.

But I asked Ward in turn about the comments of people like Marlon Brando and Dolly Parton that Hollywood was ruled by nothing but Jews, that Jewish children were used in virtually every film, sitcom, and commercial possible that required children and young people especially whether they fit the part or not? Was that strictly the bias of Brando and Parton? If so, one still couldn't discount the fact that for such a small number numerically, Jews were vastly disproportionate, and very effective, to their numbers in such categories. Was it strictly bias to acknowledge the truth of this? Was I, like Brando and Parton, to be labeled anti-Semitic for knowing and acknowledging the truth of this?

Ward was knowledgeable and honest enough to agree that my analogy was correct, that he knew I was certainly not anti-Semitic; but like most people, he didn't make the connection between homosexuality and child molestation or the impact of homosexuals propagandizing their cause through Hollywood productions and personalities. But if he had had a molested child, if he himself had been molested, he wouldn't have any difficulty making the connection. He could acknowledge the truth concerning such inordinate Jewish influence in Hollywood without being anti-Semitic, but not the homosexual influence.

As to his consternation and genuine, friendly concern about my continuing to live in the Valley, I explained it had nothing to do with being a big frog in a little pond. Though even Ward admitted this had some validity and useful utility. And much as I miss the cultural amenities of a large metropolitan city, Ward could understand that as a writer there are many stories of real life to be found in my small corner of the world with which I might not have such intimacy in a large city.

While I am ever mindful that Damon Runyon seldom lacked for material along The Great White Way, even he had to resort to manufacture at times through the very lack of the kind of small town intimacy that finds a place in many of my stories. Ward has read enough of my writing to understand how much I am given to the personal, human dimension in my writing. It is my mixing it up with real people, often the small people of no distinction that gives my writing such realism. And as a poet, I have a distinct tendency to see the ordinary and ordinary people in an extraordinary way.

Recently a beautiful woman asked my help. I have known her for quite some time and was willing to credit the story she told me which necessitated my helping her. It was late at night when Sheriff's deputies had stopped her because one of her headlights was out. But she had been at a bar with friends and one was well known to the deputies. At this point, it became a case of guilt by association.

The girl had limited her drinking and knew she wasn't drunk. She wouldn't, I know, drive drunk; if not from a moral motive most certainly because of the very heavy fine of a DUI which she couldn't possibly afford. She's an intelligent and responsible girl and wouldn't risk such a thing happening.

According to what she told me, the deputies delighted in patting her down and calling her names like "Sweetcheeks". Because of the attitude of the cops and their treatment of her, she refused a sobriety test and, instead, demanded a lawyer. She told me she felt so humiliated because of her treatment by these deputies that she simply lost it and couldn't think of anything else to do. But there is nothing that so arouses the ire of cops than to have their authority challenged. Especially if they know they have not followed proper procedure. The deputies called the CHP.

The Chippie who arrived is well known throughout the Valley. None of the officers insisted on the girl taking a sobriety test, none Miranded her; the Chippie just put handcuffs on her and hauled her off to jail where she sat for four hours before being released. She was made to sign a form declaring she wouldn't drive until after her court hearing. And still no one insisted on her taking a sobriety test.

She showed me all the paperwork. It was obvious the cops had bungled their job. In fact, in the interim the DMV had given her a temporary license based on the shoddy paperwork, obviating the declaration she had been forced to sign before the police would release her. The whole thing was so obviously a case of harassment that I took the girl to the public defender's office. After he looked over the papers and heard her story he told the girl they were going for a jury trial. His comment to her: It seems these guys just didn't have anything better to do than harass you. I don't know what the outcome of the jury trial will be. I'll let my readers know in the next issue of TAP.

Those who know me well know I am usually on the side of the police. In fact, because of my own background and experience, I'm a member of NAPO (National Association of Police Organizations). I've often said the police have an impossible task. More than one officer has told me that they are doing a garbage job. And that's largely true.

But to repeat, I hate and despise bullies, especially those who abuse their authority. And to further repeat, this is the basis of my hatred for the child molester. This is the basis of my hatred of Clinton who has abused the highest office of the land and brought all of America into disrepute before the whole world! Much as I commiserate with the police, I have known many of them personally and will never forget that Chippie who gave me the speeding ticket and lied in court about it. Or another who cited me for failure to yield the right of way when there was no traffic to which to yield. He lied in court as well. Nor will I ever forget the Chief of Police I once interviewed who told me: We're not here to serve and protect, we're here to slam the door on people!

It is true that a job with a gun and badge is an invitation to the wrong kind of people who like to carry a gun and thump heads. And much as the various agencies try to weed out such people, it is estimated that fully one-third of our police should not be doing such work (in my own experience, this figure relates to teachers as well).

In respect to the girl, the police had bullied and humiliated her. In her own words: Sam, it was as though they had raped me! She had experienced what I know all too well of the mindless primitive who sees women as prey, something that is all too often excused in society. And she had no one of any real reputation or ability to help her but me. She had no one else to turn to for help.

Much as I understand the cops enjoying patting down a beautiful woman, much as I, as a pretty normal man in this respect, would have enjoyed doing the same, there is never any excuse for any man or woman abusing their authority over others. As to sexist remarks, these are always uncalled for under any circumstances.

Had I not been there to help her, she would probably have lost her driver's license and be in jail now. But I was careful to point out to her the risk she took in such a small community of being judged by her associations with people like the guy who was with her and the police recognized.

Fortunately, there were no drugs or alcohol in the car or on their persons. That would have been the end of it. Not that some cops are above planting such evidence if the circumstances meet their criteria of not being caught doing so. But no matter the outcome, this is a small community and you can be assured the police will be watching her very carefully from now on. They won't forget. Will they be out to get her? Quite possibly.

As we waited to appear in court for the public defender to tell the judge and DA a jury trial was being requested, the girl made the comment that she wished she had had a tape recorder in order to present that as evidence of the way the cops had spoken to her in such a humiliating manner. I wished the same. But it prompted my thinking that this may yet be our lot as citizens. Has it come to the point in our society that honest law-abiding people are going to have to travel with recorders in order to protect themselves from the police? Will automakers begin to see this as a marketing device, an option along with those tracking systems and burglar alarms, in cars? Will carmakers begin to offer an option that keeps a timed recording of the speed you are traveling? I sure could have used that item in the past. And still may. Come to think about it, these are not bad ideas. But what a commentary on life in America!

The camcorders in police cars have proven to be invaluable. How about for the ordinary citizen? But it's more likely that Big Brother will require motorists begin wearing helmets before the auto industry catches on to what is happening when it comes to some of the police abusing their authority toward the motoring public.

I have this acquaintance that is a real electronics and computer wizard. But he has this little problem that prevents his working regular hours at a regular job. He's a little nuts. Binge drinking in the past has resulted in his having cirrhosis among other things and being unable to focus on ordinary matters. He was fired from his last high-tech job after his third accident in three months in SoCal while driving drunk. And this didn't include a trip to the Valley when he had demolished a car during the same time frame.

I nursed him through his last drinking bout, which nearly killed him. Refusing to see a doctor, he laid on a pallet on the floor of my cottage for nearly a week, barely able to crawl to the bathroom to relieve himself. I visit him occasionally just to compare notes because he does stay abreast of the developments in computers. They are his greatest passion. He does have another problem besides being a little nuts and his failing health. He seems to attract some undesirables, a bum magnet as Vivian put it in Pretty Woman.

Since he lives alone, these people often take advantage and I never know whom I will encounter flopping at his place and sponging off him.

He's been ripped off and taken advantage of so much I wonder he has never learned the lesson. I went by one time to find his front window broken out and someone had kicked a hole in his front door. He said some disgruntled and drunken woman had done it. But considering he has been married nine times, I just figure he's a professional victim as well as a bum magnet.

A couple of months ago, there was a young skinhead in attendance, one Timmy. I knew Timmy was a real wrong number and only stayed a few minutes. I left wondering if my acquaintance had switched from women to young men? It was, I knew, a possibility.

I went by again a week ago and Timmy was gone. I asked about him and was told he shot and killed a guy in a drug deal gone sour, had been caught and was going to prison for life. Seems the shooting was the third strike for Timmy.

Well, I know a lot of interesting people and will always be mixing it up with real people including the druggies, prostitutes, thieves, murderers, and Wise Guy wannabes as well as people like my Hollywood friend, Ward. My Birds book is replete with the stories of such associations. No end of material for a writer. Life is more than many in polite society and church pulpits realize except for what they see in Film at Eleven.

And in spite of my more unsavory associations and the advice about being known by those with whom you associate, I'm well enough known in the community to obviate this. An educated man who doesn't drink or do drugs, who is a writer and has some better associations than ex-cons, I am able to dance to a different tune. But there are risks attendant with this kind of music.

A big burly guy, an ex-con with a violent past and temper, once wanted to be my bodyguard; seems he knew enough of my associations, the work I'm doing and the threats made against me, to get the idea I needed one. I explained my reasons for refusal to him and he took it well. Just two weeks ago, he dropped dead of a heart attack. He was only forty-two. You never know. Apart from a propensity for wanting to tear out people's lungs, he was a nice guy.

When I'm not traveling, I usually try to make it to the Club on Friday and Saturday nights for the live music and dancing. Oscar and Jerry have been providing the music there for years and we know each other well. I've even played with them on occasion.

Because Oscar and I know many of the same Kern County musicians, past and present like Odell Johnson and Buck Owens, famous and not so famous; we always have something or someone to talk about; and the music.

We never tire of talking music. And about the various bar fights, generally over women, that usually accompany the C&W in honky tonks.

But the women get their licks in also, as Oscar and I know full well. The ladies often give a floorshow well worth the price of admission. I'll never forget one beautiful girl I knew busting a house stick over one barroom Romeo's head. The reason she used a house stick was because the guy had taken her McDermott and wouldn't return it. Better a house stick. Not long ago I watched as another girl I know tried to punch the lights out of some guy who didn't understand NO!

The other night at another club, the barmaid had to take the barbat to another guy who didn't understand NO! A couple of the patrons took him outside and finished the job. When the paramedics and cops arrived, it was called a clear case of self-defense. But knowing how dumb this guy is, he'll probably be back.

Some time ago, Oscar decided my special song was to be "Cool Water". Now, every time I'm at the Club, I get treated to Cool Water. It is a great tune and I always appreciate Oscar's playing and singing it.

While I might have made a terrific librarian, loving books as I do, or an archaeologist, art or museum curator, loving art and culture as I do, I think about my other experiences of life, of mixing with real people, and I know my calling has always been that of a writer and poet. And, I suppose, I'll keep mixing it up as long as I continue to recognize the Timmys and remain agile enough to dance and duck in time. Fortunately, I still go out and my back doesn't.

I often get material from sources like The Creation Research Society. I was once invited to become a member/teacher for the Society. The readers of TAP know of my fascination with particle physics research and just recently a friend sent me something from the Society having to do with this most important area of science.

Now granting that the Society has a distinct bias, it is one that I share in respect to believing in God and believing in His special creation of humanity. I definitely believe in Children of God. Of course, I believe in Children of the Devil as well. And the distinction really opens a can of worms when it comes to any discussion of the distinction, which has to do with Dualism and the origin of evil.

The material my friend sent deals with quantum concepts in physics. There are many good mathematicians, researchers and scientists in the Society and I once shared a podium with one of them. I have great respect for the Society and its members.

I have written extensively of the theories and findings in particle physics because I believe that this area of research will eventually answer many questions of creation that presently fall into religious superstitions. I've mentioned my fascination with the study of fractals, which are a part of the over-all understanding of how patterns of hugely complex mathematical precision develop in all of creation.

The mathematical basis and precision of creation is the basis of our understanding of the universe. When the mathematics fails to explain, it drives the curiosity of researchers.

But we work at a disadvantage knowing our understanding of mathematics is not complete. And in some cases, is even contradictory. For example, the infinity of pi, 3, 6, and 9, the discrepancy between fractions and decimal fractions and how this impacts on every area of science.

1+1=2 and 1x1=1, 2+2=4 and 2x2=4, and while 3+3=6, 3x3=9.

The utility of such a system belies the enormous complexity of mathematics and the deficiency of our present knowledge. And there is even a philosophy of mathematics that has grown out of our deficiency of mathematical certainty and precision in some cases.

I've used the illustration of firing a bullet straight up in the air. The data needed to determine its impact point falling to earth within an acre would be small. But the data needed to predict an impact point within a square inch would be truly astronomical. In matters of precision, obviously the amount of data needed varies in proportion to the degree of precision needed. Precision of one-tenth is a simple thing. Precision of one-trillionth is quite something else.

And if mathematics seems daunting, extrapolated to human behavior it becomes profoundly complex in the extreme. My idea for a mathematical model of human behavior is one I continue to contemplate. A simple number line with the indicated extremes of love and hate are an example. When you try to quantify an emotion, you may need a line light-years in length. The studies in astro- and particle physics become simple by comparison. But a lack of precision is the reason that psychology is, at best, only a quasi-science.

One of the most fascinating things in creation is light. Very early studies of light showed it had properties of both waves and particles. But these were contradictory characteristics; which only proved we still had a long way to go in understanding the physics involved. And still do. But recent work with sonoluminescence is, if you'll forgive the pun, shedding much light on the subject.

Genetics: The potential for fulfilling the dream of Dr. Frankenstein (or Dr. Mengele). As work progresses in the mapping of the human genome, the possibilities are truly mind-boggling; both for good and evil. To envision the possibility of actually making babies to order is a fearful proposition!

This brings to mind the Dark Ages and my contention that humanity still lacks wisdom. Only wisdom is able to direct things like genetics and atomic energy properly in a beneficent way. Lacking such wisdom, as human beings we are perfectly right in fearing some of the advances in science. But such fear is a perfect reflection of those Dark Ages when science was made subordinate to religious superstitions. This lack of wisdom led Michio Kaku and others to warn that we stand in danger of not surviving number 92 of the periodic table, that if other civilizations existed on other worlds, they didn't survive past this point either.

Does this mean wisdom is unattainable? I don't think so. If I am right in my equation of Knowledge+Wisdom=Peace, it is only a matter of determining just how, exactly, we learn wisdom? I maintain this begins with doing something no nation in history has ever done: we prioritize children as the most important priority in the world; and unless we do so, we are indeed doomed to Armageddon!

That it has never been enough to recognize evil, action is required, so wisdom must overcome a mere abstraction and become reality. And for wisdom to become so, action is required. It is my belief that the proposed Amendment is a beginning to learning wisdom, an action that has the promise of removing wisdom from an abstraction and making it a reality in our lives.

When superstition and ignorance, religion and bigotry, unfounded fears drive law, the kind of society that evolves from such law is not one I want to live in. But give me a society that is no longer fearful because it has placed the emphasis of law on the cherishing of its children, ah, that is a society ruled by wise law and leaders and one in which I would have no fear.

Can we expect a quick solution to the problem that has haunted us throughout all of history, the problem that will most certainly doom us if not solved in time? I believe the Amendment to be the start of the solution. But like the man said: If you're not paranoid, you just don't see the whole picture! No, I don't believe I am being paranoid because of what I consider to be a logical view of the facts. The fact that humanity has not gained in wisdom but has the knowledge to destroy itself is not paranoia.

So we continue to come back to the fact that without wisdom, we most certainly will destroy ourselves. And I will continue to maintain that the proposed Amendment is the place to start in becoming wise, that a philosophical abstraction can become a reality by this New Way, a new way that has never before in history been attempted.

Fearful as it is because of so many unknowns, fearful because of a Dark Ages mentality that infects so many; the Amendment still holds promise of avoiding Armageddon. But just try to find someone with whom you can have an intelligent discussion beginning with my equation for peace. In most cases, you get a vacant, glassy-eyed stare. This is the basis of my fear of our running out of time. Books have proliferated on the concern about the intellectual loss in America. We could hardly be called a nation of intellectuals. The hearings in Congress alone give one cause for fear on this basis.

But where is the book that emphasizes the need to prioritize children? A lot of abstract lip service but no specific that emphasizes this need in order to avoid our destroying ourselves; neither does the book exist, apart from my own with documentation, which places an emphasis on the absolute need of women being equally involved in The Great Conversation.

Where is the wisdom of selfishly conceiving unwanted babies and then murdering them by abortion? Where is wisdom when some are too rich while others are starving to death? Where is wisdom when people are divided, and even murder each other, in the name of God or politics? Where is wisdom when ideological or racial hatreds continue to proliferate? And lacking wisdom: If not now, when?

Do I really enjoy dealing with all of this? Absolutely not! I most sincerely wish it were some other guy. And, as I often think, maybe it is that other guy, the one I blame for such thoughts and writing. I only know, as I've often pointed out, that for some reason he behaves as the Hound of Heaven who will not leave me alone. I do this by a compulsion, not because I want to.

It's Friday. We've had a good rain in the Valley but this morning the sun shines brightly through the windows where I (or that other guy) do the writing. Tonight I will go to the Club (since the churches close up shop early and aren't open on Friday or Saturday nights and if we had a museum or art gallery they would be closed as well) and enjoy shooting pool, listening to the music, and dancing with the ladies. I'll still hope I can duck quickly enough if I have to. I'll try to ignore that other guy.

I won't meet anyone who wants to discuss my equation for world peace. I will hear some new stories of love and romance, of betrayal of love, of who just went to jail or got out, and maybe there will be a fight over one of the girls. Or between a couple of them; a *catfight* as it is called. But when I come home, I know I will lay in bed unable to sleep until that other guy has his say.

The other night we were having this discussion about the real objective of learning, knowledge, and education. I say discussion though that other guy seems to do all the talking. Obviously most get an education in order to make their way in life. And that's as it should be. But what about character? Shouldn't children be learning about character as well, both at home and in the classroom? Well, I had to admit that was true. And this should be one of the objectives of learning, knowledge, and education.

Citizenship. We used to teach children to be good citizens. What did that mean in the context of what children are actually learning about America and its leadership today? I shuddered at that. Come to think about it, now that that other guy had me thinking again, curse him, when I was a child good citizenship was one of the goals of education and emphasized at home and at school. When had that passed away?

Like good manners and correct, civilized speech. When had those stopped being objectives of education? Well, the albatross of that other guy led me long ago to start thinking about the last time poets worked in America, the time of the great Broadway Musicals. Seems America was losing sight of good citizenship, good manners, and correct, civilized speech as objectives of education about the same time. Both at home and in the schools.

I had given a copy of one chapter of my novel to a girl and she later told me: "Sam, I don't know how you wrote this! I had forgotten I had such thoughts and dreams when I was a little girl. And you're a man, a grown man! It must have taken a lot out of you to write that way."

Admittedly it does take a lot out of me to write that way. But as I recently shared with a friend, thank God I can still think and dream like a child! It hasn't been beaten out of me yet and I thank God life has not made me hard, cynical, and callous. I still delight in the magic of childhood, in Santa, the fairies and elves, enchanted forests and glades, I still believe in the best of Camelot, of Knights and their Ladies. I still delight in birds and animals, looking through a kaleidoscope and watching butterflies, baby bunnies and duckies.

But these things, admittedly as well, make me all too often guilty of the accusation of one of my ex-wives: A nice man with no common sense. I'll still leave off the practical things and turn aside at the call of quail or the bark of a squirrel. And some particular tree or rock in the forest, a pristine trout stream, will always have more allure for me than the most magnificent structures or arts of men.

I was sitting next to a fellow the other night at the club. He was drunk; and getting drunker. He told me he was dying of colon cancer and was passing blood. He refused an operation saying he was afraid. "You know", he said, "I'm afraid of the operation and I'm afraid of dying."

Well, death is never a fun subject, drunk or sober. But it called to mind the many fears of those Dark Ages. And I was reminded once more that the Amendment causes a lot of fear in people; fear in part because of the evil in their own hearts, fear in part because of the unknown. Martin Luther King, Jr.'s memorial reads: "Free at last, Free at last, Thank God Almighty, I'm Free at last!" A fitting epitaph and memorial; but is it true? Only God knows.

The unknown: But for those of us who believe, there is great comfort in not accepting death as nihilism as long as we have tried to live by the rules.

But how, do you suppose, did cannibals learn to like eating other people? Where do people learn to take pleasure in inflicting pain and suffering in others, in abusing and molesting children? Where do people learn to take pleasure in abusing their authority over others?

Learn wisdom. Well, of course! If we would only learn wisdom, the fear of the unknown would pass away. And cruelty would cease and love and compassion would become the norm for the first time in history. Do I know this? Of course not; but I believe it. After all, where does the fear of death originate if not from our personal fear of not having done right?

Certainly there is the normal fear of cessation of being, of the great unknown of the grave. But most of us have a hope or belief beyond the grave. A part of the foundation for such a hope or belief is our natural tendency to pray. People pray; they believe God hears prayer. And for those of us with such a hope or belief, for those of us who pray, doing right in our lives is of most paramount importance.

Because of this hope, I can't think of anything better to do with my life than work for passage of the Amendment. If, as I believe, children are the closest thing to the heart of God Himself, how could I think of any better way to please Him than giving my life to such a purpose?

But it isn't pleasing God that compels me. I wish I could say it was. It is watching the suffering of little ones that compels me, it is never being able to get away from the image of two little girls who were tortured, dying alone of thirst in a dark dungeon in Belgium who God Himself couldn't help in spite of their screams and, eventually, their swollen-tongued whispered prayers for death to deliver them from such unimaginable suffering, that compels me. It is knowing it is my responsibility not God's to do all I can to make sure such a thing is never forgotten and will never happen again!

Imagine, if you will, someone putting a cat or dog alive in a box or cage and leaving it to die of thirst. Imagine the hue and cry that would be raised against such a monster that could do such a thing! Most would say such a monster wasn't fit to live! But we will let such monsters continue to live who do this to children. Where is wisdom to be found in this?

Someone had to tell cannibals it was wrong to eat other people. More than telling them, they had to prove it. Well, this was really impossible. So, the force of law was applied. And, in time, cannibalism became virtually extinct.

The fact that it was just simply wrong to murder and eat other people didn't carry much weight with cannibals. But living under law and its penalties began to have the desired effect of enforcing a social view by the courts. In this singular case, most would agree with the law, that it was good law.

We have a form of cannibalism going on throughout the world in the singular case of molestation. Only law will change the practice. The weakness of the present laws should be obvious. They are far from universal and the average term in prison for child molesters is only 2.2 years!

That figure proves how little concern society has for children. We lack wisdom. But a universal law, the Amendment, will eventually teach wisdom. And, like confronting cannibalism, the learning of wisdom begins with just and universal law and its penalty. What will not be done for the sake of conscience must be done by law. Wisdom will follow if the law is just.

CHAPTER THREE

So long as there be beautiful and virtuous women, so long will there be poets inspired to extol their beauty and virtue.

As I write, it is coming up on Valentine's Day. This is the day, of course, when some with a mean streak have a chance to get even with those insufferable people who deserve getting even with (and you thought I was going to start this issue of TAP with some sentimentality regarding the day).

For example I know one guy in the Valley who is sure to get a Valentine signed: "From A Secret Admirer". It's going to drive him absolutely nuts because he is such an insufferably oafish braggart who acts like he is God's gift to women. It will undoubtedly be the only Valentine he will receive and it is sure to have him climbing the walls. While yours truly is far too kind to engage in this kind of deviltry, I did suggest the sender put a drop of perfume on the card. Nice touch, huh? I guess I'm just an incurable romantic after all.

Being interested in our local history here in the Kern River Valley, I've discovered why the Indians that used to inhabit the area became extinct. It was their name. The tribe was called the Tubatulabal. What woman in her right mind wanted to be called Mrs. Tubatulabal?

Well, with the end of the NutBowl, FruitBowl, FingerBowl, etc. ad nauseum, football season has officially ended with SuperBowl XXXIII (which, because of some events and commercials surrounding the game, I have elected to call The ToiletBowl).

As an inveterate despiser of the obscene salaries paid grown men playing children's games, I nevertheless accepted an invitation from friends to watch the game. It was that or see the latest Hollywood smash hit The Brave Little Toaster Goes to Mars or sit home and listen to my new CD of 24 Gregorian Chants by the latest hot group of monks; culture and refinement vs. watching a bunch of guys trying to knock each other's brains out. Tough call but being with my friends made it worth the while to watch the game (and, I have to confess, I'm not all that keen on Chants or Renaissance and Baroque music no matter how hot the licks. The Brave Little Toaster, on the other hand...).

Interestingly, since one of the football players was arrested the night before the game for soliciting oral sex from an undercover cop (female, I assume, though one can't take such a thing for granted these days), we can expect to hear of a Clinton Defense that it wasn't really sex.

Undoubtedly, this issue, thanks to Clinton, is going to make it to the Supreme Court that will be expected to act on the definition of sex. This ceases to be funny in any way, shape or form, at that point.

And Americans will have Clinton and football to thank for the Supreme Court's intrusion into their personal sex lives and, eventually, into their bedrooms.

It was his attack on a fellow evangelist, one Marvin Gorman that brought Jimmy Swaggart down. Because of Swaggart's personal attacks on him, Gorman's son trapped Swaggart with prostitute Debra Murphree. Murphree would pose provocatively in the nude while Swaggart masturbated. This, according to Swaggart, wasn't really sex. I'm sure Clinton would agree with him; but the Supreme Court?

Murphree was paid $210,000 (before taxes) from Penthouse for the story. Monica will do even better. It warms the heart to hear of poor working girls making good. But to quote Murphree re: Swaggart: To me, he was kind of perverted. I wouldn't want him around my children. I couldn't agree more with Murphree's assessment of Swaggart. But then I wouldn't want Clinton around my children either. And, concerning Murphree's concern for her children, calling the kettle black most certainly comes to mind.

Curiously, Swaggart's defense wasn't masturbating in front of a nude woman not really being sex. Not that the Assembly of God churches would have bought such a defense and been any less unforgiving in such a case, but it does pose some interesting questions a la Clinton and that football player. Yessir, the Court is going have some fun with this one. But will Americans find it so funny after the decisions come down?

I made the statement some time ago that Clinton may well have said, and truly believed, the Bible didn't count oral sex as real sex. So with Swaggart who had written pornography titillates and captivates the sickest of the sick in his book Rape of a Nation.

All of this simply to prove that the Devil (and his servants like Clinton and Swaggart) knows how to corrupt the truth to his own ends. He certainly knows how to put the right words in the wrong mouths. Though thinking people will continue to understand sex as sex regardless the twisted interpretations given by those like Clinton and Swaggart or even surveys like those in JAMA. But the Supreme Court will eventually sort all of this out- it will be forced to. And Americans will be forced to live with the decisions thanks to people like Clinton and Swaggart; and that football player.

On a more gratifying note, researchers in Britain have determined that sex, the real thing, sweeps out bad mutations. They estimate 1.6 to 3 bad genetic mutations are left on the cutting room floor through normal sex. In what is called life's biggest non-regulated (so far) lottery the bad genes usually cause immediate death, eliminating many mutations at once.

For those who might tend to agree with Lord Chesterfield who said of sex (and didn't hypocritically pose any self-serving distorted and twisted ideas about what he meant by the word): "The pleasure is momentary, the position ridiculous and the expense damnable" or James Thurber who asked why it was necessary rather than the easy and relatively antiseptic parthenogenesis; it is a relief to hear researchers say something nice about the real thing at the scientific level.

For my part, I will never understand any man (or woman) who is willing to settle for anything less than the real thing; all or nothing at all. I remain a devout believer in the real thing as the greatest invention in the world and wouldn't trade for a purple pig. And I'm not so old that I'd even trade for a talking frog.

I was at the Club the other night when one of the girls I know well walked up to me and pulling her sweater open exposed a T-shirt with the message: "If you don't feel good, feel me!" So I did. And felt better immediately. I told her later that it beat the T-shirt that read "In case of rape, this end up!"- A hopeful message that only the ugliest girls employ. Well, so much for an esoteric subject in which there is so little interest and which excites only prurient minds; shame on us.

I have suggested to Dean Culpepper of Weedpatch University that the school should open an obedience school for chinchillas, frogs, and ducks. My daughter Karen has had so much success with her Rottweilers; it just seemed reasonable for the University, representing Kern County, to do the same thing for chinchillas, frogs, and ducks.

After all, a county like Kern with famous and cosmopolitan cities like Weedpatch, Bakersfield and Oildale should gain some renown apart from Buck Owens and the fame associated with steel guitars and adenoidal, twangy voices (though lyrics like *I'll be over you when the grass grows over me* sung by an adenoidal voice to the accompaniment of twanging guitars and fiddle does speak for itself; admittedly a tough act to follow.

I'm particularly keen on the possibilities with frogs. Just look at what they have done for Calaveras County? Readers of TAP know of my crusade for better treatment of these noble amphibians that have been so discriminated against.

But Dean Culpepper hasn't shown much enthusiasm for my suggestion as yet. Oh, well, I'll think of something worthy of consideration yet to add further glory to the University, Weedpatch, and Kern County. And I still believe frogs are going to find their rightful place of nobility.

I know I am not the only one who has taken one of those cardboard store-bought pizzas out of the oven only to dump it upside-down on the floor. Or a toaster waffle you have just covered with jelly or peanut butter. Why do such things always seem to fall with the goodies face down; one of those enemas of life. It's still a bad start on your day regardless.

Assuming you are familiar with the hamster and carpet-layer joke (or even if you aren't), you will appreciate what happened to me the other day. Being a relatively civilized man, I make my bed every morning because I hate getting into an unmade bed at night. But to be honest there is another factor: not knowing when I'll have company of the female persuasion (and you thought I was going to leave the subject).

Well, the other morning as I was making the bed, there was a lump in the middle. I gave it a whack to smooth it out and was rewarded by a screeching yowl sufficient to curl the chrome on the ball of a trailer hitch and by a frantic scramble by Furrina, the cat. Infrequently (alas) does my bed evidence such frantic activity under the covers.

Unobserved by me, she had crawled up under the blanket while I had been getting my morning cup of coffee. For those not familiar with cats, they have a marvelous repertoire of distinctive cat-sounds and behavior which can only be fully appreciated when you have thumped one, still largely wild, under the covers while it is sound asleep.

I've always liked cats and find them fascinating critters. Furrina was dumped at my place and was a quite young and feral feline when I took her in. Her wild streak was fully in evidence when I inadvertently gave her a hearty whack in bed.

Cats like comfort. One of the reasons I am taken by them. But I never suspected Furrina had domesticated to the point that she was trying to take over my bed. I'll be more careful of thumping lumps in my bed from now on. And maybe Furrina will be more cautious about where she seeks warmth and comfort.

I'm one of those people who do everything wrong before going to bed. If I feel like eating, I eat. If I want a cup of coffee, I have a cup of coffee. If I feel like eating chocolate, I eat chocolate.

The plus side of doing these bad things just before turning in is that I'm able to grumble about them to Furrina in the morning. It is part of being a professional grumbler, something in which I take great pride. Why? Because as long as I grumble I'm not taking life or myself too seriously.

J.B. Priestly was a grumbler's grumbler. His essays The Grumbler's Apology and On Vulgar Optimists comprise the handbook of professional grumbling, a fine art if there ever was one. Accused of having a saurian eye and being taciturn with a perpetually outshot lower lip, J.B., however, makes the valid point that professional smilers like many preachers have done more to turn people to agnosticism than any others.

It is a gross mistake, a typical one of the non-cognizanti of true grumbling, to mistake this for complaint. True grumbling is never to be construed as complaining. A good grumble, like a good groan in the morning, is worth its weight.

I grumbled, albeit in a very educated and professional manner, in my doctoral dissertation concerning education. I made the valid point, a point my committee grudgingly accepted, that as long as the same people who created the problems in education were being asked by politicians for solutions, education reform would prove impossible.

Now, twenty-five years later, politicians are catching on and beginning to say the same thing. I recently pointed this out to our new California Governor, Gray Davis. I did so because he, like most politicians, is making noise about being concerned for educational reform. But will he be any more successful than so many others? Not likely.

Once he finds out that he confronts the things I covered in my dissertation so long ago, I'm sure he will accommodate himself to the universities, the NEA, and the teacher unions; business and politics as usual. And, of course, the schools will continue to fail to give children an education. Before I leave Priestly, I must commend his essay "All About Ourselves" to every reader. The request that resulted in the essay was that of a young woman who asked J.B.: "Tell me all about yourself."

Like J.B., the ordinary requests and questions about myself give me ample opportunity to lie with the best. A well-contrived and told lie, like a good grumble or groan in the morning, is of inestimable value. Sam Clemens, to whom all red-blooded American men owe so much, was the quintessential expert in such lies.

Put me with any group swapping lies and I can always hold my own. But require me, as with that young woman to J.B., to tell all about myself? Instant mental pandemonium! As with J.B., I'm always prepared with the lion's part written. But faced with the roar of the nightingale, the lion becomes mute.

Like Clemens, I have known good men, honorable men, even men of the cloth, who knew nothing (or pretended not to know) of that most distinguished game of real gentlemen, Draw Poker. And I have known good men, honorable men, even men of the cloth, who had no facility with the telling of a good and well-contrived lie. So much the pity I feel for such culturally starved and deprived creatures so lacking in the most essential, useful quality and sensitivity of true, moral character.

How, now I ask you, is a real man, a man of distinguished culture and refinement, of real sensitivity to the finer things in life, to hold a legitimate conversation with a beautiful member of the opposite sex without facility in one of the most useful and essential devices in any man's armory in such cases? Why the poor soul without such is, above all others, most to be pitied!

Women are marvelous in playing their part. They expect a man worthy of their consideration to be able to hold his own with the best in the use of this device. They are naturally attracted to those men who have proven skill in the ability to command their interest by such a time-honored facility in the use of this mechanism directed at them. It makes the woman feel appreciation for the kind of man who would go to such trouble for her benefit alone.

But just imagine the poor soul so lacking in probity of wit, not equipping himself as a gentleman of the first cloth, so lacking in perspicuity and perspicacity as to deny a woman her right to hearing delicious lies in tribute to her beauty. Such men are most certainly no fun at cocktail parties and are invariably boorish oafs.

Ah, but for a woman to request I tell her all about myself. That, my friends, as J.B. so well documents in his essay, is another kettle of fish. That forces me to consider telling the truth, a truth for which I find no solid ground.

Plato said truthfulness was the first and most important thing to be considered in the governor of his republic. Would that this was the most important thing to be considered in ours!

All of which leads me to comment from the father of the modern essay Michel Eyquem de Montaigne who wrote in his Of Giving The Lie: "Lying is a base vice that one of the ancients paints in his most shameful colors when he says that to lie is to give evidence of having contempt for God and at the same time of fearing men." Montaigne considered his own age so corrupt he was compelled to write this particular essay in an attempt to confront it. One can only think with a shudder what he would have to say of our age.

Francis Bacon, far more remarkable than lovable it was said, of whom Alexander Pope quite accurately commented: ... the wisest, brightest, meanest of mankind, followed Montaigne with his essay Of Truth:

"But it is not only the difficulty and labor which men take in finding out of truth; nor again, that, when it is found, it imposeth upon men's thoughts, that doth bring lies in favor; but a natural though corrupt love of the lie itself... There is no vice that doth so cover a man with shame, as to be found false and perfidious...."

Quite obviously, this describes Clinton perfectly as a coward who fears men and is contemptuous of God. Small wonder Bob Barr walked out of the Prayer Breakfast with Clinton as the speaker. I wouldn't be able to abide such hypocrisy either. And it doesn't speak well of any church that makes a man as contemptuous of God as Clinton is welcome! Or a country that wants to keep such a man in the most important office of America!

And, like those so well known for being false and perfidious liars, Clinton has proven his love of lying. As with all such lovers of lies and contemptuous of God, he evidences no shame for his lies and perfidy though covered with shame.

Both Montaigne and Bacon were careful, however, to distinguish the lie which is designed to both deceive and do injury as per Clinton as opposed to exaggeration or embellishment. For example, to tell a guy you've caught more and bigger fish than he has lied about quite obviously isn't in the category of which Montaigne and Bacon wrote. Clinton, equally obviously, is.

Nor are the civilized lies men tell women or other men (or those that women tell) which are not in the category of intending to both deceive and do injury. Thus Clemens, Priestly, and I in our justification of the well-contrived and told lie which is foundational to all good prose, poetry, and the civilized and mannerly games men and women play with each other. You don't have to tell a new mother: "Good grief! That's the ugliest baby I've ever seen in my life! Was its father an orangutan?" You can say: "My, now that's a baby!"

Well, that's a depressing, though necessary, line of thought. So, let's talk about the weather. Monday, January 25, Bakersfield had the heaviest snowfall in its history; three inches. Now that small amount of snow to people suffering from five-feet of the stuff is laughable. But it was no laughing matter to people living in Bakersfield, a city where snow on its streets is nearly unheard of. The city has never had, nor needed, a single snowplow. It created a problem much like you might expect if the stuff had fallen on Honolulu.

But here in the Kern River Valley where I live, we are used to snow. Not the huge amounts one anticipates in places like Lake Tahoe, of course (which doesn't make it any less cold), but at least it is familiar to us.

The snow covering the surrounding mountains of the Kern River Valley is beautiful. It often reminds me of some of the beautiful, but cold, women I have known. I prefer to admire and appreciate the snow (and such women) from a comfortable distance. I hate the cold, so it was much comfort to me to learn that Punxsutawaney Phil didn't see his shadow. I may light a groundhog in appreciation. After all, if Thoreau could eat a woodchuck....

Snow on the mountains makes it very cold in the Valley. And while beautiful, about as much fun as having a catheter removed. It makes the winter pajamas the kids gave me for Christmas all the more appreciated. Since I don't like to sleep with a heater on, I awoke the other morning to find the water in the glass on my nightstand had frozen. Interesting. It took a while before the water pipes in my cottage thawed since they had frozen as well.

But as a boy living on the mining claim, it wasn't unusual to have to thaw out my Levi's before I could put them on in the morning. They would actually be frozen stiff if the backlog in the fireplace had died out overnight, which, in spite of every precaution, would happen on occasion.

And if we ran short of water in the cabin or it had frozen on especially cold nights, some had to be heated on the wood stove in the morning then poured over the pump at the well in order to thaw it out before we could pump more during the day.

But I'm not a boy anymore; seems such things like frozen Levi's and thawing out the pump are a tad more difficult for me now. Not unlike discovering that lizards became a little faster and more difficult to catch as I got older. Curious: something to do with the evolution of lizards, no doubt.

Life in the Valley means being disconnected occasionally from the big city, Bakersfield. Right now, a boulder of several tons the size of a house is being blasted from where it fell onto the roadway, closing the canyon to traffic. A similar boulder had to be blasted last summer. Fortunately? Only one person I know of personally has been killed by falling rock in the canyon; lot of near misses, however; makes for interesting driving, together with the tractor-trailers, plain idiots, drunks, and druggies driving the road. The Killer Kern, as the river is known, has nothing on the road alongside it.

Few people seem to know of Bakersfield's infamous position regarding pedophiles. Just recently a man was arrested for downloading child pornography and using it with children. Where did he find the children? He was working in a home for abused children; the fox in the henhouse. Not unusual at all, of course, for perverts.

It would seem obvious that a thorough background check would be SOP for people working with children. Not so. In fact, this is seldom the case, whether for teacher aides, school janitors, or any other position, including those of certificated teachers, Child Protective Services, Juvenile Hall and probation workers, where perverts are naturally going to look for work which will give them ready access to children.

But a thorough background check will do nothing to eliminate the homes that are set up by perverts for perverts. Or about pervert judges who place children in such homes. Or about pervert pedophile rings which are sometimes discovered like those in England and Belgium. Such places are only the smallest tip of a very large and filthy, shameful iceberg.

And while on the subject of a lack of wisdom and justice, by now virtually everyone has heard of the travesty of Missouri's Governor Mel Carnahan commuting the death sentence of triple murderer Darrell Mease to life in prison at the personal request of the Pope. And Carnahan claims to be a strong proponent of the death penalty and a good Baptist! This gross injustice prompted me to write the following letter to Carnahan:

Dear Sir:

This is a painful letter to write but because I have a profound belief in justice and am of the conviction that the death penalty is essential for justice in some cases, conscience demands that I write it.

By now, you have most certainly heard much about your decision to commute the sentence of triple-murderer Darrell Mease. The pundits are right. Because this was such a blatant case of kissing the Pope's ring and toe, particularly condemnatory in the case of your being a professed Baptist, your decision makes no sense, morally or practically.

One of real conviction concerning justice and the death penalty cannot help feeling somewhat like George Marion, a friend of the victims, who is quoted as saying of the Pope's part in your most ill-advised decision: I'd cock him straight and sure in the mouth! I am sure Mr. Marion and others have the same feeling about you; and with justification. You and the Pope denied the victims, both dead and alive, real justice.

I congratulated Governor George Bush as a man of proven principle on his decision when he was being confronted by the Pope, Pat Robertson, and Jerry Falwell in a similar situation not long ago. How I wish I could have done the same in your case when men of real principle are so sorely needed in America!

Well, if I felt like punching the Pope in the mouth or nose, it wouldn't be on the basis of his opposing the death penalty. Many good people have the same reservations and I respect their opinions in spite of my belief there can be no real justice in some cases without it.

Though in specific cases like that of Mease, one cannot help but wonder at the Pope's ridiculous argument that it serves the cause of justice that the cold-blooded, triple murderer may eventually repent of his crime. That is the party line of religious, and I add ridiculous, dogma, and can be expected of professional bleeding hearts and religionists like the Pope.

But then his so-called Holiness never married nor had children, he never had to worry about one of his children being molested or murdered, or a wife being raped and murdered. Easy to be on the side he has chosen in such a case. It costs him nothing.

No, I feel like punching his so-called Holiness in the nose for making so much noise about the death penalty yet studiously avoiding the issue of child molestation; and why? Because the hypocritical pontiff knows it is rampant in his own church and he refuses to deal with it! But he practices his own peculiar form of perversion by taking his position in regard to the death penalty and refusing to deal with the subject of child molestation.

It was 1849 when Henry David Thoreau's small treatise On the Duty of Civil Disobedience was published. Now, a hundred and fifty years later, it has more relevance than it did when first published. And comparatively few have read it.

Friends and readers of TAP know of my kinship with my soul brother, Henry. For over forty years I have been reading Walden and Civil Disobedience. And the conversations and arguments with Henry have never abated. He is as fresh in his thoughts to me now as he was those forty years ago when I first read him.

To this extent, Henry is never dated because, to repeat, his ideas are as relevant now, and even more so in my opinion, than when he was alive. E.B. White said much the same thing in his excellent essay marking the 100-year anniversary of Walden. It has always been a comfort to me to read White's essay as confirmation of the friends Henry has always been able to call to himself through the passing years. And, in agreement with White's suggestion, I would give a copy of Walden to every college graduate together with his or her diploma.

For example, rather than the best government being that which governs least would be that government which governs not at all. But Henry realized the evil that men do requires some government; a necessary evil in itself because of the evil that men do.

I have always been of the mind that it was a great tragedy that Henry never had a wife and children. Like Kierkegaard, Henry lacks this dimension of the human experience that could have contributed so much more to his insights. But what he did contribute is of inestimable value to all of us. There is always something fresh to be found in his legacy of writings because we live and grow, and are in a constant state of learning, ourselves. By its very definition, life cannot be static and continues to be a learning process whether that learning is right or wrong.

Much is said of wisdom in the writings of men with their philosophies and scriptures. And much of what they have written concerning wisdom is true. But I have come to the conclusion that the wisest of men who do not include women on an equal basis with them, who do not place the priority of wisdom on children, have missed the real basis and foundation of wisdom. This led me to say that wisdom has been lacking throughout the whole of human history. If Knowledge+Wisdom=Peace, this equation proves my contention.

It has often been said by men of genius like Newton and Einstein that if they have seen further than others, they have stood on the shoulders of giants in order to do so. But while these men have made great contributions to knowledge, such contributions have not made a commensurate contribution to the acquisition of wisdom in the application of such knowledge. I then have to ask myself, if wisdom is found crying in the street, an orphan from knowledge, where is the genius of wisdom to be found?

Some point to Eastern philosophies. Even my friend Henry was fond of doing this (though I strongly suspect this was due in large part to his observation that his fellow citizens profaned God in sermon and song). Some point to a Buddha, Jesus or Mohammed. But such philosophies of men have never put any substantive emphasis on prioritizing children, let alone made any substantial attempt to make women the equal of men in the Great Conversation.

Historically, after many thousands of years it has only been a blink of the eye since slavery was acceptable in America. Not long ago, cannibalism was acceptable in some cultures. And we still have millions of devout believers in Astrology and many other superstitions of religion and philosophy.

In short, we remain a demon-haunted world lacking wisdom. And that is inviting the Armageddon of number 92 of the periodic table.

I recently sent the American Civil Liberties Union the following letter. Then, I sent copies of the letter to Kathleen Parker, Arianna Huffington, California U.S. Senators Dianne Feinstein and Barbara Boxer:

The following proposed amendment to the United States Constitution has been submitted by me to the President, every Governor and United States Senator as well as a number of national and international personalities:

Proposed amendment to the U.S. Constitution

An adult convicted of the molestation of a child will be sentenced to prison for a term of not less than ten years.

If the child dies as a result of the molestation the person(s) convicted of the crime will be sentenced to life in prison without the possibility of parole.

A child as defined by this article shall be one who has not attained their sixteenth birthday.

The Congress shall have power to enforce this article by appropriate legislation.

It is my contention that children, in this singular and most important respect, have been denied equal protection under Section 1 of Article 14 of the United States Constitution. For two years now, I have been working for this most basic right of children to a lawfully protected, innocent childhood to be included in our foundational charter of government.

No nation in history has made children such a priority. To me, this is most shortsighted. If Knowledge+Wisdom=Peace, it is the lack of wisdom evidenced by not placing our priority on children that denies us peace. I believe America has an obligation to be the first nation in history to place such a priority on children.

It is well said that no nation that fails to cherish its young can survive. Nor does it deserve to. I believe the proposed amendment will have the effect of proving to our children, and the world, that America does, in fact, cherish its young. God knows our children, all children, desperately need such a message of concern and hope! The children, and adults, of the world, I believe, will take heart by such a message. Considering the work you have done for civil rights, I believe this will be of interest to you and your thoughts will be most appreciated.

***

Those of my readers who know of my feelings about the ACLU may find it curious that I sent them such a letter. Suffice it to say that I will certainly let readers know of the response, if any, to my letter.

If Marx had seen TV, he'd have changed his mind about religion being the opiate of the masses. Not that religion has retreated in this respect. Regarding the Pope's popularity, we're reminded once more of the power of religion to keep the poor from killing the rich. For this, the rich are, naturally, very grateful.

As to the Pope, if I were looking for spiritual guidance of a human instrumentality, I think I'd go to a Mother Teresa rather than a guy who is insistent on keeping women in their place. That place, of course, being subordinate to men, especially men like the Pope. In this respect, the Pope has much in common with Mohammed.

But Clinton might as well kiss the ring and toe of the Pope; he's looking everywhere he can for absolution; publicly, at least. And if the Baptists don't offer what he's looking for, why not try the Catholics? A more convenient religion you won't find. At least I found it so. Go to confession, count your beads and bingo (no pun intended), instant absolution with a clear conscience; so much for conscience being a reliable source of moral behavior.

However, it is a constant source of wonder and consternation to me that such an intelligent and educated man as the Pope can subscribe to so many myths, superstitions, and fairy tales as are encompassed in Catholicism. That a man who speaks for nearly a billion people should have so much knowledge but still be so ignorant and naive and be so lacking in wisdom is a real conundrum to thinking people. But he evidences the need to believe in myths and superstitions on the part of even intelligent and very well educated people; which only proves intelligence, knowledge, and education alone are not going to deliver humanity from a Dark Ages mentality. One of the grave faults of such a muddy belief and faith in these things divorced from wisdom is the inability to confront and overcome evil by appropriate action. The attempted genocide in Rwanda is a case in point.

For those who recall the Frontline presentation of what happened in Rwanda, the message should be clear. An estimated 800,000 people were massacred in only 100 days while the world and the Security Council of the United Nations looked on. Long after the killing stopped, Clinton had the effrontery to go to Rwanda and apologize, an apology akin to that with which he insulted the American people.

A part of the thinking, a part about which no one will speak, of the Security Council, including America, Russia, and China, was the fact that as long as ignorant Africans were killing other ignorant Africans, so much to the good; that many more unproductive mouths to feed. Parts of Africa and places like Bangladesh represent a negative drain on world resources, an attribute of Social Darwinism of which John C. Calhoun would say concerning the killings in Rwanda, as he did of slavery: It's the natural order of things.

A logical and pragmatic view of the deaths of so many unproductive mouths would be, necessarily, that it was to the good of the world overall. Given the inability, so far, of the world to learn wisdom, there were those who believed it wise to let those unproductive mouths in Rwanda kill one another unhindered; and in those dark, even unbidden thoughts of civilized people much of the "So what? Let them kill one another!" attitude is to be found.

We have become so accustomed over the years to watching the vacant-eyed zombies camped or marching through desolated wastelands like Ethiopia, we have become so accustomed to watching and hearing of mass murder and starvation, of famines in Africa and Bangladesh, that we are jaded and inured to such suffering and death on massive scales. But for those Americans who live in comfort, far removed from such suffering and want, there seems little realization that the same zombies may be seen in Los Angeles, New York, and Atlanta. And if you feel helpless to do anything to alleviate such suffering and want, why make yourself uncomfortable by becoming knowledgeable of it? Unless you are a person who wallows in self-misery or sick-mindedly enjoys the suffering of others, who feeds on such reminders of these things? And if they are politically and economically unimportant, nothing will be done to help in any event, either in America or abroad.

If you really want to lay awake nights worrying about those things over which you have no control, just watch the Frontline presentation concerning the potential, if not downright probability, of suitcase nuclear bombs being brought into America by terrorists. Personally, I vote for DC being the target, since, like Thoreau, I often find myself going about with murder of the state in my heart.

Slavery is still a fact in places like Sudan. Women and children are still bought and sold as sex slaves to depraved monsters. Tours are arranged so these monsters can sexually abuse children in parts of the world. A modern age? Not as long as such demons are still permitted to haunt the world.

The Pope, being a large and significant part of the problem, tries to be on the side of God and the angels and seems to be blissfully unaware of his contribution to the work of the Devil and a demon-haunted world. But how do you tell someone like the Pope he is full of it? He seems such a genuinely nice (not to mention very powerful) guy.

Governor Carnahan of Missouri commuted the death sentence of Mease because the Pope made a personal appeal for the triple murderer. Now why do you suppose the Pope didn't mention little JonBenet Ramsey or little Melissa and Julie of Belgium? Because the Pope (apart from the problem in his churches already mentioned), as with the world in general, lacks wisdom, the real wisdom that comes from love and compassion, together with a devout hatred of evil.

***

James Michener is a good storyteller and a good novelist. A good, well-written novel is a sharing of dreams. The best of novelists are interpreters of dreams.

Some time ago someone gave me a copy of Michener's The Novel. This has helped me somewhat in my struggle, as a writer of non-fiction; with the novel I am attempting Donnie and Jean: an angel's story. Being a first edition hardback by Random House, it was surprising to find some glaring errors in Michener's book. For example, on page sixty-two, a sum of $200 is mentioned. On page sixty-three, this becomes $100.

As a writer and publisher, I am very knowledgeable about the book business. I know who has responsibility for what; the writer, the publisher, the various editors, agents, lawyers, artists, printers, etc. Michener does a good job of covering the ground in The Novel. I strongly suspect he wanted readers to know how fiendishly difficult, complicated, even mercurial, the book business is. And he used his book to make some of his complaints, legitimate complaints I add, known.

For example, on page thirty-four he makes this statement: "Despite my firm conclusion that American publishing was falling into disarray, I had not the vaguest conception of what might be done to stop the decline, and I could only lament: The time is out of joint...."

And for those unacquainted with the world of professional writing and publishing, Michener does a service by pointing out, regardless his motive in doing so, that there is a very distinct difference between a good book and a saleable book, and that because of the enormous amount of work involved in making even a good book a saleable book, only one in nine-hundred manuscripts makes it to publication. That's extremely long odds. But it is the reason it is virtually impossible for a beginning writer to find a qualified and reputable agent. It is also the reason that unless a writer is getting at least twenty rejections a month he isn't really serious about getting published.

If Michener were not a popular and successful writer, however, I doubt The Novel would have made it to publication because of its unevenness and preaching format, of his often clumsy attempts due to obvious biases to objectify abstractions. And in his book, The Novel, he acknowledges the rule of comity while at the same time ignoring it.

Another real, and too typical, weakness of the book is Michener making the mistake of trying to make a character like the Grande dame Mrs. Garland, ignorant of Ezra Pound. This is akin to one of the flaws in the film Pretty Woman when Vivian, sitting in Edward's spacious penthouse enjoying strawberries and champagne, says she doesn't think he can afford the $300 for her spending the night with him (As an aside, while the strawberries were necessary for the flossing scene in the bathroom, I consider it an affectation. I've never found strawberries all that essential to accentuating the flavor or bouquet of good champagne).

But while Pretty Woman succeeded in spite of such relatively minor flaws, Michener was too intent on his own biases to recognize this glaring incongruity of Mrs. Garland's ignorance of Pound in his book where literature and intellectualism (which the latter, unfortunately, comes off as pretentiousness) are the focal points.

However, I find it incredulous his editors didn't catch this glaring incongruity of Garland's ignorance of Pound. But if they did, Michener might well have ignored them. He was in a position to do so and was adamant in making his point regardless of the obvious incongruity; which I found an insult to the intelligence of the reader. And while not according Michener anything like the genius, which I think even Michener's ego would not accept, anything even remotely close to that of a Melville, the curse of dualism dogs his work as it does of most moralizing writers.

But Michener may be right about better novels being written (an arguable point) but read by fewer people. As depressing as that thought is, it is one of the reasons I believe I have to complete my own novel. If I think I can write a book which will move the hearts and minds of that select few on behalf of children, I have an obligation, a duty as it were, to do so.

Nothing can detract from Michener's genuine knowledge and appreciation of the world of the novelist and publishing. And he knows how the reader reacts to a good book. He is certainly correct in describing the way a reader feels regret when approaching the end of a good book, how some will even ration those last few pages.

But Michener isn't the only writer by any means that cries out for understanding in the voice of his character Lukas Yoder: Writing is what

I do! I have to do it! And every one of us who writes because it is what we do, we have to do it, can't help wishing there were someone like Yoder's wife who will tuck the blankets around us as we fall asleep. Writing of the nature Michener describes in The Novel is a very solitary and often lonely, demon-plagued business.

Michener wrote The Novel in 1991. Things are even more out of joint now, especially with the purchase of large publishing houses by Hollywood (and foreign conglomerates). I mentioned this some time ago in TAP. It gives Hollywood first chance at good (i.e. saleable) stories. It is also the reason that many a good writer will prostitute him- or herself to writing for TV rather than a reading public that is ever more becoming a non-reading public.

Time out of joint: Yes. For those of us who want to write in a mannerly and civilized way for a mannerly and civilized readership. With this in mind, my heart could not help going out to Michener. But he shouldn't have tried to be an intellectual in The Novel. It must have proven an embarrassment to him and I like to think he wishes he hadn't written it. In part because he breaks his own rules, rules of all good novelists such as preaching and trying to objectify abstractions in the kind of novel he wrote, the latter a decidedly difficult task in any case.

To exemplify the problem, imagine the weighty tomes that have been written in attempts to objectify the abstractions of the best government or world peace! Further, he commits the sins of preaching about his obvious infatuation with Hollywood and attempts to justify perversion by trying to make it seem, as with most pervert propaganda, that Hollywood and the arts are best represented by intellectuals and artists who are either Jewish or queer (if I were Jewish, I would especially resent this!).

As a result of his prejudice, Michener praises Jews and perverts, seemingly ignorant and oblivious of his equating both, to the near exclusion of intellectuals and artists who are neither. The prejudice is easily seen as such by the fact that by far the greatest number of intellectuals and artists of history are neither Jewish nor perverts in spite of the number of those who were.

No one has a greater appreciation than I do for the great artists who have given us such magnificent music and art regardless of whether they are Jews, perverts, or blond, blue-eyed Nordics. It should always be a case of appreciation for genius in spite of the character or lack thereof of the individual. In some cases, I can easily appreciate the art and despise the character of the artist. For me, the music and the art are the things.

I must add that I in no way despise Michener. And I'll always be grateful for his providing the story that led to one of the best of musicals: South Pacific. But I would warn Michener and others like him not to attempt to propagandize thinking people through the mechanism of prejudice and bigotry. It is a fraud and an affront, an insult, to our intelligence. Worse, it only contributes to continuing hatreds and prejudices that are certainly counter-productive. One only has to look to what Hitler did with such propaganda to make the point.

A good example of Michener's prejudice is a pervert professor of English literature in his book. Michener has this teacher praising the Greeks for providing the foundation for literature never seeming to recognize the fact that Homer, Aeschylus, Sophocles and Euripides were neither Jews nor perverts. And, of course, the professor doesn't present the fact to his students that the acknowledged greatest of English writers, Shakespeare, and so many of those following, were neither Jews nor homosexuals.

As with all propaganda, whether for good or evil, you ignore or castigate and denigrate those and what is not to your purpose. And as we see on a daily basis, if you capture Hollywood and the universities you have the most powerful propaganda machines in history at your disposal. So much so, these would have Hitler and Goebbels salivating (not to mention a lot of TV evangelists).

In this respect, Michener betrays his own prejudice by doing just what Tom Hanks did in Philadelphia. Every Jew and homosexual is a genius of extraordinary sensitivity and artistic ability that would never hurt a fly. And just to prove it, they are going to sue the hell out of any sexually normal Gentile who gets in their way!

And if you are a skilled propagandist, as in the case of Philadelphia, you simply have to have a Negro lawyer representing the pervert; the nice touch being to have the pervert sensitize and raise the consciousness of the Negro toward perverts. After all, the theme propagandizes: We are both victims of blatant discrimination! Brothers!

So the theme of the propaganda of Michener, Hollywood, and the universities is to equate a normal revulsion of perversion on the part of normal people with bigotry, prejudice and discrimination. To further enforce the message, there are the many films like A Time to Kill where a good, sensitive, Caucasian attorney bucks the always prejudiced South and rescues the Negro. Unfortunately, the excellent point of the film, that the abuse of children is equally heinous irrespective of the race of the child, is lost in the stereotypical preaching against white Southerners.

This is where Duvall, fine an actor as he is, lost it in "The Apostle". His lack of the actual background and experience in the subject, of never having been a true Pentecostal, charismatic religion believer, doomed his effort and The Academy recognized this fatal weakness in the film.

The bottom line: Men should never say they know what it is like to be pregnant and give birth. Whites should never say they know what it is like to be black or vice versa. And normal people should never accept perversion of any kind as simply an alternative of any kind! If perversion is not wrong, then nothing is wrong! And in saying this, it's perfectly acceptable to call people like me names such as racist, anti-Semitic (a peculiar class of racist illogically distinctive and all to itself alone) or homophobic (another thoroughly illogical epithet) for telling it like it is; especially since I am a non-Jewish Caucasian male of normal sexuality. Let's beat up on those uppity, white, straight, normal, Gentile males! There's nothing special about them and we can get away with it.

Just recently, parents in Los Angeles were demanding a Caucasian principal be removed from their school because of the population being largely Negro and Hispanic (I can certainly relate to this situation). Not because he was a bad principal, but solely on the basis of his being Caucasian!

You can easily imagine what would be happening if Caucasian people were demanding the removal of a principal on the basis of his or her being Negro or Hispanic? It would get the attention of every form of news media imaginable! CNN and People Magazine would be on this like flies on gravy! And you sure wouldn't have Hollywood making a picture glorifying this white principal for his taking a stand against discrimination directed at him for his being white!

Concerning the insane illogic of proposed hate crimes legislation, if I'm murdered by a Negro, Jew, Moslem, or pervert just because I'm a plain old ordinary white man, do you imagine the same rules would be applied in my case? Hardly. Face it. I am what I am by accident of birth just as you are. I don't get up every morning and thank God I was born a sexually normal, white male. But I do thank Him I was born in America. Still, I think it is an affront to women and God Himself for those Jews and Moslems who pray thanking God they weren't born a woman! I think that is just plain wrong and has nothing to do with such men being Jewish or Moslem. It is wrong for any man to pray in such a fashion.

But if you are to find fault with me because of what I am by accident of birth, it makes as much sense as such a prayer and is equally inexcusable! Why should anyone hate or even find personal fault with another on the basis of race, religion or gender? Such is plainly despicable, ugly, ignorant bigotry and prejudice!

It is the purposeful exclusion of foundational facts of the history of literature that makes Michener's The Novel, pervert and Jewish propaganda. I say this while acknowledging "Fiddler on the Roof" being one of my favorite musicals because Tevye overcomes his prejudice in the end in spite of the dreadful circumstances of prejudice directed at him. In confronting the situation with his daughter and a Gentile, he says if he bends that far he will break. He loves his daughter deeply. But how, he asks himself, can he turn his back on his faith? Well, Tevye didn't break. People who are motivated by love rather than hatred don't break. And the lesson learned is that any so-called faith that makes God a Jew, Christian, Moslem, Hindu, etc. is a faith of Satan, not God!

The remarkable bottom line of Fiddler, that a father could not bring himself to deny his own child, is the basis of the hope I have for the Amendment. If humanity can finally exercise wisdom in prioritizing children before any ideology, only then can we get on the right path and hope for world peace.

There most certainly is no wisdom to be found in glorifying any ideology of race, religion or politics to the extent of persecuting others. This is too much like the ignorant, stupid person who declaims his pride of things that he enjoys as accidents of birth.

In too many respects, Michener comes off too much like Hitler's toady propagandist Goebbels. And having espoused the party line, it is difficult to recuse oneself or retrench. If I am picking on Michener there is a very good reason beyond the obvious. His story of the two brothers who separate on the basis of religion, in this case Amish and Mennonite, who disagree over the wearing of suspenders on religious grounds, is a point well made.

The superstitions and bigoted prejudice too often associated with religious beliefs need to be confronted. The basic fault with Michener is that he recognizes this and at the same time he castigates it, he approves it in another form. Sum zero.

Another reason for my picking on Michener is his denigrating writers of the stature of Hemingway and Dickens among some others of great and proven merit. The envy of these on the part of Michener displayed in The Novel is so blatant it is obvious that, to use one of my grandad's expressions, he had them stuck in his craw and tried to spit them out.

But "The Old Man and the Sea" and "Great Expectations" will outlive, I am quite certain, anything Michener has written. Dickens and Hemingway will still be holding their own when Michener will only be a quaint hobby for literary antiquarians. Somehow, I think Michener knows this; which would make someone like Michener's not so thinly veiled acerbic vitriol directed at these writers understandable; and equally unforgivable.

In view of this, I found it surprising he didn't go after America's greatest woman poet, Emily Dickinson. As to Dickens in particular, you have to wonder if Michener even knew the esteem in which both Tolstoi and Dostoevsky held him? And if he did, what does that say of Michener's criticism of him? It hardly commends his credentials as a critic of real literature in any event.

For those of us who were raised loving good books, good literature, America has indeed fallen on hard times. And time is indeed out of joint due to the low estate of intellectualism in America. But writers like Michener, in spite of his hand-wringing preaching concerning the loss, only contributes to the decline of good literature and true intellectualism by vainly attempting to present himself as an intellectual and seeming to decry the loss while at the same time he attempts through his own prejudice and bigotry to justify the very things that have brought America to this sad state of affairs.

But just try calling this to the attention of the typical professor of literature in any college or university and you will get an F in the course. That is, if you're not first hooted down and kicked out of the class; so much for Michener's self-vaunted fairness and liberalism or that of colleges and universities.

This all brings to mind a statement by a homosexual that the fields of medicine, the arts and sciences, would collapse if all the perverts were removed from these. People like Michener would have you believe such an asinine and clearly self-serving statement. But, of course, he includes Jews in such a category as well. This hardly does Jews a service and if I were Jewish or homosexual, I would have sense enough to call any to account that practiced such counter-productive and hate-mongering propaganda as Michener's.

I will never forget one English professor, an exception to the rule whom I had as an undergraduate, who tried to buck the system. He lasted only that one semester I had him. But on one of my papers, he had written: "I welcome you as a fellow moth drawn to the flame." And in spite of his sensitivity and love of literature, he wasn't even a homosexual.

His remark concerning the moth proved to be true. And since that time, my wings have been singed many times. But so far the flame has not yet consumed me. The Amendment may be the flame that succeeds. I realize now that I have always had an uneasy feeling, concerning the work and writings of the great artists and philosophers, that something was missing. This became such an uneasy thing in my life because of my genuine love of great art, music, and literature.

Because of the Amendment, I now recognize a kind of paranoia that surrounds and permeates the great poets, philosophers, and artists. They themselves recognized they were missing something, their genius insisted on their recognizing this fact. It left a void they attempted to fill by many devices. That this void was true wisdom did not seem to occur to them, however. Yes, many felt the lack of wisdom very keenly. Many talked and wrote about wisdom extensively which was only natural, but it remained an elusive thing and this is evidenced by their many attempts to seek wisdom.

But like looking for love in all the wrong places, the best of genius that denies an entire half of humanity, women, of equal value to men cannot find and learn wisdom no matter how earnest the seeker. Nor, I came to realize, can wisdom be divorced from an emphasis on the priority of children in all human affairs. This, I believe, accounts for the mentioned paranoia.

Just the other day while at the grocery store, I watched a young mother with her little girl. They were in the line at the checkout counter. The little one couldn't have been quite two-years old. She was beautiful. She was seated in the grocery cart and looking about with wide-eyed innocence; her little hands on her face as though she was trying to understand her surroundings and what her mother was doing in this strange and marvelous place of so many wonders, the Supermarket. As I always do, I thought with somewhat of a pang and not a little wistfulness of the many things this little one had still to learn, of how life would be a constant learning experience filled with so many wonders. Until.

And it is that *until* that always grabs at my heart. Was this little girl going to be one of the one-out-of-two who are molested? Where was her father? Did he even live with her and her mommy? Was the young mother on welfare? Was there some dead-beat bum, alcoholic or drug addict, living with them who would molest or even murder the little one? So many hurtful questions plague my mind because I know too much. But there is never denying the love I experience whenever I see these little ones. And I have to ask myself: How can anyone not love such precious little ones?

Then I came home, turned on the news at five and another so-called man, one Guadalupe Gomez, the live-in boyfriend of a so-called mother, one Jamie Ornelas, has been arrested in Bakersfield for beating the woman's little boy Abel Ramos, only one-and-one-half year's old, to death. But going on in this vein tasks me too much. And I turn to other things like an old film, music, a good book or the writing to escape (though the last too often results in things such as I am writing now). At least momentarily.

And speaking of escaping, one cannot escape the irony of our living in a time of quantum expansions in the information field coupled with the increasing loss of intellectualism. I think most gratefully of the Internet, of web pages and e-mail, of being able to use the marvelous word processing capabilities of computers. I am grateful for being able to put an entire book on a diskette or being able to send an entire book to someone electronically with a few keystrokes.

But while knowledge increases, wisdom languishes. Few see the bottom line of wisdom while knowledge offers material and comparatively immediate payment. Since such payment is short-term, and always has been, and wisdom is future-oriented, most that are impatient and shortsighted will take the money and run. This also distinguishes the politician from the statesman.

As a moth drawn to the flame, I know my comments on Michener are inflammatory, a case of the moth lighting the very fire which will consume it.

Like Ezra Pound, whom I in no wise excuse of his bigotry, I may be the poet condemned to a St. Elizabeth.

But as Confucius pointed out, if a government or a people are corrupt, the honorable place for honorable men and women is the prisons of such a government or people. It is then an honor to be counted among the dangerous or mad that are imprisoned by such a government or people.

The Amendment most certainly casts me in the role of the moth, the dangerous madman with whom society must deal. The question is what my society, my government, will do with me if I continue on my present course? Most especially if I am perceived as making any real headway in such a course.

Unhappily, like the moth, there is far more of instinct involved with my present course than a normal sense of self-preservation. There is far more of the Hound of Heaven involved than what most would call my madness or, more charitably, lack of common sense.

Because I am a Caucasian American male of normal sexuality, I know there is little I can say which cannot be construed as being prejudiced, bigoted, or discriminatory against Negroes, Jews, homosexuals, Moslems, Hindus, Buddhists, Chinese and Japanese, etc. This in spite of the fact that I am none of this, that I accept people as people regardless of race or religion, that I appreciate the contributions of those who are gifted in the arts, music, science, medicine or whatever even in spite of despicable personal character in some cases.

But like the illogical thinking concerning hate crime legislation, it is far too easy to call people like myself names on the basis of prejudice from others, prejudice of which they themselves are often ignorant but guilty. But no one will ever be able to find me guilty of condescension or of being patronizing to others on the basis of race or religion. And as with giving credit where credit is due, I will equally find fault where that is appropriate regardless of race or religion. Curiously, it is this very lack of prejudice or bias on my part that causes me much grief. Too many people require that I be on their side. And if I am not, they find something of which to accuse me and call me names.

You would be amazed at the names I am called and the actual hatred directed at me simply on the basis of my saying that there can be no hope of gaining wisdom, no hope of peace, unless women are accepted as of equal value to men and children become the priority of the human race. It surprises some people to know of the hatred I generate toward myself by the Amendment.

Some people castigate me for standing up for civilized manners and speech. Illogically, they presume the right to be offensive but have no thought of either my rights to be protected from such or the harm bad, uncivilized manners, and profane and vulgar speech have on our future as a society.

This accusation was made against one of the close friends of Sir Richard Steele: His taste of books is a little too just for the age he lives in. I have had the same accusation made against me.

Such people obviously have never read Samuel Johnson's definitive essay "An Author's Writing and Conversation Contrasted." And, somehow, I don't think Michener read it either. If he did, he ignored some of the best advice ever given a writer by one of the most brilliant men who ever lived.

One quote from Johnson's essay should suffice: "This much at least may be required of him (the writer), that he shall not act worse than others because he writes better, nor imagine that, by the merit of his genius, he may claim indulgence beyond mortals of the lower classes, and be excused for want of prudence or neglect of virtue."

Failing to heed Johnson many express surprise or wring their hands over the lack of things like civilized speech and manners in our society and the failing intellectualism in America! But considering the universities decided in the sixties that children knew better than adults and were looking for an excuse to replace civilized manners, speech, and intellectualism with perversion and vulgarity, the loss of civilized manners, speech, and intellectualism isn't surprising at all. Situation Ethics and If it feels good, do it! There are no real moral absolutes or standards!

We truly do deserve Clinton. We earned him. He exemplifies the moral standards of America and its universities. I am tempted at times, due to the insufferable hypocrisy of Clinton, to have a bumper sticker reading: Nostradamus and Edgar Cayce Suck Eggs. A picture of Clinton will be a part of the bumper sticker. Why? Because any that believe a man like Clinton deserves to be in the White House has to be, at best, a believer in utter nonsense!

Speaking of which, we have a battle going on in Bakersfield that deserves mention in this regard. The bumper sticker reminded me of this. Virtually everyone knows of the Sign of the Fish, a time-honored and hallowed symbol of Christianity. Virtually everyone has seen these affixed to automobiles in some way or another.

Well, the Darwin Fish is coming into vogue. Shades of the Scopes Trial! The Darwin Fish is the same fish symbol but the fish has legs and the name Darwin is written inside the fish. As one local TV commentator pointed out, with the problems we are already having with road rage, this isn't going to help matters.

I visualize a cartoon showing a primitive hunter dressed in animal skins with a bow in his hands. At his feet lies a flying saucer, about ten inches in diameter, with an arrow stuck through it. The point being that primitive, ignorant hatreds and superstitions can easily overcome knowledge and technology. Faced with the very real threat of ignorant, hate-filled terrorists bringing suitcase nuclear bombs to America (for the glory of God, of course), we had better get on with the getting of wisdom before it is too late! Knowledge and technology will not save humanity. Only Knowledge+Wisdom can do this!

CHAPTER FOUR

You know things are really getting rough in L.A. when newscasters reporting traffic accidents are unconsciously often using the word *wounded* instead of *injured* for the parties involved. That bumper sticker "Pardon my driving, I'm trying to reload" stops being funny at this point.

Bakersfield is apparently attempting to reach parity with L.A. in carjackings and home-invasion robberies. Personally, I think this is only pretentiousness on the part of B-town because of jealous homeboys, the native criminals and gang members.

Weedpatch University, ever the heart and soul of social consciousness and conscience, is meeting this threat with the appropriate course offerings in things like Urban Guerrilla Warfare and How to Properly Maintain Your AK47, M16, and Uzi. Also covered in this fascinating course are things like how to perform common pre-driving bomb searches of your automobile. There are many little details of this nature of which the average person has little knowledge often leading to embarrassing situations that could easily be avoided by attending this important class.

One particular course in which I, as Chair of Men/Women Relationships, have real expectations is one in which questions concerning modern marriage such as *Husbands; Do You Know Where Your Wife Keeps Her 9mm?* are answered in depth. More than one husband has been put at a disadvantage when he has not been able to meet and counter his mate's determination to put holes in him by overlooking such seemingly inconsequential details of modern, wedded bliss.

A seminar especially designed for the business owner is *How to Keep the Homeless and Winos From Going Potty in Your Planters and Sleeping in Your Doorways*. Because of the mounting problem this has posed for businesses, the subject has been removed from its traditional place in the Home Economics Department and has been designed as a seminar for the busy businessman and woman.

This new emphasis on contemporary day-to-day living by WU has been met with enthusiasm by the Kern County Chamber of Commerce and local housewives (though the latter have expressed a little reticence about the course covering things like the whereabouts of their 9mms).

Like Time, WU marches on! (And if you remember that slogan you also remember when the line wind up the cat and throw out the clock was funny).

I got up this morning feeling like I had just watched Deep Impact, Armageddon, and Pulp Fiction in series non-stop. Bet a lot of you know just how this feels. Not good. Ah, for the good old days when The Texas Chainsaw Massacre was the criteria by which Hollywood masterpieces and America's cultural level of appreciation of the fine arts was judged. But how I felt this morning probably had something to do with my writing the following:

I Don't Want to Know!

As with the ingredients of some foods (?) like wieners and sausage, I never wanted to know Noel Coward wrote Mad About the Boy with a man in mind singing the song. And I never wanted to know Barry Manilow wrote and sang Mandy as a tribute to his dog. And I didn't really want to know about Admiral Byrd's polar winter in Antarctica in 1934 being spent solo out of fear of rumors, good and knowledgeable sailor that he was, about homosexuality otherwise.

But with scientists tinkering around with genes and medical researchers dinking with certain DNA altering drugs, maybe if I got loaded up with enough estrogen I'd start carrying a purse and wearing lipstick. As a boy, girls always gave me the impression of thinking they were better than boys were. The strange creatures exhibited a kind of disdain for boys and seemed to have an inordinate desire for cleanliness and dressing and smelling nice. Most didn't even spit. I sometimes wondered if they could or even knew how? They didn't play games in the dirt like shooting marbles and I could never envision a girl putting a frog, lizard, or potato bug in my desk at school.

And that little ditty. How it rankled. Little girls are sugar and spice and everything nice. *Little boys are sniffles and snails and puppy dog tails* while *Little girls are Sugar and spice and everything nice.* Boy! What a put-down! Well, with puberty everything changed and I had to accept the fact that girls were just different, not unlike aliens from another planet. And I didn't need a book like Mars and Venus to tell me this. I was a pretty quick study by this time.

Ah, but when I had daughters, I finally understood. They were indeed little aliens; and the most precious of little aliens. The most wonderful things I appreciate and love about women, I learned from these precious little aliens. Pity the poor father with only boys, who has never had one of these little creatures to teach him the best part of being a man, of the soft and gentle influences a little girl brings into his life.

I wouldn't trade for my boys (most of the time), but my daughters? Ah, they are special in such a very unique way to a man. I love my boys; but my girls, they are to cherish. And when little girls are grown and married, their husbands should cherish them.

But, alas, girls and boys are not learning such things anymore. With the loss of romance, parents don't seem to know how to teach such things to their little ones or how to be the examples of such in their own lives. And families certainly aren't getting any help from the government, the universities, Hollywood, or society in general.

But obesity doesn't do much to encourage romance either. Didn't you get a kick out of that fat protest in San Francisco? In case you missed it, a bunch of fatties were protesting a fitness center that had put up a large billboard declaiming: When they come, they will eat the fat ones first!

Well, that went over like a lead balloon with the porcine. For people like me who are blessed with thin genes and have never had to worry about obesity, it's difficult to relate to the plight of lardos, most especially with the ones we all see using food stamps in the grocery store.

But let's face it, fat isn't pretty or attractive. And by now virtually everyone knows it is very unhealthy as well and a main contributor to heart problems and diseases like diabetes. Still I couldn't help laughing at the billboard; this more out of the sheer stupidity of anyone who would use such a tasteless ad in the mistaken notion that it would attract customers. However, admittedly it is funny when you think about alien invaders with a sweet tooth for porkers. I remember more than one SciFi story and show with this theme and I'm sure more will follow.

Modesty, such as that of the Apostle Paul's concerning his own familiarity with angels and outer space, forbids my going into details about my own space travels and interaction with extraterrestrials, but none has expressed any desire to me to dine on humans, fat or otherwise. I trust my own expertise and experience in this matter will put some minds at ease.

The really unfunny part of all of this is that it raises the question of when Caesar may begin to treat the enormously expensive problems of health care for the obese in the same manner in which he and his legions of lawyers attacked the tobacco companies. Can't happen? Don't kid yourself!

Speaking of dumb advertising, don't you love those products that invite you to enter contests that advertise "No purchase necessary." Then, you read on the package: "Details inside." Makes you want to rip open the package, remove the details, and toss the product on the floor. It does make me curious, however, as to how the storeowner would react? No, questions I already know the answer I don't need to ask (we learn this from childhood when we first want to do something and we know mom and dad are going to say No!).

Now why does this contest come-on remind me of that tasteless and asinine Budweiser commercial showing two disreputable looking dorks trying to make up their minds (?) between the purchase of toilet paper or a six-pack and then choosing the beer? Quite sensibly, at least, the beer maker didn't include the blonde, chewing gum or not, in the choices.

It is now widely known that pornography is the best selling, number one item selected on Internet web sites. How come that dumb free contest and beer commercial seem to go with this? Maybe it's because it is commonly claimed that men are thinking of sex 85% of the time? Talk about a statistical monstrosity!

Now seriously, fellows, listen up. What I want to know is this: Just what are you wasting the other 15% of the time thinking about? Beer? Football? Tofu burgers?

Now that I think about it (as a sexually normal man, do I have enough brain-time left to think about it?), maybe it's a good thing men do think about sex so much. With so many things going to hell in a basket throughout the world, can you imagine how much worse it might be if men were using more than that 15% of the time thinking about other things? Now, given that possibility, if you ladies would only be a little more charitable toward us men and.... Oh, well, just a thought.

Inquiring (and normally prurient) minds have wondered and want to know if there has been sex in space? Well, I never did think NASA was being altogether truthful about wanting to give women equal opportunity with men, based on things other than their sex, in space. This had more to do with PR, with the NASA image of fairness, than anything like equal opportunity for women in my opinion. And since neither Jimmy Swaggart nor Clinton ever made it into space, we can at least assume the sex was normal.

A recent survey in JAMA found 43% of women considered themselves unhappy sexually. Makes you kind of wonder what makes the other 57% happy, doesn't it?

Well, my Birds book covers the subject in some depth. And, not surprisingly, the happy women were happy with their mates. Makes sense; and I didn't have to have JAMA tell me this. And I don't think it comes as any surprise to any woman.

But, let's face it. What makes a woman happy with her mate is an extremely complex problem. It reminds me of the number one complaint of women about men; that men don't listen to them. Yet, when asked what it is that women are trying to say that justifies their complaint, you get almost as many answers as women answering. However, the confusion is rooted in the fact that women know men don't take them seriously and never have. Women over the centuries have become used to men not listening to them so it isn't difficult to understand their quandary when a man asks them in all seriousness what it is they are trying to say.

If women, however, will not act like ladies, if they are willing to put up with crude speech and manners by men, we can't expect things to get any better. Imagine some boy saying to a girl: "Hey, let's suck face." You can't expect much of romance to blossom in the environment of such vulgarisms.

Nor can romance be expected to blossom when the girl's face looks like a cheap thrift store with her tongue, lip, nose, and eyebrows perforated by and dangling various kinds of hardware. Do they get this idea from ignorant cultures where you buy a wife with pigs, cows or chickens and she wears her dowry on her face? Or could it be that many girls don't know they are associating themselves with barbaric cultures in this manner, cultures that hold women are nothing but a commodity? A large part of the problem is the fact that too many girls and boys are learning about so-called love and romance from vulgar and obscene TV and films (and Clinton) rather than from their parents and good, decent literature. Before leaving the subject, I will point out in all seriousness that with virtually 50% of girls in America being molested, this goes a long way in explaining our high divorce rate and the unhappiness of so many women in their adult relationships, especially marriage.

Pro Wrestling gaining in popularity? Yes indeed. Even Ted Turner has gotten into the act big-time. Well, some caustic (and not a few perverted) souls are saying it beats those old gladiator movies. And we do have Hulk Hogan and Jesse Ventura to help, somewhat, redeem the image of pro wrestling. But as a commentary on the tastes of the general public, God help us!

The more charitable might say we are trying to get in touch with the ancient Greek and Roman cultures. If so, once more: God help us! We may yet attain to such sophistication as those ancients in watching people killing one another or battling bulls, lions, and bears in an arena with cheering crowds in attendance (makes you wonder about cultures like those in Spain and Mexico where bullfighting is still so popular?).

Tragically, and fearfully, my thoughts concerning the lack of wisdom throughout the whole of human history seem to be justified on an increasing scale. It is this very lack of wisdom that has placed America at such risk due to the failure to remove Clinton from office. To the everlasting shame of Congress, an acknowledged criminal and an embarrassment and laughingstock of a President remains in office.

The Supreme Court is going to have to deal with new definitions of perjury and obstruction of justice. The appeals of those in prison for these crimes are certain to be voluminous. Sexual harassment may become rampant and any accused of such are certain to point to Clinton for justification.

As we recently celebrated President's Day shortly after a spineless and immoral Senate found Clinton Not Guilty, none could miss the tragic irony of the day. Thanks to those Senators so lacking in morality and a real sense of justice, so utterly lacking in wisdom, America has a President still in office that has soiled the office of Washington and Lincoln in an unimaginable way.

I just received a letter from Senator Dianne Feinstein in which she gave her reasons for voting to acquit. Giving her credit for at least attempting to label Clinton for what he is, it is cold comfort that those with a real conscience failed to carry through or carry the day. History, I am certain, is not going to treat Congress or Clinton in any way flattering to either.

Don't you just love those *Please watch responsibly* messages on TV. Especially when the commercials are worse than the program. To our great surprise, it has been discovered that there is more sex on TV now than two years ago (this is commensurate with the growth of the popularity of pro wrestling). Why, any kid could have told us that. And why is this? Same old story: Sex sells.

Imagine my surprise to learn that the biggest success on the Internet is pornography. The public, apparently, not only wants Clinton, they want more sex on TV, the net, and film. At a time when so many feel they are getting an education from watching Jeopardy rather than the regimen and self-discipline required for obtaining a real education, it shouldn't be surprising that America is fast becoming a nation of ignoramuses.

Speaking of ignorance, TV, and Madison Avenue, just when did the interior of an automobile become a cabin with a cockpit? Did cars suddenly sprout wings? Madison Avenue is tuned in on the increasing ignorance of the buying public. As silly as it seems, all advertisers have to do is make people fantasize that buying the right car and driving it makes them Top Gun graduates. Like the Nike advertisement that makes young people think they can leap tall buildings with a single bound or beat out a train or tractor-trailer on Nike roller blades; a little dangerous, that; and thoroughly irresponsible on the part of Nike.

The dumbing down of America as evidenced by TV should be a wake-up call to the whole country. But it isn't, and not likely to be so. When people are trained like Pavlov's dogs and crying for Bread and Circuses, it's a little difficult to wean them away.

Certainly there is some good programming on TV. But who is watching? Given the choice between National Geographic, Nova, 20/20, 60 Minutes or Frontline as opposed to a show filled with steamy sex and violence, guess which gets the numbers?

Just recently, 60 Minutes did a great job of exposing Ford's cover-up of the flaw in the cruise control in some of their vehicles. This flaw resulted in the sudden and uncontrollable acceleration of some vehicles that caused many injuries and some deaths. But when some of the documentation was shown, I noticed some misspellings and words like *form* were spelled *from* and vice versa. Many is the time when I will type one instead of the other simply because of the arrangement of the keyboard and what is going on in my mind at the time. These are commonplace errors. But these were not simple misspellings or juxtapositions; they were the result of the writer using a spellchecker computer program and the final document not being properly edited by an actual person where such commonplace errors would normally be discovered.

One does wonder, however, how the word *Athletic* came out *Atletic* on Simpson's Heissman trophy? How many people checked that out before it was given to Simpson? Granted the eyes see what the brain is trained to interpret. And in some cases such a word as athletic is so common the brain will often supply missing information. But in this singular case of the Heissman, one does have to wonder?

But eye/brain function is a huge field of study all to itself. The errors of communication and interpretation that occur between eyes and brain account for the differing stories by witnesses to accidents and other events, for example. Such errors have a lot to do with people seeing what they want to see as well; UFOs and space aliens, chariots of fire, various miracles, etc. *I Want To Believe* has a significant relationship to such things and has made a tremendous impact on history; and continues to do so.

However, back to the subject of spelling errors; we are all subject to human error. Who among us is so righteous and pure of hand and mind as to be able to cast the first stone for the sin of forgetting a pot of eggs boiling on the stove (but, as I keep repeating, bachelors are a sorry lot)? Just recently I wrote the word *plague* when I meant *plaque*. I won't go into the mental mechanisms that might have gone into making a possibly Freudian slip of this nature in this particular case, but of course the spellchecker program didn't catch my intent and recognized the word plague was spelled correctly.

It took proofing with the human eye to catch the error. So what? might be the first reaction to such a thing. And such a reaction would be a correct one. It wouldn't normally be of much consequence. But I immediately thought of the old film Fail-Safe. What if the dumbing down of America continues to increase in part by a reliance on computers and results in a nuclear, chemical or biological catastrophe simply because a document was not carefully checked for proper spelling or punctuation by a well-qualified human being?

This is by no means as far-fetched as it may appear at first glance. America and Japan went to war on the basis of a misunderstanding of the meaning of one word: *China*! And this happened before the computer age! How much more likely is such a monumental misunderstanding or mis-communication to happen when we are becoming so dependent on machines to do our thinking and speaking for us?

As a classroom teacher, I opposed the use of calculators in basic math classes; and for a very fundamental reason. Children had to learn how to do arithmetic without mechanical aids or they would never learn the basics of math. That was only common sense. But I would be the last person in the world to accuse the educational establishment of being guilty of common sense; quite the contrary. So when the universities began to preach the dogma that there weren't any really right or wrong answers and there were no moral absolutes, it only mattered if Johnny and Susie felt good about themselves, it wasn't difficult to predict where this would lead; exactly to where we are now academically and sociologically.

In my professional religious days, I subscribed to the doctrine of the Great Assize. While I no longer hold this view, I do believe there is a judgment of God to come on an individual basis of how we lived our lives. In harking back to some of my previous beliefs, I still believe there are going to be a lot of surprises when God calls us home. For example, many good people are going to be surprised I'm not in hell. Now how do I know that? I don't. But if so, it would be nice to surprise these good folks of their expectation. Naturally, I'll be somewhat disappointed if I fail to do so.

And speaking of good folks, I'm often reminded of something that great evangelist John Wesley wrote in his Journal. He stated he had read some 600 books and didn't suppose he had been bettered by the reading of them. Some questions always plagued me about this statement. Why didn't he realize this after reading the first one hundred? Was he a glutton for punishment? Were his reading habits deplorable? Were the books that bad? Or, could it be even remotely possible that such a spiritual giant was engaging in a form of braggadocio due to his own assumed perfection? Nah.

The readers of TAP and I share a love of literature and music, the study of history and science. You may recall my recently quoting Faulkner when accepting his Nobel for literature, that the only thing worthy the blood and sweat of the artist is the human heart in conflict with itself. How very insightful of Faulkner.

And you may recall how Sinclair Lewis on the same occasion in 1930 blasted the Academy of Arts and the universities for their moribund pseudo-intellectualism because of the attack on him, Van Dyck actually telling the Nobel Committee that giving the award to Lewis was an affront to America! Well, this reminds me of what Thomas Mann said of Freud's concept of the Id: "It knows no values, no good or evil, no morality."

Even though the newborn infant of necessity is the personification of the Id, I have known, and know, as you yourselves probably, grown people who seem to act in just the manner of the Id, without moral restraint. There is a phrase for this: *Moral Anarchy*. As a result, we try to teach the child the meaning of morality, values, and responsibility.

But when I meet a moral anarchist (Clinton immediately comes to mind), I know I'm dealing with thoroughgoing, utterly selfish childishness in the worse sense of the word. This is when I confront Ovid's Maxim: It is a duty to learn from the enemy. And without question, moral anarchy is the enemy.

I well remember one man becoming incensed when I mentioned moral restraints being necessary for a civilization to progress. He claimed to hate moral restraints. Yet, when I pointed out to him that without such, he could not honestly find fault if someone robbed him or burglarized his house, if people took advantage of him, what right would he have to complain without such civilized, i.e., moral restraints? His real complaint against morality was his selfish desire that such restraints should not be applied to him, only to other people; how very selfishly shortsighted, and how very common in respect to Mann's Idish comment.

Unquestionably many crimes against humanity have been committed in the name of moral order. While in the scheme of things the murder of one seems of little consequence, except in the Stalinist sense that the murder of one constitutes a crime while the murder of millions a statistic there are two murders, apart from that of Jesus, that stand out in my mind in the context of moral order; the burning of Servetus at the stake by John Calvin, that highly moral church leader and those equally moral church leaders who hung Mary Easty in Salem. And I've often asked myself what, of moral value, do such murderers have to teach me concerning morality? Yet multiplied millions have paid homage to Calvin and venerated some of the leaders of Salem such as Cotton Mather. And many continue to do so. While Luther fumed against Copernicus, the Inquisition burned Bruno alive and imprisoned Galileo for life out of the religious attempt at moral order.

Americans seem to want someone of equal morality to Calvin and Mather, one William Clinton, in the White House. But as the Whore of Babylon smacks her painted lips and says "I am in need of nothing, I have it all and have done no wrong in the acquisition," she is still covered with shame for the entire world to see. And while the Emperor thinks himself clothed in glorious array, he is still naked in the pure and innocent eyes of a child. The sins of some bring immediate judgment, others later. But I am a firm believer in the certainty of sin finding out the sinner.

To those knowledgeable of the Bible, I don't quote the familiar verses or give the references. Why not? Because the theme was there long before the Bible was written. It was a common theme of the ancients. And since the Bible is a book written by men, why give it such a priority just to show I know the verses are there? Not to mention the fact that far wiser men than Solomon, for example, preceded him. But this is just another example of how successful propaganda can be in overcoming the truth.

And as to actual wisdom, it is largely missing in the stories and writings of all the ancients including some of those of the Bible. They passed on much knowledge, but little wisdom. And considering their glorification of war, their beliefs in myths and superstitions, and the contempt shown for women in most cases, how could it be otherwise?

It seems a kind of lunacy can grip a whole nation at times. America seems in the throes of this at present. Our own Puritan past with the insanity of a Cotton Mather being seen as a marvelous man (as per Clinton) and then our own Civil War. Germany and Japan during WWII certainly prove nations can suffer a chronic and pervasive insanity.

Yet, Hitler was a moralist as was Mather; and his faith that of moral order through the mechanism of propaganda; together with a contempt for the inability of the common people to think critically for themselves. But Hitler's words ring too true: It is possible by means of shrewd and unremitting propaganda, to make people believe that heaven is hell - and hell heaven. Of course, Hitler wasn't alone in his low opinion of the masses, as you well know. Emerson said: "The sluggish and perverted mind of the multitude, always slow to open to the incursions of Reason."

But I will point out something to which Adam Smith bore witness and with which Emerson would agree: "An instructed and intelligent people are always more decent and orderly than an ignorant and stupid one. They feel themselves, each individual, more respectable, and more likely to obtain the respect of their lawful superiors, and they are therefore more disposed to respect those superiors. . . In free countries, where the safety of government depends very much upon the favorable judgment that the people may form of its conduct, it must surely be of the highest importance that they should not be disposed to judge rashly or capriciously concerning it."

Smith's point and its relevance to our present condition in America should be obvious. And desperately needs to be heeded! Notwithstanding the caveat of Adam Smith, history bears unqualified testimony to the truth of Hitler's maxim. Tell the lie big enough, often enough, and people will believe it. That is, until they are educated enough to engage in critical thinking. And this isn't going to happen until we learn wisdom.

When the legend becomes fact, print the legend. This sage, but cynical, advice is often followed by Hollywood which knows the bare, unadorned facts are often too prosaic. It is the format of those who would make their heroes larger than life with this modification: When the facts become legend, print the legend. In just this manner, many taboos and totems, the Torah,

Bible, and Koran came into being. The Bible, for example, is filled with such legends.

But we must not worship a book, making it an idol. And weaknesses and errors, myths and legends, must be acknowledged for the sake of the truth, most especially the demon of dualism that haunts all religions.

Fabulous stories must be confronted as well, stories of commandments written by God on tablets of stone given to a supposed Moses, Joshua commanding the sun to stand still, Elijah going up in a chariot of fire, a man revived from death by his body touching the bones of Elisha and so many other fables which are devoutly believed by many even in these modern times in the mistaken notion that believing such fairy tales is a matter of faith and honors God, must be confronted for the harm they do! And this is not going to happen until we learn wisdom. But this thing of the children; we say they are the future but we turn a blind eye to the devastation caused by molestation. Thus proving we have not learned wisdom.

I watched a marvelous special about Grand Central Station in New York. What wonderful memories it evoked. I well-remember the old radio program featuring GCS and the 20th Century Limited. I can still hear the introduction to the show: Grand Central Station, crossroads of America!

You know, it is marvelous to have such nostalgic memories of the past. And I often wax lyrical on the subject of wonderful experiences, music, and films of the past. But there is no mistaking the price paid for such memories. I am reminded of this every morning when I get out of bed with a groan instead of sprightly springing up with a hearty and shouted *Huzzah for Aurora!* on my lips (not that I seem to recall ever doing quite exactly this. But I'm sure you get my point)!

My brother and I had the privilege of seeing this marvelous cathedral of Grand Central Station, which was erected to the glorification of trains and travel, and wandering about it during WWII (since getting around the country by any means was so restricted at the time, a step-father with some clout in the service enabled us to have this experience). We got to travel on that beautiful train and I remember seeing Jeff Chandler. No mode of transportation can compare with the trains of the past. How I wish Carole Lombard had chosen the train rather than that plane. By the flip of a coin, she chose and sealed her fate.

This reminds me of Destiny and DNA; and Furrina. When Furrina hops into my lap, I ask her (often engaging in conversation with animals, as is my wont): Do you really want to show you care about me or are you just looking for comfort? Are you showing affection or just responding to the source of your food and shelter? Are you being just like a woman who wants to be petted when you want to be petted, not when I want to pet you (sorry about that one, ladies)?

Well, it would be nice to think Furrina really is showing affection. But she's a cat. And I know cats. And I don't hold it against her because she is so utterly selfish and only cares about her comfort. That is the nature of cats. Would a cat ever seek its own comfort at the cost of mine? Now that really is a rhetorical question.

And if I lift her and place her in another chair so I can write and I tell her Stay! I don't wonder when I get that Kiss what? look from her. She's a cat, and being a cat she just jumps back in my lap as soon as I sit down again and start writing. We have repeated this procedure at some length at times. This is a game, I think, to her. Or maybe she enjoys playing with what I somewhat euphemistically call my mind; cats being such arrogantly selfish, cunning and devious creatures who knows?

But if I put her in the middle of my bed, letting her think I am making a supreme sacrifice by giving her the whole bed, ah, she seems quite content with that. As I have said many times, I am an incurable romantic (the more astute reader will know what I am really talking about. And to know them is to love them). But would Furrina really care about me if I tried to beat her into doing so? Pretty doubtful. Just another rhetorical question. Then why do some men behave in such a fashion towards some women (The Quiet Man notwithstanding)? And why do some people try to beat their children into caring? From the behavior of some so-called adults, one might come to such a conclusion, insane as it is. Destiny? DNA?

Just recently, I learned of a case being argued on this basis. A young man is on death row in Arizona. His father is on death row in Arkansas. Neither had seen each other since the young man was a baby. As an infant, the young man had been adopted.

But the adoptive parents, good solid citizens, had nothing but trouble with the boy as he grew up. He started a life of crime in childhood and went to juvenile hall when he was eleven. Crime became a way of life for him and he was finally caught and convicted for murder. Through circumstances, he and his father learned of each other and began to communicate by letters. Their lives had followed very similar patterns of crime and violence. The young man's attorney is arguing that his client is a genetic criminal; that he was genetically wired to commit crime, even murder.

This is going to be a continuing and growing problem in our society. As we learn more of genetics and brain function, we are going to be asked to consider ever more complex questions about personal responsibility for human behavior.

Many are hedging by trying to discriminate between a predisposition to certain behaviors versus being hard-wired to such. Being a well-qualified behaviorist, I find such studies and research captivating. I have long-known predispositions to certain behaviors do exist. I was one of the first to suggest that a predisposition to alcoholism might account for many alcoholics. This was some time before the field of genetics began to burst wide open.

Even in my most fundamentalist, self-righteous, and judgmental religious days, I didn't totally discount the possibility that genetics might account for some criminal and pervert behaviors.

Some time ago, I began to write extensively about the discoveries in genetics and brain function, particularly of how these were opening fields of investigation into abnormal, self-destructive, and anti-social behavior. The serial killer, for example, has long been a fascinating subject of behavioral science (I use this word knowing full well it is far from being a science).

Most of us have known children who seemed to be devoid of what we call conscience. I say what we call because we do not understand what conscience is. When I was a boy, I knew several such children. One in particular seemed to enjoy torturing animals. I was only about three but I remember this boy throwing some newborn kittens over a clothesline to fall and hit a concrete walk. He laughed as he did so.

There is an on-going debate concerning homosexuality, whether such behavior is hard-wired genetically. The debate is going to heat up as to whether certain criminal behaviors are hard-wired in such a fashion.

But for me, there is a bottom line. No matter what the source, some behaviors must be controlled, even curtailed. No civilized society wants, or can allow, murderers and rapists walking their streets. Since such behaviors are as old as the human race, laws became necessary to provide needed controls in order to sustain a normal and civilized society. The question is, then, not one of whether such behaviors are genetic, but how to deal with them; and, as humanely as possible with justice for victims.

The Amendment proposes breaking the chain of molestation in society by ridding ourselves of molesters through imprisonment for life. We imprison murderers and rapists because we know such evil behavior cannot be allowed in our society.

That boy who enjoyed torturing and killing the kittens should never have been allowed free intercourse with other children. Some behaviors are learned. And such a boy undoubtedly went on to teach some children that it was acceptable and fun to torture and kill animals.

Indisputably, all living creatures are genetically hard-wired for procreation. But the question arises whether perversion is genetic? The Marquis de Sade became proverbial in respect to perversion. Was he such a creature due to his genes? Creatures like Jack the Ripper and so many others?

Whether genetic or not, perversion can be a learned behavior as well. I have gone into depth on this particular subject in my books and won't belabor it here. Suffice it to say that some behaviors, whether genetic or learned, cannot be allowed to infect a society; thus the need of the Amendment to break the chain of the perversion of molestation.

Once the whole genome of humans is mapped, what changes in particular cases will be suggested, even made, in some people? Controversy is storming even now because of some of the possibilities in this area of science. Eugenics finally coming into its own? A rather horrifying thought!

If number 92 doesn't do us in first, the possibilities are truly mind-boggling! As are the ethics we will be asked to consider on a mounting scale. And the recent failure of the Senate to remove Clinton from office does not bode well for ethical considerations to hold sway on the part of any of the institutions of America including the institutions of medical science (as to our escalating the glorification of sex and violence in our society, that speaks for itself as a portent of the future for any ethical considerations)!

The parents want a white, blue-eyed, baby boy with curly blond hair and an IQ of 160. Made to order. Not impossible futuristically speaking. But will the practice of such science be wise? Is it wisdom to enable women to bear sextuplets, even octuplets? Ah, that indeed is the question, a question easily answered in part, but only in part. Especially if my equation of Knowledge+Wisdom=Peace is correct and wisdom is derived from love and compassion together with a perfect hatred of evil.

I write a good deal about the necessity of civilized manners and speech; but these are learned behavior. James Boswell bears quoting on this subject: "There is no doubt that there may be an excess of luxury by which the more solid properties of man will be weakened, if not annihilated. In observing individuals, we find that a keen gratification of appetites and tastes, as produces exquisite pleasure of an inferior and slight kind, which can be repeated with frequency, indisposes them for steady, noble enjoyment; and to borrow an admirable metaphor from Goldsmith, in his life of Nash, their minds shrink to the diminutive size of the objects with which they are occupied. A mind so shrunk and shriveled, as to take in only petty delights, is averse from those extensive satisfactions that are suited to the dignity of human nature, in that state to which, amidst all our imperfections, it can at times be raised."

Well, if Boswell had been aware of Hollywood and TV, he would most certainly have expanded his excellent and sage comments on the ability of petty entertainments and luxuries to shrivel the intellect as well as good manners and speech. Are such things being annihilated in America? I think they are.

And I further believe this has kept Clinton in office. The corrosive and cancerous disease of the petty pleasures of entertainments and good times to the exclusion of thinking of our future, our children and their welfare, of what is really best for our children, as opposed to what is noble, will most assuredly and ultimately destroy us if not cured in time. Bread and circuses are as much a part of human nature now as they have ever been; just another proof of our having never attained wisdom.

But what Boswell wrote is knowledge, not wisdom. And it is knowledge which humanity has possessed from the very beginning though Boswell states it in quite memorable words with his own peculiar and quite distinctive genius for doing so.

Obviously any person or society that gives themselves over to petty entertainments and petty luxuries is never going to advance in truly civilized speech and behavior. These require the restraints of self-discipline. But only wisdom can possibly lead to the effective application of such knowledge, to the effective restraints and disciplines needed. And America sorely lacks wisdom.

If anything, Boswell perfectly illustrates that the facts of even correct knowledge do not automatically lead to wisdom and the two should never be confused. This is very much like my continued warning to people that they should never confuse what they believe with what they know. The result is chaos and bigotry in too many cases.

I have always gotten a chuckle out of the story about the meeting between Dwight Moody the great American evangelist, and Charles Spurgeon the great English pulpiteer. At one point during their conversation Moody points to Spurgeon's cigar and says: "Brother Spurgeon, don't you know that is sin?" Spurgeon riposted, poking Moody's more than ample girth: "Brother Moody; that is sin!"

And while it was obvious Spurgeon never missed a meal, there is no doubt that Moody dug his grave with a fork. And his remark to Spurgeon always reminds me of the story told by J.Vernon MaGee of the dinner where American Christians were hosting a group of German Christians at a large restaurant in Los Angeles. The Americans were thoroughly condemnatory of the Germans drinking beer. The Germans were outraged at the American women dressing like sluts. Well, a little self-righteousness always goes a long way.

In my library, I had the complete set of The Metropolitan Pulpit, the encyclopedic set of Spurgeon's sermons. I also had and read his multi-volume commentary on the Psalms. Not having been formally educated, Spurgeon spoke better than he wrote. His sermons, while printed in full by The London Times, weren't models of erudition. But his preaching held parishioners spellbound. He was an orator, not a writer.

The Times also printed the sermons of Joseph Parker, one of Spurgeon's contemporaries and held in great esteem. Unlike Spurgeon, Parker was well educated, very erudite, and a very good writer. I had the complete set of Parker's commentaries (as encyclopedic as that of Spurgeon's sermons) and they were very good and quite enjoyable to read.

A reporter for the Times was interviewing Spurgeon and asked somewhat jocularly: "Sir, do you expect to see Joseph Parker in heaven?" To which Spurgeon replied: "No, I do not."

The reporter, aghast at Spurgeon's reply, asked: "Sir, why ever not?"

Spurgeon, lowering his head, replied: "I expect he will be so close to God Himself that I will be too far removed in order to be able see him."

Now I got to know both men very well from their writings. I also read extensively the secondary material from varied sources about both men. I would like to believe the story about the reporter from the Times; I would very much like to believe Spurgeon was quite sincere in his self-deprecating and extraordinarily humble observation concerning himself and Parker. Such humility, as opposed to so much self-righteousness that abounds among the religious, would be a real tonic and can't fail to bring a tear to the eye.

Because of this, I would occasionally use this anecdote in one of my sermons. And how I liked to believe Spurgeon's humility was matched by my own in those days. How wrong can you be!

My problem with the story, once I came to realize and accept the fact that I was only a common, garden variety sinner, was this: Successful men get caught up in their own press (often self-manufactured) and begin to believe it. This is deadly.

Because of my familiarity with Spurgeon, though hoping I am mistaken the skeptic in me knows he was quite capable of playing the expected role of the humble servant of God. And he knew his reply would be of great credit to him in such a capacity. It also put Parker in his debt. And I will always be in debt to that great man, Charles Lee Feinberg, Ph.D., Th.D., then Dean of Talbot Theological Seminary and my friend and mentor, for early-on warning me of the false humility and all too real actual chicanery to be found among the religious. I realized some years later that he must have recognized the propensity in myself to engage in such behavior and was attempting to warn me of this as well. It took awhile, dear Uncle Charles, but I did finally learn the lesson you tried to teach me. And I'll always be supremely grateful for your having borne with me.

My experience in the churches, my great familiarity with the Bible, which remains my primary textbook, my formal education and the education I have received at the hands of the real world cause me to question motives. I not only question my own wisdom, I am constantly questioning my motives in nearly everything I say and do.

One thing of particular interest to me, and one which I bring to my readers because I know they will be interested as well, is the subject of death. Philosophically, it is argued that we don't have much time or get much of a chance to develop living to a high art, life being a very personal and singular thing and of comparatively short duration.

But we get far less of a chance to practice dying or develop the art since it is a one-time only and terminal event. Besides, who in their right mind would want to practice the art of dying? I am so very familiar with religion that I can say without fear of being disputed that the basis of religion is the attempt to formulate a philosophy of death ever as much or more than a philosophy of living.

Oh, I credit religion with attempts to formulate a philosophy of life as well. But whether death comes as a gentle friend to relieve suffering, or a mad and ravenous beast to rip, tear and devour, a philosophy of death is at least of equal importance to people as a philosophy of life since the one serves to interpret the other for us. As a result, the very real and inescapable issues of life and death are the focus of religion and philosophy. Because of this, I draw a great deal of my writing from these two sources of inquiry.

Good and evil, life and death, these are the fountainhead of religion and philosophy, of art, of the grandest or the most corrupt, of human endeavors. In humankind's search for wisdom, however, often grievously erroneous religious and philosophical concepts have led us a wrong path. They are great and grave errors to confuse belief with knowledge and to confuse knowledge with wisdom.

A formal and disciplined education in religion and philosophy most often leads people to believe that in the study of the great thinkers throughout history, one is studying and learning wisdom. Not so. What is being studied and learned in most cases is knowledge. And while so very beneficial, and essential, it should not be confused with wisdom.

James Boswell and Charles Lamb are excellent cases in point. I very much wish all people would read the great English and American essays (I don't include the great German, French, and Italian writers because that would be lifting hope to a dizzying, ethereal height which would be, to say the least, unrealistic). There is so very much to be learned from doing so. I have certainly not become so anile as to fail in continuing to derive much knowledge from this salubrious exercise of my mind.

Having quoted Boswell, I give you Charles Lamb. In his essay "Witches, And Other Night-Fears", Lamb points out that just as there is no law to judge of the lawless, there is no canon by which a dream may be criticized. Credulity is the man's weakness, he says, while being the child's strength.

Just so, a careful reading of the works of Boswell and Lamb will quickly apprise the reader that, indeed, there is nothing new under the sun. What was before still is. Yet it remains for one generation to pass on the knowledge of the one to the next. And there will always be, hopefully, those of genius who will use the right words and phraseology to do so.

And it remains the responsibility of the new generation to learn what is beneficial from the old. But having said this, the cautionary word remains that belief never be confused with knowledge, that knowledge never be confused with wisdom.

It is well to weep over those things, at times, that we cannot remedy. Such deeply rooted feelings in those sensitive to such things can help in our race for wisdom. And it is a race, of that I have no doubt. Number 92 looms too ominously on the immediate horizon. And not to dispute Lamb, it is my waking dreams that trouble, that make me a poet, the maker and the teller of the stories that are needed to make the ordinary, and ordinary people, extraordinary.

It is, after all, the ordinary and ordinary people who are the stuff of the real tale of life. Marvelous men and women come and go. But the ordinary, the real heroes and heroines, remain to carry on at their lasts and anvils, the raising and caring for children, the next generation in the story and from whom the marvelous men and women of the future are to come.

And speaking of those things we may weep over and lack the means to cure, I am glad Studs Terkel is still speaking out about the homeless. Knowing some of these choose their lifestyle rather than being productive members of society, one cannot help feeling more should be done for those who don't seem to be able to handle the rat race. A social conscience is needed where real need exists. We need those like Terkel to prick our consciences and remind us of the need for compassion toward those truly unfortunate and deserving of our charity.

I count it one of the real blessings in my life that I have not had to wear a watch in years. But I worked hard all my life to reach such exalted status and have earned the right to go without wearing a watch. My time is my own. And it being the most valuable thing I possess, I try to use it to the best effect. For me, that best effect is the writing and the work for the Amendment.

So I shun appointments like the plague. I revel in spontaneity. And having punched a clock for so many years, I never take the liberty I enjoy for granted and I thank God daily for it. But I also realize the great responsibility I have for using this blessed time wisely; at least as wisely as I have the light to do so.

It is with this in mind that I mention those like Terkel and his own social conscience. As writers, he and I have an obligation and a duty to exercise such a conscience. We are blessed with the liberty to write about things like the homeless and poverty, the awareness of which contributes to such a conscience.

But it is essential that writers like Terkel and me keep mixing it up with ordinary people in order to write with a conscience ourselves. It is too easy for me to escape into the music and literature, the beauty of creation, and avoid the ugliness that is too often so much a part of the human condition.

I was at the club enjoying the music and dancing when I noticed what had to be a couple of plainclothes cops wander in and take a seat at the bar. The girl with whom I was dancing, an attractive redhead and being the daughter of a cop, noticed them as well and we nodded knowingly to each other, not even having to say anything.

When I had arrived at the club, I had been sitting at the bar having tonic on ice, my usual virgin gin and tonic with a twist of lime. Looks like the real thing, anyway. A couple of attractive young women I didn't recognize came in and took a seat next to me. They seemed already pretty well lit. When the band started, they became the life of the party.

Fortunately the cop's daughter came in shortly after and she and I took seats at one of the tables away from the bar. With my departure the two young women began hitting on a guy I knew. Soon after, as the girl and I were dancing, the plainclothes came in. There was a pretty good crowd in the club and things were really getting lively when some more friends of mine came in and we all went over to shoot some pool.

Then the cocktail waitress (I still call them barmaids) came over and collected the ashtrays. We have this new law that prohibits smoking in the bars but the club had ignored it until this night. Not long after that, the owners of the club showed up. That was most unusual.

To make a long (and very interesting) story short, the cops cited the gal behind the bar for serving a couple of guys who were already quite drunk. One of the two young women was arrested for drunk and disorderly (she got a little combative with one of the cops) and the other for soliciting (she had propositioned the cops). Not surprisingly, the girls were also found to be in possession of methamphetamine as well so a drug charge was added to the other charges. They were taken to jail in Bakersfield.

The owners were cited for allowing smoking in the bar. This, with everything else, pretty well put a damper on the rest of the evening (we especially missed the two girls. They had been putting on a good floorshow).

It was about 38 degrees outside that night. It was a pretty cool environment in which to have a cigarette.

The Valley is a relatively small place. But that Saturday night there were 46 arrests for public intoxication. Ten people were arrested for DUI, and another bartender was cited for serving persons who the cops had determined had already had too much.

I mention all of this because there are some very complex issues involved. Of course it isn't right to give more drinks to drunks, raising the legitimate issue of drunk drivers. But are bartenders always able to recognize when someone has had too much? Especially when bars are where people usually go to drink and two beers are too much for some people? I know the barmaid who was cited can't possibly afford a thousand-dollar fine. The fines can reach ten thousand dollars for allowing smoking in bars. And bar owners can lose their liquor licenses for a number of reasons.

As with my wondering when Caesar will target obesity like he and his lawyers did the tobacco companies, I can't help wondering when it will become illegal to drink in the bars? Insane? Sure. But stranger things have happened, and are happening right now. But, then, Caesar knows he is dealing with an illiterate population who cares more for Bread and Circuses than the future of America.

Who would have guessed allowing the F word so long ago in the schools by the cry of academic freedom and not raising our children as hothouse plants would result in the word becoming a synonym for the vulgar, profane and uncivilized manners and illiteracy of an America given over to promoting sex and violence as the hallmarks of our society?

Well, those with a real education, a social and moral conscience, and a genuine love of the arts and sciences, a genuine love of family and children and their future, that's who. But they were shouted down. And being so utterly lacking in real wisdom, good people never have learned the lesson that evil must be confronted by the good with an equal determination to win!

The anti-smoking lawyers, having made fortunes from prosecuting tobacco companies, are now targeting (no pun intended) the makers of firearms, bragging they will do the same thing to Colt, Smith & Wesson, Sturm Ruger and others, that they did to tobacco companies. Lawyers like Mayor Daley of Chicago are smacking their self-righteous lips over this with visions of making millions off this latest attack on American liberties.

Governor Davis of California and President Clinton are making deals with Mexico. A war on drugs? Who's kidding whom? Not when so many politicians, lawyers, police et al., are making so much money from the drug trade.

As to the drug war and California, it is widely known that the Central Valley in the state produces 90% of the methamphetamine in the U.S. Its manufacture right here where I live in the Kern Valley is so prevalent it has become a sorry joke to us natives.

Who suffers the most from all this government intrusion into our lives? The poor; those with no voice in politics; and who really benefits? Certainly not the fast-disappearing middle class; but Caesar is depending on the diminishing capability of the middle class to think and act. Caesar is fully aware of the loss of intellectualism in America.

Now that the universities have succeeded in making it politically incorrect to speak directly to the issues destroying America, things like perversion for example, and opposing gun ownership and the use of tobacco (these for the public good, of course), the politicians are having a field day dispensing with real, civil liberties. And whatever you may believe about Linda Tripp, she is certainly correct in her assessment that what was done to Vincent Foster can be done to anyone by the ruthless such as Clinton et al. who hold and wield power over the masses.

I warn about the loss of real intellectualism in America for a most important reason: Once Caesar has control over people's minds, which is his ultimate goal, the war is won. He has control of the universities and Hollywood, the two most important mechanisms for successful propaganda. With these powerful tools, Caesar can accomplish his ultimate agenda. He can take away the guns of citizens making them impotent in confronting the tyranny of government; he can successfully propagandize this as being for the general welfare.

He can successfully propagandize that perversion is acceptable, only a difference in lifestyle and sexual preference. The propagandizing phraseology wears the usual guise of fairness, freedom, equality, and anti-discrimination that is intended to directly undermine any concept of moral absolutes. Let's face it: the Devil can quote Scripture, and in the process, make people believe heaven is hell and vice versa.

Caesar can accomplish the enslaving of a free people through the tried and true mechanism of propaganda making the majority believe that such people as me are racist, homophobic, anti-Semitic, etc., etc. Thus the death knell of true intellectualism by the simple mechanism of making people such as me enemies of the state. And, of course, by this time Caesar will be absolutely correct in his assessment. But, of course, not for the reasons he gives through his propaganda.

If I go about, as Thoreau, with murder of the state, Caesar, in my heart, it is for the same reason as that of Thoreau's, a thorough and perfect hatred of slavery! The very same reason that I have such perfect and thorough hatred of the child molester! True wisdom would deny Caesar's accomplishing his diabolical agenda. But if I am right, true wisdom can only be gained by first making children our real priority and by women actually being accepted as of equal value to men.

Are we genetic lovers of war and perversion? There are many that would agree with this assessment of human nature. In spite of this, knowledge would have people nod their heads in the affirmative as well that I am correct concerning women and children. But that knowledge is not being acted upon. As a result, a critical element of the equation for peace is not in place and humanity still behaves as though war and perversion are inescapable evils.

Our history isn't very promising; nor is our contemporary world. The Amendment is the approach to an ideal of civilized society. But unless such an ideal is realized, what is our hope of transcending the Beast? What is our hope of beating number 92? Quite obviously a new way, a new path for humanity such as the Amendment envisions and promises, is essential. The traditional methodologies repeated endlessly have been consistent failures and still we have not learned wisdom.

William Hazlitt made the observation: "Things near us are seen of the size of life: things at a distance are diminished to the size of the understanding." And while in the distance some ideas, like cities, may show themselves *With glistering spires and pinnacles adorn'd,* upon close inspection the gold is seen as brass and the glistering appearance becomes tawdry. And thus the history of the human race, a repeating cycle of war and perversion.

But not having any expectation, how can we fail of expectation? Nothing new under the sun? Not so far as the history of humankind being one of war and perversion. Our lack of expectation, as a result, is rooted in having been thoroughly indoctrinated (brain washed) into believing that nothing new is possible for humanity.

We are seeing more of the failed methodology of the past in teaching our little girls and women to fight and defend themselves against predatory boys and men. And I believe this is essential for girls and women to learn. Just as I believe girls and women should be knowledgeable of mechanics and receive equal pay with men in the work they do.

But in the end, nothing will change for the better for humanity. It is a failed methodology. Women are to be the equal of men on the basis of the compatibility of differences, not in combativeness or competition to men on the basis of those differences. Boys and girls should be raised on the basis of the compatibility of differences, not in combativeness or competition to each other on the basis of those differences. That is the ideal in the case of both children and adults.

The inability to pursue the ideal with hope and expectation of success is the basis of my statement that humanity has not learned wisdom because Knowledge+Wisdom=Peace. And to work effectively toward the ultimate goal of Peace requires Wisdom. And where is the hope presently to be found for humanity to realize such an ideal?

Lacking any substantial hope or expectation for peace, we will teach our little girls to fight. It is not an answer, it is a doomed methodology; but lacking wisdom, it's the best we can do. Nations, lacking wise leaders, will have their cannon and muskets and keep teaching boys and men to fight. And, increasingly, girls and women. And the end result of this methodology will be the end of woman being the antithesis of war.

Because I am a member of The National Rifle Association and the National Association of Police Organizations as well as receiving information from several gray groups, I believe I am better informed concerning some things of which the average person is not aware and which don't make Film at Eleven.

Much of the information is certainly in the category of I Don't Want to Know! But such information from diverse sources provides a mosaic, a pattern, which evolves and leads to some conclusions I wouldn't be able to reach otherwise.

It is easy to damn Congress and Clinton for some things like sharing secrets of military technology to China, for example. The problem of the Kurds is making news and North Korea is a growing problem as well. It is equally easy to find yourself stomping ants while the elephants are rampaging through the village.

Leaders of nations know that dedicated fanatics of many stripes abound throughout the world. They know some of these have, or will have, the potential for acquiring suitcase nuclear bombs (why call them devices?). These leaders also know of the possibilities for chemical and biological terrorism.

But you can well imagine the effect a single, small, nuclear bomb exploded in America by a terrorist would have. National martial law would be the least of the effects. Conspiracy buffs are having a field day with the various scenarios. But no conspiracy is needed in the face of actual possibilities.

The point being that unless We the People are willing to pay the price for acquiring wisdom, for being willing to be the leader, in fact, for paving the way to peace, it is only a matter of time when we will run out of options for the failed methodologies that have been the history of the human race.

Like questions of what to do for the homeless and hungry both in America and throughout the world, the very scope of the problem makes us want to pull the blankets over our heads and say: Go away! I can't deal with it and I don't want to know! But such things left without a civilized solution will always find their solution in bloodshed. That is a historic axiom.

CHAPTER FIVE

Ok, so I have a wit which I only use half the time. But even at that, I believe I have more on the ball than a Congress that has tried to gull the public with its terpsichorean display of fancy foot-work which has only resulted in making it look as equally shameful and ridiculous as Bwana Clinton.

While you can train a dog to dance, you can't make it look as though it was natural for the dog to do so. Just so with Congress trying to appear as though it deserved the title Honorable. On the contrary, viewing and listening to some Representatives together with the Senate voting to acquit, I was reminded of how appropriate the remark of Sam Clemens that Judas Iscariot was only a premature congressman.

And as for Congress trying to put the best face on its actions (or, in the case of Clinton, the lack thereof), you still can't teach a pig to sing. First, it can't be done. And secondly, it only annoys the pig. If ever I needed an example of a thoroughgoing lack of wisdom on the part of those professing to be wise, those who have spent all this time and taxpayer money trying to teach a pig to sing, Congress is the best example anyone could wish.

As I and others have pointed out, the Supreme Court is going to have a more than full plate handling new definitions of perjury, among other things, due to a spineless and shameful Senate letting Clinton off the hook.

Monica lied and got away with it. So far. Now there is Juanita Broaddrick. Most people, including myself, believe this woman in spite of her lack of personal morality. And no one, by this time, would put rape beyond such a creature as Bill Loophole Clinton. But Broaddrick, Jane Doe Number Five, lied under oath as well. How will that be handled in view of Bill and Monica getting away with it? So far.

As for Clinton, he has raped the office of President and the Congress has let him get away with it. Why expect his raping a woman be thought of any greater consequence to such a Congress?

And I won't separate the two houses. All it would have taken to convict Clinton would have been for some of those Democratic Representatives to have joined Republicans during the impeachment. But by making it a Republican Vendetta, and not ignoring the partisan tactics of some Republicans, Democrats themselves put politics ahead of morality and assured the acquittal of Clinton.

And what of those polls? Isn't the real tragedy for America the fact that so many Americans, in spite of Clinton's arrogant and thoroughly shameful betrayal of his office and the people, still wanted him to keep the office of Washington and Lincoln? What does this say of the morality of America to our children and to the whole world! Well, it all calls to mind the old adage: Ya can't make a' egg without breakin' a few omelets.

The rather large, colorful but raucous twitter-tweets, the peacocks, are still around; and still terrorizing Furrina. I know, it should be pushy cat, not pussy cat for cats are, indeed, pushy critters. In the case of the Peacocks and Furrina, it's Fraidy Cat.

My mentioning the big bust in the bars of the Valley elicited a few responses from readers. And the one that predominated: What was I doing there?

Well, my presence was necessitated because the churches, art galleries, the opera house and museums are closed at that time of night on the weekends. Meeting girls and dancing (hoping to get lucky like any normal bachelor); shooting pool really had little to do with it. Well, maybe just a little.

The writing, mixing it up with ordinary people; well, even I have to admit it is far safer to write about a fictional Walter Mitty life you've never lived rather than the real thing that I have always insisted on living outside the sanctuary. But, beyond this, even I have to admit to liking John Wayne movies. And largely because of Maureen O'Hara, "McClintock" remains one of my favorites; so much for any pretensions on my part, through such a shameful admission, of culture and refinement.

It may seem of little consequence to many people but I wonder how you feel about airbrush revisionist history in regards to smoking? Most would agree that the Stalinist revisionism of history utilizing technology to eliminate figures from photographs and films that did not meet Stalin's and Communism's political correctness was not only totally unscrupulous but very damaging to the record of actual history.

Here in America, it is becoming common to eliminate the cigars, pipes and cigarettes in photos and some films of famous personages. But can you imagine Casablanca without cigarettes or F.D.R. without that trademark cigarette holder or General MacArthur without his pipe? Well, if the Political Correctness Gestapo has its way that is what is going to happen.

Even granting that not a few ex-husbands and ex-wives would like to avail themselves of this technology, obviously it isn't of much consequence if we are only talking about smoking in respect to such artistry. Just airbrush away that part of history. It isn't important that sending cigarettes to our boys overseas was the patriotic thing to do during WWII and tobacco sales were of such importance to the war effort; that tobacco advertising was so important to the early history of radio and TV, and doctors used to recommend their favorite brands. It isn't even important that the early colonies depended on tobacco to settle what was to become The United States of America.

When you think about it, maybe making such history disappear isn't all that inconsequential; but having said that, I would be among the first to describe smoking as a fool on one end and a fire on the other. I cannot think of a single redeeming thing to say of tobacco. It is unquestionably a terrible addiction and ruinous of health and were it within my power to do so, I would banish it from the face of the earth! And I say this as a smoker myself. Especially because I am a smoker myself! My legitimate fear is that the intrusions of Caesar and those of the blue-nosed, self-righteous prejudicial disposition of a Billy Sunday will, as with prohibition, make the cure worse than the disease.

In the last issue of TAP I mentioned the raids on the bars in the Kern Valley where I live. By the time the dust settled, a total of 51 people were arrested. Some simply because they protested the arrest of others and tried to stick up for them! It was: "Ok, outside! You're going too!"

Most people don't know that the Alcoholic Beverage Control (ABC) agents don't need to give any kind of drunk test for them to arrest people by observation only. As a consequence, not a single one of the 51 arrested was actually given any test of any kind. They were arrested, handcuffed, and hauled off to jail in Bakersfield on the basis of observation only. This cost a lot of people, including the taxpayers, a lot of money. And the only recourse of those arrested is to make out a complaint and go to court against the police; something few of those arrested can afford to do.

Well, it's the old story of whose ox is being gored. If you don't go to a bar or drink, who cares? If you don't own a gun, who cares? If you don't smoke, who cares? If it wasn't you or your child molested or murdered...? And in all fairness, there is too much of what is so well depicted in the film "A Civil Action" that prevents many good people from joining the fight against Caesar. But let's be honest; it is due more to apathy than any other reason. Who cares?

But what of the more substantial changes Caesar with his PCG has in mind in the name of political correctness and his New World Order? For example, just like Stalin and his cohorts, what if Caesar with his PCG, following in the footsteps of Stalin, starts making actual people begin to disappear from American history, people not representative of Caesar's vision of a new world order? And, naturally, if you make the people disappear from photos and films, like tobacco, they must be eliminated from history books as well.

My particular bias in this regard: I vote for making Clinton disappear. And Janet Reno. And Chicago mayor Richard Daley. And.... No, that way is madness! There are just too many I would like to see disappear who have been, and are, a blight on America and humanity. I'm not that weak of stomach but every time I see and hear Clinton on TV I want to vomit! And the same goes for Janet Reno! I'm not about to forget Ruby Ridge or Waco any more than I will forget an equally conscienceless, lying hypocrite of a President!

If Caesar has his way, these acts of murder by Reno will be erased by the PCG as well (Vincent Foster? What Vincent Foster?). But as long as I have life and means to do so, I'm going to keep letting Reno know I haven't forgotten her acts of atrocity or her victims! Anymore than I will stop letting Clinton know I won't forget his own criminal behavior and the way he has shamed America before the whole world! And I won't stop writing and speaking of it and posting this message on the Internet for the whole world to see! And my Memorial Wall of Shame still stands out front with the names of the little victims of an America, which continues to turn its back on them; an America filled with good Americans who Don't Want to Know! It took a Clinton, a person of such despicable lack of conscience and character, to make the phrase I share your pain repugnant! Virtually everyone I know now cringes at the phrase.

I take great comfort in the rumors that Hillary plans to divorce her draft-dodging, didn't inhale, womanizing and abusing, thieving, despicably arrogantly shameless, conscienceless perjurer and philandering embarrassment of a husband as quickly as possible (I deleted some of the worst pejorative adjectives for the sake of the more sensitive reader and brevity). She realizes he will be an albatross around her neck in all her future plans. Not to mention the potential financial disaster he poses, and the potential for his eventually winding up in prison. But she will, hypocritically, play the role of the long-suffering Stand by her man innocent victim as long as she is forced to do so and as long as it suits her purpose.

There is a ray of hope in all this. When I worked in the shops, I saw a few people die quite unexpectedly. I watched as one fellow machinist simply sneezed and dropped dead! The autopsy showed he had broken a blood clot loose in his nose and it went straight and immediately to his brain.

One morning, the guy who worked right next to me didn't show up. Later in the morning, we were told he had been riding to work with another fellow and the passenger door of the vehicle had inadvertently popped open. He fell out of the vehicle onto the road and a truck ran directly over his head. Another fellow was electrocuted because of a poor ground on a piece of equipment. And yet another was killed when a heat-treat furnace exploded in his face. A fellow pilot I knew very well fell out of the top bunk of his camper and broke his neck. He died instantly.

I could relate many such incidents of people I knew well suddenly dying or being killed. I could relate stories of those I knew well that died of heart attacks or wasted away from cancer or died at their own hand. If you live long enough, you are going to witness such things in the ordinary course of living.

Death is no laughing matter. But life is no joke either. Though filled with the events that make up the Divine Comedy including the tragedies, life is often confronted by the unexpected for which no amount of preparedness will suffice to meet.

Looking back, I should have been killed or badly injured many times when I wasn't. I've been cut and shot at more than once; I have survived dynamite, a rifle possibly blowing up in my hands, being shot at, and a major motorcycle accident that should have killed me. A seemingly slighter accident did kill my eldest daughter, Diana.

I have missed death or serious injury many times in circumstances such as bullies who have wanted, and threatened, to kill me, circumstances that have left me shaking my head over the seeming incongruity of the events or people that kill or injure some while not touching others. Guardian angels, but where are they in some cases like that of Diana? Who wouldn't cry out at the unfairness of such things? What really loving parent wouldn't gladly and even gratefully exchange their life for their child's if such a thing were possible?

I have been deeply involved with some dangerous occupations and hobbies. The mix of explosives, machine shops, construction, peace officer, guns, planes, boats, motorcycles, wandering wild and desolate places, is guaranteed to rub up against possible death or serious injury. And when you are so involved with so many things portending danger, you practice as much caution as you can.

But what of the ordinary, mundane, everyday circumstances and accidents of life- I was once riding with a friend when I noticed the lane we were in ended and we were headed directly toward a telephone pole. Occupying the passenger seat, the pole was straight in line with me! I couldn't believe my buddy didn't see he was headed directly at that pole! Only my sudden gasp at the last instant before crashing into the pole caused him to jerk the wheel just in time to avoid the disaster!

Where was his mind? It obviously wasn't on his driving. Once, I had to actually reach over and jerk the wheel of another driver to avoid going over the side of a canyon. Where was his mind? Such things leave me wondering there aren't more accidents than there are. And, why I am still alive? Of course, a few such incidents cured me of being too polite to say anything or take appropriate action when some idiot seems bent on killing me by his lack of attention to his driving.

An old buddy and I developed a suitable phrase for such occasions since we both were pretty idiotic about our own driving: *Is this where we die?* It's one thing to have pedal to the metal and purposely driving like an idiot with a death wish; but in the ordinary and sensible course of travel?

To repeat, if you live long enough, you will see people die, be killed or badly injured. And you will see these things happen by even the most mundane and ordinary circumstances of every day life.

Not to be depressing but rather factual, if you are going to talk about life and everything else the everything else is death. As the old saw has it, none of us is going to get out of this alive. Death is an absolute. Granted, no one in their right mind dwells on the subject. Still, it won't go away by ignoring it.

William Hazlitt's essay "On the Feeling of Immortality in Youth" is one of the finest pieces written on the subject of life and death. A very familiar theme throughout history, the subject is treated by Hazlitt in a most sensible way to which all can relate.

Unquestionably, as I mentioned in the last issue of TAP, life and death, good and evil, are the fountainhead and themes of religion and philosophy, as well and understandably they must be. These are the themes of art and literature. They are the themes of the best and worst of human endeavor. Curiosity, as the driving force of many inquiries into the subjects, has opened some interesting, and largely erroneous, paths for humanity.

The need to find explanations for phenomena has been the driving force of scientific inquiry. The myths and legends of human history invariably have their sources in some facts that were unintelligible to people at one time. Or, in events which were equally unintelligible. Why did pre-homo sapiens bury their dead with ceremony?

The great men and women of history were commonly made larger than life. This was usually the task of the poets of antiquity. The scriptures of various cultures came into being in just this fashion; as did the gods, goddesses, ceremonies, prophets, and shamans of such cultures.

Astrology, for example, has its roots in the need to believe in the supernatural, in the need of people in many cultures to make sense of the insensible; such as, for example, trying to make Destiny of the accidents of life.

I often find myself lying in bed having conversations with God. Most would call this praying. I call it conversation with my Heavenly Father. I don't know that God and I are conversing. But I believe this. And I find great comfort in such a belief.

Just the other night during such a conversation, something came to me that someone had recently said about my work for the Amendment being the work God has called me to. Well, several people have made this observation and it is, admittedly, a humbling thing. And I freely admit I would really like to believe this.

It is, admittedly as well, a tremendous work, far beyond the capacity or capability of any one individual. And I don't think it was my idea. I don't think I have that kind of genius for the Amendment (or the Equation) or even that kind of genuine love or concern for others, that I would have come up with the idea myself.

So who did that leave? God? Perhaps. I don't know. But it would be nice to know. That would let me off the hook. It's God's idea, not mine. It's always nice to be able to blame others for your seeming madness or stupidity. And God has always been a convenience for such blame. Sadly, He doesn't get much credit for being sensible or reasonable.

But as I was lying in bed, the fables of Shaharazade and Penelope came to mind. The literate know that Shaharazade kept herself alive by telling stories in To Be Continued format to King Shahryar. Penelope kept her unwanted suitors at bay for three years while she waited and hoped for the return of Ulysses by weaving a winding sheet for old Laertes and undoing the day's work at night. This ruse worked until her maids betrayed her. Fortunately, as we know, Ulysses showed up in the nick of time.

I freely admit of the wistful wishing to believe in myths and legends rather than have to face such fearful realities as Number 92 of the Periodic Table; or the ugly realities of Clinton and Reno. So it came to me: Suppose the Amendment and its corollary Equation were of God and He was keeping me alive as long as He needed me to do the work and the writing in support of them?

But of course I wouldn't be unique in believing in something so strongly that the very belief in such keeps one alive. This is called the placebo effect or, in some cases of delusion, the need to believe. And I don't delude myself that I am immune to these. Quite the contrary, I want to believe. But I credit myself with not wanting to believe lies; not even the lies purporting to be of God. Most especially not such lies so common to religion told and believed by good, even loving, well-intentioned people.

By definition, I could never call the things I was taught as a child by loving people, lies. And never in the sense of a lie that is told with the intent to both deceive and do injury. Yet, I was taught many things that later proved to be untrue. But because of these things being so well intended, and because these people loved me so very much, it was the most difficult of tasks to finally admit to myself that these things were untrue. And though told and taught me by those who did love me, they did great harm though caused unwittingly by these loved ones. The intent was good; the result sometimes disastrous.

It is coming to grips with the truth of this that has forced me to admit to believing many things I even taught my own children, that I later learned were not true. This necessitated a ruthless honesty in admitting of this to my children first and foremost. But I have tried to impress upon them and others that a mind not subject to change is a most dubious asset at best.

It is my own history of errors, both believing and committing, and lack of wisdom, that necessitate my being honest in my writing in spite of whose ox I gore in the process. Including my own. Far better to fear God rather than men, far better to be ruthlessly honest with my children and my friends than paint myself other than I am.

Still, as Charles Lamb so well said: ... there is no canon by which a dream may be criticized ... and Credulity is the man's weakness while being the child's strength.

Being a fairly normal man in most respects, I would heartily resent any accusation of either credulity or childishness. But I do have a dream, if you will, for the Amendment holding the potential for peace in the world and the salvation of humankind. Not a bad dream; though just a tad grandiose some would say. But I'm sure all would admit it's not a bad dream.

In spite of the normally-to-be expected criticisms of equally normal people, it is a dream kept alive by the best part of the man, the child within that desperately cries out to be heard! And as Lamb points out, there is no canon by which the dream may be criticized (though this obviously does not prevent criticism. Which, given the nature of such a dream, is perfectly understandable).

Nor would any that really know me attempt to justify any accusation of childishness or credulity in the man; I'm fully aware at all times of the part of the man and poet in his dream, that part which must recognize and deal with the ugly realities of life. The acceptable credulity of the child in this respect, his strength, is his wide-eyed wonder at the hearing of fabulous legends, his believing in magic and myths, Knights and Ladies, fire-breathing dragons, witches, sorcerers, and heroes larger than life. But most important of all, is the child's believing faith in goodness.

Belief comes easy to a child. And well it should. The tragedy is in the loss by the adult of the best of such belief. To lose the wonder of a rainbow or a butterfly, to lose the belief in the healing power of a mother's kiss, to lose hope that goodness can prevail, is such a tragic loss.

All things are possible to a child. I believe this is why Jesus said we must be born again. Jesus was no god except in the sense that we are all gods as he himself pointed out. But he was a man who recognized the special gifts of children, gifts of God that we squander as adults as the best part of childhood, the part we should hold on to, which is soon squandered in a prodigally profligate manner and wastes away but must be reclaimed. Hence the expression Jesus used.

One of my favorite childhood characters was Tarzan. The marvel of being Lord of the Apes, Lord of the Jungle, always fighting for the right, just like Superman, appealed to my child's sense (and actual knowledge and wisdom, I would say) of justice and fairness.

The air of mystery that surrounded that magical place called Africa filled with adventure and excitement, how I wished I could be there with Tarzan and help him do battle against evil-doers. There were so very many champions of justice like Tarzan, The Lone Ranger, and The Phantom in that by-gone era of WWII; they were the good guys who were always there, and always waged battle and won against the bad guys.

The domain of childhood is being able to believe in fairness and justice, knowing with a child's faith and wisdom that these are real, to believe in those who stand up against the bullies who prey on the weak and helpless who cannot defend themselves, just as it is the domain of childhood to believe in Santa and Christmas. These last are peculiar to children; they have virtually no meaning apart from children. Consider what either Santa or Christmas would be without children. They simply wouldn't exist, as we know them.

Certainly fantasy and imagination are the hallmarks of childhood, but there is a supreme reality to such things that begins in childhood which only a child understands, which only make sense to a child, and is all too often and all too soon lost to adults.

But it is the underlying reality of fantasy and imagination that begins in childhood that makes us such an exceptional and marvelous species. As adults, we are unlocking the secrets of the universe and beginning to look to the potential reality of such things as star travel. But we don't seem able to credit the child within us for making such miracles possible. We too soon lose the understanding and the believing faith and wisdom the child possessed. I think Jesus and others recognized the need for us to keep the best of the child alive in ourselves. This is the basis of Jesus saying that unless we become as little children we can never enter the Kingdom of Heaven.

But there is another part to this which Jesus and all the great thinkers and philosophers before and after him missed. But all had an intimation of it as Jesus himself by quoting a well-known, ancient Greek proverb (which, undoubtedly, the Greeks had picked up from some more ancient culture): "Wisdom is justified by her children". There was the thought, but it had never come to fruition. Why not?

Christians will be upset by this but there was virtually nothing in all Jesus said, or at least all that was credited to him by the men who wrote of him, that didn't have currency long before he was born. In this respect, there was indeed nothing new under the sun. It was his confronting the religious hypocrisy of his day, much as did Socrates of his society, that sealed his fate. As such confrontation has sealed the fate of many good men and women throughout history in a similar fashion; and continues to do so in even our contemporary world.

It has long been irksome to me, as it was to Thoreau, that people in the West are so abysmally ignorant of the Bibles and Scriptures, myths and legends of ancient and foreign cultures. But then I once had a college professor give credit to Shakespeare for a King James Bible quotation.

The point being that too many are so very ignorant they will point to the Bible, Torah or Koran and credit these with something said by some far more ancient writer or philosopher. But it's an ugly, bigoted and ignorant prejudice that says I have all the truth I need from the Bible (Torah or Koran). I don't need any truth beyond it!

But if that's all the truth you know, if these are all the books you read and study, if all you read and study beyond these is derived from those that agree with your sources of truth and fact, obviously an ugly, bigoted and ignorant prejudice is the natural result, though no one can rightly call themselves "educated" who has not read the Bible, the one book that has had more influence in the world than any other.

Another reason that the truth of the Amendment and the Equation have been missed is that men and women have always had the need to believe, the need for their gods and goddesses, aliens and UFOs, Astrology, witches, ghosts and goblins, messiahs and prophets, etc. The deification of Buddha, Jesus, and Mohammed for example, has kept much of the human race from earliest times, including the vaunted Greek and Semitic cultures, in the abysmal darkness of mind that has kept it ignorant, bigoted, hate-filled and prejudiced. Small wonder, when you really think about it, that the history of the human race has been one of warfare and perversion.

But even with the understanding of such things keeping minds in darkness, it had become an increasing oddity, even an aberration, of history to me that so many of the thinkers of the past, including Confucius, Socrates, Plato, Jesus and so many even in modern times, skirted around the question of finally attaining wisdom but kept missing it. Naturally, a very large part of the problem derives from the things I just previously stated.

However, it finally came to me that wisdom cannot be attained by men, irregardless of the genius of the individuals, by their excluding a full one-half of the human race, women, from what is called The Great Conversation. And no matter how eclectic your reading and study, regardless of what sources of truth and fact are chosen, there is no way of getting around this inescapable fact.

This seemed so obvious on the very face of it; I was stunned when I first confronted it! But there it was right in front of me and the truth of it could not be denied.

Accepting the obvious and inescapable truth of this fact, a very natural corollary suggested itself. Children were excluded as well. All the great philosophers including Jesus had given lip service to the importance of women and children, but none had seemed to realize the absolute necessity of including them on the basis of equal value to men.

Delusions can be sparing of reality and thus bless ignorance; but at what cost, at what price? Even escaping into madness can be a blessing for some for which the reality is too unbearably and torturously cruel to live with.

But if something rightly disturbs my conscience, haven't I the duty to disturb the consciences of others? This provided that my own conscience is disturbed by actual facts and events rather than the result of a bias or prejudice on my part. By any standard or definition of fairness and justice, should not the blood of the innocent, as is so well written in Ezekiel 3:18 of the wicked, be required at my hands if I fail to warn the ignorant of their way?

All of these things mentioned were a part of the reasoning that went into the Amendment. So the reader will begin to understand what I mean by the Amendment being such a monumentally complex and profound approach and first step to world peace, impacting as it does on so much fallacious thinking throughout history, impacting as it does virtually every legal and sociological basis of civilization!

It has taken some two years after the Amendment framed itself in my mind for the equation Knowledge+Wisdom=Peace to suggest itself as its corollary. I realize now that these two years of working for and thinking on all the complexities of the Amendment were the requirement for the Equation to shine through with all its genius of profound simplicity.

And, like the Amendment itself, the Equation seemed so simple and obvious on the face of it that I was amazed I hadn't seen it sooner, that it had not already been discovered by those good men of the past? They had hit all around it (as I had done myself); the words and thoughts were there. But they, as me, had missed the actual target! Their aim had been off due to not considering the need for women and children being accepted as of equal value to men, by excluding them from the Great Conversation, in finding a solution to the historically intractable problem of world peace.

The Equation is so obvious that once I had actually written it out and began to share it with others, I began to get responses like "Why, that's in the

Bible!" Or "Why, my mother or father taught me that!" Or "Why, of course, everyone knows that!"

Well, first of all, it isn't in the Bible and no mother or father ever taught this to their child. And if everyone knows it, they most certainly haven't stated it as an equation or lived it and acted on it. Nor has any nation in history done so!

But I began to realize that it is in the literature of the past though not stated in the exact form of an equation. It had been known and hinted at, but never actually expressed as an equation. It is a part of people's thinking and when once presented as an equation as I have done, the immediate and reasonable reaction is: Why, of course this is true!

What is not obvious to people is the fact that while it is at once such a reasonable and obvious thing once presented, while it must surely have been so stated by someone at sometime in the past, this is not the case! Surely it is to be found in books like the Bible, surely my mother or father must have told it to me, etc. Incredibly, none of this is true! Talk about not seeing the forest for the trees! The thought was there all along, it was indeed such an obvious thing that it simply wasn't possible it had not been stated as I have stated it by someone long, long ago! But it hadn't!

When I first wrote it out and stared at it, this was my own reaction. It simply wasn't possible that the great thinkers and philosophers had missed something so very patently obvious! Surely I had seen this somewhere in the thousands of books of my acquaintance. But try as I might, nothing came to mind. The equation simply did not exist until I had written it out. An exhaustive search by Internet resources failed to produce the equation as such in any of the literature in any of the libraries of the world. To state the obvious: If it isn't there, it doesn't exist!

Yet, it strikes people as so fundamentally right that no one, including myself, finds it easy to accept that it has never existed. But I was reminded of my letter to the UN asking if anything like the Amendment was to be found in any charter of any government in the world? There wasn't.

It was a real struggle in my mind to accept the fact that nothing of the nature of the Amendment existed in any foundational charter of any nation's government either past or present! But, as with the Equation, this proved to be true. It was equally difficult to accept that the Equation had never existed until it came to me through the Amendment and the work for it, the constant turning of it in my mind in so many different ways.

As time passed, I came to realize, understand, and appreciate how truly enormously profound and complex the Amendment was in the myriad ways it impacted society both sociologically and legally. With the Equation, as with the Amendment, the most profound thing about it is its seeming simplicity.

So simple on the face of it in fact, that it makes the originality of it all that much more difficult to accept.

But I came to realize that it took a great breadth of study in both science and the arts, in human behavior, in religion and philosophy, and most importantly, a real desire for truth, a genuine appreciation of the need of women and children to be included in The Great Conversation and accepted as of equal value to men, in order to put the facts of all these things into the form of an equation.

I recalled some time after I had offered the Amendment, I had written about it comparing it to a large multi-faceted diamond that refracted and reflected the light in a thousand directions as you turned it about in the pure light of the sun. As to the originality of the Amendment and its corollary Equation, I was encouraged by Melville's comment to the effect that only the most obtuse (i.e. stupid) and coarse would say there was nothing original left to be discovered by humanity; which, naturally, would seem to immediately come into conflict with the expression that there is nothing new under the sun.

But this expression is only true in the context of the wrong path of war and perversion which humanity has never been able to redirect. The Amendment offers another way, a new way and path for humanity; which, of course, is so fundamentally revolutionary beyond anything ever attempted by any nation in history; it immediately comes up hard against the wall of the prejudicial mind-set of a humanity that has never known any other path but that of war and perversion.

Given this, even the word revolutionary applied to the Amendment is far too mild a term. But as with e=mc squared, all the essentials were there. And as simple as it appears on the face of it, a world of information, data, went into Einstein's equation. But my equation for peace had these same elements of deriving from an enormous amount of data and information. Still, somehow, no one had put all this data and information into a workable, sensible equation that balanced, which any workable equation must, and caused all of the data and information to coalesce and focus into the coherent and succinct form of an equation. And as with e=mc squared and the Amendment itself, the very seeming simplicity of the Equation for Peace belies the enormously profound complexities encompassed.

And just as Einstein had to do, the terms for my equation had to be defined. First and foremost, the requirement to define wisdom presented itself. This, I came to realize, had to be defined as deriving from love and compassion together with full knowledge of evil. It must include accepting and including women and children as of equal value to men. And knowledge must be correct knowledge and not confused with wisdom which so many of the thinkers of the past have done. So much so, that many people today do not separate the two and confuse the one with the other. Very much as people confuse what they believe with what they know.

This confusion of mixing belief and knowledge, of confusing knowledge with wisdom, led to my questioning the wisdom of others. Not because it was different than mine, but because I began to question my own. I began to realize that I had been no different in confusing these things myself.

The great hope at the turn of the century was that science and technology were going to be the salvation of the human race. Those who placed their hope, their faith, if you will, in these things failed to recognize that while these great scientific discoveries and advances contributed mightily to knowledge, they contributed nothing to wisdom, and quite reasonably not. After all, knowledge is not wisdom. But the confusion of the two is commonplace and always has been.

In defining the terms of the Equation, Knowledge is the factual and true, material part. Wisdom is the factual and true spiritual part. It is the combination of the two that equals Peace.

We should know that the science and technology of nuclear energy is knowledge, not wisdom. It takes wisdom to direct the discoveries and work of science and technology properly. It is the lack of wisdom that makes men like Michio Kaku, I, and others fearful of number 92. Humankind has the knowledge and power to destroy the world. And lacking wisdom, will most assuredly do so because to put it as simply as possible, we are fast running out of time!

Beating the same dead horse generation after generation, constantly repeating the same mistakes of the past, humankind has yet to attain unto wisdom. But we have reached that point in history when we will learn wisdom, and quickly, or Armageddon is no longer a possibility, but an absolute certainty!

In the last issue of TAP, I mentioned the propensity of humankind to give itself over to the stomping of ants while the elephants are rampaging through the village. Is it possible that the elimination of the first and second amendments of our Constitution, the entire Bill of Rights, in fact, could fall into the category of the stomping of ants? Yes. This will be the case when that first suitcase nuclear bomb goes off in America! Whether as an act of terrorism by foreigners or homegrown, or even by Caesar himself? As insane, as thoroughly improbable such a thing appears, I find myself believing I wouldn't put it past Clinton with his arrogantly megalomaniacal Stalinistic/Hitlerian attitude toward people and America.

And having put that thought in words and really examining it, it's not a bad plan; one small nuke and instant martial law throughout the nation, and if I can figure this out being a simple country boy....

As Caesar tries his best to accomplish his diabolical agenda of making us slaves, make no mistake: he does so with the best of intentions. Caesar, just as Stalin and Hitler of their people, believes Americans are too ignorant and selfish to be trusted to govern themselves any longer. And he is fully aware of the danger, the immediate danger, of number 92 though, as I suggested, I wouldn't put it past him to try to use it to his own purpose. Just who was behind the murders of J.F.K. and his brother Robert? And were Ruby Ridge and Waco orchestrated? History has never suffered a lack of Caesars.

The world has become a very dangerous place. Who could blame Caesar for doing all he can to defuse or overcome the dangers? Our Constitution, just as happened after our Civil War, becomes only a scrap of paper in such case; for the Greater Good, of course.

After the debacle of the silicon breast implants through the abuse of the tort system, and causing major companies like Dow Chemical to cave in, Caesar and his legions of lawyers went after the tobacco companies using the same tactics and succeeded. Now, Caesar is going after the gun manufacturers. And I have no doubt he will succeed in his goal of disarming American citizens, using the same proven tactics of bankrupting abuse of the tort system of law.

The wholesale arrests here in the Valley recently disabused many people that they have any real rights when confronted by Caesar's Gestapo. These citizens were packed off to jail like common criminals. No Miranda, no tests for alcohol, just the authority of Caesar. They were guilty by observation alone. And that was all that was necessary under California Penal Code 647 F, simple observation on the part of Caesar's Gestapo authority is enough to jail anyone. And when you are released from jail, you get your day in court to prove you aren't guilty.

Lacking wisdom and faced with number 92, Caesar's only option is reacting to the law of expediency. The danger is immediate. So the program of Caesar's enslavement of Americans has a great urgency. Airbrush revisionism of history is a part of that program of enslavement. As is the Bread and Circuses format of the present Caesar in the same manner as that of his predecessors. He knows that Americans are increasingly ignorant, selfish, and given over to petty entertainments and pleasures, those things that shrivel the intellect, dull conscience, and starve the soul. The recent Grammy Awards and the increasing popularity of pro wrestling by themselves most certainly serve to prove Caesar's contention.

I pointed out to a fellow just the other day that, lacking wisdom, reform in education was virtually impossible of attainment. And certainly not even desirable to Caesar and his universities, given their agenda. As I have often said, you don't solve problems by asking the very people who created the problems for solutions. That is insane! But, lacking wisdom, insane desperation and the law of expediency become the norm. And this, of course, leads to anarchy, enslavement, and destruction.

But reform in education, as with issues like abortion, the loss of an armed citizenry, even the loss of the franchise and a free press, considering the present circumstances of number 92 become simply stomping ants by comparison to the preservation of the species. No matter the magnitude of the problems, no matter how righteous the causes, unless we give ourselves quickly to the pursuit and attainment of wisdom, all else pales into insignificance because number 92 looms immediately before us! And that one small bomb in America is all it would take! And as long as Americans are given to Caesar's program of petty pleasures and entertainments, the dumbing down of Americans, they will be at the mercy of Caesar's wisdom which dictates the enslavement of We the People for the sake of the Greater Good! Now, where have we heard that before?

But how to free ourselves of Caesar and pursue wisdom; and quickly? The Amendment, I believe, is the place to start. We must make children, the children of the world, our priority! And the Amendment depends on We the People, this is where We the People can take personal responsibility and start on the path of putting Caesar in his place, caging the Beast and denying his version of the Final Solution.

It was my focus on the exclusion of women and children from The Great Conversation that led to my writing the Birds book and my books "Women: The Missing Half of Humankind!" and "Hey, God! What went wrong and when are you going to fix it?" Though I know it isn't God's place or responsibility to fix things it is ours, as I make plain in the book.

I realize now that these books were the foundational works to the Amendment and the Equation. Had I not begun in the writing of these books to examine, in depth, my own biases and prejudices, neither the Amendment nor the Equation would have suggested themselves.

And if I had not had so much education academically and in the real world, had I not had so much curiosity about so many diverse things in creation, the arts, and sciences, had I not been possessed with the soul and spirit of the poet, had I not had the childhood I had, the many relationships with women, had I not had children, especially my daughters, had I not mixed with so much of the evil that people do, especially to children, the Amendment and Equation could never have formed in my mind.

And most essential of all, had I not determined to face my own ignorance and prejudice, with God's help and encouragement I believe, and started being honest with me, my children, and my friends, none of the aforementioned would have availed.

Through all of these things mentioned, the result was that children became the focus of my attention. I came to realize that it is the loss in the adult of such things as the beliefs and the saving faith of childhood that has led a wrong path for humankind; that has led humankind to never put the proper priority on children as the path to world peace!

As I said in the last issue of TAP, not having any expectation, how can you fail of expectation? We become deluded as adults that there can be no new thing under the sun, that good guys finish last and we must accept human nature as inherently selfish and hopeless of change, in need of divine redemption, that we cannot possibly save ourselves, that we are, in fact, DOOMED!

A part of my daily prayer is thanks to God for hope in the face of seeming hopelessness. I get up each morning thanking God for a new day and life to live it, for His giving me hope in the face of seeming hopelessness. So it is that I continue to write in hope, often driven to do so by the child within who so desperately wants to be heard, who cries out to be heard, with this message of hope that derives from the child's knowledge and wisdom, the faith of the child that fairness and justice are real, that the evil can be overcome by the good if only the good will meet the evil with determination to win!

It is my task, then, my duty and responsibility as a man, to give a voice to that child while at the same time avoiding the fault of childishness, by my being a real man who understands his duty, his obligation and responsibility, and performs accordingly. The what-should-be-obvious-but-equally-obviously-isn't lack of wisdom on the part of the ancients, of the history of humankind, is the failure of adults to give such a voice to children.

Some of you know exactly what I am talking about. You have looked into the eyes of children and you see there the message of hope with the needed knowledge and wisdom shining forth. There in the eyes of children is the redemption and salvation of humanity! To protect and preserve the best for which God created us, the protection and preservation of innocence, that innocence which is the very heart and soul of the very best of humanity made in the image of God Himself that truly possesses saving, believing faith, that is the duty and responsibility of every adult! And in the fulfilling of that duty and responsibility, to save ourselves! That is our redemption; that is our salvation as adults, that is true wisdom and our only hope for peace in the world!

Some will say: Ok, Heath, you've preached your sermon, now leave us alone!

Ah, but I've not done yet. What preacher or teacher ever is? There is so much else to say. The child has sermons never heard from any pulpit that he has yet to make intelligible to the man. And, given the enemy we face, given all the ugliness and cruelty yet to be confronted in the war, there are many battles yet to be fought and won! Shaharazade does not dare conclude her story until she melts the heart of Shahryar and Penelope must continue to weave in hope and the anticipation born of believing faith, until the arrival of Ulysses.

For my part I have only pity for those who have been so successful in silencing their child within who so desperately wants to be heard. As we grow into adults, it seems we perversely become dedicated to childishness, spending our lives for those things that will never profit by giving us happiness or satisfaction, let alone peace. It is the rule, rather than the exception to cast our pearls before swine; to squander our lives and at the end say "It is naught, it is naught!"

Of how very many we can discern the legion of demons within, those for whom no amount is ever enough! And in the end, they die and the truth of the proverb "A living dog is better than a dead lion" comes to fruition.

Ah, but to truly live as a lion and then die! That is something else altogether. But none can live as lions who have lost the best part of being a lion, the power of the child within, that power of real courage and faith of pure innocence which recognizes both beauty and evil for what they are, which is able to confront, do battle with, and overcome the evil while at the same time never losing the sense of the beautiful and true for the sake of which war is waged and the battles fought!

It is the domain of the best part of humanity, the child within, which eagerly fights against evil with determination, and believing faith, to win!

***

After writing the above, I had to get away for a while. I had been drained emotionally and physically. For those who think writing is only a sedentary occupation, you are wrong. It can be one of the most demanding of tasks and often leaves me weary in mind and body.

But this is not complaint. After all, I'm a writer; writing is what I do. It is, as I've said many times, a compulsion, a fire that burns in the bones. It isn't like I have a choice. I really believe I don't; at least not in the sense in which we usually mean and use the word. This is where the suggestion of madness intrudes itself.

It's just that I never anticipated taking on such monumental tasks as those of the Amendment and Equation. It isn't a job I would have chosen. So the reader must forgive my occasional jests at myself, and others at times, my occasional flights of fancy that help me maintain what balance is possible for a madman.

With this excuse and a plea for charitable understanding made, I have always thought Robert Redford did a good job with his film "The Milagro Beanfield War." I particularly envy the old man having a friend who had passed on with whom to have conversations and even play chess. The ending of the story is superb as the old man's friend shows him a shortcut. And so the old man gently departs this mortal coil and goes home in the company of his friend.

I often hold conversations with those like my grandparents, my daughter Diana, and my brother Ronnie. There is a lot of comfort in such conversations with my loved ones already gone home ahead of me, this in spite of the obvious unfairness of Diana and Ronnie preceding me.

It is the belief in these loved ones watching over me that often prevents my doing things of which I would otherwise be ashamed. Lacking such real morality, goodness or genuine love of the truth in myself, it is believing this of my loved ones that often prevents my being anything but truthful in many of the things I do or say and write about myself as well as of others.

And naturally, I most certainly don't want to shame my children by being someone of whom to be ashamed as their father. Though I do cause them embarrassment at times, I know that truthfulness is the one real safeguard against shame even though being truthful often causes me embarrassment as well. But far better being embarrassed than being a liar! And if I truly believe God sees and hears, how much more circumspect and honest before both God and men, as well as my children, should this make me (of course, I have to excuse the common, polite and civilized lies men and women tell each other in the pursuit of playing the mating game)?

But, of course, such a belief doesn't prevent my insisting on being foolish or my committing errors. And, alas, it doesn't prevent my getting out of bed some mornings feeling like I've been hit by a truck. And this often without even the excuse of having a really good time the night before! Creaky and cranky comes to mind on such occasions. But in all fairness, I have to admit the long hours of writing are not conducive to preventing many of my aches and pains. It's just that once I get started, the hours flee without particular notice. Until I get up.

And like you, I have my good days and my bad days. On my bad days, I will confront the religious for their hypocrisy, but I try to temper it somewhat. But since I used to be so fundamentally orthodox in my own religious beliefs and so expert in playing the game of the Elect, on especially bad days I feel like telling them, since I know the routine so well and used to be proficient in it: Don't try to convert me or save my soul, keep that sanctimonious, superstitious religious claptrap and mumbo-jumbo about grace (a manufactured label in lieu of understanding like so many religious terms), Jesus, a Jesus whose memory you defame, and the Bible to yourselves when you haven't even written your Congressman on the behalf of your America, let alone on the behalf of the children you say your God and Jesus loves!

Why try to save my soul in order to make brownie points for yourself with God when your own is in such dire peril and jeopardy by your proven hypocrisy! Like those Pharisees of old, you will offer God the tithes of dregs and keep the best for yourselves! Then have the gall to serve a sop to starving conscience by preaching to benighted infidels like me whom you deludedly believe are in need of your corrupt brand of salvation while you, through your refusal to get your hands dirty in the real work for the children of the world, feel you have done your duty and honored God!

And you will go from me, after I have said these things to you, convinced you have confronted the devil and done battle against the enemy; you will leave convinced you have suffered for the sake of truth and righteousness, and the great swelling evil of pride in your own humility as a humble servant of the Most High will eventually witness against you on that day when you appear naked before Him with whom we must all reckon and to whom we must all give account for how we have lived, to whom we must all give an account for the deeds done in the flesh!

Doesn't the blood of the children, like that of Abel's, cry out from the earth to God? And how is it that God can hear while you, made in the image of God and claiming kinship in whatever fashion whether Jew, Christian, Moslem, Buddhist or Hindu, are deaf to such cries? NO! They that are God's own hear the cries of the children and respond to their cries with determined action against the evil done to those closest to the heart of God, to those who are the most innocently precious in the sight of God, the children!

But this is only on my especially bad days. I suppose my bad days, both the bad and the especially bad, are brought on in the main because of the apathy of so many concerning children. Children keep disappearing and they are often found, if found at all, tortured or murdered. But the beasts that take these children and torture or murder them know Americans do not cherish their young, they know the laws (which vary so widely from state to state) treat horrendous crimes like molestation as of little consequence.

Far too often crimes against children don't even merit the same punishment as those committed against adults. It is easy to nod the head in the affirmative that No nation that fails to cherish its young has a future as a nation. Nor does it deserve one! because this is knowledge. And it is common and correct knowledge that has been affirmed from the beginnings of human history.

But that is usually as far as it goes with the majority of people. And this also has been the case from the beginnings of human history. Thus proving my contention that America, and the world as a whole, has never attained wisdom; for only wisdom motivates people to take determined and concerted action in the cherishing of their young, the very future of our species! But, then, to be future-oriented rather than ruled by the immediacy of I want mine now and to hell with everybody else and the future! is one of the criteria of wisdom. And one only has to look at the utter hodgepodge of laws and their application, both state and federal, to determine the lack of genuine concern for children together with the utter lack of wisdom on the part of the legislators who pass such laws.

At the federal level, look at the puny effort of Megan's Law; to think that child molesters are going to register with the police when they get out of prison, if they are caught and convicted at all, is naivete carried to the point of maliciousness! In fact, as I've often pointed out, we have evolved into a society that seems to actually hate children!

Paul Robeson was one of the best known and most influential people of this century. In spite of his many films and world-wide concert tours, and his role as Othello, most will remember him from his appearance in Show Boat and his unforgettable singing of Ol' Man River.

Robeson suffered mightily during the McCarthy era because of his politics. In spite of his world renown and his efforts on behalf of America before, during, and after WWII, he was vilified and blackballed because he kept harping on Peace, not Bombs, and because of his association with communism and communist leaders. Looking back, Robeson appears naive concerning his work and aspirations for the brotherhood of all mankind. Like Martin Luther King, Jr., Robeson had a dream for peace and brotherhood.

Robeson would be one of those figures Caesar would have disappear from history by airbrush revisionism. He refused to cave in to Caesar, he refused to swear an oath against communism in order to get his passport reinstated, he stood his ground as an American in spite of all the threats inveighed against him by individuals, groups, and his own government. His was a rare courage.

It is hard to believe that just a short time ago people were going to prison in America if they did not supply J. Edgar Hoover with two names of friends who might be communists. In spite of Robeson's naivete, how very naive of people today to believe such a thing cannot happen again in this country!

It is the mind-set of the Hoover's and their abuse of authority that make it possible for beasts in the form of men to drag a man to death behind a truck just because of his race, and for a radio disk jockey to make the remark concerning the Grammy Awards that one singer makes such unspeakable acts of inhuman behavior understandable!

Civilized people will applaud the death sentence being handed down in such a case as that in Jasper, Texas. And well they should. But they will virtually ignore the cruelty being visited every day and night on children as of little comparative consequence! Never realizing that it is an America ignoring, even hating, its children that provides the fertile soil for the ignorant and despicable hatreds of bigotry and prejudice which produce monsters such as those in Jasper!

Civilized minds reject the disk jockey's attempt to justify himself on the basis of humor. He was only joking, he said. But it takes an intellectual mind to make the connection between this and the vulgar and obscene humor so prevalent and acceptable today, it takes an intellectual mind to make the connection of this to the ads for Victoria's Secret and Calvin Klein children's underwear, it takes an intellectual mind to make the connection between such things and excusing the inexcusable in a President of the United States! In short, it takes an intellectual mind to recognize moral anarchy for what it is and what it leads to!

But it has to be admitted that America no longer produces intellectuals or encourages intellectualism. Quite the contrary, the cry for Bread and Circuses prevails. It has always been the delusion of humanity that such things as racial hatred can be made to go away without the children, all the children, becoming the priority of nations!

I draw particular attention to Robeson not only because of his rare courage in standing up for his principles, but because of his music. His was a rare talent. And because music, as with mathematics, is supposed to be a universal language, it will be difficult for Caesar to make Robeson disappear altogether through revisionism of any kind.

I have no doubt Caesar would like to make the Amendment disappear because he recognizes that this is the consummate form of true intellectualism, the greatest threat of all to Caesar, it is the intellect married to the spirit. But as long as the Amendment and the Equation are widely publicized, this becomes increasingly difficult for Caesar to accomplish.

But this doesn't mean Caesar isn't going to try. It doesn't mean that there may not yet be a price to be paid for standing up for the Amendment and its corollary Equation. I would like to believe, however, that had Robeson known of the Amendment, he would have supported it. But I am sure the time will come when it will take the courage of people like him to stand up for it, that a price will be demanded.

I believe this because I believe Caesar fully recognizes the danger to him in the Amendment. I believe he knows that the Amendment strikes at the very root of his claim to power. After all, if the way is opened to peace in the world, where does that leave all the Caesars?

If you watched the excellent presentation of *Too Rich, the secret life of Doris Duke* starring Lauren Bacall, you couldn't help being moved by it. The tragedies in the life of "The richest woman in the world" have to move hearts. The desperate search to be loved, the theme of the presentation, is one to which most people can relate. And while most would quite sensibly choose to be rich rather than poor (just like Tevye in *Fiddler on the Roof*), it has always proved a problem when it comes to love and friends.

Having taken a vow of poverty early on as a writer (not really by choice, it just seemed to happen that way), I haven't had to be too concerned about love and friends on the basis of great wealth. But neither too rich nor too poor is good thinking, I believe. And that pretty well describes my own situation because I also believe a wise person lives simply. The recent rash of kidnappings in Mexico is a good example of why it doesn't pay to live ostentatiously; most especially in a poor and corrupt country like Mexico.

I cannot ever get away from the nightmare of two little girls being tortured and left to die alone of thirst in that black dungeon in Belgium. Nor can I ever get away from the nightmare of the dreadfully abused and beaten little boy who asked me: If I die will they love me?

I know I am an intellectual because so many accuse me of being one. Just as I know I am a poet for the same reason. Well, this is hardly justification since I've been accused of being a lot of things; even things worse than these. Many of those who claim to be intellectuals would point to the nightmares I have used as illustration and say of them with up-turned noses: Emotional Propaganda.

But neither Paul Robeson nor Doris Duke would see it that way; each for their own reasons. But both lived through an era of history when people had a better sense of good manners and civilized behavior. But they certainly were not unaware of the evil people do; they saw it and bore the brunt of it in many ways and forms.

It is an all too common fallacy that true intellectualism must be divorced from feeling. While facts are most stubborn things and not subject to change as the emotions are, when you combine factual knowledge with the spirit you have wisdom, true intellectualism.

Knowledge dictates that you cannot have rapists and murderers roaming a civilized society. It likewise dictates that you cannot have monsters left free to prey on children. Knowledge dictates that you cannot find an answer to the problems facing the world unless women and children are accepted as of equal value to men on the basis of honoring the compatibility of differences. Knowledge dictates you cannot have world peace unless nations place their priority on children and thus actually work for a future for all of humanity.

But these things are common knowledge; those thinking themselves intellectual would be quick to agree with these things. Then what is missing? Wisdom. These things of knowledge have not been melded into the spirit. And only when this is done will humanity be able to act on the knowledge it possesses and achieve peace. The Amendment is a first step in that melding of knowledge and wisdom, a step taken by the active process of true intellectualism enabling the good to meet the evil with equal determination to win!

Well, the sun is shining brightly through the windows at this corner of my little cottage where I write. It's Friday so I'll be going to Slugger's and Arlie's tonight. As usual, I'll try to get the bad taste of so many bad things out of my mouth as I shoot pool, listen to the music, dance and visit with friendly people who don't know and don't want to know.

However, some will know: the girls who were molested when they were children. Some of them will have been raped both as children and as adults. Some will have prison records, both men and women. Some will be doing drugs. But, as usual, the churches, the opera house, the art galleries and museums will be closed. And I will continue to get the stories that make up so much of what some people call Life. And for these, to think on Peggy Lee, that's all there is.

CHAPTER SIX

The weather is moderating here in the Kern River Valley around Lake Isabella. It has been a beautifully mild day with abundant and glorious sunshine. This evening after sundown, I was able to take a turn around the grounds of my little cottage. An occasional bat would flit about the oaks while a coyote barked in the distance and was answered by some closer neighbor's hound. Doves, quail, and other assorted birds had roosted for the night. It was time for the bats, raccoons, skunks, owls, and other nocturnal occupants of this small corner of my world to take their turn in company with me and begin their rounds.

The soft mildness of the evening following the mild weather of the day was a real tonic to me. It was good to be able to be outdoors so late and enjoy the reflective mood such weather and such an evening always calls me to. For some reason, I found my mind dwelling on Harper Lee's To Kill a Mockingbird.

As I watched the first stars begin to appear, a slight, night breeze began to stir the leaves of the trees with just enough hint of a chill to remind me that winter had not yet had its full say. In fact, a storm is being forecast for this weekend.

I most reluctantly went back inside, pausing only to look up once more at the stars through the now black-silhouetted branches of the tall, old pine next to the cottage, and settled down to the writing.

It is difficult to get back to work after such a tranquil evening, but duty calls; so with prayer, and a pack of Zantac handy, I plunge ahead.

Kern County, especially Bakersfield, has made its mark again nationally. No, I'm not talking about Weedpatch University, Buck Owens or the rock group Korn. This time it is a book by one Edward Hume entitled Mean Justice. The Kern County DA, Ed Jagels, is featured in the book (in a most unflattering way) and is not happy. Especially since so many ugly rumors continue to circulate about this DA

Admittedly Kern County has a deserved reputation for being tough on crime. And we have a lot of it to be tough on. From the city of Oildale being featured by Time Magazine as one of the top ten cities in the U.S. for racism, to the daily shootings among and between minority gangs over drug turf, Kern County is quite a mix of crime. Invariably, in such a milieu of wrongdoing, the cops catch a lot of flack. And it has become a commonplace to scream Discrimination! Racism! with the equally commonplace lawsuits to follow whether the cops got it right or wrong, whether in Bakersfield or L.A.

Books will continue to be written by well-meaning and not-so-well-meaning people with the various authors' solution to the problem. When welfare (in its many and varied forms of Bread and Circuses) and prisons are a nation's growth industries, the social problems are easily predictable. But, like most books of the nature of Mean Justice, it doesn't tell the whole story, distorts some stories, and there is an observable bias. Still, as long as we have freedom of speech and freedom of the press let the books be written. We need the gadflies of society to help keep us honest.

But I certainly don't intend to read Monica's Story nor did I watch her TV regurgitation to Bawah Walters. I hear enough self-serving stories and lies in the normal course of events. For the same reason, I wouldn't be interested in a similar Clinton's Story. Heard all I need to hear, and more, from him.

My favorite non-fiction book, as readers of TAP know, is Thoreau's "Walden". But it has been a while since I mentioned my favorite novel, "To Kill A Mockingbird". It, together with Walden, occupies a space on the table next to my bed. And perhaps it wouldn't be a bad idea to give both books to college graduates along with their diplomas.

One reason for my keeping Harper Lee's wonderful and masterful novel so close at hand is the fact that I was a contemporary of the era Miss Lee describes; and I was born into, and raised in, the identical culture with the identical kinds of people straight out of the Dust Bowl and Grapes of Wrath with the identical ignorance and prejudices all around me (and diet and idiomatic dialect), described in the novel.

And thanks to my maternal great-grandmother and grandparents, I am most familiar with the best of the values, sense of justice and fairness, good manners, and civil behavior so characteristic of the best of Southern people like Atticus Finch. And I am ever grateful loving people so representative of him raised me. But I am also well acquainted with what cruel poverty and ignorance can do to any people of whatever culture or race.

I repeatedly watch the film as well as read the novel, never tiring of the film with its marvelous score by Elmer Bernstein nor failing to gain inspiration from hearing the little girl's singing to herself, and her happy, giggling laughter during the introduction of the film, for there is no sweeter and joyful music this side of heaven than a child's singing and laughter. And I don't doubt God chooses children for His choir.

The poignant scene of a little girl drawing, and tearing, her crayon picture of the mockingbird accompanied by her singing and laughter, is an unforgettable adumbration of the events to follow, the ugly events which have been, without let throughout human history, so successful in inevitably stifling, silencing, the voice of children's singing and laughter.

God knows how badly, how desperately, children (and adults) need the Aunt Maudies and Calpurnias, the Heck Tates and Atticus Finches! And we desperately need them far more than all the great men and women of history, far more than all the great philosophers and artists of history, none of whom, including all the manufactured deities, messiahs, religions and prophets, have provided the wisdom that would deliver the world from the continued abuse and murder of children or led the world to peace!

Few people know of Harper Lee's childhood association and friendship with another child, Truman Capote, and her using that childhood friendship in her novel. For that matter, few seem to know that Miss Lee's first name is Nelle. Since I have gone into an examination of the novel in so much depth in time past, I won't repeat myself. But I have had some new thoughts about it that I would like to share at this time.

When I first read the book so many years ago (it was published in 1960), and then saw the film starring Gregory Peck, it never occurred to me that a madman, Boo Radley, would become so influential and important to me. Long before I was able to fully appreciate the true social implications of the book, I was taken by the charm of childhood Miss Lee made so convincingly real through the eyes of little Scout. Nor was I aware when I first read the book that I would be going through a similar metamorphosis as Miss Lee in my own writing, trying to awaken the child both in myself and in others.

For those who have seen the film but never read the book, you have been cheated of some of the most important points that make it a truly great story told in a masterful way and you will never be able to understand how truly powerful the message of the story is, a message told in such a way that removes it far away from being the usual morality play. And told in such a way as to be so very deserving of the Pulitzer Prize Miss Lee was awarded.

This is not to denigrate the film, for the film is great in its own way. But the film is very, very far from the whole story Miss Lee has told in the book, a story that in its entirety was worthy and deserving of the Pulitzer. The film, while addressing the monumentally important issues of racial prejudice and injustice, could not, due to its brevity, tell the whole story in spite of Peck's Oscar-winning performance. Though if the Oscar were awarded to children, my vote would have gone to little Mary Badham who played the role of Scout.

I've said that Harper Lee wrote better than she knew when she used a madman to balance the scales of justice. Certainly she knew this of the children and Boo Radley, of Boo, Tom Robinson, and the evil Mr. Ewell.

But she didn't see that such a madman as Boo would be needed to balance the scales of justice for the children of the world against all the Ewells. That would have been too far a reach. It would take a madman such as me to reach so far and Miss Lee was too civilized and anything but mad.

Then too, when it comes to such madness, far better a man such as myself than a lady like Miss Lee. The whole point of such madness is to free children so that boys can be gentlemen and girls can be ladies. And this is the responsibility of madmen, not madwomen, since it is men who bear the primary guilt of the decisions that prevent children from becoming ladies and gentlemen.

What inept civilized law and law-abiding citizens could not do in confronting evil with determination to win in order to protect children, only a madman could, and would, do. So I credit Harper Lee, as well as Tolstoi and Dostoevsky, for planting such a thing in my mind, for driving me to such madness.

Mr. Dolphus Raymond does not appear in the film. After all, the makers of the film were not interested in saving the children of the world. Their attention was on the adult issue of racism apparently not realizing, or ignoring, the fact that it is a children's issue long before it becomes an adult issue. But to let the reader know how important the real point of the novel is, here is an excerpt as little Scout relates it of Mr. Raymond:

I had never encountered a being that deliberately perpetrated a fraud against himself. But why had he entrusted us with his deepest secret? I asked him why.

Because you're children and you can understand it, he said, and because I heard that one-

He jerked his head toward Dill: Things haven't caught up with that one's instinct yet. Let him get a little older and he won't get sick and cry. Maybe things'll strike him as being - not quite right, say, but he won't cry, not when he gets a few years on him.

Cry about what, Mr. Raymond? Dill's maleness was beginning to assert itself.

Cry about the simple hell people give other people - without even thinking. Cry about the hell white people give colored folks, without even stopping to think that they're people too.

Harper Lee knew there were things children understand that adults don't. She knew children weep over injustice and lose this wisdom as they grow into adulthood. Adults excuse this loss, this forsaking of wisdom, by claiming it is a part of growing up, a part of the real world, never realizing that their real world is a world of their choosing and making, a world that has ever failed to attain unto wisdom, the wisdom they, in fact, had as children. And having forsaken such wisdom, contributing so much to this loss is the resulting failure of good people to confront injustice, to confront evil with absolute determination to win!

Every child recognizes and resents a bully. This is because children have the wisdom to believe in justice and fairness. Let's examine a very small point in justification of my criticism:

In my pious and devout, albeit thoroughly misguided, days of religiosity, I attended a church, North Redondo Chapel that was fundamentalist orthodox. We had a guest singer one Sunday who was very pompous and full of himself. He sang to the glory of God, of course, not himself. Just as so many preachers preach for the glory of God and the sake of others, not to be praised for their much speaking. Of course.

But wanting to impress the congregation with his range and the magnificent virtuosity of his voice, this fellow did Ol' Man River (which neither he nor Frank Sinatra should have ever attempted. If you ever heard Paul Robeson you know what I mean). But in order to make it suitable for such self-righteous people as he and the members of the congregation, including myself, he changed the word drunk to happy. Talk about straining at (out) a gnat and swallowing a camel!

Well, even being at least as pharisaical and self-righteous as any member of the congregation, I was nevertheless critical of this sop to religious conscience in the singer's taking such advantage. I think in my more lucid and honest mind, I had recognized the hypocritical dishonesty of doing such a thing with the notion of supposedly making it more acceptable to God and the Elect. It was a lie! And it was a lie ostentatiously perpetrated against God Himself in the so-called House of God! And for the sake of one man's ego!

Sadly, even tragically, it was a lie I was to witness over and over again without the slightest exception in all the churches in which I worked (only I called it ministered in those days. Wonderful how you can excuse so much delusion and deception, not to mention poor theater, and blame God for it on the basis of this word ministry). And to my own shame, I participated in some of these lies; all to the glory of God and the work of saving souls of course.

Telling of this, I recall another singer who emasculated a lot of Elvis music for the glory of God with the rationale: Why should the devil have all the fun and good music? In fact, the guy was an Elvis wannabe and the only audience he could get was church congregations. Last I heard he was still making pretty good money doing this.

But I have written a great deal about the need even the religious people feel to get into Broadway and Hollywood but not having the talent to make it; and, as a result, providing insipid and even outrageously poor, when not downright insulting, theater in the name of God. This, of course, reminds me of the great majority of religious books written with the same lack of talent and for the self-glorification of the petty egos involved.

This has not a little to do with the loss of ethics worldwide, the loss of ethics, for example, on the part of the International Olympic Committee and our own Congress. As for the world looking to America as an example of ethics, well, we can forget that now. And, of course, it isn't all the fault of Clinton and Reno by any means. They just epitomize such a loss, a loss that evidences itself in the failure to bring the murderer of little JonBenet to justice, a failure that is so closely connected to politics, the kind of failure due to Caesar's lust for power that makes things like Ruby Ridge and Waco, bankrupting suits against businesses like Dow Chemical, tobacco companies and gun manufacturers, a part of his agenda.

Harper Lee, since she was quite well educated, prefaces her book with a quote from one of my favorite essayists, Charles Lamb: "Lawyers, I suppose, were children once."

Granting the extreme difficulty we face in giving lawyers any credibility as being human, let alone once children, Miss Lee nevertheless chose Atticus Finch as the preeminent humanitarian and a man who kept the best part of the child alive in himself.

But Atticus had the extreme good fortune of having little Scout (Jean Louise) to keep him honest. It is Scout who, innocently, and because of such innocence that must be cherished, is the best part of her father's life and compels him to stand up and be counted for truth and justice. Being a good man, how could he ever betray such believing and saving faith, trust, and innocence as that of his little girl!

I haven't forgotten Jem (Jeremy) in this. But Jem is growing up. And Miss Lee gives Jem a lot of credit for his own sense of truth and justice. But Lee knows how little girls differ from little boys. As she has Scout say at one point "I began to think there was some skill involved in being a girl."

Harper Lee epitomizes the need to include women and children in The Great Conversation. There is indeed some skill involved in being a girl. And boys and men are in desperate need of such skill on the part of girls and women. The constant refusal on the part of men, who were once little boys, to accept women and children as of equal value to themselves is at the heart of the problem which has kept the world at war and without wisdom, and as a result, without peace, throughout history.

Harper Lee must have recognized this. But it must not have been as conscious to her as a grown woman as it was to her as a little girl. And how could it be otherwise when men still exclude women and children from The Great Conversation?

To say she has forgotten is not a criticism of Harper Lee. The little boy in me is far more aware than the man of the things Harper's little girl knows that she had forgotten as a woman, the things that are in fact the wellspring of intimations and hope of immortality.

The question confronting humanity is whether we will reach the stars or destroy ourselves? Unless the equation K+W=P is put into practice, #92 will do us in. There is no middle ground between the two, any more than there is between vice and virtue; humanity has run out of the failed options of the past. It will either be K+W=P or #92!

For example, it is obviously unwise to exhibit so-called adult themes such as the perversion of homosexuality, among others, in cartoons and cartoon characters that children mistakenly think belong to their world. But propagandists know their targeted audience: Children. China uses this format very successfully in indoctrinating children to various themes and issues. Joe Camel made an easy target on this basis. But we must ask why promoting perversion is excused on the same basis? Where is wisdom in such a thing?

I mentioned the social implications of Harper Lee's novel. But what was the real impact? Certainly it had an impact on me; both because of my own background and because it wasn't long after the book was published that I found myself teaching in Watts at Jordan High.

The results of the Watts riot were fully in evidence and I was a part of the whole milieu of that time in our history. You might say I was at Ground Zero during the 60s. But decades after the riots, what has changed for the better? Nothing. If anything, things have only gotten worse in respect to Negroes in America; and for children; the future of America and the world.

Riots and rhetoric, films like To Kill a Mockingbird, A Woman Called Moses, Mississippi Burning, Ghosts of Mississippi, A Time to Kill, The Tuskegee Airmen, Miss Evers' Boys, and Amistad, have not changed things for the better. And the world lacking wisdom, how can they? Nor can Hollywood have it ways, pretending to fight discrimination on the one hand and supporting perversion on the other.

Nor can we ignore the fact that so many Pulitzer and Nobel Prize winning works have failed to make any substantial changes for the better, including To Kill a Mockingbird. To quote the Chicago Tribune (one of many such sources of praise) about the book: Of rare excellence ... a novel of strong contemporary national significance. And as the reviewer for the Minneapolis Tribune said: The reader will find ... a desire, on finishing it, to start over again on page one; and so I have; many times.

Abundant and well-deserved praise was heaped on Harper Lee and her extraordinary novel. But far too often do great themes such as hers concerning inequities, injustices and discrimination, find the deserved applause and rewards of good people while never accomplishing the avowed goal of righting these inequities, injustices, and discrimination.

And one can go back into the furthest distant past to find the same themes being declaimed by good and wise men. There is nothing new in these themes. Doesn't it puzzle you, as it did me, why this should be so? Since I have a pretty healthy ego myself (i.e.: I'm nuts), I think I know.

In Harper's novel, Tom Robinson was convicted of a crime that he did not commit and died by the ugly and hateful mechanism of racial prejudice in 1935. And sixty-three years later, more than a generation later, a Negro is dragged to death behind a truck driven by monsters posing as human beings solely on the basis of his being a Negro. Recently two others, one on the West Coast and another on the East, were unarmed but riddled by police bullets. What, any civilized person has to ask him or herself, has changed for the better in this respect for Negroes in the last sixty-three years? Or since 1960 when the novel was published?

Before you say anything, I am fully aware of the problems Negroes have created for themselves, problems acerbated by Negro leaders not accepting responsibility for these problems and for speaking directly to them, problems like the necessity and encouraging of birth control, for example. Not the least of these problems is that of molestation which is literally pandemic in many Negro communities. But this is largely hushed up.

The sustaining of racial and religious prejudice is by no means peculiar to America. It is, in fact, far, far worse in other parts of the world where whites are killing whites, blacks are killing blacks, Christians kill Christians and Moslems kill Moslems.

Knowledge is abundant. But Wisdom is, as ever, conspicuously absent, an orphan from knowledge! Since true wisdom is derived from perfect love and compassion with a perfect hatred of evil, it isn't surprising that the world lacks wisdom and people continue to torture and murder for the sake of ideological differences and in the name of God. It should not be surprising that the same crimes and cruelties continue to be repeated without end in spite of all the great books and apologetics designed to overcome the hatreds, ignorance and prejudices that continue to make their contributions to an increasingly demon-haunted world.

Once more, my point that knowledge is confused for wisdom is made by even the best attempts to meld knowledge and wisdom without facing the fact that until women and children are accepted as of equal value to men, and until children become the priority of nations, wisdom will continue to be orphaned from knowledge and unachievable!

Nor should it be surprising that knowledge dictates we must become wise or we will most assuredly destroy ourselves! But at the same time we are reaching out to heaven, hell is abundant throughout the world, a world as much and even more of a demon-haunted world as it ever was on the basis of ignorant and prejudicial hatreds thousands of years old! Wisdom? Who's kidding who?

I was in one of the local bars when a guy walked up to me and asked about the names of all the murdered children in front of my house? He didn't even recognize the names of Polly Klaas or JonBenet Ramsey; which only underscores the magnitude of my task on the behalf of children and the Amendment in the face of so much apathy and ignorance concerning the threats to children in America, of the actual evil being perpetrated against children because of such apathy and ignorance!

But then, such apathetic and ignorant people care nothing about the evil of such things as the corrosive social cancer of pornography which serves the Devil and Caesar equally well as their handmaiden to the destruction of sound minds and true morality, to the evil perpetrated against children!

On the appropriate holidays, I have displayed a small American flag on my Memorial Wall with the names of the murdered children. I do this in spite of an America that always talks a good game for children but fails to follow through. The other day, someone brought me a larger flag. I was very grateful for this most thoughtful gift. I am fortunate to have such thoughtful friends. But I am acutely aware that my greatest fight for the Amendment is a battle against the prejudices of good people. The overt evil is well known; that evil which possesses good people is far more successful in remaining hidden.

It is the kind of evil so well recognized by Benjamin Franklin in his friend George Whitefield, the Evangelist. When Franklin offered Whitefield lodging during one of his evangelistic crusades, Whitefield thanked Franklin on behalf of Jesus. Franklin would have none of it and rebuked his friend with the words: "Make no mistake, my offer is based on my affection for you and Jesus has nothing to do with it."

Whitefield exemplifies the evil Franklin felt, in all honesty toward his friend and before God; he could not allow credence and had to rebuke. And so it is with me toward such friends who would try to salve their consciences by blaming God in the name of Jesus for their apathy. Or even try to obligate both God and me through their gifts by giving anything in the name of the superstitions of religion.

There is always the hidden agenda of such good, religious people that they are glorifying God and making brownie points with Him by trying to obligate God and me to them by petty efforts and gifts. And I know they often do these things in the deluded idea that they are somehow going to bring me around to their way of thinking. But that is their agenda all along, that through their petty efforts and deluded, often self-serving prayers and gifts, I am going to finally be drawn from my benighted state of unbelief in their peculiar deities, whether Jesus or whoever, because of their oh, so well-intended, even sacrificial (?), efforts on my behalf in the name of God. They believe.

But such things are usually nothing but selfish ego at work and have absolutely nothing whatsoever to do with any love of God, let alone any love for me because of the work I am involved with on the behalf of children. Such people believe they will get their reward in heaven even if they fail to convert me by their good works.

For people to be so deluded that they can convince themselves that God has truly done a work in their hearts on behalf of children, and then practice such deceits in the name of God would seem to be the height of hypocrisy. But seldom do such good people recognize this in their lives, let alone repent of it.

I often have to point out the obvious to such people: If children are the closest thing to the heart of God Himself, how is it that you live as though there was something of greater importance? And all too often these other things done in the name of God are absolutely contradictory to the welfare of children! The time would fail me to list such things, things I have been guilty of myself!

Now, before you criticize me for such remarks, I know full well whereof I speak. Because I am expert in such thinking myself, having practiced the very same way of thinking for many years! Having worked for years under the very same self-delusion as that of Whitefield, I easily recognize it in others. It took extraordinary measures on the part of God, I believe, to get me to understand and accept Franklin's point of view and repent of my own dead and self-serving works in the name of God and Jesus.

So it is that my battle is most often fought against the good people who, in their deluded minds, think, as they have throughout all of recorded history, that if they do things in the name of their peculiar beliefs, God is somehow obligated to honor their good intentions, even their petty and back-handed gifts and efforts.

I have several friends and acquaintances that sometimes stop by for coffee and a chat. One of these always tries to intrude God in the name of Jesus into the conversation. And I feel my blood pressure beginning to rise. After he leaves, it takes me an hour of quiet time to get back to normal.

Though his visits are sometimes unwelcome because I know his not-so-well-hidden agenda so thoroughly, I still love this man and hope he will eventually come to his senses. But I also know there is slight hope of this. I might as well try to change the mind of the Pope. People who have come to believe lies, who have lived these lies all their lives, are not likely to change. As I said, it took extraordinary measures for me to change.

But my blood pressure goes up now because I know the real evil in them that prevents such good people from being effective in the cause of children and wisdom, the real evil of their living in the darkness of religious delusions and superstitions. And these have been the greatest obstacles to world peace throughout the entirety of human history! Such good people, religious or not, will spend their time, money and energy stomping ants while the elephants rampage through the village. Every time.

Harper Lee makes some very good points concerning this in her novel. She also recognizes the religious animosity toward women for example. That of the Moslem and Jewish religions is patently obvious. But when Harper Lee points out the preaching of the Women are unclean and a sin by definition doctrine of Christianity, she hits the nail on the head! And most ministers would certainly get their backs up over her accusation that ministers are preoccupied with the subject. But I believe she, and all thinking people, realize why this is so.

Sex by any definition is still sex, whether cloaked in religiosity or not, whether God is profaned in the process of preaching such damnable doctrine or not. You think and preach that women and children are of lesser value than men? You take that kind of thinking and preaching right back to the pit of hell where it originated!

Yet good people, including women, are going to try to convince me that religions such as Christianity and Judaism are working toward world peace by denigrating women (when not each other or other religions)? Just who is kidding who?

A fair and sensible mind, a rational mind, has to reject such deluded, self-serving and lop-sided propaganda. Just as the rational mind has to reject the claims of those who say they do good in the name of one they call the Prince of Peace, Jesus, when the misuse of that name by its deification has been the cause, and continues to be the cause, of so much divisiveness and misery in the world ever as much as the names of Mohammed, Allah, or the Jewish YHWH (Yahweh) or Jehovah.

I've often related the story of the old Indian I knew as a child. He had a pistol, which he said had been used to commit a murder. Every night he would place it under his pillow. In the morning, it would be covered with blood. He would clean it, and the following morning the blood would be back again.

As a child, I had been taught it wasn't proper to contradict adults. So I didn't. Besides, the old Indian was a source of many marvelous and entertaining stories. Did this old man really believe this himself? He certainly impressed me as believing it. And I have known many adults who believed such stories,

stories like blood coming from statues for example. Or believing stories like the talking donkey in the Old Testament, and confirmed in the New.

We can certainly be understanding of the fantasies of childhood. But carried over into the adult, we call such things childishness; and for good reason for so they are. In spite of the obvious point, at no time in history does humanity seem to have suffered so much separation anxiety over the loss of their brains from the beliefs in UFOs, astrology, to you name it. As a consequence, the superstitious beliefs of humanity continue to be the bullies of humanity.

The wisdom of childhood causes children to separate from bullies if at all possible. Children will not play with bullies. So it is that so many good people evidence the lack of wisdom of the child in allowing themselves to be bullied by superstitious beliefs that hold them in bondage. And so it is that such good people are so representative of why the good has never been able to triumph over the evil! Such good people do not recognize the evil within themselves that they serve and to which they are held captive! We are very often, as a consequence, the victims of the well intentioned. The result: God save me from the good intentions of others, from well-intended people! It is no wonder Thoreau said he would run away from any such person intending to do him good.

Benjamin Franklin, reputedly the wisest man in America of his time, refused to be bullied by the beliefs of people like his friend Whitefield. And so do I. But the reader can certainly appreciate the enormity of the battle to be fought against this enemy of humankind, the beliefs that holds so many in bondage to the darkness of their minds; a darkness that constitutes the real evil and is the enemy of enlightenment and the enemy of the liberty of wisdom!

In retrospect, there wasn't any real difference between the old Indian's pistol and many of the things I was raised to believe, there was no difference between the story of a bleeding pistol and a bleeding statue, a talking donkey, the parting of the Red Sea, tablets of stone written on by the finger of God, the resurrection of Jesus (though I will not discount this entirely), or any of the other fabulous stories of the Bible. There was no difference in any of these and beliefs in astrology and flying saucers. The source of all such stories and beliefs is ignorant, prejudiced, self-serving, self-righteous, and superstitious ego.

We are all born with a desire to be the center of attention. And we will get that attention by any means possible. It is natural for a child to demand attention. Children need the attention of parents, for example, in order to grow up with essential and healthy self-esteem.

But far too many adults demand attention in childish ways. The charismatic churches, especially, are successful in allowing and encouraging adults to be childish. The childishness is no less evident in the liturgies, ceremonies, and various religious impedimenta of all churches, high and low.

As a formally trained behaviorist, I find it amusing, when I don't find it thoroughly repugnant, to watch grown men and women behaving in such childish ways, from the speaking in tongues to the mode of dress like men who love the vestments of holy office and wear their collars backwards, to the lighting of candles and repetitious prayers as though by their much speaking they honored God by believing and practicing superstitious lies.

Some will demand attention through various experiences, epiphanies, miracles, visions, and voices of angels and God. Some will have actually seen or have been abducted by UFOs. But when such childishness with its stories and beliefs come into conflict with truth, fairness, and justice, when such stories and beliefs become confused with knowledge and become the enemies of wisdom, preventing wisdom, then they become the source of every kind of wickedness and evil! It is a very disturbing fact that books about angels are the number-one selling books in America. People actually want to be deceived.

I would disabuse anyone, no matter how noble they consider themselves, no matter how noble they consider their institutions and their beliefs or their efforts in the name of their institutions and beliefs to be, of the thought that they can hang onto lies for the sake of the truth; that they can ever attain unto wisdom by such. Sounds sensible and logical enough; it is most certainly rational thought. But just try putting it into practice and discover for yourself what conflicts arise; some quite surprising!

I know I have used very strong language in confronting the myths and superstitions of good people, some even whom I love. And while I have explained my reasons for doing so, there is something else which motivates me. We are running out of time. I firmly believe this.

Because of the very real and immediate threat of #92 we have run out of time for the failed options of the past, we have run out of time for the polite civilities of: Well, you have a right to your opinion or But look at all the good he or she or the churches or this or that institution does. We have run out of time to be polite to well-intended fairy tales and well-intended people and groups. We have run out of time for anything less than being absolutely and ruthlessly honest and truthful!

During the battle of Gettysburg, General Lee finally realized he was in the most important battle of the war. He desperately needed information from Jeb Stuart but Stuart was late getting to Lee. The General upbraided him and Stuart offered his resignation. Lee told him: "There's no time for that!"

The point was well made. At some point in time the war becomes such that the ordinary civilities and amenities have to be suspended. There is an abundant failure on the part of good people to recognize the fact: There's no time for that!

America cannot keep hordes of illegal aliens from entering our country. America cannot keep tons of illegal drugs from crossing our borders. And yet Americans are so naive as to believe that terrorists cannot bring a nuclear bomb into our country! It's just a matter of time. And we are running out of time!

In respect to the kind of madness that seems all-pervading and prevents good people from seizing the initiative in acquiring wisdom, in Harper's novel she has Calpurnia telling the children: "You're not going to change any of them by talkin' right, they've got to want to learn themselves. And when they don't want to learn there's nothing you can do but keep your mouth shut or talk their language."

And sure enough most do not want to learn and not only have no interest in talkin' right they want me to talk their language no matter how ignorant or self-serving, to be polite to their idols, myths, and superstitions no matter how harmful to wisdom. The worst of these insist on everyone either talkin' their language or they will mount a jihad in order to destroy anyone who does not! In spite of how very, even selfishly, ignorant their own language may be, they not only do not know better, like the ignorant Ewells of the novel; they have no interest in doing any better.

When the jury in the novel, because of ingrained, ignorant prejudice, finds Tom Robinson guilty of a crime he so very obviously did not commit, Dill and Jem cry. Scout would have cried if she had been just a little older. She was just old enough to realize a great injustice had been perpetrated, but still young enough to not understand and cry about it. She would learn to cry about such things later. And when Jem asks his father how the jury could have done such a thing, his father tells him, as Mr. Raymond told Dill: "I don't know ... when they do it - seems only children weep." It is, once more, the wisdom of the child that Harper Lee brings out so clearly, vividly, in her novel.

As an adult, I have a rather normal and healthy reluctance to being lynched or shot. Notwithstanding the target I make of myself by the names and sign in front of my house, and writing and speaking as I do, even mixing with some of the people I do. I am not a John Brown and would far rather go along to get along; I would far rather live peaceably without conflict and confrontation. But good people filled with their inept and counter-productive good intentions and ignorant prejudices and beliefs will not allow of my doing so.

In spite of my wanting to live peaceably, I began to realize it was the prejudicial ignorance of good people, good people who believe lies ever as much as those good people who constituted the jury for Tom Robinson, who would be the most difficult enemy I faced in the cause of the Amendment. And so it has proven to be.

For example, when I first proposed the Amendment, many thought organizations like The Christian Coalition and men like Pat Robertson and Jerry Falwell would be in favor of it. I knew better. I used to be one of them. I know their thinking: If the idea didn't originate with them or someone like them, it couldn't have any real merit. Most especially since it came from a benighted infidel such as me who isn't even a Christian!

As a result, the Amendment has not suffered the kiss of death by bearing the imprimatur of such men or organizations. Just one more reason I am more than a little inclined to think the idea for the Amendment may very well have come from God.

If, instead of the names of murdered children, I had painted *UFOs! Inquire within* on the side of my shed I would have people, good people, flocking to my door. But no one stops by to inquire about the names of the murdered children or my sign: IT SHOULDN'T HURT TO BE A CHILD!

But I'm fully aware of why people don't stop and inquire. They don't want to know. They would rather hear about UFOs (or angels, the latest miracles, etc.). They are interested in UFOs, not what they can do to stop the molestation and murder of children, not what they can do in the pursuit of wisdom.

The foundation of effective teaching is repetition. The art of teaching is being able to practice this by not seeming to be repetitious. Being a well-qualified and experienced teacher, I know how vital it is to repeat essential points and lessons. As a result, some of these points and lessons occur with some frequency in TAP. My readers of some years will forgive this necessity of repetition knowing, themselves, both the purpose and necessity.

People do forget. Had a guy come by the other day that fancies he knows somewhat about being a teacher by virtue of the fact that he did some substitute teaching. He claimed to know what I was talking about in respect to the necessity of repetition from his college training, forgetting that I had told him this long ago. But he is one of many I know that cultivates a convenient memory.

And being so familiar with the schools of education on university campuses, I also knew he wouldn't have learned this from them, let alone have learned how to do it. The art of teaching fundamental lessons is in how to be repetitive without seeming to be repetitive. This isn't always possible, of course, but a teacher should always keep it in mind.

But this fellow conveniently forgets many things I have told him, not wishing to give me credit for them. He has a not-so-well hidden agenda of trying to put me down and convert me from my benighted state. But he's a likable sort and I tolerate him. Occasionally. This in spite of the fact that he invariably leaves feeling self-justified that he has been noble and pure of heart in his efforts to save my soul.

Over the years, I have become accustomed to people trying to take credit from me, even stealing ideas and writings of mine and claiming them for their own. But this invariably has come back to haunt them because of their lack of ability to follow through.

Recently I had one of these fellows come by and tell me that my equation for world peace K+W=P was in the Bible, a claim several people have made since I first came up with the equation. Of course it isn't, so I challenged him to show it to me and never heard back from him on the subject. What made this particularly rancorous is the fact that he knows I know the Bible from cover to cover and far better than he, I know perfectly what is, and what is not, in the Bible. But his prejudice insisted on being heard. He is representative of those who are going to give the Bible credit even if he has to lie in order to do it. I've known many such people and am used to such holy lying; done enough of it myself in time past.

I encounter a lot of this prejudice and outright theft on the basis of the Amendment and the Equation. Such people, being so egocentric, don't realize that I could care less as long as the message gets out there. To paraphrase the Apostle Paul; whether of good or evil intent, thank God the gospel of the Amendment is being preached!

Such people remind me of something Atticus says in the novel: "Naming people after Confederate generals makes them slow steady drinkers." And there is nothing like naming someone The Pope, Reverend, Rabbi or Ayatollah to accomplish the same result of making men drunk with their own egos and self-importance.

Jem and Scout are only children. But they talk about people, about issues of life arising from the trial of Tom Robinson. They wonder why people can't get along together? Jem suddenly says to Scout: "I'm beginning to understand why Boo Radley's stayed shut up in the house all this time ... it's because he wants to stay inside."

Over the years, I have come to love Harper Lee; I have come to love Scout, Jem, Atticus, and Maudie. I lay in bed last night pondering this and talking it over with God. Like Boo Radley, as Jem had it figured, I realize I would prefer to dissociate myself from many of those who think themselves sane. I most certainly wouldn't have gotten on with those who considered Cotton Mather a marvelous man. And I don't get along with those who consider Robert Schuller, Kennedy, Copeland, Robertson, Falwell, and the Pope, et al. marvelous men. There is too much of the stench of Cotton Mather about them.

If I could be a child again wearing my bib overalls, walking barefoot in the alkali dust of a Weedpatch or Little Oklahoma road in Bakersfield, just kickin' it once in a while to make the dust fly, enjoying the honest warmth of it between my toes and just doin' nothin', how delightful that would be. Maybe I'd be carrying my Genuine Daisy Red Ryder Lever-action Carbine BB gun, the one I earned selling garden seed and Cloverine salve door-to-door.

I was really proud of this; though it was accompanied by the usual and familiar dire threat about putting out the eyes of all the children in the neighborhood. One of the mysteries of childhood was why adults thought the sole purpose of BB guns was that of shooting out the eyes of children. But, then, it did seem adults engaged in a lot of morbid preoccupations of this nature intended to either frighten us or make forbidden fruits all that more desirable.

Maybe I'd be thinking, like Scout, that there really wasn't much more to learn when I grew up than what I already knew except, possibly, algebra. And like Scout, nothing would be really scary except what I read in books.

The thing is, I have had this experience of childhood and I know what I am missing. I know and love Scout and Jem and Dill and I long to join them. I know they would welcome me. But I can't, and it makes me feel I've lived too long and know too much. There has been more to learn than algebra and I know all the scary things are not just in books.

Like Atticus of Jem and Scout, I wish I could spare my children, all children, the pain of growing up in a world with ugly, ignorant, and hate-filled prejudices and hypocrisy, a world that has little concern for children, their future, or the monsters that prey on them. But I could no more do that than Atticus could of Jem and Scout.

I don't want to write as I do of the pain and suffering of children; I want them to play and I want to write of their playing. I want to go play as I did as a child, I want my occupation to be that of child: to play. But the ugliness remained for Jem and Scout long after the trial of Tom Robinson. It remains today and it hurts to imagine Jem and Scout as adults, facing a world that had not changed for the better no matter how hard their father had tried to make it a better world for them.

Like Atticus, I wanted to make it a better world for my children. But I finally realized this couldn't be done unless it became a better world for all children. But to accomplish this, I can't be the child I long to be. I can't join Jem and Scout and Dill at play. I'll never be able to walk that dusty road again barefoot just doin' nothin'. I've lived too long and I know too much.

Humankind, as nature, remains red in tooth and claw. And as long as it does, I can't live just doin' nothin'. I have even had to give up the toys of adulthood, the things I used to play with that only filled the time and gave me the illusion that they were somehow of importance.

It's all well and good to comfortably intellectualize the truth of such a thing and it's been done many times. I've done it myself. It is easy to intellectualize the proverb: A wise man lives simply (unless you begin to deal with the fact that such sayings always exclude women and why. And don't try to make the term man generic when it isn't intended).

But it's hard to live it, this thing of putting aside the toys and focusing on the things of real importance. And this is new to me; I am trying to grapple with it, understand it, every day now. It's a hard thing and I fervently wish I didn't have to do it, that like Boo, I could just stay in the house and avoid the ugliness outside. But when the circumstances demanded it, Boo did come outside and face the ugliness, the real madness, of a society believing it sane.

While there may be guardian angels I believe adults have all the responsibility for children, no part of which may be sloughed off onto supposed angels in any way. As I do not blame God for my failures, so I will not accept the blaming of God or angels for the failures of others.

As Boo watched the children through cracked shutters from the confines of his lonely, dark tomb, their lives began to be a part of his. He became their guardian angel, a mad angel, from time-to-time placing small treasures for them to discover in that hole in the tree.

How was it possible for a madman to know the children were in danger? One has to suppose that such a madman can know and sense things sane people cannot. As the film "Rain Man" so well portrayed, savants are the product of some forms of madness.

Boo was a kind of savant in respect to the children. The genius in his madness made him their guardian angel, an angel who could plunge a knife into the evil Mr. Ewell who was intent on revenging himself by attempting to murder the children. And undoubtedly would have done so had Boo not been there.

The children never knew they had such a guardian angel until that moment in their lives. Nor should children be expected to know of such angels. They had, in fact, been warned of him, warned by dire threats and stories to stay away from him. He was the neighborhood bogeyman of their childhood. How very strange that a bogeyman, a madman, becomes an angel of light.

Scout was mistaken in her sadness that she and Jem had never given Boo anything in return for his love and gifts, his kindness to them, even saving their lives. The children had given a madman the most precious gift of all: A reason for being, a reason for living. Imagine that! Reason in a madman: and reason because of children. But then that has been my point all along, hasn't it?

But To Kill a Mockingbird is only a story. Well, at least it was only a story until the real message of it struck me and I finally realized that it would take just such a madman as Boo Radley to balance the scales of justice for all children. To personify the Amendment, it is the Boo Radley that children need as their guardian angel, an angel to protect them from all the Ewells who prey on children.

What loving parents wouldn't wish for their children such a guardian angel as Boo? An angel who watches over their children when circumstances, circumstances of which the parents are all too often unaware, puts them in harm's way?

I look at the computer with which I connect to the world via the internet and web pages wishing it were someone else's task, that someone else had the job, not me. I never wanted the blasted thing in the first place. But those things of duty and responsibility nag at a man. Especially a man who knows he has lived too long and knows too much. And just as Atticus could never tell Jem or Scout to be obedient to him if he failed to perform as a man, neither can I of my own children or others should I fail to do so. Children all too soon learn the difference between those who only preach and those who do as they preach.

I often enter the world of the novel and film and lose myself in them. The novel describes little Scout taking Boo home after he has saved her and Jem from Ewell. Boo has asked her to do this. It's as though he is a frightened child himself, frightened to be separated from the children, frightened to once more enter his dark and lonely place apart from them.

But Scout refuses to lead Boo home by the hand. She has him offer her his arm, just like a real lady and gentleman would do, and Scout makes sure that any neighbor who might be watching will see that the madman who has saved her and her brother's lives is a gentleman. And she is a lady, a little eight-year-old lady, on the gentleman's arm.

And I think to myself: A little child shall lead them. But the prophet failed to recognize the fact that the *them* are madmen like Boo Radley. And how could he? Women and children were not, and never are, the equal of men to such prophets. But little Scout on the arm of a madman, their roles now reversed; it is a scene that never fails to bring the sting of tears to my eyes and a lump in my throat as I realize it is the little ones like Scout leading me.

The producers of the film, the script writers, had enough sensitivity and artistry to have Scout walking Boo Radley to his house with her hand in his arm, as though he was escorting her, rather than her leading him by the hand like a child. I suspect Harper Lee may have insisted on this.

It was too complicated to explain the purpose of this in the film as Harper Lee did in her book. Perhaps the filmmakers depended on the sensitivity of viewers to catch this. But like the shadow of the heart in the courtyard of Gigi, very few do. You have to have read Harper's account in her book to understand the whole significance of little Scout realizing that to tell the truth about Boo would be kinda like shootin' a mockingbird, to understand how a little eight year old girl could understand the significance of insisting Boo offer his arm to her, rather than his hand, in order for her to take him home.

Even as I write of this, in spite of the many, many times I review this whole scene in my mind's eye, I always feel the sting of the tears and the lump forming in my throat. And I feel the longing to flee the man who has lived too long and knows too much, to flee back into a time when the boy, not the man, had such love and wisdom as that of little Scout. And a madman.

But when I put the book down or the film comes to an end, when I begin to write, the reality of Now is there to greet me. And I face the fact once more that it is, after all, just a story. There are no Boo Radley's; only children who die daily for the lack of them. And myself as the man who in his own madness is compelled to warn the world of the lack of them.

But speaking of a little child leading, what of the lynch mob little Scout disperses by the simple but ever miraculously profound ingenuousness of being a child? Don't adults need the leading, the love and wisdom of guardian angels in the form of children? Oh, how very badly, how very desperately, we need them! We need the saving faith of their love and wisdom when our own fails so miserably! How often the world appears to me as a mad lynch mob in need of the love and wisdom of a child to disperse it, of children to be the leaders of love and wisdom into sanity!

I believe the hope and optimism with which I greet each day is of God and is based on my belief that if good people know better, they will do better. If I could learn, so can others. If I can be led of a child to see and understand the need of the Amendment from Harper Lee's story and the cruelties perpetrated against children everywhere, so can others. If in spite of the hardness and darkness of my own heart I can be so moved and feel the sting of tears about such things as I have described, so can others.

I learned long ago through many futile attempts on my part that good people needed something to give them hope that they could actually do something substantive to change things for the better. Many good people give themselves to causes in the hope that this will prove to be the case. I needed such hope myself. But I also came to realize that there were just too many things in need of change, that good people often felt impotent in the face of so many problems of ever-growing magnitude.

But why, as Thoreau pointed out, should there be a thousand hacking at the branches of evil to only one hacking at the root? But so it has always been. This is why the evil has always prevailed. Good people are too busy stomping ants.

It was when I began to really research the origins, the root, of evil that I realized what was needed, that I realized why so many were fruitlessly hacking only at branches, stomping ants. Women and children had to become part of The Great Conversation; they had to become accepted as of equal value to men. I began to write of this and book followed book.

Finally, the proposed Amendment came into being. It was the result of a very arduous and time-consuming process of many diverse factors coalescing into a single thing, a single thing that held the promise of good people coming together in concert with hope of success because it confronted a single issue, a single but most fundamental evil, on which all good people could agree. It had absolutely nothing in it of a divisive nature such as religion or politics. I knew that all the people of the world have at least this in common: Parent's love for their children. If the focus of the world could be brought to bear on children, it could be the basis of dialogue between all nations of the world.

Granted, I knew there would have to be an enormous amount of time given to educating good people to the necessity of such a Constitutional Amendment and the domino effect it would have in overcoming so many other evils of humanity. This is a new thing, a thing never before done in all the history of humankind, working through the mechanism of making children the priority of a nation in its most fundamental and basic charter of government. As such an original, complex, and enormously profound thing, both legally and sociologically, I knew it would be first rejected out of hand, just as I had first rejected it.

But the Amendment addresses an issue about which all good people throughout the entire world agree. For the first time, I had an idea of an issue and something that could be done about it that held promise of good people coming together in common cause to fight for something good with hope of success! The enormity of that alone was truly mind-boggling! But I also realized it was an issue that would not have the support of men; it would take women, the momma bears, to bring such a thing to pass. And, sure enough, men have stayed away from it in droves while women respond.

The equation recognizes this. Because wisdom is not quantifiable in the way of knowledge, love and compassion with a perfect hatred of evil has to be universal. And it cannot be so unless women and children are an equal part with men. And this cannot come to pass as long as humanity is held in mind-

and heart-darkened bondage to such a witch's brew of hateful prejudices, superstitions, and ideologies which in their various forms become ever more deadly to humanity! But children can change this. And only children can change this!

I sow in hope with every book written, with every issue of TAP written, mailed, and posted on the Internet, with every letter and email to various columnists and politicians. I do so knowing some will, flattering themselves, think I am picking on them personally. But I'm really not.

Harper Lee addresses many things in her novel which made the story and her way of writing it worthy and deserving of the Pulitzer, many things not brought out in the film and deserving of in-depth analysis such as the interactions of the various people involved with the courtroom proceedings of the trial of Tom Robinson and the real point of Mrs. Dubose and Mr. Raymond as characters in the book. But I have written extensively about these things and won't belabor them now.

Suffice it to say that the awarding of Miss Lee's Pulitzer was largely based on the social injustices she addressed in such a masterful way, not on the things I have shared with you about Boo and the children in this issue of TAP. The world easily recognizes, and always has, though throughout history been impotent to prevent, such injustices as the crime committed against Tom Robinson. As I mentioned previously, it is a familiar theme throughout history.

But I believe the real story Harper wanted to tell was the one I have emphasized. I believe she was listening to the little girl within herself who was crying to be heard. And Harper responded to that little girl she used to be, who still cried out to be heard, in a most astonishing way! But the Pulitzer and Nobel are not awarded to children; nor are they given for the wisdom of children.

If this was simple cynicism, I could deal with that, I understand that. But the cynical blindness of humanity is beyond my capacity to heal, in any other, beyond the ability of any one individual or myself. I will say that I believe my eyes have been opened somewhat because of what a little girl in a grown woman's book has said to me. And maybe Harper, consciously or not, was trying to reach men with this message.

And in my own plodding way, I fervently want to help that little girl to be heard. To do this, the little boy within me must have a voice. It is that little boy who perfectly loves that little girl and understands what she is trying to say. It is that little boy who understands the relationship between Scout and Boo Radley, the relationship between these two angels; each in a very distinctive way, the guardian angel of the other. But isn't this the way it is supposed to be between all children and adults?

141

In the meantime, the civil war in Sierra Leone is heating up. Children as young as seven years old are being used in the fighting; if you can imagine an AK47 or an Uzi in the hands of a seven year old. Not to worry, the UN is working on a treaty forbidding nations to use children as soldiers. They figure it might have a chance of passing, maybe, in about ten years or so.

And China really has no ulterior purpose in mind for the nuclear weapons technology they are plunging ahead on with secrets sold them by American scientists; or just given as a gift through Clinton's generosity and superior knowledge of foreign affairs.

Leaders with superior wisdom press for federal hate crime legislation making it a more heinous crime to murder homosexuals, Jews, or almost anybody else than to murder plain old ordinary white people or children; in fact, if these leaders have their way, such crimes will carry the federal penalties so steadfastly denied of crimes against children.

But I see Jem and Scout and Dill. Jem and Dill are on their clandestine and fearless mission in the night to try to get a surreptitious peak at Boo Radley. They have not yet discovered that it isn't a madman like Boo they should fear, it is the insanity of the world, the insanity of their own small society in Maycomb that will condemn an innocent man to death just because he is a Negro, a society that will do this and still allow the real monsters such as the Ewells to continue to run wild and prey on the innocent and defenseless.

Scout is afraid and I hear Jem telling her: "I declare to the Lord, you're gettin' more like a girl every day!"

As a man, I can laugh at Jem and still understand his aggravation. It will take time for him to grow out of his aggravation toward Scout and to appreciate girls, for him to appreciate what little girls become as they grow up. But Jem has the advantage of a father who will teach him to respect girls, a father who loves his little sister and will teach Jem to show her due regard as she grows up. Not all children have such an advantage. But they should.

And should Jem grow up and become the father of a little girl? Oh, my! What he will learn about girls he would never learn otherwise. He will learn as a man what it is to cherish. But this is only for those like Jem to learn for only those like him are capable of learning such a thing.

But if little boys and girls are taught and encouraged to respect each other, they will grow into ladies and gentlemen. Provided they are given the love and affection that is their due as children and don't fall into the hands of real monsters. All children should be able to have the advantage of mysterious missions in the night without fear, of play involving daring exploits of courage, of finding nothing scary but what they read in books.

I have so much yet to learn. But the children are more than willing to teach. As I reach the end of this issue of TAP I feel the melancholy of not putting the message of the children in the words they would use. But I live with the disadvantage of being all grown up.

Like dear Harper Lee, all I can do is try. And pray God and the children will still bless and overcome my shortcomings of age, overcome the many years of cynical disillusionment with so many of the dreams I have had, so many of which turned into the nightmares all parents live with.

It has been said that all children deserve better parents. And to a certain extent, I have to agree. But I believe this goes back to my thought that if good people know better, they will do better. And maybe if I am ever successful in giving a real voice to the children, if I am ever able to get in touch with the loving wisdom of the children and can reach others with that loving wisdom, goodness will yet prevail over the evil. But this presupposes that the message will be successful in preventing the Mayella Violet Ewells ever growing up so love-starved that they will put their hands on a Bible and swear a false oath condemning another human being to death.

The challenge the message of the children presents is that of awakening the consciences of adults to the all-too-often silent cry of children who cannot be heard. What happened to a little girl that produced a woman like Mayella as opposed to a little girl like Scout and her so very different prospects as a woman? I know the Amendment confronts this monster and exposes it. But the message can only be truly effective once it is able to find expression in the voices and language of the children. And the truth of that fact is, at times, almost more than I can bear.

CHAPTER SEVEN

I am pleased by Governor George Bush of Texas running for President. I have been encouraging him to do so, as readers of TAP know. You also know of my urging him to ask Elizabeth Dole to be his running mate.

During the course of our corresponding, the Governor has acknowledged the value of Elizabeth Dole but has not yet indicated whether he will choose her for his Vice President. I can only continue to advise him to do so and hope this will happen. As I wrote him last, it is far past time that America had a woman in such a leadership position. And by having a woman Vice President, finally begin to acknowledge the value of women and the need to include them in this top representative position of government.

In my last letter to the Governor, I concluded with these words "It is too easy to miss the forest for the trees and it would seem that all the good intentions of good people will not avail until a new way, a new path, is taken by humankind. I propose America take this new way and path by making children the national priority they have never been.

"I have asked this question of good Americans and I ask that you consider it as well as you begin your campaign: If children are the closest thing to the heart of God Himself, how is it that good people live as though there were something of greater importance?"

I hope the readers of TAP will write Governor Bush and encourage his asking Elizabeth Dole to run with him. It will, at the least, make for a most interesting campaign in the next presidential race. Whatever happens, whether you agree with me or not, we can hardly do worse than what we presently have in the White House.

I think Governor Bush choosing Elizabeth Dole as a running mate will accomplish flushing out some of the vermin. It would not only be good for America, but it would make those who only give lip-service to the equal value of women to men put up or shut up!

The present occupant of the White House is certainly helping people make a name for themselves. And money. The tell-all books and talk show appearances are giving Americans and the rest of the world a good look at the kind of people politics attracts. Like insects to a lamp in the dark.

The self-serving rats leaving the sinking ship of state and now trying to save their own backsides saying that if they had known what a rat Clinton was they would never ... Just fill in the blanks, it all has a familiar ring to it throughout the history of politics. Birds of a feather still flock together. One thing is abundantly clear: America better get it right this next time!

The fellow I mentioned in the last issue of TAP who came by to tell me my equation k+w=p was in the Bible still hasn't delivered. I reminded him of this recently, saying to him: The most reliable reports of late have it that Hades has not as yet frozen over but you may depend on it happening when you find the equation in your holy book. I could have simply told him: Put up or shut up. But such people are immune to the obvious. And being a relatively civilized man, I try to keep sarcasm to a minimum.

And I don't usually resort to such sarcasm, but exercising the prerogative of age I find I have less and less tolerance for those who insist on being fools, treat it as a virtue, and expect me to countenance it as such. It is such an attitude that sometimes leaves me as cantankerous as though someone set my outhouse on fire. And I was in it at the time. Not unlike getting up in the morning to discover your pet marmot has died or someone has called you some ugly name like Okie lover!

And speaking of being cranky, like any normal addict I have to get that first cup of coffee down in the morning in order to restore the power of speech. Should anyone call or come by before I get my fix, they are likely to be treated to my equivalent of expertise in the Mesopotamian dialect or what one would normally expect from the inarticulate and guttural sounds of your average Mongoloid idiot.

But with the elixir of life doing its magic number on my tongue and brain, within an hour I face the day with the kind of exuberant speech and intelligence one usually associates with your average idiot. I really don't mean to brag or boast, in spite of the praise I heap upon myself from the foregoing comments, but I've always said that if I want an intelligent conversation I'll talk to myself. Now some carping and super-critical souls might find that statement somewhat egotistical. On the contrary, it is meant in the most self-effacing way. I'm one of the few people I know that loses arguments with himself in this manner.

Having lived alone for some years with only the occasional hiatus in my bachelor status, I've noticed that my conversations with myself have increased somewhat. Of course, I know that a guy who goes around talking to himself is not always a paragon of mental health. And while I don't hold it against anyone who has lengthy conversations with the resident cat, it has to be admitted that there are some eccentricities associated with living alone for an extended period of time notwithstanding the benefit of not bumping into things in the dark.

I have shared with my readers that the most used expression in my vocabulary is: I don't know. But I haven't mentioned several others that usually find their way into my conversations with myself. They are: What should I do? I wish I knew what to do? What can I do? Should I do anything? This last one is of particular significance because I have discovered over the years that there is no problem of whatever magnitude which, with very little effort on my part, I can't make worse.

These phrases are so common of my conversations with myself that no intelligent conversation with myself fails to include them. It seems they are repeated endlessly at times. At that, I don't think I'm as bad off as the fellow who stopped by the other day, who has seen flying saucers. I know a few of these people but this fellow is exceptional. He is brilliant when it comes to computers, for example, and has been quite helpful to me on occasion.

But having a good mind and an outstanding education, or even being expert in computers, is not a preventive of self-delusion. Regardless of the mental equipment, training, and experience, people choose to believe what they want to believe. And, quite often, see what they want to see. For this fellow, it's flying saucers.

Since he is very intelligent, he does try to follow my explanation of how something a person wants to believe can become an experience to that individual. It works in the same fashion as the placebo effect. If you believe something exists or will be beneficial, it may become a part of your experience. And you will relate such things with great sincerity since you believe them.

A person's belief in Tarot cards, astrology, and avatars of all description falls into this category; along with all the myths and superstitions to which many people subscribe, including that of religions where similar beliefs become articles of faith. I was raised with many fascinating and marvelous tales which were as much a part of my culture as hot water bottles, asafetida, Snuffy Smith, Li'l Abner, Brown's Mule, and Carter's Little Liver Pills. My maternal great-grandmother and grandparents were a fount of ancient lore and myths. The people of my childhood, many of them immigrants to California during the Dust Bowl era, were sources of many fabulous stories.

As a child, my imagination thrived on such stories and I couldn't get enough of them. If anyone was ever prepared as a child to later believe as an adult in flying saucers or hot steams, ghosts, witches, and goblins together with Nostradamus, Edgar Cayce, the Resurrection, the Second Coming, and the miracle-working efficacy of Vicks Salve, I was. I also had the benefit, thanks to my mother's rather heterodox marriage habits (she married six times), of being well indoctrinated in both the Protestant and Catholic religions. Somehow, in some mystical way, faith in a religion was different than being faithful to a marriage partner and my mother told me that I shouldn't confuse the two.

But I was only a child and had great difficulty with this. As an adult, ex-wives would later straighten me out on the subject. The Catholics have it all over the Protestants when it comes to believing in myths and legends. But thanks to the charismatic forms of Protestantism, the Protestants are fast catching up.

In retrospect, I came to learn that I believed what I chose to believe. Like anyone else. I may now cringe at some of these things, but there is no denying I believed them and preached them as gospel truth to others. In time, as a result of my confronting these myths in my own life, my conversations with myself began to take on a curious turn. I began to win more arguments with myself than those I lost. It didn't make me right, of course, but it has become a comfort to me.

When I began writing books, I quickly discovered that I was far more interested in writing than selling my books. It is true that a writer does not want to divert his or her mind from writing and, as a consequence, are poor promoters of their works. When Thoreau bought back those hundreds of his book that did not sell, he wryly turned it into a joke. The Vanity Presses thrive on the gullible that think they have written books that are bound to be best sellers. But unlike Thoreau, such would-be writers are not likely to be appreciated after they die. And I'm not sure how much Thoreau himself is comforted by the fact that he has been vindicated and so much appreciated after his death. I told you so! may be beneficial to the living, but the dead? I'm still normal enough to want the flowers and the praise of my good works before I die.

Only the most sensitive, intelligent, and thinking people read TAP (place pat on back here). Therefore it is assumed on my part that such good and intelligent people are thoroughly conversant with To Kill A Mockingbird; that they have read the novel as well as viewed the film, and not just once, but several times. So naturally I write of my thoughts about the book and film with this assumption. This is a pretty thin veneer of attempted concealment for my real message of: If you haven't, you ought to be thoroughly ashamed and do something to correct such a monumental dereliction of cultural and intellectual duty and address the deficiency immediately! With that off my chest, I return to the theme involving the novel, which I introduced in the last issue of TAP.

A good book, as with a good film, can become a close friend; in the case of To Kill A Mockingbird (the book and the film), as with Walden, it has become one of my best and closest friends. As I love Thoreau, so I have come to love Harper Lee, little Scout, Jem, Dill, Atticus, Calpurnia, Miss Maudie, and Sheriff Tate. And Boo Radley.

A Pulitzer winning novel is always deserving of special notice, so much so that they become the subjects of college and university seminars. But such a novel may not become a close friend. I am maintaining that Harper Lee's novel is especially deserving of our notice, even our friendship, that there are especially significant things of profound import in it which will serve us well in love and friendship, in wisdom, if they are fully understood and applied.

A substantial part of the genius of Harper Lee was in her being able to present the monumental truths she was conveying in such a subtle and cunning way. The reader becomes absorbed in the simplicity of the story-telling format of the book, the simplicity of language and plot, and isn't really aware, at least not from the first reading of it, that these great truths are there.

This is the evidence of a work of real genius. And the Pulitzer committee was fully aware of this. Those on the committee are no slouches in the good brains department in spite of the fact that they occasionally hit the target and miss the real mark. Such was the case in TKM.

The Pulitzer was given Harper Lee for all the right reasons. At least all the right reasons adults were capable of knowing. But the real mark Harper Lee was aiming at was the story behind the story as I attempt to make clear. And it is this story behind the story seen through the eyes of the children, especially little Scout, that equates a mad guardian angel, Boo Radley, with the Amendment. And further makes little Scout the guardian angel of a madman.

In the last TAP I noted the fact that in spite of all the great books and philosophers, the world has yet to attain wisdom. The indisputable truth of this being that the world has yet to know peace; and wisdom is the foundation and the source of peace. I also noted that until women and children are included in The Great Conversation, wisdom is impossible of attaining.

There have been a number of books like Uncle Tom's Cabin which have changed the course of history but, in the end, have not led us to wisdom. To Kill A Mockingbird is a great book. It stands right there with the best of Tolstoi and Dostoevsky in spite of its deceptive simplicity; a simplicity of real genius. Harper Lee did even better than these great writers did, or any others such as Hawthorne, Melville, Hemingway, Steinbeck, Faulkner, Inge, Williams or Miller, in reaching my own heart and mind.

I would be drummed out of any litt class for comparing Harper Lee with Tolstoi and Dostoevsky. But I don't mind. Having been a litt major, I know the party line of the universities and would be the last to accuse them of much in the way of being a source of creativity or original ideas.

It is a commonplace of uncommon genius to be unaware of its own genius. Like all great writers, Harper was inspired to write better than she knew. Because of this, together with the fact that I am able to personally relate to the time and people of which and of whom she wrote and interact with their culture, speech, and manners, I felt I had a duty to attempt to explain some things that only the little girl in Harper Lee knew and the little boy in me could respond to, the things that are essential in leading to factual knowledge, wisdom, and peace.

I am able, for example, as a point of strictly critical literary analysis, to appreciate and understand why Harper Lee had to say waked up rather than awakened in the last sentence of the novel and it had to be used in the film. It takes an appreciation of the genuine charm of Southern culture and people to understand why Samuel Clemens had to say rose up rather than rose or arose. In this context, it led Sam to say: Some things are unlearnable. And when it comes to some parts of Harper Lee's masterpiece, for some people some things are, in fact, unlearnable. But I write in the hope that the most important things she writes of are learnable to most people. But in addition to things of this nature, I can also relate to little Scout's observation of Mrs. Grace Merriweather sipping gin out of Lydia E. Pinkham bottles. It was nothing unusual for, as Scout observes: Mrs. Merriweather's mother did the same.

When Scout's aunt Alexandra descends on the household in order to help Scout become a lady and she is asked by Atticus how she would like her auntie staying with them, she admits: "I said I would like it very much, which was a lie, but one must lie under certain circumstances and at all times when one can't do anything about them."

Regardless her tender years, Scout is no fool. So when the reader encounters my remarks about the innocence of childhood, I am not talking about innocence of the foibles of life that come with the territory of childhood. As Scout remarks of adults by trying to comfort Dill at one place in the book: "They don't get around to doin' what they say they're gonna do half the time."

Children maintain their marvelous, nearly miraculous, innocent wisdom in spite of such things, in spite of their keen observation of adults which early begins to acquaint children with unfairness, injustice, and the typical hypocrisies practiced by adults; and taught to children as they grow.

A truly great book, because it is inspired, is in turn an inspiration to thinking people. It causes such people to analyze many things to which such a book relates. There are lessons to be learned from TKM. And I am a qualified teacher. In that capacity of teacher, I am learning myself. And it is my fervent hope that I will learn the lessons of the novel well and be able to pass them on to others.

Of great encouragement to me was the comment of a gracious lady eighty years of age who recently told me that the last issue of TAP had given her some insights, and thanked me. This is high praise and I felt rightly humbled by it. And I once more took stock of the truth of the phrase: You are never too old to learn. It made me wonder what I would be learning at eighty? Shudder.

But as we talked, we shared the fact that longevity is no guarantee of wisdom any more than it is a guarantee of continued marriage, only an opportunity. And at no point in life can we fold our hands and say: That's all there is.

Those fathers who are blessed as I am with daughters learn things about women not learnable in any other fashion. The intriguing little alien creatures are, undoubtedly, unquestionably, from another planet. I am so taken by little Scout in TKM because she is so very much like my little girls Diana and Karen. They grew up. But daughters, unlike sons, never grow up to fathers. They always remain a father's little girls.

And I suppose this is why the change from daddy to dad and father left me with a melancholy. I never wanted to stop being daddy to my little girls. The compensation of little girls growing up to the need of a father rather than a daddy doesn't lessen the melancholy.

Because they were little aliens, I often found myself torn between cuddling my girls and treating them with the courteous detachment described of Scout's father, Atticus. I don't think a man ever learns quite how to act with or around his little girls. Not surprising since they come from another planet.

But like my little girls, Diana and Karen, Scout required a great deal of understanding from Atticus. Harper Lee did a terrific job, as a woman, trying to make Atticus appear understanding. But since men will never be able to think as women about some things and vice versa, there were some problem areas for her. As Maudie in frustration exclaims to Atticus at one point, "Atticus, you're never going to raise those children!"

Harper did create Atticus as a father any little girl might envy any child having as a father; particularly in a home missing a mother. But we have to face the fact that there are some things only mothers can do. Harper has Scout make the observation at one point that her father tried to do something that only women can do.

I might have done as well as I could as a man and father without a wife, but I failed miserably as a mother. Scout was right; there are some things that only women can do. But Harper did not intend this as a criticism of men. She understood all too well her own limitations as a woman.

Things are difficult enough for children when a parent dies and the other is left alone to do the job, as was Atticus. But divorce is quite another thing and easy divorce has done more damage to children by far than anything else in American society! Children are not thrown into a turmoil of allegiance between a dead parent and a living one; children are not left wondering as with divorce what terrible thing they did that drove their parents apart. And their natural fathers seldom molest little girls and boys.

But in respect to things that only women can do, this is by no means to say that there are not things that only men can do. And Harper gives full recognition to this. It takes two parents to really do the job. I know this. But my girls always seemed to need a father in a very special way, somehow special in a way that could never be found in a mother. Harper makes this clear as well. The biological facts of a mother and father concerned with differing roles and needs are there, of course; but there is far more to it than this, things of a nearly mystical significance in regard to little girls and their fathers. One of the results of the way a little girl can really get into a father's heart differently than boys is that fathers have an especially difficult time in disciplining girls.

I was basic with my boys, Daniel and Michael. No slack. But the girls? The boys rightly perceived the girls got special consideration and treatment from me. It was the most difficult thing in the world for me to spank my little girls and I may have done it only twice, if that. And that was twice too much.

I think fathers are aware, in a way that mothers and boys are not, that there is a special treaty between fathers and that alien planet from which little girls come. No spanking. Boys are different. They were born right here on earth; as a result, no special treaty for them. My girls, however, kept me afraid for them more than the boys did. As a man, I knew my little girls were prey and boys and men the predators. Naturally, this made me far more protective of my little girls.

Tragically, we have evolved into a society that approves, even encourages, early sexual activity. And in spite of how you may love your children, in spite of the fact that such early sexual activity is destructive to girls especially, no lone parent can overcome such insanity of an entire nation's approving this destruction of our little girls and the babies resulting from this insanity!

As parents, you can sit your little girl (or boy) down and tell her: Early sex is wrong! But society, the schools, the government, Hollywood and the universities are telling her it is perfectly normal, natural, and if it feels good, do it. And to hell with what your mom and dad say! And these days, since parents have no way of legally enforcing discipline and responsibility, your child may very well tell you to go to hell! And if not in so many words, most certainly by their actions.

In Scranton, Pennsylvania parents are going to jail for not making their children go to school. In the individual cases, the parents may very well be to blame. But the insanity of the situation is in trying to enforce laws of school attendance while at the same time the parents have no authority to make their children attend school! This is a situation of Caesar at his very best!

It has always been the peculiar madness of kings to consider themselves wise by virtue of position. Quite often the delusion of position becomes, in such thinking, the equal of wisdom. And lunatic kings are well known to populate history.

The leadership of America indulges this kind of lunacy. The leadership of America has proven it does not cherish our children: The leadership would continue in the insanity that children can be encouraged in early sexual relationships without consequence. Thanks to the universities, the leadership believes and teaches that moral absolutes are not necessary to prevent such destructive behavior on the part of children; or to the future of America.

This is one of the main reasons men oppose the proposed Amendment. Men would like to maintain the status quo of little girls becoming sexually active at the earliest age and being the hunting preserve for boys and men. As a consequence, the moral restraint and absolute of the Amendment is not to men's liking.

Men would like to maintain the status quo of it being a man's world, a world without the equal influence of women or the emphasis on cherishing children. The Amendment strikes at the heart of this as well. Men who lead religious empires, the Pope, Pat Robertson, Jerry Falwell, the churches, typically male-dominated, hate the idea of the Amendment for the same reason. If you attend a church or synagogue and doubt this, just try getting the leadership of your place of worship to support the Amendment! This is why I keep repeating that it will take the Momma Bears to pass the Amendment. Men oppose it for their own selfish, licentious, and prurient reasons; even when these men try to cloak these reasons in quotations of scripture and other ecclesiastical impedimenta.

At one point in the novel, Scout starts using the words hell and damn. She thinks this will move her father to allow her to stop going to school. She has been having some real problems in school and tells Atticus she is picking up such language from this source. Hearing such words from Scout, Uncle Jack says to her, "You want to grow up to be a lady, don't you?" To which Scout replies, "Not particularly."

Scout is only about seven years old at this point in the novel. Lacking a mother, she is influenced more by her father, Jem, and Dill than by girls and women, and at this time in her life isn't particularly impressed by the role of ladies in her world. In fact, Scout describes her attitude about becoming a lady in the following words when her aunt comes to visit with this express mission in mind: "I felt the starched walls of a pink cotton penitentiary closing in on me, and for the second time in my life I thought of running away (I'm sure Diana and Karen harbored such thoughts themselves)".

Harper does a magnificent job in pointing out some of the failures of the school in its attempt at innovative designs in teaching and learning, beginning way back in the 30s. The destruction of public education has a long history in this country, a destruction designed in the universities. Little Scout reacts to this by wanting to get out of going to school; as she puts it in her thoughts to herself, she doesn't think the state of Alabama really intends her to go through twelve years of unrelieved boredom.

Scout thinks events like Burris Ewell's squishing the cooties from his filthy, unwashed hair between his fingers and threatening their first grade teacher and calling her a slut might make school mildly entertaining. But she rightly perceives that it obviously isn't an institution really intended for teaching children; except as a place of incarceration and to learn words like hell and damn, words only excused and acceptable from pulpits.

Scout fights and is always ready with her fists. Lacking a mother to settle disputes with Jem, she and her brother are quick to fight. She splits the skin of a knuckle on a cousin who calls her father a nigger lover and a disgrace to the family because of his defending Tom Robinson in court.

At one point early in the book, Scout describes her relationship with Dill in the following manner:

He had asked me earlier in the summer to marry him, then he promptly forgot about it. He staked me out, marked as his property, said I was the only girl he would ever love, and then he neglected me. I beat him up twice, but it did no good, he only grew closer to Jem- Which only proves some lessons of childhood do not always carry over into adulthood.

Scout lived in dread of being called: *Only a girl.* She realized she was a girl. But not just Only a girl. It took a lot for Scout, without the support of a mother, to sort things out to the point where she had the feminine wisdom of a girl, a little girl only eight years old, to become the lady who would refuse to lead Boo Radley to his home by the hand, to make him, for his sake, offer her his arm like a gentleman to a lady.

The film does not tell you of a madman's whispered plea to little Scout: "Will you take me home?" The film doesn't go into the thought processes of little Scout's realizing that while she could lead Boo by the hand like a child through their house and out to their porch where the Sheriff and her father are discussing the situation, once she took him home in view of neighbors, she has to insist on Boo offering his arm to her and their walking together like a lady and gentleman, the gentleman escorting the lady.

But as I pointed out in the last TAP, I don't think it was possible for the film makers to go into the profoundly complex things that led to Scout realizing she couldn't lead Boo home by the hand; certainly not without making the film much longer in length in order to do it justice. And many other points in the book would have had to be included to do this. Harper's novel focuses on children. But I think the filmmakers knew an epic four hours or more in length about children wouldn't be saleable. Concentrating on sex and violence at epic length? Yes. Children? No.

And it would take a film of epic length to achieve what Harper Lee did in her novel culminating with Scout walking Boo home in such a fashion. Perhaps Harper herself didn't fully realize she had achieved the zenith of the romance of wisdom in describing this the way she did. I wonder if anyone ever commented on this to her? Whether or not, I have to believe this was the effect she was aiming for all along.

It is obvious to me that the deepest part of Harper's heart went into this part of the book, that at this point in her novel she exposed her innermost desire and yearning as a woman for the purity and nobility of the real love and romance of the wisdom of childhood. She not only wanted this for little Scout, she wanted it for all little girls and for all the women such little girls would become. Just as she wanted to make it plain that little girls like Scout, exercising the skill of being girls, were necessary for boys like Jem to grow into men like Atticus.

And I don't doubt those on the Pulitzer committee were moved by the way Harper closed her novel in such a fashion, whether consciously or not. But it isn't the kind of thing men like to talk about or even admit to recognizing. It hits too close to the point of the Amendment.

Children like Scout epitomize the love and romance of wisdom. And it attracts the monsters that prey on children like Scout, the beasts in the form of men who would destroy such innocence because they hate it so! It clearly and indelibly exposes these monsters for what they are!

My comments about this culminating part of the novel should not be taken as denigrating the film. It is a great film. And like all great theater, books, art, and films, it makes certain demands on the viewers. But my criticism of the film still stands. It exaggerates the adult view to the minimizing, and at times ignoring, that of the real emphasis and importance of the book.

To this extent, the film can rightly be called superficial compared to the book itself. But this just criticism does not take away from the value of the film in its own right; having said that I still emphasize the fact that to have only seen the film is to miss the real import and real significance of the book, an import and significance that moves me to place it right up there with Tolstoi and Dostoevsky.

For example, the film does not address the following except in the most superficial way: At what point in a little girl's life does she begin to realize as Scout there might be some skill involved in being a girl? And more, when she begins to realize that she wishes to be a lady instead of not particularly? As

Eliza Doolittle pointed out, if you treat a flower girl like a Duchess, she will act like a Duchess. And as Scout was to discover, it often takes a little lady to make a gentleman.

As Jem begins to enter puberty, he is increasingly aware of his responsibility to Scout as her older brother. Harper Lee does a magnificent job of describing this transition and Scout's quite normal resentment of the change in Jem, of the change in their relationship as brother and sister.

Opposed to Jem's accusing Scout of acting more like a girl all the time is Jem beginning to tell her to act more like a girl; admittedly very confusing to Scout and a source of resentment. It was bad enough to be lacking the talent to compete with Jem and Dill after the children's unexpectedly surreptitious observation of Mr. Avery's awesome performance when emptying his bladder; but Scout had to begin to accept some of the other facts of life that had condemned her to being only a girl.

But Scout is learning. And there are those like Maudie and Calpurnia to help her during this transitional period, to help her begin to understand and appreciate that there might be some skill involved in being a girl. Little did Scout realize, nor could she, how much boys and men are in such desperate need of the skill involved in her being a girl.

She is beginning to acquire a dim understanding of this, however, when she thinks to herself that Atticus needs her presence, help and advice: Why, he couldn't get along a day without me, she thinks to herself at one point. Atticus has made his love for his little girl so plain to her that she feels important and needed by him. That, folks, is successful parenting!

But it was Scout's very skill as a girl that made her father the kind of man and father he was, the kind of skill that would make Jem want to be the very same kind of gentleman their father was, that would make Jem far prouder of his father as a gentleman than of his father's talent for shooting. It was this skill in being a girl that Scout was learning that had made Atticus a gentleman, which would cause Jem to admire his father and want to be exactly like him. It was this skill as a girl that would cause little Scout to both understand Sheriff Tate's verdict regarding Boo and to refuse to lead Boo home by the hand. And it would be this skill that would defuse and disperse a lynch mob.

In the last issue of TAP I brought up the point that it took a little girl, Scout, to disperse the lynch mob. And I mentioned my own view that the world itself seems a lynch mob that can only be dispersed by the saving faith of the innocent wisdom of children. If the world would only cherish its children, it wouldn't behave like a lynch mob.

When those men in the mob were confronted by the best that humanity holds promise of being in the form of a small innocent girl, each individual comprising the mob had to look at himself as an individual, something that lynch mobs are not inclined to do. But once having done so, conscience had no choice but to bow to that innocence, an innocence in which fairness and justice rule with wisdom and where the Beast has no place of concealment; he is exposed and laid bare to those all-knowing pure eyes found reflecting the wisdom of an innocent child.

If the wisdom of childhood had ruled in that court and jury box, Tom Robinson would have been restored to his wife and children. Scout had saved her father from being harmed; she had saved Tom Robinson from being lynched. At that, it took the goodness of her brother Jem insisting on standing by his father to give Scout a chance to innocently confront the mob. But Jem alone could not have prevented violence. Only the skill of a little girl could do that. This is one of the things that separate girls and boys into what should be honored as the compatibility of differences.

Harper Lee knew with her feminine wisdom that men make war, not women. Women do not bear children with the idea of sacrificing them on the altar of the wars men make. If it had only been Jem and Dill there with Atticus to confront the mob, this would not have worked. The all-male makeup of such a thing would only have acerbated the situation. Harper knew this. As a woman, she knew it would take the skill of a little girl, little Scout, to defuse the situation because there are some things that only women can do. Or, in this case, only a little girl could do.

This whole scene illustrates one of the most profound characteristics of wisdom. It is one thing to speak of wisdom being comprised of love, compassion, and an instinctive hatred of evil. Atticus and Jem are incorporating all the aspects of wisdom in confronting the lynch mob. But one thing is lacking, the wisdom of that other half of humanity without which wisdom is incomplete.

It is that part of wisdom, the instinctive hatred of evil that little Scout so well represents in a way that only an innocent little girl can, that accomplishes confronting the mob peacefully and successfully. Atticus and Jem know full well the evil the mob represents. But Scout is innocent of this. As such, her knowledge and confrontation of the evil is totally innocent! And, victorious! This is wisdom in action; this is wisdom at its best!

The genius of the Amendment is based on this fact. Once the mob confronts itself as individuals in the face of such representative innocent knowledge and instinctive hatred of evil as little Scout so well exemplifies; the mob will look into its heart on an individual basis and return to sanity. The melding of knowledge and wisdom is accomplished, and peace is the result. But the world lacking in wisdom, neither Scout nor Jem (nor Atticus) could save Tom Robinson from a caste system and perverted judicial system of evil constructed stone by stone and brick by brick through the determined and dedicated labors of evil men.

In the case of Tom Robinson, it was a system that put even good people in a no-win situation. In fact, women were not even permitted at the time to serve on juries in Alabama and some other states. If the jury found Tom Robinson innocent, it would be calling two white people liars against the word of a Negro. Unthinkable! The good people of that jury would be ostracized from their own society! And only madmen are capable of confronting the kind of sanity that leaves good people in this no-win position.

Some weeks ago I wrote of a girl I know who was pulled over by the local police and had to go to the sheriff's office where she was detained for over four hours before being released. I knew she was beaten before she started. The police pulled her over at night for a broken headlight. But she had come from a bar and was with a disreputable fellow well known to the police. She was subjected to humiliating behavior from the cops, especially as they searched her and made sexist remarks like calling her "Sweetcheeks".

But she was confrontational with the cops, a real no-no, even demanding a lawyer, and it came down to guilt by association. She admitted having been to a bar and she was with a guy the police recognized. Unfavorably. The public defender seemed to be on her side. But when she appeared in court, this disreputable looking fellow she had been with was the only witness for her. And the jury looked at him and found the girl guilty. There was little the public defender could really do. Police testified against her and the jury couldn't keep their eyes off the guy who was the girl's only witness.

Unfortunately, people are not educated to the facts of our judicial system. And when they are confronted by it, it is usually too late to get an education. Lacking money for a good attorney, the common people, the great unwashed, are at the mercy of a system that has little mercy for such people as this girl.

Let's face it: You are judged by appearances and you are judged by those with whom you associate. You are judged by your use of language, your vocabulary and your pedigree; and your money. The girl will do seventeen days in jail and will be on five years probation. She is now in a system that will permit the police to pull her over at any time they choose; to search her and ask her anything they want. Her life is no longer her own. If she complained of having no rights as a citizen before, she is going to learn how little she really does have now.

In this manner, the system of the 30s that condemned Tom Robinson hasn't really changed all that much. But as I told this girl, until good people get together to confront it, those who have the authority of Caesar will pick them off one by one. Hang together or hang separately. This has not changed.

I freely admit that had I not known this girl personally and I had been on her jury, I would have found her guilty. I am no more immune to appearances than any other is. And faced with having to choose between duly constituted authority and the word of this girl and the guy she was with, admitting having come from a bar and her demanding a lawyer instead of submitting to a sobriety test, or even requesting one (which she should have done if she had not been drinking), it would be, in my mind, a just verdict of guilty.

But the system is designed to militate against anything less than the amount of justice you can afford. It is designed to favor the rich against the poor. And that is why I bring up this particular case involving the girl. Guilty or not, given our judicial system, she couldn't win if Caesar really wanted her. To this extent, it was like shooting a mockingbird.

When that good man Sheriff Tate rendered his verdict that Bob Ewell fell on his knife, that it would be a sin to tell the truth then abruptly leaves, Atticus looks at Scout and says (this in the book, not in the film) "Scout, Mr. Ewell fell on his knife. Can you possibly understand?"

Scout runs to him and hugs him and kisses him with all her might. She says to her father "Mr. Tate was right." When Atticus asks her what she means she replies "Well, it'd be sort of like shootin' a mockingbird, wouldn't it?"

As parents, we are never really sure of what our children understand of adult thinking. Little Scout is only eight years old now but she remembers what her father had said two years before about it being a sin to shoot a mockingbird. Another loving and responsible adult in the children's lives, Miss Maudie, reinforced this. And Scout is able to make the connection between this and the way fairness and justice could be best served in the case of the madman who has saved her and Jem's lives.

The main concern of a loving father was that his children would misunderstand; how they might perceive the excusing of what amounted to vigilante justice in the case of Boo Radley killing Mr. Ewell in order to save them. But Scout does understand. To tell the town that Boo had actually plunged the knife into the evil Ewell would, indeed, be a sin as Sheriff Tate had said. And children know far more of actual sin than do adults. It takes the innocence of a child to really recognize sin for what it is with an instinctive hatred of it. And in the two cases of Tom Robinson and Boo Radley, the hateful sin of killing a mockingbird.

A madman had balanced the scales of justice and Scout understands this, as only a child is capable of understanding it. Atticus had nothing to fear on this score. There would be no taint of hypocrisy to come back to haunt him in his relationship with his little girl. And it must have reassured him further to know his little girl had every bit and more the sense of fairness and justice he had himself.

An obvious conundrum presents itself in spite of this. Jem and Scout will be able to understand the necessity of not telling about Boo. But the case of Tom Robinson remains. That justice was served by a madman is something children can understand and accept. But for adults, it remains vigilante justice. The law required telling of Boo killing Ewell in order to save the children and the Sheriff and Atticus are civilized representatives of the law.

But these outstanding civilized representatives of the law could not save Tom Robinson. And they could not prevent the evil Ewell from stalking and murdering the children. Only a madman could do this and get away with it. But given the option of having all the ladies in Maycomb knocking on Boo's door and bringing him angel food cakes, Sheriff Tate and Atticus had only one choice: To ignore the law, to, in fact, become lawbreakers themselves!

This is a point I have hammered in time past. It needs another hammering. Scout understands and accepts what was done in the case of Boo. She will never be able to understand and accept what happened in the case of Tom Robinson.

We will applaud the vigilante with the fast gun who comes in and cleans up the town. But we refuse to face the fact that it is perverted laws that make such a thing necessary! And as long as the vigilante remains necessary and is applauded, so long will the world lack wisdom. So long will Scout be unable to understand what happened to Tom Robinson. I need to repeat a couple of quotes from the novel that I used in the last issue of TAP in order to make a point. Please bear with me:

Mr. Dolphus Raymond does not appear in the film. After all, the makers of the film were not interested in saving the children of the world. Their attention was on the adult issue of racism not realizing, apparently - or ignoring - the fact that it is a children's issue long before it becomes an adult issue. But to let the reader know how important the real point of the novel is, here is an excerpt by Mr. Raymond as little Scout relates it:

I had never encountered a being who deliberately perpetrated a fraud against himself. But why had he entrusted us with his deepest secret? I asked him why.

Because you're children and you can understand it, he said, and because I heard that one-

He jerked his head toward Dill: Things haven't caught up with that one's instinct yet. Let him get a little older and he won't get sick and cry. Maybe things'll strike him as being - not quite right, say, but he won't cry, not when he gets a few years on him.

Cry about what, Mr. Raymond? Dill's maleness was beginning to assert itself.

Cry about the simple hell people give other people - without even thinking. Cry about the hell white people give colored folks, without even stopping to think that they're people too.

Harper Lee knew there were things children understand that adults don't. She knew children weep over injustice and lose this wisdom as they grow into adulthood. Adults excuse this loss, this forsaking of wisdom, by claiming it is a part of growing up, a part of the real world, never realizing that their real world is a world of their choosing and making, a world that has ever failed to attain unto wisdom, the wisdom they, in fact, had as children. And having forsaken such wisdom, contributing so much to this loss is the resulting failure of good people to confront injustice, to confront evil with absolute determination to win!

Every child recognizes and resents a bully. This is because children have the wisdom to believe in fairness and justice. When the jury in the novel, because of ingrained, ignorant prejudice, finds Tom Robinson guilty of a crime he so very obviously did not commit, Dill and Jem cry. Scout would have cried if she had been just a little older. She was just old enough to realize a great injustice had been perpetrated, but still young enough to not understand and cry about it. She would learn to cry about such things later. And when Jem asks his father how the jury could have done such a thing, his father tells him, as Mr. Raymond told Dill: I don't know ... when they do it - seems only children weep. It is, once more, the wisdom of the child that Harper Lee brings out so clearly, vividly, in her novel.

The point I want to emphasize from the above is how brutal it is to betray the innocent wisdom of a child. To betray in such a way that a child does, eventually, lose the wisdom and ability to weep over unfairness and injustice. And I could weep thinking of how little Scout will be forced when she grows up to deal with the difference between what happened to Boo Radley and what happened to Tom Robinson.

As a mere man, I have to confess that had I not had daughters, I would never have paid that much attention to the lessons of TKM, I wouldn't be nearly as sensitive to the lessons men need to learn from children and women. But when it comes to trying to convince most women to take an active role in being examples of the lessons Harper Lee teaches in spite of the attempts of men to keep them in their place, in most cases I might as well be preaching forty acres and a mule!

The Equal Rights Amendment was a doomed effort, a failed experiment in equality because women had it wrong. Until children become the priority of America, nothing else is going to work; which only proves it isn't men alone that are the problem.

There is no royal path to knowledge; and most certainly not to wisdom. In spite of Brookings, SRI, etc., no think-tank has come up with the equation k+w=p. But the universities and think-tanks are not given to solutions. They excel in stating the obvious and muddying the waters. The reason for this failure of such vaunted institutions is, in fact, very obvious: They don't concentrate on women and children as of equal value to men. For such institutions, it is business as usual by not including women and children in The Great Conversation.

Is it reasonable for fourteen and fifteen year old girls to be unmarried and having babies? Is it reasonable for a society to be encouraging and approving of this? No. It is patently insane! Recently, a flap in Bakersfield has occurred over parents removing their children from a class taught by a pervert. The parents do not want their children exposed to this pervert teacher. But Caesar says parents do not have the right to remove their children from this pervert's class.

At the same time, some people are protesting their recent arrests by ABC agents in the Valley. They are carrying placards and protesting in front of the courthouse. But they seem blissfully unaware that Caesar has made them his slaves by the mechanism of taking away the rights of parents to remove their children from the influence of perverts. Once more, it is business as usual for Caesar who is totally dependent on his power, which rests on whose ox is being gored, of good people refusing to accept the dictum that we will hang together or hang separately.

This calls to mind the point I made in the last TAP that good people are overwhelmed by the magnitude of the problems, the magnitude of Caesar's power, and feel helpless to change things. What good people are consistently overlooking is the fact that Caesar must destroy the single most basic foundation of America, the family, in order to achieve his ultimate goal of enslavement of all Americans. He is already largely successful in this destruction of families. And it is Caesar's most powerful tool against parents and children, the schools, which he is using to destroy families. As I have mentioned, parents no longer have any real authority over their own children. And the schools, being such powerful instruments of Caesar, are teaching this to children at an earlier and earlier age.

I recently shared some of my views with our new California Governor Gray Davis. Governor Davis talked a lot in his campaign about his giving education reform the highest priority if elected Governor. He replied thanking me for my input. But will anything change for the better? Not if I am the only one making any noise to the Governor. It will take a lot of people making the same noise.

The Amendment gives good people the chance to take back the power of government. But it is a daunting challenge to educate good people to see the connection, to see the connection between the power of Caesar through the schools, to arrest without cause on the basis of observation only, the power of Caesar to prevent good people from removing their children from the influence of perverts in the classroom, and the power of the Amendment to redress these abuses of Caesar.

Are Americans so spoiled and naive as to believe that they can save their cake and eat it too, that we can succeed as a society without moral restraint and without exercising personal responsibility? Yes. Insane! Within such an insane society, there is an obvious need for the Boo Radleys; there is an obvious need for the Amendment, the personification of Boo Radley, as a first step toward restoring sanity to America and to the human race.

But Caesar is depending on Americans giving themselves over totally to Bread and Circuses, to petty pleasures and entertainments, to anything but making children our priority, in order to succeed with his agenda of total enslavement!

We desperately need the skill of all the little Scouts of being girls. I believe in the power of the Amendment to give all little girls the chance to learn and develop this skill, to give all children the chance to develop all the skills of childhood. And I believe the Amendment gives all of humanity the chance to make that first major step toward finally achieving the wisdom which will make this possible for children.

For example, there is no more precious line in TKM than the one Harper gives to Jem during Scout's first day at school. It is his little sister's first recess and Jem is checking on her to see how she is doing. Harper has little Scout describe it this way: *Jem cut me from the covey of first-graders in the schoolyard.*

Only a woman could and would describe this action of Jem by such a precious phrase in such a precious way. Harper Lee had obviously acquired the skill of being a girl. And this is so very evident from this special line in the book, together with her sensitivity to all the things little Scout represents of the best of girlhood and its impact in bringing out the best of boyhood.

Every little girl needs to be cut from the covey by one that loves and cares for her; and demonstrates it by doing so. Little girls are designed of God to bring out the best in boys and men, to cause them to cut little girls out of the covey when they need to be. It is a demonstrative form of cherishing.

When a man chooses a wife, he is to cut her from the covey and cherish her. But the woman had better have learned the necessary skill of being a girl while she is a child or it isn't going to happen. I may only be a man but I have learned and know at least this much about women.

The Amendment, by protecting children from the most vicious evil of all, molestation, will enable children to be raised in protected innocence, the most fundamental and basic right of humanity. Parents will be able to focus on teaching their little girls to be ladies, their little boys to be gentlemen. Beginning with the Amendment, Caesar will begin to lose his power and We the People will begin to take back our government, our America, by making children the priority they deserve to be and must be.

In my former life I was a well qualified, card-carrying, chauvinistic redneck religious and political conservative. I wielded the Bible (and the flag) like a club to beat everyone into submission to my brand of wisdom and truth. And I could quote chapter and verse with the very best. Those who knew me well back then will vouch for this.

It is nothing short of miraculous that I think and write as I do now; most especially about women and children and the need for them to be accepted as of equal value to men in order for the world to attain to wisdom and peace. In the old days if anyone had suggested to me that Jesus not accepting women as Apostles may have been a mistake on his part, that in not doing so he was as guilty as any other man of his time in placing a lesser value on women, I would have condemned the person to the outer reaches beyond redemption! Then I would have followed through with the appropriate sermon denouncing such a thing from my pulpit warning women in the congregation that the flames of the pit awaited any woman who did not agree with me!

After all, if women were of equal value to men, well of course Jesus would have chosen some to be Apostles. But they aren't! Didn't Sarah win the approval of God by referring to her husband Abraham as Lord? Didn't Paul, speaking for Jesus, say women were to keep silent in the churches; that it was a shame for them to teach or speak; to learn in silence and if they had questions they should ask their husbands when they got home? In short, keeping uppity females in their place was part of being a Christian and a pastor. And I could always count on the men in my congregations agreeing with this and supporting me.

There is another side to this; the women that do not want any responsibility in the decision-making process. It's a convenient way to make sure men always get the blame when things go wrong. This was the problem with the ERA. Women wanted to save their cake and to eat it too.

If I could believe the Amendment is God's idea not mine, it would at least make some sense to think, speak, and write as I do now. But I don't know. But I can't deny the Amendment makes sense regardless the source. It seems the sane way out of the madness which grips, and has always gripped, the world, making the world a lynch mob.

Nor can I deny how very important little children have become to me over the last few years, how their very innocence has penetrated my own dark heart, how the fate of those two little girls in Belgium, Melissa and Julie, gave me the nightmares that drove me to the Amendment and the Memorial Wall with their names and so many others in front of my house for all to see.

Intellectually, it has its attraction. I can, with great interest, contrast my former beliefs and state of mind with my present and I spend a good deal of time doing so. It is far safer, and far more comfortable, to intellectualize this and hold my emotions in abeyance. But there is always the message of TKM to confront. There is always my former life to confront no matter how I try to bury it. And I may get away from these during the day when the sun is shining, but when I lay my head on my pillow in the darkness, they are still there. It is at such a time I think of what little Dill said when Scout asks him, "Why do you reckon Boo Radley's never run off?" Dill replies, "Maybe he doesn't have anywhere to run off to."

It isn't any fun to admit at my age how wrong I have been about so many things. I was always ready to credit myself with more intelligence than to be taken in by hypocrites, thieves and liars. Now, having to admit to such things, especially being guilty of these things in the name of God, is no easy task as you can well imagine. To have to admit to having been expert in the art form of holy lying and begging, worshiping and using the Bible as the instrument of my own unrighteousness, is a hard thing. And, to repeat, it is nothing short of miraculous that I have been able to see this and admit to it in my case.

Somehow, the children became my focus of attention. As I intellectualize it, I could write a book of my educational progress and experiences of life of which I could say, "These are some of the reasons". I say only some of the reasons because in my heart and soul I know these things alone cannot account for my present honesty, an honesty that is misunderstood by many good people, even close friends, and has hurt me so badly in so many ways. It is a very lonely position that no man in his right mind would choose.

Recently there was a TV special hosted by Maury Povich about the tombs of Egypt. Anything about the ancient past of Egypt, especially the pyramids, has always held a fascination for people. Those like Edgar Cayce were entranced by the subject. Theories abound concerning the ancient monuments and tombs, the kings and queens, curses, the various deities, the enormous amount of time, money and energy devoted to the afterlife.

From the first excavations of archaeologists, to Cayce, to Chariots of the Gods, to Indiana Jones, to Povich, the fascination grows. Books, theories and films proliferate. Especially popular are the theories of ancient space travelers coming to earth and being either the builders or teachers of many of the ancient wonders. Theories of connections to lost civilizations like Mu or Atlantis abounds as well.

Curiously, it seems that ancient peoples or space travelers never got around to attaining wisdom. Natural disasters seem to have been unavoidable to these ancient cultures, regardless of their science and genius, as well. I have had to ask myself, in confronting so much gullibility on the part of so many people, why these ancient cultures, whether of earth or the stars, were so given to war rather than peace? Not only is there no record of any ancient culture which is not a record of war, there is no record of the kind of wisdom which would lead to peace. Whatever myths, legends, or actual records you resort to, war is there. For the UFO and X-Files aficionados, no interplanetary influence has ever been proven to be, let alone to have been, the source of peace in the world.

Of course, the easy way around this fact for me in the past was my belief in blaming God for the whole mess and preaching that the Rapture, Second Coming, and the Great Assize would sort things out. Pie in the sky by and by was an easy and comfortable out; a lot easier and simpler than accepting personal responsibility for the mess.

There is a point to all this. The record of humankind is one of blaming God, regardless of the religion or beliefs, for our own lack of wisdom, to blame God rather than taking personal responsibility for the evil in the world. The Amendment, I believe, confronts this lack of responsible wisdom on our part. It puts to the test theories of ancient cultures being so far advanced. They didn't survive for one simple and basic reason: They never attained wisdom. And k+w=p is the proof of this.

The world has never had the wisdom to overcome the case of Tom Robinson. As I said, Scout could accept the wisdom of not telling about Boo Radley being the mad guardian angel of the children. It would, indeed, have been sorta like shootin' a mockingbird. But the case of Tom Robinson remained. And still remains. It always has. What Scout could never be asked to understand was the real difference between Boo Radley and Tom Robinson?

We can credit everyone connected to the case of Tom Robinson with sanity or we must charge the entire society with insanity. You don't try to explain this to a child whose own wisdom cannot possibly credit sanity to those responsible for the death of Tom Robinson. To a child, such a thing is obviously insane!

I have said that the Amendment is the personification of Boo Radley, the madman who acted with sanity. But he certainly appeared to be insane. He had committed an insane act against his own father. But his kind of insanity made children his priority.

The *insanity* of the Amendment is in making children, for the first time in history, the priority of a nation. And until this is done, the case of Tom Robinson remains unresolved and insane. Not just for Scout and Jem, not just for 1935 in Maycomb, Alabama, but throughout the entire world throughout all of history, and throughout the world today.

There seems no end to the list of insanities we face today. For example, I just got a letter from Mrs. Mattie Jane Futrell asking my help for her son, John Futrell. He was one of the police officers involved in the shoot-out at a North Hollywood bank in 1997. Family members of one of the robbers who murdered an innocent bystander in cold blood are suing him. The officer is being sued because he had the innocent victims given ambulance priority over the robber/murderer.

Well, it takes a special form of vermin, like the robber/murderer and his attorney, to bring out the best examples of the kind of insanity we confront as a society. But it is the kind of insanity the Amendment confronts. If Americans are more concerned and interested in Egyptian tombs and flying saucers than children, if Americans continue to believe it is God's job and not theirs to protect children, if they continue to stomp ants while the elephants rampage through the village, so long will the case of Tom Robinson remain unresolved, so long will the little Scouts be unable to make sense of it all. And so long will the Ewells be the cause of injustice for the Tom Robinsons and be the stalkers, molesters and murderers of children.

Children need responsible action by adults on their behalf. Children need a guardian angel like Boo Radley in the form of the Amendment. But as long as Americans think themselves sane and the Amendment madness, so long will children and the Tom Robinsons suffer and so long will humankind fail to attain wisdom.

It is no small matter to offer people hope, hope that things can be done to save our children and our world. The Amendment offers such hope. But as long as men love darkness rather than light, so long will all of humanity remain at risk from the power of such darkness.

My closest friends remain those like Henry Thoreau and Harper Lee. They see through the darkness and offer me light and hope in a very dark and dangerous world. If, in my sharing this light and hope with others, I am seen as the madman for confronting my own sins and those of others, I confess this leaves very little hope of things changing for the better; because I know it will take an army of people who share my dream (my madness?) of changing things. It will take an army who shares my belief that if good people know better, they will do better, to accomplish the purpose of the Amendment.

But if good people will let the children make their voices heard, this can happen. In the meantime, I will continue to read Walden and TKM, I will continue to try to hear little Scout and listen to what she has to say and try to shut out the sanity all about me that confronts my madness.

It's a hard thing, this thing of being all grown up. I can't help wishing I could join Scout and Jem and Dill at play. I want my business to be the business of a child, to play. But there is the rub. I know it can't be a better world for my children until it is a better world for all children. And there is no getting around the fact that I am all grown up, and that we adults are the ones who have the responsibility of making that better world.

CHAPTER EIGHT

Years after the filming of To Kill a Mockingbird, several of the makers of it as well as those who played in it were interviewed. It was agreed that there were two truly magical moments in the film. The first is at the very beginning: the title sequences with the little girl humming and singing to herself, the use of the box with its contents like the rolling marble, together with the little girl drawing and then ripping the crayon picture of the mockingbird accompanied by her little girl's lyrically musical, giggling laughter. The whole scene draws you into the magical world of a happy child, the happiest of all worlds imaginable.

The second occurred early in the film. It is bedtime and Scout is in bed and Atticus is listening to her read. As she is getting ready to be tucked in to go to sleep, she asks to see Atticus' watch. The mystical, magical bonding between an innocent little girl and her father, little Scout's stretching and yawning, the way she holds her father's watch in her small hands and reads the inscription, cuddling her teddy bear while being tucked in and the sleepy questions to Jem about their mother is not only magical, it is the most touching scene of the film. It is the reason Mary Badham was nominated for an Oscar for virtually no one with a good conscience and a genuine love of children can help being touched by the captivating and precious tenderness of such a thing. It appeals to the very best in all of us as human beings.

But as Mary said years later, she wasn't acting; she was just being a little girl. And that is always magic. But it isn't the kind of magic to which the world awards its plaudits of recognition and praise. We adults don't reward the natural gift of the art and wisdom of childhood; we reward the adult who has to work hard at even pretending they still have this magical and natural art and wisdom.

The producers of the film in this interview that occurred so many years after the making of it were right. There has never been another film like To Kill a Mockingbird. There is no other film like it. And while all the superlatives have been used in attempting to describe it, I especially like what one person, I believe it was director Robert Mulligan, said of it in eloquently classic and elegant understatement: It is a very particular film.

But most of the major film studios wouldn't touch the book in spite of it being a Pulitzer Prize winner and so popular with the reading public because they couldn't see any real story in it that would appeal to moviegoers. The consensus of the studios, and to quote one executive, was: There's no story; there's no action, no romance, no obvious sex or violence. This, of course, was an early indication that To Kill a Mockingbird was a book of far greater depth than anyone really knew notwithstanding its Pulitzer status. But it would take time for this to be discovered.

In its film form, it took the genius of people like Horton Foote (who won the best screenplay Oscar for his work), Elmer Bernstein, Robert Mulligan, and Alan Pakula to make the story, and it took the talented genius of those like the children and Gregory Peck to make it come alive on-screen. It took real artistic genius for the makers of the film to accomplish so very successfully the transporting of an audience back to the time during which the events of the film take place, wonderfully enhanced by Bernstein's superb musical score and the exquisitely distinctive and natural Southern charm of Kim Stanley's voice as narrator.

But while Gregory Peck was an undisputed natural for the role of Atticus (and won an Oscar for his performance) the most difficult task confronting the producers was to find the right children for the roles of Scout and Jem. Hundreds of children all through the South were tried before Mary Badham and Phillip Alford were selected, only to discover they lived within four blocks of each other in Birmingham but had never met.

If miracles ever occur in film making, this was one. The two children were not only perfectly suited for the roles of Scout and Jem, even having the necessary family resemblance; anyone watching the film cannot fail to appreciate how naturally the two children interact as though they are, in fact, brother and sister. Another miracle was in the totally innocent and naturally unaffected talent of little Mary Badham, this really setting the film apart from all others and making it what it is: a truly great film.

I certainly agree with those who say that there has never been a film like To Kill a Mockingbird. It stands alone and has a peculiar and distinctive place all by itself in the whole of the history of filmmaking. The film and its history are a worthy study in and of themselves.

But if there is a single most important aspect to the film, it is this: While Peck was given the Oscar; it should have gone to Mary Badham. It wasn't Peck who made the film what it is; it was Mary. What makes this so very significant is the fact that adults still lack the wisdom of childhood. And adults made the film claiming to try to capture things through the eyes of children. They didn't. And the Oscar went to Peck. But as I mentioned in the last issue of TAP, the film while a work of art in its own right, couldn't tell the real story of the novel, the real story Harper Lee captures so vividly through the eyes of the children, especially little Scout.

The film comes close during the title sequences and in that early scene between Atticus and Scout. And it shows, but without telling the why, little Scout walking Boo to his house with her hand in his arm rather than leading him by the hand. But as I also said, it would have taken a film of epic length to explain things like this and the film makers knew the film would only succeed on the basis of adult issues and behaviors, not those of children.

Further, it can be argued that in 1962 no filmmaker would dare touch the real issues of the book in the way Harper does in the novel itself. I would argue it isn't even possible now. And I am certain Harper had to hold herself in check at times, which is clearly evidenced by some of her hints and allusions of things and issues that people even today don't want to recognize or speak of.

However, I give the film makers and those who played in it a lot of credit, and most especially little Mary Badham, for creating a work of art that stands alone among films in its artistic greatness. But to repeat, it didn't, nor do I believe it could, tell the real story of Harper Lee's novel. And it is that real story, or rather, I believe, the story behind the story, told the way Harper tells it, that makes her book stand alone as a work of genius which I compare with the best of Tolstoy or Dostoevsky; and even exceeding these in the very genius of the simplicity of its greatness. But, then, I maintain greatness is a simple thing, almost ingenuous if you will.

For example, the real test of greatness is time. The novel came out in 1960. I have had all these years of reading it and am still learning things from it. The story, the way Harper wrote it, is a treasure hunt; one I can compare with Thoreau's Walden. You may go over the same ground many times and miss a gem. Then, at some point in your life, simply due to the experiences of life, while you are going over such familiar ground your eye suddenly catches the glint of some exquisite jewel you missed so many times before.

I have only to look at the notations that I have made over the years in my copy of the book, the pages now fragile and yellowed by time just like my copy of Walden, to realize this. And, as with my copy of Walden, I am still making new notations every time I read it.

The thrill and excitement of discovery is often enhanced by the realization that in some cases Thoreau and Harper Lee missed the whole import of these things as well, that they wrote better than they knew. But as I have learned, one of the characteristics of genius is to often be unaware of its own genius.

This is why I believe Harper Lee, especially, wrote better than she knew. As she has Dill say (probably due to the influence of her childhood friend, Truman Capote, who was a kind of model for Dill) after the trial in spite of his weeping earlier: I think I'll be a clown when I get grown...There ain't one thing in this world I can do about folks except laugh.

Little Dill is already beginning to learn the wisdom of adulthood and lose the wisdom of a child; and much more quickly than Mr. Raymond had prophesied. Adult wisdom is already beginning its dirty work of destroying the child's wisdom of fairness and justice and replacing it with the adult wisdom of the cynicism: There's nothing you can really do about overcoming evil. And so it is that the history of humankind has been one of unremitting hatreds, prejudices, and warfare, by forsaking the wisdom of childhood.

Adult wisdom amounts to this: There's no use being a child unless you know the world is going to eventually break your heart! To which I reply: What's wrong with this picture? But even as I say the words, I know it takes wisdom to figure this out, wisdom the world has yet to attain.

I have said I am normal enough to want the flowers and the praise of my good works before I die. Emerson's eulogy of Thoreau was too late. It would have served both Emerson and Thoreau far better to have had Emerson recognize the preciousness and special gifts of his friend before he died. But too often the flowers and praise come too late, too late for the living, that is, who don't realize what they had in someone before they are gone. And the realization of this comes back as a specter to haunt in the midnight hours.

Or it can come when the sun is shining brightly and some familiar thing causes the loss of that loved one to assault us in an instant and explode full force upon our senses. And so it is with so many things and people in our lives that we fail to appreciate in their season. But as we live and grow, both as individuals and as a species, it does seem humanity would learn some of the lessons of such wisdom.

Harper Lee wrote at the end of her novel: Neighbors bring food with death flowers with sickness and little things in between. And this is all part of life, and it is as it should be. Family, friends and good neighbors, these make up the most precious part of life. And it often seems so very unfair when parents have to bury a child, when the good die young, when the wicked prosper and perverted laws and leaders rule over good people.

I find it passing strange that I am the kind of man who loves books and films like Terms of Endearment and Steel Magnolias and still be the kind of tough-minded, hard-edged man I am in so many other ways. I believe it was my children who saved me from becoming callous, cynical, and bitter. And though I failed them in innumerable ways, it was my children who brought out the best part of me as a man.

After little Scout's miraculously ingenuous dispersal of the lynch mob, Atticus makes this observation to Jem and Scout: "So it took an eight-year-old child to bring 'em to their senses, didn't it? That proves something - that a gang of wild animals can be stopped, simply because they're still human. Maybe we need a police force of children...."

An intriguing thought, isn't it, a police force of children. But that is exactly what the Amendment represents personified as Boo Radley, a mad man whose whole essence of being, his only focus of life is concentrated on the children. The Amendment is further personified as Atticus, Jem, Dill, and little Scout together confronting the lynch mob of the world.

What will not be done for the sake of civilized and sane conscience, the law must do. Just law is for the uncivilized lawbreaker, the lawless who act without conscience, and not the law-abiding who have no fear of just laws. On the contrary, the law-abiding, the good and civilized people of good conscience, applaud and support such laws. Which made it all the more impossible for Scout, Jem and Dill to understand how that jury could have found Tom Robinson guilty; such a verdict was so very obviously totally unfair, unjust, without conscience, and in fact, insane to them!

But a mob is often made up of one's friends and neighbors as Atticus points out to the children. Whenever I confront friends and good people with their own sin of hypocrisy by their agreeing that children must be the closest thing to the heart of God Himself and then live their lives as though there were something of greater importance, I am not thanked for the service I do them.

If I point out that the world itself behaves as a lynch mob because the greatest minds throughout history have lacked the wisdom to cherish children, that the greatest civilizations have warred and met destruction repeatedly because the greatest leaders of history have lacked such wisdom, that the particular cases of Boo Radley and Tom Robinson are evidence of things having never changed for the better for children, I certainly don't do so for the applause of the world; but if not, for what? Because I am compelled to try to speak for the children.

Now before anyone resorts to trying to tell me or anyone else how easy it is to be on the side of the angels, you try it. Try it in this manner, as I do: Try making converts to the Amendment. You won't find any children who in their wisdom wouldn't agree with the Amendment. You find the enemies of the Amendment among good adults; even fine, upstanding, church-going, flag-waving American citizens. Don't even try to tell me that children don't need someone to give them a voice or how easy it is to be on the side of the angels when you attempt to do so. These are lies. As are the lies preached from the pulpits of politics and churches of how truly concerned good people are for the children but live as though there were something of greater importance.

The mob that wanted to lynch Tom Robinson was composed of friends and neighbors of Atticus, many of them calling themselves, and undoubtedly even believing themselves, God-fearing people, Jesus-and-Bible-believing and loving people. And had not the children intervened, these good friends and neighbors, these God-fearing, Jesus-and-Bible-believing and loving people, would have hurt Atticus to get to Tom Robinson and kill him.

But these very same people comprised the jury that found Tom Robinson guilty, it was composed of good people, God-fearing people, Jesus-and-Bible-believing and loving people, the same friends and neighbors who would have hurt Atticus and lynched Tom Robinson had not the children intervened.

The most difficult part of the message of the Amendment I have to teach and preach is that it confronts good people, good people that as a mob or unjust jury will condemn the innocent. But if good people will allow little Scout to confront them individually, the wisdom of a good and pure conscience will prevail.

It is on an individual basis that good people prove their ability to respond to the need to protect that wise innocence of children which is the single most precious thing that is the responsibility of adults to protect! Once that lynch mob was confronted by this fact in little Scout, they came to their senses. The challenge is to direct these good individuals to come together in concert for the good of children, all children. The Amendment gives good people the opportunity to do just exactly this. But not in the name of their peculiar institutions or religious beliefs, not in the name of Democrats or Republicans or any other; but simply because it is their duty and responsibility as adult human beings, simply because it is the right and wise thing to do!

This is one of the things that mitigate against people supporting the Amendment; they cannot hang any of their bigotries, religious or political prejudices on it. It carries no baggage beyond it being simply the right and wise thing for people, all people, to do.

But the lynch mob, the unjust jury, the comfortable congregation, is led of a pack mentality, a pack mentality that includes the insanity of group-think. Or, in such cases, the group insanity led of the prejudices that make good people so utterly lacking in wisdom agree together to commit evil in the hypocritical corruption of the very names of God, justice, and fairness.

Scout points out how Atticus needed her, how he couldn't get along a day without her helping and advising him; Atticus had done a marvelous job as a father raising his little girl to think in such a way. He had made her feel important and needed.

Of course Scout couldn't know as a child of the things that really made her so important and needed to her father, the things he responded to in his little girl that led her to believe he relied on her help and advice. She couldn't know how important and needed it was to Atticus for her to climb up on his lap and hug him, how important and needed it was to her father for him to be able to tuck her into bed and kiss her good night, and how important and needed she was in making her father a real man, a fair and just man, a real gentleman, who didn't dare betray his little one's love and trust.

We men need our boys. We want to be able to teach our boys to be men. But we need the cherishing of our little girls to make us men soft in the right places so that the melding of the hard and soft results in the right alloy of toughness to both be able to love as well as be able to confront, fight, and overcome evil.

There is absolutely no greater influence for good in the life of any man than to have his child climb onto his lap seeking the warmth of his love and protection. No king on any throne can possibly possess such wealth and power as a man with his arms about that trusting little one he is holding. And no man with such memories can straightaway go out and go about doing evil. God meant children to be this influence for good in men's lives, to bring out the best in the best of men.

And knowing this how is it possible that the world has never attained to the wisdom of such a thing? How is it possible that humanity still behaves as a lynch mob? How is it possible that humankind still looks to God or some messiah to deliver it from its own seeming helplessness and inability to confront evil and overcome?

But it is a self-imposed tyranny of evil through blind, ignorant, and hateful prejudices that makes good people seemingly impotent in the face of evil, that has prevented enough good men and women in coming together in common cause for the common good of all humanity. Through this self-imposed tyranny of evil good people have failed to make that common good of all humankind, children their priority. Then, rather than accept personal responsibility for ridding themselves of this tyranny of evil, good people will turn to blaming others, institutions, and even God, for the evil!

And then good people will tell themselves that had they sat on Tom Robinson's jury they would not have caved in to such an injustice, that they would have stood up and been counted. And these same good people will say their prayers at night and go to sleep with an easy conscience while the children continue to be molested and murdered without hope of either protection or justice.

After the trial, Jem and Scout are asking their father how such an injustice such as that committed against Tom Robinson was possible in the face of his obvious innocence. In the course of trying to explain, Atticus tells the children, "It's all adding up and one of these days we're going to pay the bill for it. I hope it's not in you children's time."

My greatest fear for my own children is that humanity is running out of time; that the bill is due. But if in fact the only two choices are k+w=p or #92 of the periodic table, shouldn't good people be getting the message that concerted action by them is required if we are to survive and progress, if we are to insure a future for humanity, our children?

Jem and Scout retire to Jem's room to discuss some of the things their father has told them. At this point in the novel, Jem is entering puberty and the change is confusing to Scout. He has become moody and their relationship is changing; and not to Scout's liking.

For example, Jem tells Scout to try to get along with their Aunt Alexandra; that she is only trying to help Scout become a lady, something Scout heartily resents, in fact, when Jem says to Scout "Can't you take up sewin' or somethin'?" Scout's immediate and direct reply is "Hell, no."

Scout is only eight and has no real command or understanding of invective. She innocently uses the profanity because she thinks this is how she has to react to a big brother who is trying to push her around, insisting she become a lady, a traumatic change from Jem accusing her of acting like a girl such a short time ago, and this is the only device she knows to stick up for herself without mother or sister, or even a close girl playmate, in her male-dominated environment.

But things settle down between them and the children begin discussing what makes people different. Their aunt has told them they come from good people of good breeding, that some others like the Cunninghams are trash, and fine people like themselves, the Finches, should not associate with them.

Scout particularly resented this; in fact it infuriates her, causing her to lose her temper. This helps to account for her using the word hell; she was angry with her aunt and she became angry with Jem when he seemed to be trying to boss her. She likes little Walter Cunningham and would like to have him visit. But this brought on the comment by her aunt concerning what she considered suitable friends for the children. And Scout's resulting furious resentment.

Scout's resentment and anger is also borne of another source, one she simply cannot understand. Her father would never call anyone trash; he treated everyone alike, often going out of his way to be polite to people whom his sister, aunt Alexandra, obviously thought and spoke of as trash. How could her aunt be so different from Atticus? It didn't make sense. And all this fuss about background and ancestors, why should such things make a difference between people, why should such things be so obviously important to aunt Alexandra and not to Atticus?

Aunt Alexandra and Atticus were brother and sister. How could they be so close and think so differently? Scout and Jem sometimes wondered about stories of changelings.

As Scout and Jem calm down and begin reflecting on what their aunt has said and trying to work through the differences between people, Jem says in evaluating their aunt's remarks: The thing about it is, our kind of folks don't like the Cunninghams, the Cunninghams don't like the Ewells, and the Ewells hate and despise the colored folks. Neither of the children can really understand why this is true. They just know it's the way things are. But they also know as only children do that there is something plainly wrong with this and are trying to make sense of it. Scout says she thinks folks are just folks and that's the way it ought to be.

Jem's face grows cloudy and he says to Scout, "That's what I thought too ... If there's just one kind of folks, why can't they get along with each other? If they're all alike, why do they go out of their way to despise each other? Scout, I'm beginning to understand why Boo Radley's stayed shut up in the house all this time ... it's because he wants to stay inside."

What normal adult can't understand the confusion of Jem and Scout? And who of us can't relate to Jem's conclusion concerning Boo Radley? How many of you, like myself, haven't wanted to stay in the house, pull the blankets over our head, and tell the world to just go away?

I'm as normal a human being as any in this way. Which makes it all the more inexplicable that I would be doing as I am in regard to the Amendment. But as a reasonably honest and responsible man, I can't get away from little Dill's cynical conclusion, "I think I'll be a clown when I get grown...There ain't one thing in this world I can do about folks except laugh."

This hurts too much. Children should never have to become so cynical or have the wisdom of childhood destroyed by adults who have given up the fight, thrown in the towel, and give countless and very practiced excuses for their forsaking their own personal responsibility to confront evil.

I repeatedly hear of this or that person doing good for children. But when I pursue these stories, too many times I discover such people often don't even know the name of their State or U.S. Senator, they don't even know the name of their Representative in Congress, they have never written a letter to an editor of their local paper or their legislator; local, state or federal. Some, God help us, aren't even registered to vote! And many that are registered don't bother!

Is it that such good people think they are really making a difference when they are not involved in the political process; but so many of these good people are the first to complain against unjust laws and corrupt legislators. This is hypocrisy which good people fail to recognize as such!

No matter how many good works people think they are accomplishing by teaching in a public or Sunday school or working with children in any capacity, they are doing nothing of any lasting value unless such people are actively involved with the political process at all levels: local, state, and federal.

I grow weary of the stories of this or that one, of how much of an effect they are having for the good of children when such people haven't so much as written their local supervisor or editor. Don't delude yourself that real change for the better for children can ever be accomplished without good people being politically active. It isn't going to happen. The Devil and his wicked servants seem to know this even if good people don't!

But it is far easier to delude yourself that you are making a real difference by teaching a class of some kind. There you are, actually working with children and thinking all the while you are making a difference. It's a lie. You aren't. Making a real difference is being a responsible part of the power of We the People to change government so that you are a part of the solution for all the children, not the few you are working with. I spent many years working with thousands of children and suffering the same delusion that I was making a real difference before I realized the truth of this.

Go ahead and become an Albert Schweitzer or Mother Teresa, go ahead and build an orphanage, go ahead and become a teacher, be a foster parent, a Big Brother or Sister, a mentor, a Scout leader. These things are good, noble, and worthy works for children; for humanity. But they won't change anything! They never have and they never will!

As good and noble, as needed as such things are, in and of themselves they will never accomplish the goal of the Amendment in changing things for the better for all the children. The magnitude of evil, the size of the Beast, if you will, is too great for any single effort, or combination of efforts now existing because they are so fragmented and most often working at cross purposes, to overcome.

I wish I could get good people, We the People, to understand that unless we have good government, good leaders, and good laws, nothing is going to change for the better no matter how much time and energy they expend on all their other good works, no matter how many children they think they are saving. I wish I could get good people involved in the political process, that good people would recognize the Amendment is the way to accomplish something of substantive and lasting value for all children. As I came to realize, I could never make things really better for my own children until things became better for all the children.

Good people throughout history have allowed the insanity of their own prejudices to overcome the wise sanity of prioritizing and cherishing children, all children, and the result has been a history of the insanity of hatreds based on prejudices and always leading to the insanity of every description of lynch mob and war rather than the wise sanity of peace.

Looks simple enough on the face of it, doesn't it. Then what's the problem? The problem is the prejudices of good people who consistently fail to recognize or admit of such prejudices, good people who refuse to admit of their prejudices or face them for the evil things they are and consistently confuse what they believe with what they know. The problem is the same one throughout history that has always led to the need of the vigilante and Boo Radley, and to good people who will become a lynch mob or a jury condemning the innocent like Tom Robinson to death, to good people who will kill one another in the name of God, race, or political ideologies.

But when little Scout climbs up on her father's lap, when that little one knows she is protected, needed, and loved, ah, what a difference that makes in a man. No man with that memory, no man with such power and wealth in his arms, no man who loves as Atticus loved his children, is going to let any prejudice rule his passions. Such a man's passions, and his mind, already have a monarch, and one who rules with the wisdom of love, God Himself, through His most precious little agents of love and wisdom: Children.

Simple enough? Just try preaching this sermon. Watch good men, for example, nod their heads in the affirmative of the need of the civilizing influence of women and children to contravene war. Then watch good people, most especially men, in their hypocrisy go on about business as usual.

It is so very easy to accept the fact that there is no belief or fear of God in people like Mr. Ewell or his daughter, people who put their hands on a Bible and swear before God and all humanity to tell the truth, then lie in order to put an innocent man to death. It is easy to accept the fact that a man who will swear with his hand on a Bible, a Bible he says he holds to be the very Word of God, who swears to be truthful and uphold the Constitution and the laws of America, and then betrays that oath, has no belief in or fear of God. But it is not easy to accept the fact that obviously good people may have no belief or fear of God in them.

But logic would seem to demand this to be the case. If good people are going to agree that children are the closest thing to the heart of God Himself and then live as though there were something of greater importance, the very least such good people are guilty of is the stench of hypocrisy!

I have said that most people would say it is easy to be on the side of the angels. I have also pointed out the fact that while this is easy to say, it is very difficult to practice; particularly when you attempt to be on the side of the angels in trying to speak for the children in confronting the prejudices of good people.

I find it an intellectual puzzle that I would be attempting this work of trying to be the voice of children. I have often pointed out the fact that I have no inordinate love of children beyond that of most parents for their own. For those who believe I am on some holy quest, that the idea and the work for the Amendment somehow requires some kind of saint, I must appear at the very least an enigma, if not a downright embarrassment to such thinking because while I have done a lot of swimming I have yet to walk on water.

I wonder every day why I am doing this? Not only do I not have any really satisfactory answer, the enormity of the task is so overwhelming that, viewed as a whole, it makes me want to give up. It would be nice to believe that God needed an amanuensis and I got tapped for the job. As I've said several times, it's always a nice convenience to blame God for many things that are the fault of people. And it doesn't always take a mad man to use this device; good, normal people do it all the time.

I have tried to answer this question of why to others and myself many times because unless I can make sense of it in my own life, how can I expect others to make sense of it in their own? I owe people an explanation. The best way I can describe it so far is that it seems to be just a job. I never think of it as some noble undertaking, it is just a job that has to be done simply because it is the right and wise thing to do. I don't think I could do the work if it were anything but just simply a job that needs to be done.

Sometimes I wish I had some heavenly visitation, some epiphany or theophany that would make clear and declare from God Himself: This is your holy calling! But nothing of the sort ever happened. And I don't suppose it will.

It comes down to this. The Amendment is the right and wise thing to do. And once it formed itself in my mind and I finally accepted it, it became just a job that needed to be done. No one, I believe, has a healthier ego than I do. I love it when people think and speak well of me. I am a perfectly normal man in virtually all respects.

Quite often I speak and write of the two little girls in Belgium, Melissa and Julie. The horrible, monstrous deaths of these two little girls gave me nightmares. And still does. Something is horribly wrong with a species that could allow such a monstrous thing to be done to children! How is it that we allow such monsters to roam and prey on children in any society thinking and claiming itself to be civilized?

I hate bullies of any description. I have years of experience working with children and I have always had a natural hatred of those who would abuse children. But these things alone do not separate me from any other normal man.

When the Amendment suggested itself as a job that needed to be done, I believe that at the time I responded as any normal man would by rejecting the idea. But the idea kept insisting itself to me. And perhaps if there is anything abnormal about me as a man, I finally began to realize how appropriate the Amendment was, how important it was that humanity make children the priority of all nations.

Normal men, as I have had to finally accept, do not respond as I finally did. But as I began to dig deeply into my own motives, those which caused me to first reject the idea, then those that made me finally accept it, I began to learn many things I would never have learned otherwise; most especially things about myself as a man.

And as I learned, I began to get a perception of what has been wrong with humanity throughout history, a perception of the very things within myself that prevent good people from overcoming evil. One of the first things I learned was that I had reacted to the Amendment as a normal man would. I rejected the idea.

But if the Amendment was the right and wise thing to do, there had to be something wrong with what I considered normal! This was logical thinking. But not the kind of logical thinking I was anxious to pursue. Still, as an intelligent and reasonably honest and educated man and one who liked to think of himself as responsible, I seemed to have no choice but to pursue it.

As a writer, it was natural for me to express in print my thoughts and the things I was learning. I began to share these things with the readers of TAP; and lost many friends and readers in the process. But from the very beginning, I knew I was only a man, a very normal man, notwithstanding my new insights as to what this really meant, without any heavenly vision or holy grail to pursue. The Amendment made sense. And it was my job to make it make sense to others. And that is the only way I can pursue the work. I can't make my job anything else than just that: A job.

Most certainly the expression: It's a dirty job but someone has to do it! often comes to mind. In fact, I face that expression every day in my own thinking. Sometimes I feel it was the luck of the draw and I'm just playing the hand I was dealt, wishing it were someone else's, that the job itself were someone else's. I can at least say this much: I never asked for the job.

Years after the making of Harper's novel into the film, Gregory Peck was interviewed and said that the role of Atticus was the one he counted the favorite of his career, which he felt he had to do it and that being asked to play the role was one of the luckiest things to ever happen to him. I wish I could say this of the Amendment in my own life. But I can't.

I am an intelligent man. For this, like the natural skill of Atticus with a gun, I can take no credit; only a fool tries to take credit for the fortunate accidents of birth. It was an early lesson in my life, but one well learned, that it isn't so much what you've got, but what you do with what you've got that counts. I am also a very well educated man. For this, I can and will take the appropriate credit. This is taking what you have been given by birth and trying to make the most of it.

Because I am an intelligent and educated man, though I first rejected the idea of the Amendment, I was compelled to analyze why I opposed it. Little by little I became aware that the Amendment required I take a hard and honest look at myself as a man. Little by little it made me aware of so many errors and evils within myself as a man; I began to understand why I had been so set against it to begin with. It made me ask questions of myself that no man wants asked him. Let alone have to answer.

There were also the responsibility and accountability factors the Amendment addressed. I wanted nothing to do with these either. And yet, I had always considered myself a very responsible and accountable man. What was wrong with this picture I had of myself that seemed to be confronted by the Amendment in such a fashion that I rejected it?

Now I had had a lot of years in getting to know myself. But I had never known myself in the way the Amendment made me come to know myself. I was amazed, and at certain points, horrified! as I came to recognize so many hurtful errors and prejudices of thinking and acting in my own life, of how many of my own beliefs I had confused with knowledge.

If there is anything simple about the Amendment, it is this: It forces people, men especially, to look at themselves in such a critical and honest fashion that it also forces them to reject it at first. Just as I did. It exposed the errors of what I had considered normal. It exposed the errors of the historical definitions of normal.

I would never minimize the difficulty any person has in confronting the things I had to confront about myself in order to accept the Amendment as the right and wise thing it is. And I came to realize that there probably wasn't a human being alive that wants to examine themselves, and an entire society of which they are a part, as closely and honestly as the Amendment requires them to do.

It came down to a compulsion for me. I have no idea why I was forced to start examining my innermost ideas and feelings about the issue of children in light of the requirements of the Amendment. But it became just that: a compulsion.

Was I to commend myself for wanting to be that honest with myself? No. How do you commend yourself for a compulsion? You don't. Neither did I want to deal with the issues of such deeply held, but erroneous, beliefs of a lifetime, beliefs that I finally had to admit were nothing but prejudices, things I had been taught as a child to believe, things I wanted and chose to believe.

Then what? Why? Nothing was left to me but the explanation of compulsion; which was no answer at all. But it was all I had by way of explanation. I was driven by compulsion to accept the Amendment, to submit it to every Governor and U.S. Senator, to the President and influential figures of national and international reputation including Oprah and The Pope, to organizations like The Christian Coalition and even the United Nations.

Madness! That was the other explanation.

Was it madness or compulsion, perhaps a compulsion of madness, that forced me to decorate the front of my house with a Memorial Wall of Shame with the names of murdered children for all the world to see, for every passer-by to believe I am some kind of kook who should probably be put away and not to be trusted with sharp instruments? To post web pages on the Internet in support of the Amendment offering further support to those that consider me mad?

But I know the wisdom of the Amendment. I know this now. I didn't when I first started examining it. It came to me little by little. Early on I could accept the intellectual and logical necessity of it. But it took a woman, Harper Lee, to help me understand the wisdom of it.

Granting it took intelligence and an enormous amount of educated research to come to the realization that humanity had always lacked wisdom by excluding women and children as of equal value to men and this exclusion had doomed all efforts for a peaceful world, this was knowledge, not wisdom.

It took this knowledge together with my children; my years of working with children, and insights such as those of Henry Thoreau and Harper Lee for me to understand that it took factual knowledge plus wisdom to equal peace. I further had to come to an understanding that wisdom derived from love and compassion with an instinctive hatred of evil.

While Thoreau spoke to me about many things, about the evils of government, the wisdom of living simply, and so many other things, there was something missing. I always realized my friend Henry was deficient to a certain extent by his missing a large dimension of life through his never marrying and having children.

I also came to realize the world had always been lacking in wisdom by excluding women and children as equal in value to men. This is the reason the equation k+w=p could never be found in any of the works of men, including the Bible which, like all of these other writings of men, determinedly excludes women by treating them as of lesser value to men.

It would take the melding of both Henry Thoreau and Harper Lee to make it work for me. The two are representative of great genius, that of a man and a woman. It took such a melding of the genius of both halves of humanity for it to all come together and make sense of the Amendment. Neither, separately, could do this.

In a very definite way, it takes something of the combination of both Tom Sawyer/Huckleberry Finn and little Scout to make it work. For example, at the same time that Harper can cause little Scout to think humorously of reasons why women are not allowed to serve on a jury, she can have Atticus say: Serving on a jury forces a man to make up his mind and declare himself about something. Men don't like to do that. Sometimes it's unpleasant.

It takes the wisdom of a woman to make this kind of observation through a man the way Harper does. And nothing brings this into focus the way the Amendment does. But while the logical necessity of the Amendment is there, while it epitomizes wisdom, there is no way around the fact that every person must confront himself or herself as I did when confronted by the requirements of the Amendment. And every person will have to struggle with these requirements just as I did. And there is no minimizing the enormity of such a thing! History is against us as a species being able to do such a thing!

When little Scout reads Mr. Underwood's editorial about the shooting and killing of Tom Robinson, she thinks to herself about the due process of law that led to his conviction, his defense by Atticus and the jury finding Tom guilty in spite of his obvious innocence and tries to make sense of it all. Then it comes to her: "Atticus had used every tool available to free men to save Tom Robinson, but in the secret courts of men's hearts Atticus had no case. Tom was a dead man the minute Mayella Ewell opened her mouth and screamed."

And this has been the insane history of humanity. And it is in the secret courts of men's hearts that the Amendment will be tried. And it is in the secret courts of men's hearts that the Amendment will try them. Facts are often ugly, stubborn things. But all the wishing in the world won't change them. And the ugliest facts the hearts of men have to deal with are that they have never cherished children and they have never considered women and children to be of equal value to them.

But we can either submit to the fatalistic truth of little Scout's assessment and Dill's idea of becoming helpless clowns, we can continue to destroy the wisdom of childhood and refuse to declare ourselves thereby assuring our destruction, or we can face ourselves with the facts, accept them, and do those things necessary for finally attaining wisdom. And I submit that the Amendment is a first step in doing so.

For those good people whose hearts and minds the Amendment reaches, I would urge you to do as I have done. Get involved politically. Write those letters to the editor, your Governor and legislators. If you are on the net, chat and post your own messages or web pages.

I get many requests for support in the form of donations from individuals, organizations, and politicians. As a matter of course, I always reply by sending their material back with a flyer for the Amendment. I make a note to them: When I get your response to the enclosed, I will consider supporting you. This always accomplishes at least one of three things: They will ignore me, take me off their mailing list, or respond. A small thing? Sure. But it is just one of many small things that can add up to a major influence.

Some of you have a favorite columnist or TV newsperson or personality. Many of you have favorite actors and actresses, sports figures; many of you belong to churches or other organizations you support. Send or give them a flyer for the Amendment and ask their opinion. Don't ask for their support for the Amendment; ask them for an opinion. The support will follow if you can reach such people favorably. But first you have to get their interest; you have to make them knowledgeable that such a thing as the Amendment exists.

Equal rights for all, special privileges for none! is an ideal that has never happened. And isn't going to happen without wisdom. And until children are cherished, until women and children become of equal value to men, the wisdom of equality and denial of special privilege will remain unattainable.

Prejudice and bigotry don't make sense to children. As Scout, Jem and Dill struggle with the insanity of such things, Scout notices something strange. Her third grade teacher is a Miss Gates. During a class discussion, the persecution of the Jews by Hitler comes up. Miss Gates, a Jew herself, waxes eloquent on Hitler's mistreatment of the Jews and uses his abuse of authority to compare it to the democratic government, the freedom and equality of America and American citizens.

But after Tom Robinson's trial, Scout overhears Miss Gates making very derogatory comments about Negroes. It doesn't make sense to Scout. How can Miss Gates talk about Hitler's mistreatment of the Jews square with her obvious dislike of Negroes as though colored people were the inferiors of Miss Gates?

Children are keen observers of adults. But it isn't possible for them to understand the prejudices and bigotry of adults. Scout couldn't possibly understand the hatred engendered in those like Miss Gates, most particularly Miss Gates, because of a Negro feeling sorry for a white woman. Such a thing was not only incomprehensible to those like Miss Gates and to those on the jury, it was inexcusable effrontery! Why, it was almost as much as those people saying they're as good as us! I underline those people because you surely realize that those people could be anybody to anybody. Such has been the entire history of the human race.

I mention this ugly incident because it so clearly underscores why Scout finally realized Tom Robinson was a dead man as soon as Mayella Ewell screamed. That's a pretty tough thing to hand a small child. And when in history has it ever been any different? It hasn't. Is it any different now? No. Children throughout history have been handed this very same tough thing and it is just as rampant today as it has ever been.

But you cannot possibly fight successfully against prejudice and bigotry while at the same time condoning other kinds of perversion such as homosexuality, infidelity in marriage, abortion and pornography. Children are wise enough to know this. But if we, as adults, will confront, do battle and overcome these evils, showing children we do care about them, that we cherish them through guarding and protecting their innocence as it is our obligation to do, we will finally acquire wisdom. And it will be the kind of wisdom that will save humanity, it will be the kind of wisdom that led little Scout to insist on Boo Radley offering his arm rather than her leading him home by the hand like a child.

When Boo pleaded so pitifully to Scout: Will you take me home? She knew he was a frightened child. The man, this mad man, who had just killed an evil man in order to save her and Jem, was now only a frightened child pleading for her to take him home.

Scout had already shown the depth of her wisdom, that great part of wisdom which only a child understands fully in its depth of love, compassion, and instinctive hatred of evil, in agreeing with Sheriff Tate that to tell the truth about Boo would be in Scout's words and thinking sorta like shootin' a mockingbird.

But now as her wisdom has increased, she faces the plea of this grown man: Will you take me home? the words said almost in a whisper in the voice of a child afraid of the dark, as Scout describes them. She would lead him by the hand through the house and out onto the porch where the Sheriff and Atticus are discussing what to do. But she will not lead him home by the hand like a child. No! Let Scout describe it in her own words:

I put my foot on the top step and stopped. I would lead him through our house, but I would never lead him home.

Mr. Arthur, bend your arm down here, like that. That's right sir.

I slipped my hand into the crook of his arm.

He had to stoop a little to accommodate me, but if Miss Stephanie Crawford was watching from her upstairs window, she would see Arthur Radley escorting me down the sidewalk, as any gentleman would do.

I can feel the sting of tears and a lump in my throat as I write of this. And I'm not ashamed to admit it. For your sake I have to admit it because I don't believe any one of any sensitivity can avoid feeling as I do when this whole scene unfolds. For those who do not feel as I do about this, I have to wonder....

A mad man, a mad guardian angel, their childhood bogeyman, has saved these children's lives. And now, little Scout is walking him home, her hand in his arm, a little lady and her gentleman friend. Let the neighbors stare and wonder! They would see Arthur Radley escorting me down the sidewalk, as any gentleman would do.

Folks, that is the epitome of wisdom on the part of a little eight year old girl, it is the wisdom adults pound out of children by bowing to the wicked dictum: When they get a little older, they won't cry about it anymore, they will understand they can't do anything about the evil in the world.

And so it is that good people have always excused themselves for not confronting and overcoming evil. To tell a child: You have to take what life deals you, and then to hypocritically refuse to do your part in doing all that is in your power to make that life all you can by being a responsible adult and doing your duty is damnable!

But this has been the history of the human race. And it cannot, must not, continue! Good people are going to have to confront their prejudices, their sins, and do better! If it is sin to kill a mockingbird, for example, isn't it a greater sin to allow the predators of children to roam our world or to murder an unborn child? Where, any thinking person must ask him- or herself, are our priorities? We must ask ourselves, sensibly, are the present priorities leading to the advancement of civilized peace or Armageddon? And I believe any sensible person knows the fearful and horrifying answer to this question!

It wouldn't have occurred to Harper because of her being a woman, because of her being such a lady. She left it to me as a man to point it out and make something of it: Scout would be the only lady, a little eight year old lady, to ever grace the arm of Boo: Mr. Arthur Radley. And for me as a man, that is one of the deepest of the tragedies in the whole book. And yet...

Scout would not realize this of course. After all, she is only eight years old and should not realize it. It is one of the great benefits of childhood to not have to realize or even be aware of such things. Scout never saw Boo again. But I like to believe he died peacefully and content. He had been the guardian angel of the children. In what had to have been the sanest moment of his life, he was there for them.

But, then, the children had been his guardian angels in turn. And at no time more than when a little lady graced his arm as she walked with him and he was no longer Boo, but the gentleman Mr. Arthur Radley escorting the little lady Miss Jean Louise Finch. I believe I could die content with such a treasured memory alone.

It was only fitting that Scout should be sad thinking that in spite of all Boo's gifts to them, even saving their lives, she and her brother had never given Boo anything in return. But Harper did point out the benefit to Boo in watching the children through the close-shuttered windows of his dark tomb of a house. The joy it must have brought to him in watching them and placing those small gifts in the hole of that tree for them to discover. Even taking part in a kind of game they devised about him which he surely watched through those shuttered windows, and even enjoying the attempts by the children to get a glimpse of him. Boo shared in the children's lives and they, unknowingly, gave that degree of reason and happiness to a mad man. They became his children.

And in the end, they became one another's guardian angels and Boo became Mr. Arthur Radley and Scout became Miss Jean Louise Finch. As I said, I like to believe Boo died content with that memory to sustain him to the end; would that all adults throughout the world, believing themselves sane, were as insane as Boo Radley.

But, then, it has taken the putting of many years behind me to take the first step and begin the long and torturous journey to such insanity myself. And that first step would never have been taken if it were not for my own children and grandchildren together with the screams of pain, and finally the lonely whispered prayers for the kindness of death, to deliver two little girls in a black, cold dungeon in Belgium which finally penetrated my own hard heart and made me hear and listen to those screams, and finally, the whispered pleadings for death of those two little ones.

God has spared me the kind of nightmares which have to afflict any parent who has had a child tortured and murdered as were little Melissa and Julie and so many others. I cannot perceive of any such parent retaining their sanity under such circumstance. I believe I wouldn't have the courage to continue living with such a nightmare.

I suppose such parents who do go on living become insane. It would take such a kind and humane mechanism to enable such parents to function as though they were alive though a portion of their mind would have to be disabled. As a behavioral scientist I can accept this.

The monsters that prey on children can usually be identified very early in their lives. But the laws protecting juveniles often prohibit taking preventive action. Agencies like the schools and Child Protective Services are so paranoid and jealous of their own empires, you will find virtually no cooperation from these institutions or agencies. This is why so many agencies and institutions like the schools and CPS, intended for the good of families and children, are often at cross-purposes.

Another factor in a failure of early identification is the threat of lawsuits. We are such a litigious society that there is virtually no area of our lives that does not invite suit at one time or another. But as long as insanity rules a society, we can hardly expect things to get better. And it is insanity that rules.

The genius of Harper Lee was in using a mad man to balance the scales of justice. Civilized law, civilized people, could not protect the children against determined evil. But it was the patently insane prejudice of civilized good people who loosed this evil against the children by condemning an innocent man. It is the children who always pay the price for such prejudice on the part of adults.

Our society is determined to make conditions ever worse for children by insanely continuing to let the monsters loose to roam and prey on them. And nothing will get any better until society puts these monsters away, permanently, at the very earliest.

And once these monsters are identified, the most charitable term I can use for a society that will continue to loose them to prey on children is the word insane. And if not insanity, what? A society that simply does not give a damn about children, a society that steadfastly refuses to identify these monsters at the earliest time, a society that acts like it hates children! You try to tell me what lies between these two choices!

I recently received a couple of mailings that accentuate what I am talking about, one very conservative from HUMAN EVENTS (read: Heritage Foundation) touting Robert Zelnick's expose of Al Gore, the other from the ACLU. I could hardly ask for better examples of two extremes.

Neither will touch the Amendment. And here is the reason: Notwithstanding Emerson's failure to appreciate Thoreau as he should have, nothing can detract from his contribution to transcendentalism. Emerson, as Thoreau, had the courage to face the errors of his childhood, the errors of his age, and lend his voice to addressing those errors.

In his essay "Compensation", Emerson points out the kind of insanity on the part of good people that led to the jury convicting Tom Robinson and allowing the evil Ewell to be loose to prey on the children. It is the very kind of insanity the Amendment forced me to face and overcome in my own life.

In the era of Emerson and Thoreau, the ministry was an occupation for gentlemen. The universities were given largely to the training of promising young men for this occupation. Both Emerson and Thoreau received this university training. And both saw the inherent evils in orthodox religions and repudiated them after earnestly attempting to accommodate themselves to such teachings.

In his essay, Emerson points out a fatal flaw in the religious beliefs of most people. He had just come from a church service where the minister had delivered the traditional sermon that included the traditional promise of the Last Judgment: But the assumption of traditional religion is that judgment is not to be expected or executed in this world, but in that which is to come. The wicked are expected to be successful and happy in this world and the righteous are expected to be unsuccessful and miserable.

Yet what import, Emerson asks, is to be expected from such orthodox teaching by the churches? "Was it that houses and lands, offices, wine, horses, luxury, are had by unprincipled men whilst the saints are poor and despised; and that a compensation is to be made to these last hereafter, by giving them the like gratifications another day, - bank-stock and doubloons, venison and champagne? This must be the compensation intended; for what else? Is it that they are to have leave to pray and praise? to love and serve men? Why, that they can do now. The legitimate inference the disciple would draw was, We are to have such a good time as the sinners have now - or, to push it to its extreme import, You sin now, we shall sin by-and-by; we would sin now, if we could; not being successful we expect our revenge tomorrow. The fallacy lay in the immense concession that the bad are successful; that justice is not done now. The blindness of the preacher consisted in deferring to the base estimate of the market of what constitutes a manly success, instead of confronting and convicting the world from the truth ... and summoning the dead to its present tribunal."

The key to Emerson's remarks is that phrase: *not being successful we expect our revenge tomorrow.* This is the excuse good people use for not doing their duty to confront and overcome evil. This leads to his most rational conclusion that this further leads to the fallacy which lays in the immense concession of those supposing themselves to be good to the evil, that the bad are expected to be successful and justice is not expected to be done now. The bottom line of all such thinking on the part of good people is to blame God and not take personal responsibility for confronting evil! The perfect excuse derived from religion of good people from time immemorial.

But this is knowledge, and any reasonable person is able to understand and accept Emerson's remarks in the light of knowledge. The application of such knowledge to wisdom is another matter. And it is at this point that good people fail to gain wisdom from such knowledge for even Emerson and Thoreau failed in wisdom by not realizing or accepting the fact that ultimate wisdom is unattainable unless that other half of humanity, women, is accepted as of equal value to men.

How is it, though, that good people as Emerson exemplifies reject even such obvious knowledge? Because of the prejudices of good people who choose what they want to believe in flagrant disregard of factual knowledge! A self-fulfilling prophecy of Armageddon is thus assured by good people holding onto their prejudices by disputing and in the face of facts. That there is nothing new under the sun is the fault of the prejudices of good people who will not confront their prejudices for the ugly, destructive things they are!

Only when differences based on such prejudices are set aside will good people come together in common cause to confront and overcome evil;

which is the job of good people, not God or angels. Only then will there be something new under the sun, the prioritizing of children which will lead to wisdom and peace.

There is most certainly nothing new in Emerson's remarks. The same thoughts have been expressed by people since the beginnings of human history. They continue to be expressed now and, in fact, I have just done so. But I do so to call attention to the need of the Amendment as a first step in going beyond such knowledge that Emerson expresses so succinctly, a first step toward a New Thing under the sun.

The success of the Amendment depends on good people recognizing this and acting accordingly. The Amendment gives good people a chance to set aside all prejudices of beliefs and act according to factual knowledge.

It is the right and wise thing to do. But can only be done by the setting aside of personal prejudices and coming together on the sole basis of making children the priority they have never been. And by doing so, to take that first step toward the kind of wisdom humanity has always failed to acquire, and which will lead to our accepting personal responsibility for the kind of world we want for our children.

If, as Emerson alludes, we were able to summon the dead to our own tribunal, what do you suppose they would have to say? More importantly, let us suppose we were able to summon the murdered children to such a tribunal, what do you suppose they would have to say? Can you even suppose the children would accept our feeble excuses, those excuses based on personal beliefs in God, angels, and Last Judgments of the wicked whether you are a Christian, Jew, Moslem, Hindu or without any particular or no religious belief, in lieu of our failure to do all that was our responsibility and in our power to protect them? I think not.

A while back I wrote the following:

The challenge the message of the children presents is that of awakening the consciences of adults to the all-too-often silent cry of children who cannot be heard.

What happened to a little girl that produced a woman like Mayella as opposed to a little girl like Scout and her so very different prospects as a woman? I know the Amendment confronts this monster and exposes it.

But the message can only be truly effective once it is able to find expression in the voices and language of the children. And the truth of that fact is, at times, almost more than I can bear.

It is trying to give expression to those voices of the little ones and in their language that tries my own soul. It is the searching of my own heart and mind, the writing of such things, that makes me wish there was someone who would hold my hand, someone into whose lap I could crawl just like little Scout, an Atticus who would hug me and make me feel loved and needed.

To that extent, I am not a mad man; I am as normal as any of you. I didn't ask to be born, but here I am. I wish my childhood could have lasted longer, that I could have retained the best of childhood into adulthood. But it didn't and I couldn't.

The conclusion of this gray hair: It can't be a better world for my children until it is a better world for all the Scouts, Jems, Dills, and Mayella's as well. And this isn't going to be the case until there is no further need of the little Scouts to confront lynch mobs; there are no more juries who will convict Tom Robinson, until there is no further need of Boo Radley to do the job supposedly sane and civilized people fail to do.

Good people can make this happen. But only once they get past their excuses and prejudices, and come together in agreement and with determination to overcome the evils directed at children and for the sole purpose of bringing this to pass. As long as good people hold on to their peculiar beliefs and prejudices, making these things the priority in their lives rather than children, it will never come to pass. And if not, whom will we have to blame but ourselves?

CHAPTER NINE

Increasingly, chocolate is ever more being considered as food. Well, this is good news to a great many people, especially women and the Easter Bunny. But it has its philosophical side as well. I expect a book any day now to be presented on The Philosophy and Metaphysics of Chocolate. This, of course, will lead to government controls and somewhere down the road, lawsuits will begin to multiply against chocolate companies because of chocolate's addictive characteristics (how would you choose between your broccoli or a Snickers bar?) which these companies have unscrupulously, unconscionably in total disregard of the public health, kept secret. Undoubtedly, lawyers are already salivating over the prospects. It takes a lawyer to make a mountain (multi-million dollar lawsuit) of a pimple.

And when people begin to die of chocolate related illnesses other than terminal acne, I wonder how Medicare will handle this? And when chocolate addiction and its mood-altering characteristics become a legal matter, I wonder when the first serial rapist or murderer is going to find a lawyer to represent and defend him on this basis? Folks, it's just a matter of time.

When my own thoughts turn to a philosophical bent, I always think of one of my favorite musicals, "Paint Your Wagon", one of the most entertaining of travels through philosophical thought processes and one from which I never fail to draw inspiration.

I don't believe many knowledgeable people would disagree with the statement that the era of the great Broadway Musicals was the last time poets worked in America. And while there aren't that many musicals that would qualify for that designation of being truly great, I think it is a sad thing that so many people today can't even name the two which do qualify in which the lovers never even kissed.

Paint Your Wagon always reminds me that God is surely far more human than religion gives Him credit and isn't dead though religion does its best to kill Him when it isn't trying to make Him look either stupid or ridiculous. But this is a subject which always raises my blood pressure and leaves me wanting to swear a mighty Boy Bird Watcher's or Boy Scout's Oath so I'll refrain for now.

For those that are familiar with the sublime beauty of Sarah Brightman's operatic voice, especially if you have heard her sing Summer Time, it would usually be thought vulgar at the least to mention a musical like Paint Your Wagon in the same breath with this angel of song. And this would also be like trying to compare apples and oranges. Such is not my intention, as you will see by my calling your attention to what is sublime in the musical.

There are three really good songs in Paint Your Wagon: They Call the Wind Maria, I Talk to the Trees, and I Was Born Under a Wandering Star; this last being the theme song of my life. But apart from some good music and the just plain, often delightfully irreverent, hilarity of the musical, there are some very deep philosophical moments as well like The First Thing You Know, the philosophy of which I totally agree with without reservation.

And I can't think of a single line from any of the great philosophers that surpasses Ben Rumson's comment on the young farmer, Horton: "This boy has a talent for dissipation that is absolutely unique." When I become really depressed and about ready to give up on the human race, I remember this line and find encouragement once more.

While there are many other examples of great philosophical concepts in the musical, like it being undesirable to be found dead while drunk and muddy in the street, Ben's comment about Horton is my favorite. And after the young man has experienced his first cigar, his first glass of whiskey, and his first woman, his conclusion that the last was the best is hard to fault, philosophically speaking, of course.

And many are the times when some well-intentioned, religious friend has wanted to pray with me and I have been tempted to say, to paraphrase Ben Rumson: "No thanks, I've suffered enough." This is more polite than the familiar: "I'd rather eat dirt!" which I've always considered a little unkind.

Not that I have anything against prayer. On the contrary, I believe in prayer. But not the prayers of those who, because of their own peculiar beliefs, would consign people to the pit who didn't agree with the religious beliefs of those doing the praying.

When asked if he had read the Bible, Rumson replies that he had. But when asked if that hadn't made an impression on him concerning the evils of drink, he said it hadn't. But it had sure suppressed his desire to read the Bible any more.

Since I am not a drinker, I have read the Bible through, cover to cover, many times. But I finally came to appreciate Ben Rumson's view of it when in the hands of those who try to convert me. It is such people who make me think that liquor is a better alternative. My point is to poke fun at those who take themselves too seriously, who speak ex cathedra of things and issues as though they spoke for God Himself; and, to poke fun at myself and remind myself of the ever present danger of becoming guilty of this as well.

We are wont to look for wisdom in our sages of the past. But as I keep pointing out, wisdom is impossible of attainment as long as men refuse to accept an entire one-half of humanity, women, as of equal value, and as long as humanity refuses to make children the priority of nations. But we do find much of great value in the thoughts and writings of sages of the past, much that contributes to knowledge though wanting in that ultimate wisdom which would lead the world to peace.

People like Emerson are easily faulted for often being dogmatically didactic about things of which they obviously could have no certain knowledge, confusing what they believed with what they knew, an all-too-common foible of humanity. When they fall into this mode, they remind me of the fools who say: "God told me...."

But even Emerson, as Thoreau, was only human. And like all of us, sometimes misspoke or spoke from a bias or prejudice. Still, he had a keen, incisive, and analytical mind and much of what he said and wrote, even when his pompousness is most evident, makes good sense.

Ralph Waldo Emerson is not the daily reading of most Americans. And to our shame is, as with Thomas Paine and so many others, largely an unknown to most Americans today. But it was Emerson's opening the door to new ideas that made possible many of the thoughts that led to an unparalleled academic freedom for the universities at the turn of the century.

Though Emerson is now unread by most Americans, who are more interested in and know far more of Elvis Presley, the truly learned scholar of today still turns to him for the great thinker's ability to put complex ideas in a cogently succinct form (once you learn to read around his metaphysics). Emerson not only had a great mind for philosophical thought, he had a rare gift for being able to cut through the extraneous and get directly to the heart of a matter. I usually remark on Emerson's most illustrative disciple of transcendentalism, Henry David Thoreau, because of Thoreau's going a step further than Emerson in the actual carrying out of Emerson's philosophy into direct action.

Emerson was the preeminent idea man and Thoreau the activist. But both master and disciple proved their courage in confronting the religious and governmental tyranny of their time. Both were disciples of the idea of the ultimate responsibility of the individual to first learn to govern himself before being fit to govern others. Both believed in the need of a bloodless revolution without cannon and musket, a revolution of ideas, which would lead to a whole and entire humanity, rather than the fragmented one of history, red in tooth and claw.

The original battleground of transcendentalism was that between materialism and spiritualism. Men like Emerson and Thoreau, and women like Margaret Fuller, were giving expression to the idea that the spirit should learn and grow and eventually transcend the materialistic senses.

Of course, there was nothing new in this idea; many of the very earliest poets and philosophers were given to the same theme. What was new in transcendentalism was the confronting of established orthodoxies of both religion and government, and the confronting of these during a time when to do so flew in the face of what was considered modern progress, a modernity based on the growing success of materialism enhanced and supported by religious and political dogma.

It would be well at this point to repeat, and reemphasize, something I wrote in the last issue of TAP. I am certain the reader will be able to make the comparison between Emerson's remarks and Paint Your Wagon with the hypocrisy, which the musical exposes in such a delightfully farcical way:

In the era of Emerson and Thoreau, the ministry was an occupation for gentlemen. The universities were given largely to the training of promising young men for this occupation. Both Emerson and Thoreau received this university training. And both saw the inherent evils in orthodox religions and repudiated them after earnestly attempting to accommodate themselves to such teachings.

In his essay, Compensation, Emerson points out a fatal flaw in the religious beliefs of most people. He had just come from a church service where the minister had delivered the traditional sermon, which included the traditional promise of the Last Judgment: "But the assumption of traditional religion is that judgment is not to be expected or executed in this world, but in that which is to come. The wicked are expected to be successful and happy in this world and the righteous are expected to be unsuccessful and miserable."

During the McCarthy era, it was calling someone a Commie that tarred one. During Emerson's time, it was calling someone an Infidel or Freethinker. The convenience of labels being used to destroy reputations has a long history. Now, it is labeling anyone Homophobic who has any normal person's natural revulsion to sexual perversion. And if you dare support the Amendment or any moral absolute, you are called a Moralist.

Homosexuals have picked up on this device in order to propagandize their agenda of making perversion accepted as normal behavior. The homosexuals would have everyone believe that the normal revulsion one feels towards pervert behavior is to be condemned. So the homosexual agenda, as with that of Hitler and Goebbels concerning the Jews, is to call normal people with a normal revulsion of pervert behavior homophobic; normal people who are repulsed by pervert behavior are, by the same method of Hitler and Goebbels, to be made haters of homosexuals. The homosexual agenda is to equate normal revulsion of perversion with bigoted, prejudicial hatred and racism.

With the power of the universities, Hollywood, and Caesar's courts and legislators together with the ACLU to back up this propaganda agenda of perverts, it isn't surprising they have been so successful in their power to intimidate normal people. Who of us does not recall what happened to Anita Bryant when she had the courage to speak out about allowing homosexuals in classrooms to teach our children?

If the churches and synagogues ever had to face themselves honestly about their lack of any power or influence for good, the two issues of the success of homosexuals in our classrooms and abortion on demand should shut their mouths in shame. But I learned long ago that a feeling of shame for failure to take a stand in confronting real evil is not the long suit of the religious. But this has more to do with uncritical servility to traditions rather than a failure of individual character and lack of virtue. I continue to hope that if good people know better, they will do better. And my writing is dedicated in most part to an attempt to help good people know better so they will do better.

I do this in spite of the fact that good people are notorious for not doing better even when they know better. A good example of this is occurring right now in my home county of Kern, particularly the city of Bakersfield.

Virtually everyone knows of Edward Hume's book Mean Justice featuring Kern County in a most unflattering way. But now another Kern County matter has reached national attention: Homosexual teachers.

We all know what happened to Anita Bryant when she had the courage to confront this perverted insanity in Florida. Now, it is happening in California. And the word insane is not an overstatement of the case. What sane society would ever think perverts acceptable role models for children in any capacity, let alone our classrooms?

As to good people not doing better even when they know better, I wonder how many will do as I have done in trying to confront this evil threatening our children? And this is what I have done: I have written all my government representatives; local, state and federal. And I have written letters to the editors of my two local newspapers as well. A copy of this Letter to the Editor follows:

The word pervert is still in the dictionary and I resent the Hitlerian propaganda ploy of homosexuals to label normal people homophobic just because they have a perfectly natural and normal revulsion to sexual perversion.

I further resent the homosexual lobby trying to equate this normal reaction of normal people to perversion with the ugliness of racism. The agenda is plain enough: to make normal revulsion to perversion an act of discrimination.

Homosexuals do not belong in classrooms with and teaching children. Period. This is not discrimination; this is just plain, good old-fashioned common sense. But if the homosexuals have their way, the legislators and courts are going to equate the normal revulsion of normal people to sexual perversion with discrimination. Americans will have sent the message to children that perversion is perfectly normal and acceptable. And Goebbels will have won once more.

Pseudo-intellectuals are quite fond of crying: What is normal? To which the answer, in the case of homosexuality, should be obvious: Sexual perversion is never normal. And legitimizing it by allowing its practitioners in the classroom as role models to our children is insane at best!

***

I have to wonder just how many people, considering themselves good people, will follow this example of making their voices heard concerning this issue, an issue that dramatically impacts on our whole society. Will these good people even know who their government representatives are? Will they take the time to write the necessary letters in order to make their concerns known? In most cases: No. And the homosexual lobby is counting on this to carry the day. And evil will have once more triumphed because good people did nothing.

Why, I ask myself, should an issue like pervert teachers be thought the concern of only people like Robertson and Falwell or the Christian Coalition? This is not a religious issue. This is an issue, to repeat, that impacts on our whole society and shouldn't be carrying a religious banner any more than the Amendment.

The issue of pervert teachers for our children should be one that concerns all Americans because confronting it is the right and wise thing to do, not because of some presumed holy books or religious (or political) views. For example, many good people agree that an armed citizenry is, as Thomas Jefferson and so many others pointed out, the only means we ultimately have to confront and overcome the tyranny of a government which has become unendurable, the only insurance we have to ultimately protect our most basic freedoms.

No one has to be a good Christian, Jew, Moslem or Hindu to recognize the truth and wisdom of this. But how very few good people belong to the National Rifle Association, the only effective lobby we have in Congress for our right as private citizens to bear arms. I am constrained to say this: Unless you are politically active, unless you are writing those letters, you may be a good person but you are most certainly not a good citizen!

If my own heart has become an empty tomb where once the songbird dwelt, if I have no joy or happiness in my life, it is because of my attempting to be the voice of children who have no voice or choice but that which adults give them. But refraining from the invention of poesy, which has never prevented the abuse of children no matter how prettily phrased, I do wonder how people can be happy when children are suffering? To repeat some thoughts of mine in recent issues of TAP about Harper Lee's To Kill a Mockingbird:

It has been said that all children deserve better parents. And to a certain extent, I have to agree. My own certainly did. But this goes back to my thought that if good people know better, they will do better. And maybe if I am ever successful in giving a real voice to the children, if I am ever able to get in touch with the loving wisdom of the children and can reach others with that loving wisdom, goodness will yet prevail over evil. But this presupposes that the message will be successful in preventing the Mayella Violet Ewell's ever growing up so love-starved that they will put their hands on a Bible and swear a false oath condemning another human being to death.

The challenge the message of the children presents is that of awakening the consciences of adults to the all-too-often silent cry of children who cannot be heard. What happened to a little girl that produced a woman like Mayella as opposed to a little girl like Scout and her so very different prospects as a woman? I know the Amendment confronts this monster and exposes it.

But the message can only be truly effective once it is able to find expression in the voices and language of the children. It is no small matter to offer people hope, hope that things can be done to save our children and our world. The Amendment offers such hope. But as long as men love darkness rather than light, so long will all of humanity remain at risk from the power of such darkness.

My closest friends remain those like Henry Thoreau and Harper Lee. They see through the darkness and offer me light and hope in a very dark and dangerous world. If, in my sharing this light and hope with others, I am seen as the madman in confronting my own sins and those of others, I confess this leaves very little hope of things changing for the better because I know it will take an army of people who share my dream, my madness, of changing things, my dream that if good people know better, they will do better, to accomplish the purpose of the Amendment.

But if good people will let the children make their voices heard, this can happen. As I have pointed out, you won't find any child who would find fault with the Amendment. This is the purview of adults, since children are not permitted a voice in this matter. It is the responsibility and duty of adults to listen to the cry of the children for the Amendment. In the meantime, I will continue to read Walden and TKM, I will continue to try to hear little Scout and listen to what she has to say and try to shut out the sanity all about me that confronts my madness.

It's a hard thing, this thing of being all grown up. I can't help wishing I could join Scout and Jem and Dill at play. I want my business to be the business of a child, to play. But there is the rub. I know it can't be a better world for my children until it is a better world for all children. And there's no getting around the fact that I am all grown up, that we adults have the responsibility of making that better world.

To return to Emerson: "The voice of fable has in it somewhat divine. It came from thought above the will of the writer. That is the best part of each writer which has nothing private in it; that is the best part of each which he does not know; that which flowed out of his constitution and not from his too active invention; that which in the study of a single artist you might not easily find, but in the study of many you would abstract as the spirit of them all... The exclusionist in religion does not see that he shuts the door of heaven on himself, in striving to shut out others."

My purpose in calling your attention to the above is several fold. For one thing, writers like Henry Thoreau and Harper Lee did indeed write better than they knew. Also, those thoughts, which are above the will of the writer, often find their way into my own writing. And while often true, are often the cause of a lot of grief to me as a consequence. These are the things about which I am compelled to write even to my own hurt, the things I cannot seem to keep private, the things that come to mind unbidden and force themselves upon me because they are true.

Few would try to discount the warning inherent in Emerson's calling our attention to the need to avoid inventive exclusivity, the need to examine the whole rather than becoming dogmatic about particulars. I recommend any writer reading Edgar Allan Poe's essay The Philosophy Of Composition. But I don't recommend taking all of his thoughts as gospel on the subject. In writing, as in most of life's endeavors, it is good to look at the whole rather than concentrate on particulars to the point of losing sight of the whole.

It is in the concentration on particulars, those inventions of exclusivity, to the hurt of the whole that so many religious and philosophical ideas fail to hold together. And it is in the same manner that so many ideas that find their way into law fail as well. It was in a recent conversation with a friend that the subject of philosophy came up. Having a fine university education, he agreed that the academic study of the subject was a very valuable tool in learning critical thinking, a point I have stressed many times. But the conversation became lively when we began to discuss my equation $k+w=p$.

I shared my thought with him that while I used to believe many things were right, I had failed to examine these things in the light of whether they were wise. I mentioned my own guilt of too many occasions where I had practiced inventive exclusivity to the hurt of the whole. Oh, it wasn't that I didn't believe these things of inventive exclusivity to be wise. But that was an assumption. If it seemed right, well, of course it had to be wise as well. Not so.

We have all had the experience of looking back and wondering how we could have been so dumb as to do something that turned out horribly wrong. But we thought it right at the time we did it. The old: Seemed like a good idea at the time. In general, these things fall into the category of lacking in wisdom. They seemed right at the time, but our inability to evaluate these things as to their wisdom was the cause of their not being the really right thing to do. This, of course, is the very foundation of any culture; the dependence of a culture or society on the wisdom of parents to teach children properly, to teach them the right things to do. And when this fails the culture or society fails.

But unwise laws, causing the failure of a culture or society to encourage parents, to encourage family values, can obviate the best efforts of even the best of parents. Is it right, for example, to have a welfare system that rewards unmarried women, many in their teens, having babies? Of course not. Then why do we have such a system? Because at one time, as with slavery, it seemed the right thing to do. But it was obviously unwise.

Does it make sense to have laws that are virtually unenforceable? Of course not. Then why do we? One example is the law against marijuana. This single example, a clearly unenforceable law, has clogged our courts and made criminals of multiplied thousands of otherwise law-abiding citizens.

When it comes to laws of this nature, we might have to follow the money in order to make any sense of them. Who profits? But once that question is answered, what do we do about it? We don't want to know! That is too often the case. If our ox is not being gored, who cares; which brings us back to the issue of good people who are not good citizens. If more Americans were good citizens instead of just good people, I seriously doubt we would be having many of the problems we are.

As to being able to discriminate between what seems right and what is truly wise, this is far from simple. Many times it is a lack of sufficient data leading to a wrong conclusion that is at fault. If a course of action is based on insufficient, or in some cases even wrong, data, the result is undoubtedly going to prove unsatisfactory. This is why factual knowledge is essential to wisdom. You simply cannot expect to act with wisdom if you do not have factual knowledge or you act on data that is insufficient or incorrect. And it should be patently obvious that wisdom is impossible if you refuse facts in order to maintain a particular belief, bias or prejudice.

A lack of sufficient, factual data or the result of having made unwise decisions, which precipitate a crisis, often characterizes decisions made on the basis of expediency. Many crises of government arise because of politicians who bow to getting elected rather than acting wisely. If Emerson was right that the majority are slow to the incursion of reason (and who would disagree?), just who is to blame for this if not the leaders of such a majority? And who is to blame for such leaders if not the majority; which brings us back to the undeniable fact that there are far too many good people in America who are not good citizens, who are too busy to be good citizens. But this is why politicians consider a personal letter from a constituent the view of thousands of those who do not write. This should give you some perception of why it is so critical that you do write those letters.

Charles Dickens was a superb essayist and my favorite is his essay: Night Walks. He describes his wandering about parts of London at night and observes how so many suffer, especially children, from unjust laws, laws especially designed to make the rich richer, and the poor poorer.

We could walk the streets in any major city of America (if we dared do so) and see the same things Dickens observed in England during his era. We could travel to Appalachia and see the same conditions of extreme and cruel poverty. Whether in Watts or Atlanta you can, as I have, observe people urinating and defecating in public, you can see the protective sheet metal on doors, rusting and corroded from people urinating in doorways.

But our Founding Fathers and men like Dickens, Emerson and Thoreau, women like Margaret Fuller, would be quick to point out the fact that when a society fails in good citizenship, unjust and unwise laws that create an immoral and deteriorating society are the natural result. And it doesn't take genius to either recognize or figure this out. But if it takes genius in leadership to move a society in the direction of good citizenship, perhaps that is where we are deficient. No one is likely to accuse the present leadership of America of genius; quite the contrary.

It has been known throughout history that to be both ignorant and free is an impossibility. Given this fact, what would any rational person make of the fact that the literacy rate of Massachusetts in 1799 was greater than it is in 1999? A historian would immediately call attention to the emphasis placed on reading in Massachusetts, and elsewhere, in 1799 which was necessary in order for people to read the Bible and Pilgrim's Progress, the two primary textbooks of early America. Our early universities were training institutions for ministers and missionaries. And men like Cotton Mather.

But the educational insularity of early America was to be impacted by events in other parts of the world, particularly in France. As a result of world events like the French Revolution and scientific discoveries, America was to move steadily into another and much broader area of educational emphasis rather than that of the narrow one devoted to turning out ministers and missionaries. And men like Cotton Mather.

It should not be surprising that books would become the primary tools of education from earliest times. Reading was the single most important basis for the advancement of civilization. The churches maintained their power all during the Dark Ages by purposely keeping the common people ignorant and illiterate.

The comments of Benjamin Franklin concerning the importance of books to America are worthy of note. This wisest man in America at the time saw the need of public libraries. And a gentleman, a leader, was expected to have a distinguished library. But it must be noted that while most men would be judged by the books in their libraries, the exceptional contrarians such as John Adams, adjudged the most brilliant of all our presidents, should be kept in mind as well. I have always kept books with which I disagree for the same reason John Adams did.

My point in all of this is to call attention to the fact that America is fast becoming an illiterate nation. Americans seem too busy to read and they are too busy to be good citizens. And if a people cannot be both ignorant and free, with this trend of illiteracy Americans are fast becoming too busy to be free!

While education has never been a guarantee of individual success, the lack of education is a reliable predictor of being unsuccessful. And the lack of education can most certainly predict the doom of a nation. A lack of education leads to many hurtful things. For example, is it important to know that the venerated General Robert E. Lee proved a bad general due to his Old Dominion mind-set?

Of so many thousands of examples, why choose this one? Because the name Robert E. Lee is well known and he is well thought of. Certainly he was an exceptional man, an exceptionally good man, an exceptionally well educated man. After the war, he became president of Washington College.

When the word gentleman comes to mind, Robert E. Lee is right there as well. But he had deep prejudices that marred his thinking, prejudices that, in spite of his being a good man, a gentleman, a well-educated man, led to his making unwise decisions. Lee, like most of those with his background, believed in the righteousness of his cause. Because of this, and because he was a deeply pious and devout man, he believed he could call on God to make up for his own faulty thinking and errors of prejudice. And this proved disastrous.

It was his religious prejudices that prevented Lee from being a truly educated man. If he had had the benefit of a more open mind, the benefit of being more widely read in those books which jarred with his own prejudices, how different things might have been for him; and for the course of American history.

I find I cannot mention Lee without commenting on General Thomas Jonathan (Stonewall) Jackson, also known as Deacon Jackson (derisively by his detractors) and Holy Jack (reverently by his friends) as well as General Lee's Good Right Arm. Jackson is judged the ablest of the generals of the war. And no prominent figure of the Civil War was more devoted to children, wife, and God. It has been well said that if Jackson were to walk into a room filled with adults and one small child, he would go immediately to the child, pick it up and love it.

I do wonder, since Jackson fought for the wrong cause, if God Himself didn't have a hand in his being cut down (mistakenly by his own men) during the middle of the war in order to spare Jackson the personal hurt and calumny of carrying on in such a cause? I do wonder if God does not sometimes remove those who sincerely love and reverence Him, as Jackson most assuredly did, but who because of hurtful prejudices do both themselves and God harm by continuing in such prejudices?

If we try to excuse prejudice by using the term confused, we might be more charitable of the errors of belief on the part of those like Lee and Jackson. And there is no misunderstanding the history of America during this period; the Civil War was fought over the issue of slavery. The politics of State's Rights, the right of secession, was fought in the various legislatures; but the fundamental and divisive issue of slavery was always there and the evil of slavery made conflict inevitable.

Righteous judgment cannot be divorced from the time and circumstances of events. So it is that we cannot make men like Lee and Jackson evil because they held to an evil belief such as God's approval of slavery. The doctrine of God's approval of slavery was easily supported through recourse to the Bible, both the Old and New Testaments, by its adherents; just as the doctrine of the inherent inferiority of women is. And both Lee and Jackson were firm believers in Biblical inerrancy.

Both of these most honorable men, however, lacked wisdom, the kind of wisdom the world has always lacked. And in their defense, it has to be admitted that many churches of the time supported slavery and preached a gospel of God's approval of both slavery and the war to protect it. But there has never been a lack of such prophets preaching in defense of evil and approving it with a text. Human history is replete with instances of people killing one another with God's supposed approval, even brother against brother, in His name. The killing goes on today in the name of God.

And until wisdom prevails, until people finally admit such things cannot possibly have the approval of God but are the product of ignorant and prejudicial, superstitious beliefs and myths, the killing will continue. Nor will the world lack those with no belief in or fear of God who will take full advantage of this kind of ignorance, even fomenting it to suit their own agenda of evil.

The issue of freedom from the tyranny of a Federal government, a legitimate issue, is on the side of those like Lee and Jackson. And most Southerners of the time, if asked, would have made this issue the focus of the war, not the issue of slavery. The tragedy of the war, the confusion of men like Lee and Jackson, if you will, was the fact that the two issues of Federal abuse and slavery could not be separated at the time. Given time, slavery would have died a natural, but slow, economic death. But the circumstances, brought about by unwise choices, did not allow of this time being granted.

If we should have learned anything from the Civil War it should have been this: If America was to be a nation, rather than a collection of states with oft time contradictory and conflicting interests, it would have to be a nation united on the basis of a generally agreed national ethical morality. And this was clearly not possible as long as slavery existed in America.

But because of the murder of Lincoln and the actions of evil men intent on punishing and plundering a defenseless South following his murder and the end of the war, this agreement did not come about. And as a result of this failure, wisdom once more proved unattainable for America. And I won't excuse good men and women for the part they played, and still play, in this monumental failure. Like Lee and Jackson, one does not have to be a scoundrel to be wrong, even wrong in conscience.

Virtually no one could ever fault either Lee or Jackson on the basis of their sense of honor and morality. Their lives were living proof of their indisputable honor and morality. But they were wrong. And they were wrong to the point of actually supporting and promoting evil. And that in the name of God, a God they trusted implicitly and in whom they most sincerely believed with all their being and wished to serve with all their might!

Will people give even their lives in support of a lie? Yes. History is replete with such instances. But they die needlessly for such lies because of a lack of wisdom. Wisdom dictates that there is a human family. And harm cannot be done to one part of that family without it impacting the other parts. You simply cannot harm and degrade one part without it harming and degrading you as well. Whether in the name of God or some supposed superiority of race or gender, whether in support of slavery or ethnic cleansing, the harm done one part of the family cannot fail to diminish those who believe the lie, for cause and effect are immutable in this instance above all others.

So we know that good people can do evil, supposing themselves doing so in a righteous cause, even in the cause and name of God Himself. As a result of this fact, I find my greatest battle for the Amendment is the fight with good people, trying to convince good people that this battle for the children cannot be won in the name of their peculiar, particular, religious or political beliefs, but only on the basis of their recognizing it as the right and wise thing to do irrespective of their personal beliefs and prejudices.

The point should now be obvious. This will require real education. And real education is not gained from the reading of books alone. Nor can it be gained by reading books that only agree with your own point of view. But neither can it be gained by being ignorant of books, by not reading books, and at that, the reading of a great many books of great diversity, trade books and academic in many different fields, which is absolutely essential to a real education.

Now, if Americans are too busy to read, especially to read good books which would disabuse them of much muddy, fallacious thinking, if they are too busy to be good citizens, too busy to write their legislators and be politically active, it follows that they are too busy to be free; which brings me to the further point that we get, and deserve, the kind of leadership we actively support. If the good majority allows an immoral and corrupt minority to lead, this can only come about because the good majority is too busy to be properly enlightened and involved in the political process. And the Devil wins by default.

Benjamin Franklin, John Adams and Thomas Jefferson; brilliant men but they should have paid more attention to Thomas Paine and Mary Wollstonecraft. Certainly John Adams should have heeded his much beloved Abigail and emphasized her views when she gently chided him about the need to remember women in the crafting of the U.S. Constitution.

But the wisdom of Franklin, Adams and Jefferson did not avail in respect to slavery, and it is most doubtful it could have availed on both the issues of slavery and women being addressed at the time, the failure to do so being grave faults in our Constitution. And though Negroes and women were eventually enfranchised, this failure has still not been rectified on the basis of real, accepted equality.

These great men and women in our early history as a nation would be the first to agree that putting it on paper doesn't make it real. But as a nation of law it must start there, as with the proposed Amendment, and the reality comes with the actual acceptance and practice of equality.

My knowledge of history and literature leads me to believe that anyone can deduce the distinct failure of wisdom throughout our own American history despite the fact that many things were done well. But the distinct failure of so many things that began well, which were so well intended and seemed so right when begun, only to degenerate and at times turn out disastrously, should prove my contention.

A common expression is that of: Those who fail to learn from history are doomed to repeat it. And so it has proven to be throughout all of history.

While those thinking themselves wise will nod their heads in the affirmative, true wisdom, the kind of wisdom that would not doom humanity to repeating the mistakes of the past, the kind of wisdom that would lead to world peace, remains elusive.

But it does not take wisdom to recognize the fact that if all human beings were accepted of equal value regardless of beliefs, race or gender, peace would be the result. This is knowledge, not wisdom. It will take wisdom for this knowledge to become the reality in fact and in practice. And this is not going to come about until men and women are in fact of equal value on the basis of honoring the compatibility of differences, and children become the priority of nations.

Real education, I believe, holds the key to wisdom. And by real education I mean education that is devoid of prejudice. For it is ignorant prejudice alone that prevents real equality between people, between men and women, that prevents nations from making children their priority. And real education, the learning of factual knowledge then applying that learning, I believe, would lead to wisdom and dispel this darkness of ignorant prejudice which has been the common plague of humanity throughout all of history.

While it is quite evident that books are a vital part of education, some of them have been the Devil's tool in the past and continue to be such today. I believe it is very important to education that people be the contrarians John Adams was, that people read widely including books that are at variance with their own views.

As to being the Devil's tool, one only has to consider that writing and books have promoted great evil as well as great good for humanity. Since writing and books were under the control of leaders who had their own agendas, we struggle to find the facts among the myths in the earliest of recorded history.

And once more, the choices that are made which seemed right but were not wise make themselves known. And once those unwise choices begin to exert their influence through circumstances, expediency rather than wisdom becomes the operant though the chance for peace is, as usual, forsaken, even unattainable, in the process.

One of the most troubling facts of modern times is the growing popularity of things like astrology. But this is an indicator of people becoming more and more gullibly ignorant and illiterate; and, therefore, more and more superstitious thus making them all the more vulnerable to the unscrupulous who are always more than willing to shear such sheep. The Extraterrestrial Church of God has arrived together with my prophesied Hi-tech and Designer Religions. Who can condemn AT&T and MTV for getting in on the act when, as those who commonly embezzle money from the schools because it's so easy to do say, "The money was just there!"

Since books and writing were early used to promote points of view under the control of leaders with agendas, it isn't surprising that such leaders would be described as gods (and prophets and judges) with god-like characteristics. That this mode of writing, once in the hands of common people, was used in promoting religious and political views which degenerated into blatant propaganda is not surprising either.

It is the gravest of errors to real education, however, to ascribe facts to what are obvious fictions simply on the basis of antiquity; as Lincoln told his wife: People do lie. I would add, that people have always lied, and often with the best of intentions. And there has never been any lack of people willing to believe lies as opposed to truths which jarred with their accepted, and chosen, prejudices.

Recently the question of Thomas Jefferson's relationship with Sally Hemings has received a lot of attention. And well it should if we are really interested in the truth. But as is often the case, controversy rages about events of a mere two hundred years past, even fifty years past, and yet people are so gullible as to believe that the truth is known of events two and three thousand years past simply on the basis of their being written in books like the Bible, as valuable as the book is to legitimate studies. However, this can lead to naiveté at best or prejudicial ignorance to the point of maliciousness!

I foresee a time, provided humanity does not destroy itself first, when people will believe, as facts, fables derived from the tabloids and movies like Star Wars. One only has to consider how many people are taken in by films like Chariots of the Gods and the fact that books about angels are the best sellers. There is a growing population of people who believe what they see on TV, stories like those of The X-Files and Star Trek. Our children are being force-fed on a daily basis fiction that will undoubtedly be a part of their belief system as they grow.

But good books, scholarly books, should disabuse of ignorance and prejudice. The problem, however, is that such books are not what people are reading. As a result, as Americans we are on the road to a thorough-going and destructive illiteracy, and becoming a nation more given to an ignorant belief in space aliens and vampires on the basis of movies and TV rather than education on the basis of sound scholarship and facts.

I would submit without any fear of contradiction that no greater gathering of real genius and personal character and honor would be found in all of history than that represented by the collection of the Founding Fathers of America. But whatever favorite you may choose among all of these, you wouldn't find a single one who would claim perfection as a human being. Such perfection is the sole purview of those who believe and perpetuate myths, whether of a religious or political bias.

But, concerning the myths of films, at the same time so much of the energy of Hollywood seems intent on perpetuating religious and science fiction mythology the real facts of history are ignored. And the ignorance of Americans deepens. One cannot help but wonder when Thurgood Marshall's relationship with J. Edgar Hoover will be made into a movie and how Hollywood will interpret this.

But the vital place of film in recording history cannot, and must not, be ignored. In the recent C-SPAN series on our Presidents, I found it interesting that panelists were being asked about their favorite films concerning American history. One professor of history from Harvard said the film Glory was his favorite depicting the Civil War. The film "Amistad" was mentioned by some. Even a W.C. Fields film was mentioned by one panelist.

Several very well educated men and women on the various panels made references to popular films, incorporating these films into their remarks about subjects of academia. I expect this will happen more and more often in gatherings of intellectuals. The power of film should not be underestimated.

Given the shame attaching to our present Congress and White House, don't you wonder how Civics is being taught in our schools? How will recent events shape courses in civics? Will the teachers themselves (not to mention parents) be too cynical to try to motivate our children to be truthful and civic minded? And how will the course textbooks be handling the subject? This may be a moot point if TV and films supplant books in our classrooms.

This only points up the dumbing down of America, aided by a lack of motivation to become truly educated. Rather than books, our children are far more likely to depend on TV and films for their knowledge of history. And all too often popular TV and films, like many books, made or written for profit or a personal agenda. After all, the propaganda value of these things is real and powerful. This is one of the reasons perverts cry about freedom when it comes to pornography and abortion. Both of these issues suit the agenda of perverts.

Recently, the beautiful women of Hollywood gathered to protest the female apartheid cruelty of the Taliban in Afghanistan directed at women there, including the extreme, reprehensibly barbaric cruelty of female circumcision (not that male circumcision is any less cruel, barbaric or reprehensible). I was glad to see this protest by the femmes of Tinseltown. The barbarism of the Taliban is something that needs to be confronted by all those considering themselves civilized.

Jay Leno was right: God is not going to be impressed by his collection of cars and motorcycles. And I don't think He was impressed by Whoopee

Goldberg's one hundred plus carat diamond ring (yes, I watched the awards, one of the high points for me being Hanks not getting an Oscar).

But men like the Pope, ministers, priests, mullahs, and rabbis refuse to accept their responsibility for promoting prejudicial hatreds. They are all, like Lee and Jackson, going about doing good in the name of God and like the story of Pilate, try to wash their hands of the blood that stains their hands no matter how they try to cleanse them.

Whether by design or force of circumstances and bad choices, America is in fact becoming a two-tier system of ever increasing disparity between the rich and poor, the educated and the uneducated, which is leading to a ruling elite of those with superior education. And will this ruling elite be any better than that of the Dark Ages of religious power? It would be foolish to believe that the technocrats, nerds if you will, will inherit the earth. The inheritors will continue to be those who are able to enforce their own will over others who are too busy, and ignorant, to be free.

Over the past two years that I have been working for the Amendment, I have discovered how very successful it is in getting people to commit to points of view they would never have articulated otherwise. It has also proven an excellent mechanism to get people to evaluate their real prejudices and beliefs, to think through issues to which they may never have previously given much, or any, thought. It certainly had this effect on me.

What I feel constrained to say now will not be very welcome by good people. But it is nothing profound; only true: The lesser of evils is still evil. Now while people, all people, nod their heads in the affirmative, this is where I get into trouble in spite of the truth of this.

The cruel and ignorant barbarism of the Taliban against women is easily recognized and condemned by any calling themselves civilized. But that of the Pope and other Christian leaders is not so easily recognized because it is far less cruel and far more subtle; but evil nevertheless. You undoubtedly, as me, hate bullies. But how many of you see the Pope or other Christian leaders as bullies? Still, that is exactly what they are. And they are notorious for their bullying tactics against women.

The beliefs of Lee and Jackson concerning slavery may be attributed to confusion, to the circumstances of birth, etc., but nevertheless evil. If I point out the fact that evil remains evil in spite of mitigating circumstances, this is only accepted until I pick on those like Mohammed, Lee, Jackson, the Pope, Falwell, etc. At such a point, most good people close their ears and condemn me.

It is only for the sake of the truth that I do this. I know this new way for humankind via the Amendment cannot succeed if any group of good people tries to use it to advance their own religious or political agenda. This has made it of absolute necessity that I make myself clear in respect to what I believe would be an evil if any group should try to make the Amendment their peculiar banner.

The evil of slavery was common to good men throughout history including our own. As detractors are quick to point out, Washington and Jefferson owned slaves. These were good men who practiced evil. I am able to make distinctions on the basis of religion because I am very well educated in comparative religions and their histories, most particularly Christianity in all its various forms, both Catholic and Protestant.

Several obvious points present themselves. One of the most important is that a person chooses what he wishes to believe. And such choices do not make the person necessarily either good or evil, but may well cause the person unknowingly and in all good conscience to support and participate in evil.

From the earliest poets and philosophers the ideal has been expressed that goodness and virtue were derived from treating others as you would be treated. This has been popularized as The Golden Rule, which many mistakenly attribute as unique to Jesus, but has a history of much greater antiquity, as scholars well know.

I will never forget an account by a reporter during the Russian invasion of Afghanistan. A Russian soldier had been captured and was summarily shot by two Afghans. When the reporter asked why he had been shot, the Afghans simply replied: Because he wasn't a Moslem.

That was their justification for murder. They had made choices that caused them to support and participate in evil. Were they evil men? Probably not; but neither were they virtuous men. What is lacking in those who are good but support and participate in evil is virtue, that real virtue which is an integral part of true wisdom.

Wisdom dictates that you do not do evil in order to promote good. Wisdom dictates that the end does not justify the means. But humanity historically lacking in true wisdom always finds itself doing evil in the name of good or because of expediency of circumstances brought about by unwise (un-virtuous) choices. It is obviously no mark of virtue when any group of people chooses to think of themselves as being superior on the basis of religion, race or gender. While one culture may excel another in many ways, such as its system of government, this is not the same thing as believing oneself superior by some assumed divine decree or accident of birth.

I was dancing with a beautiful girl the other night when she hugged me close and whispered, "You're a nice man, Sam." I am always taken aback at such compliments. Not because I don't know I am a nice man; I am. And I know this. I don't kick the cat or use vulgar language; I am kind to children and courteous to women. I am civilized and always put the toilet seat down.

So I am going to deny myself the traditional self-deprecating remarks with which one attempts, and always fails, to appear properly humble in the face of such compliments.

No, what takes me aback is the fact that I know who and what I am. And when receiving such a compliment a host of things, many not so nice, immediately flood my mind. That is human; that is human nature. But since confronting myself on the basis of the Amendment, I have discovered so many errors and prejudices in my own thinking that a compliment like that of this girl's makes me uneasy now. And I start reviewing all the things I wish I could share with those like this girl.

Most of these things have to do with what I have learned about virtue and wisdom, things I had presumptuously thought I knew but did not, things I fervently wish I had learned in time to teach my own children when they were growing up. But until I confronted the Amendment, it wasn't even possible for me to learn these things. And now, it is my task to attempt to teach others. But when I view the enormity of the task, knowing how many good people are alienated in the process of such instruction, it would be easy to give up.

One of the most compelling reasons for my wanting to give up is the fact that I really am a nice man. And as a nice man, I could have brought this girl home with me. I certainly wanted to. Nice or not, I'm still a man. But the whole scene unfolded before me. There would eventually be the exchange of ideas and the whole thing would fall apart. And I would no longer be thought such a nice man because the Amendment would force conflict with this nice girl, a conflict I would rather not have happen. I would far rather she continues to think of me as a nice man.

My recent thoughts on the film Pretty Woman have a lot to do with this as well. I think I understand what virtue consists of. And I have come to understand and appreciate how misunderstood it is, how greatly I misunderstood it and failed to appreciate it. This is why I can say that men like Washington, Lee and Jackson were good men, but they were not virtuous men in the sense that virtue is an integral part of wisdom, that wisdom which derives from factual knowledge leading to perfect love, compassion, and an instinctive hatred of evil.

Few people consider the fact that it was a drawing away from the myths and superstitions of religion that gave America a running start on the kind of creativity that was a hallmark of our early beginnings as a nation. People who did not suffer the strictures of religion characterized Yankee ingenuity, for example the kind of Benjamin Franklin.

The very age of the Renaissance and Enlightenment which gave rise to so much inventiveness and creativity could never have come about without courageous men and women who began to question the myths and superstitions

211

of religion as opposed to the truth of God. But as I point out in my book "Hey, God!" the fatal flaw of dualism in religion proved insurmountable for the greatest writers and thinkers. I never realized in the writing of the book the part it would play in arriving at the Amendment. But once I had taken the position that it was not reasonable to make God responsible for both good and evil, another way, a way that provoked some original thinking about the subject unfettered by the ideas of the past, led to the originality of the Amendment.

I was blissfully unaware of this as I wrote the book. In fact, it wasn't until the information I had covered in all my books came together that the Amendment seemed to sprout instantly in full bloom. I am forced to admit that one of the many reasons I first rejected the Amendment was the fact that I early recognized it would force me to take a position in opposition to so many good people, people I loved and would lose as friends.

It is bad enough that I can't bring a girl home with me from a dance because of the Amendment. Maybe if I had been able to foresee this... But I didn't. And now it's too late. I am well practiced in the civilized lies men and women tell each other, I know the game very well. But one look at the sign on my house: IT SHOULDN'T HURT TO BE A CHILD!, one look at the Memorial Wall of Shame with all the names of those murdered children, and that would probably be the end.

Got off the track with that; but it reminds me that out of the thousands of individual facts of history, there remain organized conclusions that can make sense of these multifarious facts. And this has been the goal, largely unrecognized by myself, of my writing over the years.

Again, it has been an attempt on my part, apparently, to get away from what I must have unconsciously recognized as the danger of the inventive exclusivity of particulars to the hurt of the whole even as I practiced this exclusivity. So much so that I would have agreed with the old Virginian who, when informed that Adams and Jefferson had both died on the same day, exclaimed: "It's a damned Yankee trick!"

Slavery is evil. It has always been evil. And many good people have supported and participated in this evil. The genius of intellect and diversity that was Thomas Jefferson did not preclude his participation in this evil though he personally disagreed with it, yet it may have been the seed of America's eventual demise.

The Founding Fathers like Jefferson began with a given evil: the fact of slavery. In spite of the fact that we won the Revolutionary War, though by attrition and the difficulty England had fighting a war across an ocean and not by battles we won slavery presented a most difficult question. What to do with the slaves if slavery were abolished?

The usual selfishness of economics had brought slavery to America; but it would have been far easier, it would have been wise, to have dealt with this issue at the time of the Founding Fathers rather than later by a Civil War. It would have been far better to have done so at the founding of our nation than what we have to deal with today as a result of this failure.

Armchair quarterbacking? 20/20 hindsight? All true. Equally true is the fact that we can all think, and choose, that which seems right which is not wise. And we are going to have to do better than this!

CHAPTER TEN

It's only a rumor, I'm sure, that a new TV channel out of L.A. is going to be devoted to nothing but Felony Evading. With so many drivers wanting their moment of fame by leading police on freeway chases, it does make sense, I admit. And with the voracious appetite of TV producers and viewers for every kind of cockamamie material, who knows?

This popular L.A. sport has spawned another rumor making the rounds that Felony Evading is to be included as an Olympic Sport in the near future. All things considered, since it is further rumored that all the necessary bribes have already been paid to Olympic Committee members, the only problem I see with this is finding places with enough roadway.

Some people wonder at my criticism of the colleges and universities. But a large part of the justification of this criticism is summed up by one of America's preeminent humorists, Bill Cosby, who said: The nice thing about colleges and universities is the fact that they have nothing to do with real life. Bill must be reading TAP.

***

I Don't Know. This is my most oft-used phrase. Why? Because in most cases, I just don't know. Sometimes, it is a case of not knowing whether the girl wants to dance with you (just thought I'd throw that one out before I get into the really heavy stuff).

There you are on a Friday or Saturday night; the band is playing a beautiful, romantic ballad and you really like this one girl and want to dance with her. And, since you know her, you believe she wants to dance with you. But there's one slight problem. You don't really know. And if you're sensitive to her feelings, you don't want to put her on the spot. And to really complicate things, just before she came in, another girl had come in and taken a seat next to you. She wants to dance with you. Talk about a no-win situation. Damned if you do and damned if you don't. In the worst case, you and the girl you really want both wind up dancing with other people rather than each other.

Not exactly an earth-shattering scenario, you say. And, in most instances, you would be absolutely correct. But it is real life and this is what captures my own heart, mind and soul as a writer; real people and real life, especially how people, even good people, hurt one another and themselves in so many cases because they just don't know. And, in so many similar situations and circumstances, neither do I.

But, I remind myself, I do know a lot of hurt could be avoided if people had the courage to be really honest with themselves and with one another. Sometimes it is a matter of pride. You don't want that other person to know how much you really care. Happens all the time. But pride of this kind is always destructive and many a real romance has withered and died before it was given a chance simply because of this.

My "Birds" book materialized from just these kinds of experiences, from the years of playing, singing and dancing in so many different clubs and honky tonks. In few other environments do you experience such a real slice of life at its fullest and most intimate. I have often said it would do political, religious and education leaders a lot of good for them to spend some time in just this kind of environment if they really care about people and really want to know how best to serve their needs.

Looking back, I realize I have had one of the most unusual lives imaginable, by birth and by circumstances and choices which have led to my being involved in so many and varied relationships and activities. Many who have read my books or seen my resume have questioned how one man of my brief life span could have had the time for all these things. Don't think I don't wonder at it myself. Still, it is recorded fact.

But driven by insatiable curiosity about a multitude of things, not only seeking specific answers to minutia, but ultimate answers to the origin and meaning of life, has made my life an unsurpassed journey of exploration, an exploration exceeding in interest and excitement anything else I can imagine. Some philosophers have described this as a seeking for truth, a seeking for God. In my case, God was always there. And this has ever been a foundational truth for me.

This has saved me a lot of time in the seeking process while still mindful of the fact that my belief in God is just that: a belief. I don't know. That I believe I know but don't know is a paradoxical statement; and one that remains unresolved in all of humanity which keeps it in the realm of philosophy in spite of the many and varied claims of certitude.

Still, I believe in God, I believe He is the Creator and our Heavenly Father. And because I believe these things, I also believe God hears and answers prayer, among other things. Prayer is one of those things that are quite natural to all human beings. Perhaps this is one of the proofs, albeit totally subjective, that God is there for all of us. But I am quick to point out as well that I do not believe God is religious. I have a sign in my office that reads:

God is welcome here: Religion is not!

It is my belief in God that helps me to deal with those things that often threaten to overwhelm me. And it is my belief in God that eventually caused me to reject religious orthodoxy and became heterodox. While I believe it is absolutely essential that God be honored and reverenced in our lives, that our children be taught this, the leadership of America has failed to do so. And, too often, when God is acknowledged, people try to tie Him to their own peculiar religion or church and thereby make Him a religious figure rather than what He really is, our Heavenly Father. And by this phrase, I mean God our Creator and the Heavenly Father of all people regardless of their belief system. It is, after all, religion that divides people, not God nor a real belief and faith in God.

It was this rejection of religion on my part that led to my critique of To Kill A Mockingbird, which I describe as a personal statement of faith. I believe it would benefit anyone to write out such a personal statement of faith. Looking at ideas in written form is always helpful. To this extent, everyone should be a writer.

But the critique was something more than a statement of faith. Those who read it for themselves will determine what this something more is. I have given several draft copies to friends for their input and have gotten many different reactions to it. But one thing seems a constant: No one yet has failed to have a very strong reaction to the critique. Some are saying it is the best thing I have ever written.

Well, perhaps they are right. But it wasn't written for personal praise, it was written for adults on behalf of children. It has caused several people to read, or re-read, the novel. And this is good. Some who had not seen the film have rented it and watched it. Many that had seen the film years ago watched it once more. The critique brought out things many people had not noticed in the novel. Especially those things that focused on the children and things it had taken me years to see and understand myself.

But having finished the critique and awaiting responses to it, I needed to turn my attention to those things of vital importance which the critique addressed in my own life as well as the lives of others. And nothing is of such importance in my own life as mixing it up with real life, with real people.

As a result, this issue of TAP is reminiscent of the Birds book. I believe it is so because of how much it took out of me to do the critique of To Kill A Mockingbird. It went through several drafts over a period of months, including proofing and comments by some who suffered with me in the process of birthing the thing. And I have had to depend on the comments of others that were gracious enough to read the rough drafts and provide their input. But I couldn't have imagined the many sleepless nights, how painful and emotionally demanding and draining such a thing as the writing of the critique was going to be.

And once completed, I had to get away. I was totally exhausted from the months of unanticipated, often anguished, labor that went into this kind of work. And where was I to go to get away? To the music and dancing in the bars and clubs where I have so many friends, the environment I know so well; filled with the stories from which the Birds book materialized.

As a result, this issue of TAP has some of these stories. For a writer, the people and the stories may be similar in most cases, but for a poet the people always make the ordinary extraordinary. And while the stories have a sameness due to the commonality of the human condition, the individuals involved make them different in every case. Ultimately, it is my interest in people that leads me to write of their joys and tragedies, to try to make sense of what often seems insensible. And sometimes, I am successful.

An old friend comes to the Valley frequently to check on his father who is ninety-two. This friend has worked in the film industry for years. He has worked with men of unquestioned artistic genius; but he is also an alcoholic. But this hasn't lessened his capacity for the work. He is in great demand by the major studios because of his own extraordinary talents. I say talents because while this friend is brilliant and talented, he is not a genius, as he himself is quick to point out. But, as I said, he has worked with genius and recognizes it.

We were in one of the local bars (where else?). My friend was concentrating his efforts on getting drunk. One of the curious things about drunks is that they are the most honest people you will ever meet while they are drunk. We were discussing my critique of To Kill A Mockingbird which he had read, and the conversation became one of the most unusual I have ever had with him.

"Sam", he said, "you are a genius."

I wasn't sure where he was going with this. And having no grounds upon which to modestly dispute his keen and perceptive statement, I listened because he wasn't yet too drunk to make sense.

"What would you do with the money if I were to give you $10,000 cash?"

This was a pleasant thought. But I couldn't honestly answer the question. I knew he was serious. And my silence was more an acknowledgment of the seriousness of his offer than anything else; especially since he knows I don't have any need of his money.

Noting my silence, he continued.

"As I see it", he said, "you will eventually do one of three things. You will kill yourself, you will become a demented recluse, simply withering away in this backwater of Bodfish, or you will get the platform you need from which to speak and save the world which is exactly what you are aiming at, and I would like to help you. Besides, I'd rather have you as a live friend rather than a dead one."

I was really touched by his genuine concern for me and his wanting to help. But I couldn't accept his offer. As I explained it to him, I purposely do not solicit or accept money from people, including friends, for my work on behalf of children. Such things have a nasty way of coming back to bite you and I cannot afford to have my own motives called into question. And nothing calls motives into question faster than money. He readily understood and accepted this explanation.

But do I want to save the world? I have questioned this for quite obviously good reasons. My problem with this is the word want. I have never thought of what I am doing regarding children and the Amendment as wanting to save the world. My focus has been on children, on doing what is right and necessary for children, not on wanting to save the world. But I can't deny that in the process of saving the children, it logically follows that the world is to be saved as a consequence.

Only an egotistical fool tries to take credit for the accidents of birth such as genius. I may be mad in a sense; but while my ego is healthy enough, I am not such a fool. Besides, my own genius is hardly something I would credit as a particularly happy accident of birth because I can't ignore how closely genius is allied to madness. There is a very fine line dividing the two. But as long as I can determine where that line is, I know I haven't yet crossed it.

This line might be viewed as a kind of sobriety test for sanity. Like my continuing to be entranced by all of God's marvelous, though often inconvenient, creation. As long as I can take joy in, and marvel at, the stars and flowers, a rainbow or the flight of a butterfly, as long as I take joy in sharing such things with others, I know I'm still ok. Genius is rare; and as a consequence, largely misunderstood. So I ask the reader's indulgence as I take some time to explore the phenomenon in respect to my friend's remarks especially.

It is impossible to ignore the difficulties associated with genius, including some of its peculiarities. And my friend is intelligent and sensitive enough to appreciate the dilemmas and possibilities this presents in my case. Especially the loneliness associated with genius.

My genius is of a most singular and peculiar kind, a kind that only people like my friend recognize. My being a writer compounds it; and, as such, leading to my being a quiet man living in my head, largely alone with my thoughts. It isn't genius as most perceive such. It isn't the kind of Newtonian genius that results in new theories of particle physics or quantum mechanics.

It is a genius of seeing things like the broad vistas of human potential, for example, which most see only in the narrowest way.

It is also a genius of connecting seemingly unrelated and simple things to a far more complex pattern and making sense of them, of seeing order in seeming chaos. This also enables me to recognize flaws in what some think to be order and to separate belief from knowledge. This last, especially, has proven to be one of the most vital elements in my life.

There is no denying the necessary, and essential, orderly mathematical precision required in such things, just as it is needed in the minds of great composers and artists. The great principles governing order in all things are necessary to all workings of genius; including that of the poet/philosopher's.

But I have been most understandably reluctant to accept my genius because of the obvious megalomaniacal implications. After all, anyone who thinks he can either save or destroy the world, as my friend was quick to recognize in my case, has to be more than a few bricks shy of a whole load.

And that right there is a part of my singular genius. What genius, in the ordinary sense of the meaning of the word, is going to use such phraseology in the context of something so serious as saving the world? It is that kind of humor, and quite often a very dark humor, in the face of the most serious considerations that set me apart from most.

The very seeming simplicity of the Amendment should warn of its enormously profound legal and sociological implications. But, tragically, America has become such a non-thinking and illiterate, TV-captured and non-reading nation, that this profundity of the Amendment is lost too most. Consequently, most mistakenly see it as a simple thing.

The deceptive simplicity of To Kill A Mockingbird leads the majority of readers to miss the enormously profound truths Harper Lee presents. They are nearly subliminal. It took her genius to express these truths in such a manner. As a teacher, my critique was aimed at bringing these truths to light and give them fuller expression on behalf of children.

Since educating people to the complexities of the Amendment is an essential part of it becoming the Law of the Land, most of my time is devoted to this educational process. As time-consuming and difficult as this is, I know there is no short cut to the process. A very large part of the explanation of the Amendment is contained in my critique of To Kill A Mockingbird. A very intelligent and attractive woman recently told me: "Sam, I don't know anyone but you who would have the nerve to write a critique of this book (being a very forthright woman, she didn't actually say nerve but used a plural term descriptive of a particular and private part of the male anatomy)". She is intelligent and educated enough to know how seriously profound such a thing as the critique is, and was quite expressive of her sentiment regarding it.

I have come to depend on a lovely lady who does some of the proofing of my writing, to be my best and most honest critic. She is a real professional and doesn't spare me her red pen. When something I have written meets her approval, I know I have done a good job and it is ready for publication. So you can imagine how I must have felt when I saw her remark in one place of the critique: "Magnificent! This doesn't just fly; it soars!"

Some others, as I mentioned, claim the critique is the best thing I have ever written; while I am quite normal enough to be very far removed from being immune to praise of my work, this lovely lady's remark made me feel like I do when watching a child open a Christmas present. Money can never buy some things. It can't buy this kind of feeling.

For example, I recently gave a very beautiful girl a gift. It didn't cost much but it was exactly what she both needed and wanted. She hadn't been expecting anything from me of this nature and reacted like a little girl who had just opened a Christmas package. Money could never buy the feeling I had from her reaction to receiving this gift. Instantly, I realized God knew I needed the joy of this girl's obvious joy of receiving the gift. She had given me something far more precious than any amount of money could provide. And the memory of her joy in receiving the gift is mine forever! Few people would think of genius in such a way. But it is my singular kind of genius at work in such things. The following is another example of this genius:

In spite of appearances at times, I'm not really a fool when it comes to young women. I know my place and try to keep it. This isn't to say I'm afraid of embarrassing myself; I've done that countless times. Enough times to have gotten used to it and not take it personal.

While doing some music here in the Valley, my good friend Oscar who has a band and has been playing fiddle for many years was sitting with me during a break. "Sam", he said, "you know every beautiful girl in this Valley, don't you." Oscar had seen me with a few and while he slightly over-stated the case, I modestly confessed that I probably knew my share of them. However many that may be. It's a small Valley.

People often wonder why I embarrass myself in print by such things like Oscar's remark to me. It's really very simple. It's real life; these things happen in real life. That they happen to me doesn't make them any less real and to hide them would be dishonest.

For example, just the other night a fellow I have known for quite some time who has seen me with a few attractive girls walked up to me and said: I don't know whether it's your eyes or your money that gets to all these girls? He was more than a little crocked or he wouldn't have had the nerve to make such a comment. But as I pointed out earlier, drunks are often the most honest of people when they are drunk. But many people have commented on the characteristic of my eyes. Granted, most have been women and it was most unusual for a man to say anything about this.

Aside from being truthful about such things and telling stories on myself, even to my own embarrassment, I enjoy poking fun at myself. I am my own best source of both humor and embarrassment. God forbid I ever take myself so seriously that I fail to laugh at myself. And if, at times, I appear to flatter myself in spite of the truth of what I write, I more than make up for this by giving equal time to the embarrassing, even stupid, things of which I am just as guilty as any normal human being. Who of you will forget my telling of the time I absent-mindedly tried to put my broom in my refrigerator and put a cigarette out in my coffee instead of the ashtray? In short, I don't hide from myself. No poet worthy the name does. And like my friend Henry Thoreau said: I would not write so much of myself if I knew any other so well.

But concerning Oscar's remark, I do appreciate beauty and acknowledge it. And I do so on every occasion that permits within courteous and civilized limits. And I would be much less than human, much less a man, if I didn't admit to being pleased when in the company of a beautiful woman or I go into some bar or lounge and some attractive girl says to me, "Hi there, handsome." Now, those are words men would kill for. And I most certainly welcome them. What man wouldn't? But I'm old enough to have learned there is no age limit when it comes to caring or doing something simply because it is the right thing to do regardless of appearances. Even at the risk of making a fool of myself.

Being a song and dance man at heart, I still do occasional music at one of the local clubs or in the Old South Bay where my voice and clarinet are welcome by the bands that play in these places regularly, this by way of explaining that the music and dancing are still a large part of my life. And, sometimes, this gets me in trouble. But most of the time it is just good, clean fun.

Sitting one out so I can dance, the particular girl with whom I am dancing is a stunningly beautiful petite blonde and every guy in the joint is green with envy and hating me. As a mere man, this is particularly good for my male ego. Eat your hearts out fellows, I think to myself. They don't get any sympathy from me. But I know something they don't. The beautiful girl in my arms has AIDS.

I've known her for almost four years. She wasn't what you would call promiscuous, at least not by today's so-called standards. She had remained faithful to one guy for a long time until he took up with someone else. Lonely, depressed and self-destructive, she started hitting the bars and one thing led to another. The end result was AIDS.

She's only twenty-six; so very young to have to confront such a brutal thing in your life, to have to confront the end of your life. The band is playing one of those beautiful, romantic ballads as we dance. I draw her close in my arms and she hugs me as tightly as she can. We aren't really dancing now, we're just moving slowly and gently to the music while in each other's arms.

At one point, I draw away just enough to be able to look into her eyes and tell her, "This is magic. You are magic. This is the way it is supposed to be for a beautiful girl like you."

There are tears in her eyes as she comes back into my arms, hugs me tightly once more and presses her face to my chest. "Thank you, Sam," she whispers, "you're a kind man." I know she wants to say more. But that's all she can say. And that is more than enough.

The next day, I went to a florist shop and bought her a single red rose in a bud vase. The shop did a nice job of surrounding it with baby's breath and just enough greenery to set it off attractively. I left it for her in the club rather than taking it to her. I did this on purpose. The club owner knows the girl and knows she has AIDS. As I explained, I wanted everyone to see that rose with the girl's name prominently displayed on the card accompanying the rose. The club's owner understood and was more than willing to cooperate.

In my critique of To Kill A Mockingbird, I make the statement that I have lived too long and I know too much. Another very beautiful girl, having read the critique, called me and chastised me for this. She said I had too much to offer to say such a thing.

Maybe she's right. Naturally I would like to believe this. But I don't know. Once more. But I do know it's vitally important to let people like the girl with AIDS know they are loved and cared for in spite of this dread killer infecting their bodies. I also know how important it was for me to hold her tightly, for me to caress her hair and kiss her cheek as we danced. I know how important it was for me to make her feel like the beautiful girl she is in spite of the disease.

For me, this is my genius at work. Some would call it caring about others. But there is too little of this at work in the world today. So I credit it more to my peculiar genius than my caring. I have difficulty dealing with this subject of caring. I really don't know that I care. Still, for that matter, I can at least intellectually accept the possibility that those people are correct who accuse me of caring too much. But, once more, I don't know. But I do know that such questions automatically arise in the minds of those like me whose curiosity often transcends the easy way out of not questioning such things. People like me who live so much in their minds are never satisfied with simple answers to complex questions. Maybe it's in our genes.

I do know there is nothing wrong in wanting the flowers and praise before we die. And I know there is something definitely wrong with the people who withhold these things until it is too late. Of course, the music and the dance end and the grim realities are still there. This girl hasn't been able to escape these in spite of the magic of the moment or because of the rose. This is reality.

But the magic of the moment still lives and has a unique reality of its own. It is that kind of magic that can sustain us in the face of ugly realities. It is the kind of magic which can keep us hopeful that not everything we confront is the ugliness in our lives. It is the kind of magic that costs virtually nothing but is of inestimable value, priceless, and we all too often fail to make real in one another's lives while we still have time in season to do so. It shouldn't take genius to recognize such things. Then how is it, I ask myself, that so many people fail to recognize them and act on them? Can it be that so few people think of them? Or, even worse, that so few people really care?

Serendipity is defined as a happy and unexpected confluence of events. I like to think of it as the little miracles God is always doing in our lives that go unnoticed by us most of the time. Being in the right place at the right time often brings us opportunity to do the small things that can bring the needed joy in someone's life. But too often we miss these opportunities and, as a consequence, miss the opportunity for joy in our own lives.

I know many people who are bitter and cynical. One such man was telling me, bitterly complaining, how lonely he was and how no one cared about him. He is getting old enough to be concerned about his mortality and he fears dying alone. This is a man I know very well who has never learned to take advantage of the opportunities God has given him to bring joy into the lives of others. As a consequence, there is no joy in his own, only the fears that come from not having done what he could for others.

I got a call from the bartender where a friend and I shoot pool together. He said my friend had left something for me on his way back to Hollywood. It was a cuestick tip cutter/cleaner. Only when I held it in my hand did I remember mentioning to him that I needed one. It cost very little. But it meant a lot. There is much truth to the old adage: *It's not the gift, it's the thought.*

What a world of difference between the man who bitterly complained of no one caring about him, the man who failed to do the little things for others, and my friend. But it is a difference that makes a very real difference in the lives of people.

I had gone to one of the clubs for a pool tournament. After the game, I went to the bar to chat with the barmaid, a beautiful girl I have known for quite some time. It was going on 10:00 p.m. when another beautiful girl I had met some time past walked in. Seeing me at the bar, she came and sat down next to me. I introduced her to the barmaid and a few of the other people in the club. None had ever seen her before and the guys were immediately, and quite understandably, very attentive to her.

She was a very petite brunette with marvelous, deep gray eyes and the kind of face and figure that keeps men looking. Knowing I am a writer, she asked what I was presently working on, how the work for the Amendment was going, and so on. Since she is very intelligent, I was pleased to have her with me so we could talk. Her being beautiful didn't hurt either. I will always appreciate beauty, and in no form more than that of a beautiful woman.

One of my buddies seeing the girl and me in lively, stimulating conversation and wanting a closer introduction (and inspection) told the barmaid he was buying drinks for the girl and me. This is a favorite and time-honored ploy of Barroom Romeos in order to get acquainted with the girls. But my buddy, M---, was a really good sort and I most certainly didn't resent his maneuver. In fact, since M--- is one of the good guys, I was pleased with his thoughtfulness no matter the motive. Since I seldom drink, and never to excess, I had a cranberry juice and the girl had a Budweiser.

It was getting late and as much as I was enjoying the girl's company, I finally excused myself, said my good-byes, and took my leave of the club. One of the other girls had already come up to me and whispered in my ear in no uncertain terms, not knowing my relationship with the girl: "Look out Sam, this one's looking for a man." I appreciated her concern for me.

I was snugly in bed and sound asleep when the call from the barmaid awakened me at a little after 1:00 a.m. "Sam, forgive me for calling you but I didn't know what else to do. You're the only one who knows the girl you were talking to. Nobody here knows her and she's so buzzed-out she doesn't know what she's doing. She's fallen down once already and I'm afraid she's going to hurt herself. I don't want to call the cops and I really hate to ask but can you please come down and see what you can do with her?"

Well, I've had such wake-up calls before. And I immediately knew what the barmaid was talking about. You see, I knew the girl was a stone alcoholic and meth user. This was one of the reasons I had left the club, hoping some of the younger fellows like M--- would take the situation in hand and be able to handle the girl.

I groggily got out of bed, dressed hurriedly and drove back to the club. As I entered, the barmaid, looking enormously relieved told me the girl had become combative with the guys who had tried to either hit on her or help her. The girl was now sitting by herself, arms folded and staring into space. I sat down next to her, held her in my arms and tried to talk sense to her. She quite obviously couldn't be allowed to drive and if I didn't get her home, the barmaid would have no choice but to call the cops. The barmaid didn't want to have to do this to her and I sure didn't want her waking up in the morning in a strange bed with some strange guy from the bar.

In spite of the appearance of things, I knew the tragedy of this young girl's life. I knew of her being repeatedly molested as a little girl by a stepfather, which was the basis of her self-destructive behavior. I genuinely cared about her, about what happened to her, and she knew this. She, like so many others, deserved far better than the hand life had dealt her.

It took a while but I was finally able to get her to her vehicle, put her in it and get her keys. I was the only one who knew where she lived and one of the guys would follow us. After I got her home and put her to bed, he would bring me back to the club to get my car. It was 3:00 a.m. by the time I got home and was in bed again. But my mind wouldn't turn off. I know too many people like this girl. And it is things like this that make me think I have lived too long and I know too much.

Such things as the incident with this beautiful girl make it tough to get up in the morning and try to save the world. As I have said many times, it's not a job I would wish on anybody.

***

The following is taken from a chapter in the Birds book that deals with the impact of divorce on children. A small part of the particular chapter quoted here focused on the betraying heart and the part it plays in divorce. Of course, I selected this because of another beautiful girl who is suffering just this kind of betrayal in her own life. The sameness of the story, a tragic story, doesn't detract one iota from the personal tragedy of the girl. It never does.

I've known her for quite some time. In fact, I once told her I not only loved her, but that I really liked her. Her face became radiant at that comment. She's not only beautiful, but also a really decent and very intelligent person with so very much to offer a man. But, as too often happens, she had hooked up with some bum that had betrayed her for someone else; same song with countless verses.

I took the following part of the chapter from the Birds book and gave it to her. So many people have said it was of help to them that I decided, since excerpting it already to give the girl, to include it in this issue of TAP. I hope it will be of help to those who need it. And if so, I want my readers to know they have this beautiful girl to thank for my including it here at this time:

The basis of the Amendment for which I am fighting on behalf of children has its roots not only in any normal person's love of children but in my hatred of bullies, most especially my intense and perfect hatred of the most heinous and cowardly bully of all, the child molester. This cowardly monster, the

Samuel D. G. Heath, Ph. D.

spawn of Satan in human guise chooses his victims from the most defenseless and innocent in our society, the children.

There is no crime, or sin, if you will, so vile as the betrayal of innocence, the betrayal of the love and trust of a child. The child molester epitomizes the worst kind of bullying and cowardly behavior to be found in all of humanity.

But in my work with families and children, there are many other cowardly bullies I have had to confront as well. Among these are those adults who have betraying hearts, those adults who betray the love and trust of their marriage partner. It is this kind of betrayal that impacts so harshly not only on the one betrayed, but on the children as well. For in the larger sense, such betrayal of a marriage partner is a betrayal of the love and trust of the children involved as well.

As a professionally trained counselor working with troubled children in the schools, I always focused on the root cause of their problems that would invariably prove to be their home environment. Children from homes where they were loved and secure seldom had problems in school. Most people, I am sure, recognize why this is so. A good, loving home is the most essential thing in the life of any child.

Because of the absolute importance of a good home environment for children, much of my effort over the years on their behalf has had to do with examining the reasons for divorce that impacts so drastically and negatively on children. In many cases of failed marriages, I discovered what I came to call the betraying heart. You won't find this phrase in any college or professional text concerning psychological evaluations of inter-personal relationships. But it is there in many forms, disguised in clinical terms.

The root cause of a betraying heart is a thoroughgoing selfishness, which is evidenced by a lack of conscience. A man cheating on his wife or vice versa has no conscience in respect to the one who loves and trusts him or her. And it is a simple thing to betray love and trust. The one who loves and trusts is not suspicious. Real love and trust cannot exist in an atmosphere of suspicion.

Consider, for example, two people who are cheating on their mates. Can such people trust each other when they have betrayed their own wife or husband? Of course not. But no relationship can survive without love and trust. This brings me to what I have come to call the Professional Victim. Here again, you won't find this phrase in any textbook. It came to me through my work with battered women.

Many people wonder how women who have been beaten by men will keep returning to such a relationship. It is because such women have become Professional Victims. In such cases, many of these women actually believe they deserve such punishment. In the worst cases, they will actually encourage it.

Another class of Professional Victims among women is that of those who believe the man will change. This is very naive. Study after study has proven that once a man has beaten a woman, this pattern of behavior will keep repeating itself. In the worst cases, the woman, and even children, is eventually severely injured or even killed.

Studies of human behavior clearly show that anyone who believes a person who has betrayed love and trust will change is doomed to disappointment. The problem is that betraying heart. It isn't subject to change. It will continue to selfishly betray and use the one who loves and trusts, it will continue to be a user of those who become the Professional Victims because these victims are deluded that if they love and hope enough, the one they love will change. It isn't going to happen.

And why should the betrayers think they have to change as long as the victims keep telling them: Here I am. Use me. I'll keep forgiving you and taking you back. This is where the victim becomes what is called an enabler. The enabler, often because of low self-esteem, actually encourages the betrayer to continue in his or her pattern of being a user and betrayer of the victim. This repeating cycle only makes a bad situation worse as time passes.

Tragically, the victims seldom seek professional counseling in such cases. Only when the circumstances result in coming to the attention of some official agency such as Child Protective Services, the schools, or some police agency, will counseling become a part of seeking solutions to the problems.

But no amount of professional counseling will change the behavior of those people with betraying hearts. And, tragically once more, in too many cases the victim as enabler will continue a self-destructive course of encouraging the use and abuse of themselves in the vain hope that somehow, miraculously, the user and abuser will change.

The fact of low self-esteem on the part of the victims seems to escape them. Many even believe, like too many battered women, that they aren't worthy of any better treatment by such users and abusers in their lives. Many molested children believe they have done something wrong that encouraged their becoming victims. Many children in divorce think they are to blame for the separation of their parents. How do you convince the victims they are not to blame? You can't as long as they continue to blame themselves and excuse their betrayers.

If there is a single thing I wish I could get across to those who have been betrayed by someone they love and trust, it is this: Not all the effort, not all the love, prayers and hope in the world, can change a betraying heart. It often begins in childhood and carries into adulthood. It evidences itself by its selfishness, a selfishness rooted in the spoiled child who wants it all without giving in return.

There is no changing this kind of behavior. And anyone who believes otherwise is doomed to being a Professional Victim who does all the giving without receiving anything of value in return.

And one of the obvious things in such a relationship is the fact that once love and trust are betrayed, not all the loving forgiveness on the part of the one betrayed will ever restore that one thing so very vital to a real love relationship: Trust! Once betrayed, trust can never again be a part of a relationship. And no relationship worthy of the name, most particularly marriage, can be of any value or satisfaction without trust.

I was one of the founders of a treatment center for alcohol and drug addicts. I was professionally trained and credentialed for this kind of work. But I never really knew the whole story of addiction until I actually loved and lived with an alcoholic.

No one has any reason to have confidence in someone without the necessary experience as well as the professional qualifications. This was a hard thing for me to accept. But it proved to be true. You really do have to live it for it to be real and of benefit to others.

In the case of the betraying heart and being a Professional Victim, I have had the experience. I once believed that if I loved, hoped, and prayed enough, the person would change. She didn't. And the result was years of hurt and anguish for nothing of value in return, years which I will never be able to recover.

As vital as professional qualifications are, I think we all know there is nothing that can take the place of actual experience. We read the stories of beaten and molested children, for example. But until you have experienced such things, until you have seen these children and worked with them and tried to help them, it isn't real.

And as I discovered, until you have lived with a broken heart because of the betrayal of love and trust, you can never know the kind of living hell a betraying heart can visit on those who have been betrayed. But if nothing else, we can learn through such a living hell the lesson of compassion toward others. And, hopefully, become wiser in the process without losing our own ability to love and trust someone else worthy and deserving of our love and trust.

***

Since I do have a responsibility to readers for other realities, I reluctantly turn my attention to some of the ugly realities of politics. Because of the recent arrests here in the Valley by Alcoholic Beverage Control (ABC) agents, the issue of Due Process has become a hot topic of conversation.

Very few people in this community were aware that these agents had the police power of arrest based on Observation Only! If they thought you were guilty, not even a test for alcohol was necessary. They just slapped the cuffs on you and hauled you off to jail. Forty-three people were arrested in just this fashion in just one night here in the Kern Valley.

This is a small community and the arrests were made a major subject of debate in our local paper. But people were so outraged that the Bakersfield Californian and Kern County TV stations gave a lot of attention to the arrests as well. To acerbate the situation, David Hume's book Mean Justice which targets my home county of Kern here in California was getting a lot of play at the same time. In fact, he was in Bakersfield doing a book signing at Barnes and Noble during this time of the arrests in the Valley.

The county Sheriff, the county DA, along with agencies like the ABC, are catching a lot of flack and doing some pretty fancy dancing trying to justify themselves. But few people here where I live realize that the crackdown by CHP and Sheriff's Office, as with the ABC, is related to a Pulitzer Prize winning book. A lovely girl and I were recently having coffee together and I was explaining this to her.

She was telling me about being stopped by the police shortly after leaving one of the clubs where she had only been drinking coffee. This girl is actually the daughter of a local CHP officer. It didn't matter. The Sheriff's deputy knew her but stopped her just because she had left a bar and it was about midnight. As a result of such tactics, people are becoming afraid to drive late at night whether they have been drinking or not. If all the local cops didn't know me so well, I'm sure I'd get stopped.

The long and short of this abuse of police authority, and I know personally of this being abuse because I was a witness in one of the bars as the agents were making arrests, brings up the subject of Due Process. As I tried to explain to some friends, these agents were given such authority because good people were too busy to be good citizens. And no matter how you try to wiggle out of it, this is the bottom line to all the abuses by government. When you are too busy to know the candidates and the issues, too busy to be politically active, too busy to be a good citizen, you may be a good person but you are not a good citizen and you are too busy to be free, thereby giving Caesar the victory by default.

As to Due Process, most certainly the framers of the Constitution did not intend how much justice you can afford. But that is the system of so-called Due Process we live with today. The people who were arrested now have the chance to prove they are innocent. And this will cost a minimum of $1,200 per person for their day in court. This is a case of presumption of guilt, and guilt by observation only, as opposed to the presumption of innocence until proven guilty.

I know how this system works. I am not naive about such abuse of authority. And I know it isn't right. But to really understand how this perversion of Due Process came about, you might as well try researching the origin of evil; which I have done and it resulted in my writing a book on the subject.

And it would take a book the size of War and Peace to do justice to the subject of how Due Process became what it is today instead of what the Founding Fathers intended it to be. Suffice it to say that the phrase: First, we kill all the lawyers would be prominent in the process of understanding what has happened to Due Process.

But that would be simplistic and miss the point that if good people weren't too busy to be good citizens, such perversion of Due Process could never have come about. We The People get the kind of leadership we actively support. And if we fail in good leadership, this comes back as a failure of We the People to be good citizens or to put our time and money where our mouths are.

The squeaking wheel gets the grease. If evil gains the ascendancy over the good, this can only come to pass when good people are too busy, too ignorant and selfish, to confront the evil. Political lobbies and action committees are made up of people who put their time and money into their respective causes. When enough people and money are involved, legislators are moved to enact laws accordingly.

And we cannot blame the legislators when good people are too busy to be politically educated and involved, too busy and ignorant to write the necessary letters to these legislators. This is the reason most legislators know one letter may represent the view of thousands who do not write. As a result of this apathy, ignorance, selfishness, of being too busy to be a good citizen, the Devil wins by default. It really is as simple as this.

I know it isn't easy, at times, to become educated politically. For example, I wanted to contact Federal Judge Susan W. Wright to express my appreciation to her for her efforts for justice on behalf of We the People. Now with the national and international attention being given Judge Wright, I thought it would be easy to get an address for her. Not so!

I called the library, my local Supervisor, my state Assemblyman and state Senator, my U.S. Representative and U.S. Senator. None could give me an address of a Federal Judge. A few of the aides for some of these influential politicians hadn't even heard of Judge Wright! But I persevered because it was important that Judge Wright hear from me. Sometimes it takes a real effort to be politically educated and active. The alternative, however, is business as usual where the rich get richer and the poor get poorer and our liberties as Americans become ever more eroded. And those who ought to know better, don't do better because it takes some effort on their part. This is no excuse!

It has become altogether too easy to damn Caesar and his cohorts, the politicians, judges, lawyers and police when the real fault is that of good people who are too busy to be good citizens. And, as a result, too busy to be free!

***

All poets worthy of the name are, inherently, philosophers. So I have never taken it amiss when my youngest son Michael refers to me as: "My dad, the philosopher."

A philosopher is defined as one who speculates upon, and seeks, wisdom and truth. Society in general doesn't much like philosophers because, like Socrates (among others) who his society condemned and put to death, such speculation deriving from a seeking of wisdom and truth puts too many beliefs and prejudices to the test.

Society does not want its conventional wisdom questioned. The majority of individuals do not want their beliefs and prejudices questioned. This is why religion and politics (and the Civil War) are not wise topics in bars and should be avoided.

Still, there are people like myself and others, who seem destined as Socrates and Jesus were, who can't seem to keep their mouths shut on these topics. We know ignorance is a real killer, and errors of thinking, erroneous beliefs, cry out to be confronted.

For my part, I know how children suffer because of these errors and prejudices on the part of both individuals and an entire society. And because of this, I find myself in the most unenviable position of trying to get people, and an entire society, to confront these errors and prejudices honestly. It's an obviously thankless task and not one anyone in his right mind would purposely choose. So, perhaps, that says all that needs to be said about why I even try.

If I am seen as picking on religion, for example, this is correct. I do pick on religion because it is the source of so many of the hatreds and prejudices that have plagued humanity since the dawn of time. The fighting over Kosovo should never have happened. But the conflict is one of historic hatred between Christians and Moslems. Just as the historic conflict between Jews and Arabs, India and Pakistan, Ireland, Africa, China, Southeast Asia, Indonesia, etc. is based on religious hatreds.

I have friends who just love to be called *Reverend.* I consider this sheer egotism at best and sheer blasphemy at the worst since only God is to be reverenced and I adamantly refuse to call any man or woman Reverend. That is my belief. As a philosopher in my own right, I ask myself how any man or woman can fail to see the paradox of their professing to speak for God and peace and at the same time practice such a hypocritical deceit? Christians are notorious for touting their doctrine of Jesus as the Prince of Peace. And then they rub the faces of any that disagree with them in a doctrine of prejudicial hatred.

Many seem to believe, because they could hardly be accused of critical thinking, that the Crusades, the Dark Ages, the Salem Witch Trials and men like the various Popes, Calvin, Edwards, and Cotton Mather were only aberrations of a true and pure religion. But all religions are flawed morally. At some point, a particular religion, because of its interpretation of God accompanied by various scriptures, teaches that all who do not agree are the enemy.

A popular religious cliche is: "If God is not God of all, He isn't God at all!" Well, I believe God is God of all. But unlike religious people, I don't believe God is confused. And one cannot help but admit, apart from blind prejudice and refusing to face facts, that religion is confused. Systematic theologies are anything but.

For example, Christians have never been able to decide what God does with babies who die. Or, for that matter, why they die. Apart from having no explanation for this, there is no reason for thinking God takes any pleasure in the death of babies or even that He is to be blamed for orchestrating their deaths. Blame it on original sin? Hardly satisfactory, let alone wanting any proof whatsoever. The Bible itself is strangely silent on the subject. Catholics have their systems of Limbo and Purgatory. But these are merely religious conveniences, hardly explanations.

The Imprecatory Psalms have always proved interesting reading. But I have to confess that even in my orthodox days I had some problems with those like Psalm 137 when the Psalmist seems to delight in the idea that the enemies of the Jews were going to get theirs, and it would be marvelous when the babies of these enemies could be happily murdered by bashing their brains out against stones.

But this is too often the traditional thinking of religious people, whether Jewish, Christian, Moslem or Hindu: "God! Destroy those that don't believe in You like we do!" Or, as throughout history: "God! Help us destroy them!"

Uncritical servility to tradition is at the heart of the religious hatreds between the people of the world. If you are born into Catholicism, Judaism, Moslemism, Hinduism, etc., you are likely to be raised and believe as such.

It is a truism that children have to be taught to hate those who are different from themselves. Children are marvelously unprejudiced as I believe God intended them (and adults) to be. This wisdom of childhood seems to escape adults who believe it is their duty to teach their children to hate; both history and our contemporary world evidence that adults have been enormously successful in this.

I get Christmas and Easter cards. But some are outright frauds. These will sing the praise of Jesus all over the place; even on the outside of the envelopes. But I know these people. And I know they are doing virtually nothing for the sake of children in spite of the fact that they would agree with me that children must be the closest thing to the heart of God Himself. They are trying to make brownie points with God by doing their duty by being religious; like the good people who knock on my door, religious literature in hand, confronting my, they believe, infidel status.

Most of these people are good people. But many are hypocrites. They say and do not. For example, many of them couldn't give you the name of their local government representative. Most of them think themselves good Christians but they are most definitely not good citizens.

Because of this fact, it should be evident to even the most obtuse that it will take good citizens, not good Christians, to make America a better nation. America, I believe, desperately needs to repent and turn to God. But not to religion, which separates, divides, rather than draws people together. But this point requires critical thinking, something that is hardly the purview of the zealously religious. And how can it be when you begin with a deeply ingrained prejudice? And it is this deeply ingrained prejudice that makes such people notoriously poor citizens. Such people have a religious agenda, not one for the welfare of the whole of society let alone children; rather, only that society which is in agreement with their prejudice.

So when I get cards and letters saying: "God bless you and ACPC in the name of Jesus," I am only reminded of how great a battle presents itself to both God and me in overcoming such prejudice for the sake of the children. ACPC does not stand for Jesus; it doesn't stand for any religious myths born of prejudices. It stands for children; it stands for the Amendment because it is the right and wise thing to do. And often in the face of the obstacle of those who profess to believe in Jesus.

But what most of these people have done is tell me to be warmed and filled, contributing nothing but their own deluded sense of: "I have given a witness and testimony to that poor benighted soul (me, of course) of my risen Lord and Savior." My mind reels with sarcasms at this point because I used to be expert myself in promoting this.

Simply as a point of courteous and civilized manners, it is rude for anyone to insist their religious or political prejudices on someone else. But the fanatic is not concerned with being courteous since he selfishly considers his point of view the only correct one and has deluded himself that he really has only your benefit in mind. Or else!

Parents rightly expect their children to grow up to become responsible adults. Those claiming to be God's children have a way to go in accomplishing this. And they will never grow up, they will never acquire wisdom, as long as they hate and kill one another on the basis of their religious beliefs.

An excellent example of critical thinking would be to imagine yourself, as a parent, sitting down with a group of other parents. You are a Protestant, another a Catholic, another is a Jew, another a Moslem, one a Buddhist and another a Hindu, one an agnostic and one an atheist.

Here are eight different belief systems (and make no mistake, the similarity between Catholic and Protestant is at best superficial regardless of claims to the contrary). Now every parent, irrespective of belief, wants what is best for his or her child.

If the discussion concerning what is best for children were limited to this only, devoid of any differences of beliefs, every parent would find him- or herself in agreement with the others. This can't happen. It is the ideal, but it can't happen; and why not? Because in due course, every one of these parents will attempt to make what is best for children a process of their belief system.

The genius of the Amendment is its exclusive focus on the welfare of children irrespective of any system of belief; religious, racial or political. It is one thing that all good people can find agreement on. It can be the first step toward the ideal of peace on the basis of confining dialogue solely to the welfare of children.

Jesus is supposed to have said that everything he had been taught, The Law and The Prophets, rested on one thing: "To love God and to love your neighbor." Now without getting into the parsing of the statement like theologues or quoting far more ancient philosophers who had said the very same thing, the statement itself is not only the right thing to do, it is the essence of wisdom. To love God and your neighbor would equal peace in the world.

While it is quite evident that books are a vital part of education, some of them have been the Devil's tool in the past and continue to be such today. I believe it is very important to education that people be the contrarians John Adams was, that people read widely, including books that are at variance with one's own views.

The books of those like John Locke, Adam Smith, Montesquieu and Rousseau that guided the Founding Fathers are largely unknown to Americans today except by name only (if that) as well as the writings of these Founding Fathers themselves. But to be a good and informed citizen, a good American if you will, these are essential works.

As to being the Devil's tool, one only has to consider that writing and books have promoted great evil as well as great good for humanity. Since writing and books were under the control of leaders in history who had their own agendas, we struggle to find the facts among the myths in the earliest of recorded history.

And once more, the choices that are made which seemed right but were not wise make themselves known. And once those unwise choices begin to exert their influence through circumstances, expediency rather than wisdom becomes the operant though the chance for peace is, as usual, forsaken, even unattainable, in the process.

When choices are made on the basis of beliefs and prejudices that separate people, prejudicial beliefs that make one race or religion superior to all others, conflict is virtually guaranteed. As a result, the world has never known peace. And never will as long as there are people, even nations, that believe God favors one religion or race above others rather than being what He really is, the God and Father of all His children regardless of race or religion.

But I anticipate the calls and letters from those who will consign me to the outer reaches beyond redemption or the flames of hell for writing such things. I have come to accept such reactions from those that would rather hold on to some cherished belief rather than face their beliefs and learn to question them honestly.

It is not an easy thing to do. But until people do learn to question these things, until people become honest about them and admit they have confused beliefs with knowledge and learn to separate the two, there is no chance for peace in the world.

As with the complexities of the Amendment, it is an educative process, a process of learning, which few, unfortunately, really have any interest in. But ignorance is a real killer. And as a teacher, I can't leave it alone. When I face ignorance, I am compelled to try to teach because I firmly believe that if I could learn, so can others. I believe that if I had known better in the past, I would have done better. And I will continue to believe that if good people know better, they will do better.

And if, at times, I make myself appear naive or foolish, if I embarrass myself in the process like telling the stories on myself here in TAP, far better I do this than be anything less than honest with my readers. Whether you

235

agree with me or not, I have a responsibility to all of you to be truthful even to my own hurt.

And please don't mistake this for any kind of nobility on my part. I know I'm no better in any way than any of you. But don't you agree the world itself would be a better place if we could all practice real honesty in our lives even if we do, at times, embarrass ourselves in the process?

CHAPTER ELEVEN

Lord, grant me the serenity to accept the things I cannot change, the courage to change the things I can, and the wisdom to hide the bodies of those people I had to kill because they really ticked me off!

It may have nothing whatsoever to do with the fact that it takes a lost man an average 1 hour, 22 minutes of driving time before asking directions, but there has to be some correlation between this and the following:

There are many pitfalls for those who are truly talented, even gifted, and you sometimes have to wonder how such people can do what amounts to stupid things. But it only proves they are just like me, after all, human.

When it comes to doing stupid things, no one has a corner on the market. We are all human and we all, as a consequence, do stupid things. But as reasonable human beings, we try to profit from such mistakes, differentiating between innate, intransigent stupidity and honest errors, and do our best to keep from repeating them.

For example, I have learned from experience that my morning coffee is not supposed to contain ants or be green or purple; especially not after adding cream. But in my defense, I do make good coffee. One very lovely girl, having spent some hours in conversation with me at my little cottage, told me she was so wired from my coffee that when she got home she cleaned the entire house. My recipe for this coffee can be had by request.

And speaking of stupidity, who decided to make it a crime for us ordinary citizens to lie to government authorities, but not a crime for them to lie to us? Who decided candidates for office can lie their heads off and not be held accountable? I don't think the ordinary citizen has any difficulty seeing what's wrong with this picture. But the ordinary citizen can usually be counted on by Caesar to be as faithful as Caesar's dog. Curse it and kick it and it comes back for more. Cats, on the other hand, are smarter (i.e. more selfish and given to self-preservation) than this. However, cats are difficult to train compared to dogs. For example, in spite of my every effort to teach her better, my cat Furrina still leaves streaks when she cleans the windows of my cottage.

In addition to my expertise in coffee, I have also learned that when I mention I am a habitue of Slugger's Saloon, it raises eyebrows. People who do not know Slugger or her establishment equate the name with some den of iniquity filled with types for whom clean Levi's and T-shirts without holes in them is being over-dressed, and drug dealers and ladies of the night ply their trades.

Not so. Just the other night I witnessed Slugger send a guy packing who was trying to make a drug connection. She gave him a choice: "Leave now or I'll call the cops!" He left. Slugger's is a sociable place filled with people like the owner herself, real and compassionate people, most of whom are struggling at ordinary jobs, like many Americans, just to make ends meet.

But what's in a name? A great deal at times; and there is no denying that as human beings we are naturally given to stereotyping on the basis of names, and quite often with good reason in spite of the many exceptions like that of Slugger's Saloon. All of which brings me to the: *Bodfish Philosophical Society.*

Now at first blush, the name alone seems quite pretentious. After all: Where the hell is Bodfish? And a name like Bodfish does not seem to accommodate itself to the cultural and intellectual pursuits of a Philosophical Society. When one thinks of such things, places like Menlo Park or Concord more readily come to mind. But as Bing Crosby once told a fellow passenger who recognized him on a cross-country flight, "Everybody has to be somewhere." And every institution has to be somewhere as well; so why not Bodfish in spite of the fact that the name seems to jar with the subject?

Well, of course, there is more to it than this. Bodfish is, admittedly, an unlikely place to start such a thing as a philosophical society; and for a number of legitimate reasons, notwithstanding the name. Bodfish is a very small community, relatively isolated and without any of the cultural amenities.

But a revolution needs only a small nucleus of truly dedicated members and geography is not a determining factor though not disputing the fact that a name and location can be such. However, what I am proposing through BPS, as with the Amendment which is a natural adjunct corollary, is nothing short of revolutionary. It all began with discussions with a number of people, primarily women, concerning the critique of To Kill A Mockingbird.

California Governor Gray Davis gave the copy I sent him to State Senator Gary K. Hart who is head of the California Education Committee. Senator Hart wrote me a very encouraging letter after his reading the critique. This prompted me to consider an abridged edition of the critique to be used as a handbook for teachers.

I have now completed this abridged edition and sent copies to people like Senator Hart and Governor George Bush along with several other very influential people. As a result of writing this version of the critique, I found myself in conversation with a group of local women and from this evolved the idea for the BPS.

Unexpectedly and passionately expounding on the need for women to develop a philosophy of their own which would complement that of men, I had an attentive audience of women. It was during this discussion that I recalled something I had written about in my book "The Missing Half of Humankind: Women!"

I knew a woman who was very involved with a large group of women and they held meetings every month. I posed a question to this particular woman: The most common complaint of women about men is that men do not listen to them. I asked this lady to present this question to her group: What is it that women are trying to say to men that justify their complaint? The lady reported back to me that she had never witnessed such confusion and chaos on the part of her group as that which my question provoked. But since men have never taken women seriously, since men have never considered women of equal value to themselves, I was not surprised at such a result of my question. With this in mind, and after my discussion with the particular group of local ladies I previously mentioned, I came home and wrote the following:

The philosophical works of men throughout history have provided the foundation of all societies and their governments. It was the works of men like Hume, Locke, Montesquieu and Rousseau that provided the Founding Fathers of America the ideas that culminated in Alexis de Tocqueville calling our nation the greatest experiment in Democracy in all of history.

The Founding Fathers themselves, in turn, left an unsurpassed legacy of philosophical writings to future generations of Americans. But if one turns to the earliest origins of philosophy, there is an entire half of humanity missing and ignored in what is called The Great Conversation.

This Great Conversation is well represented by a set of books entitled "The Great Books of the Western World." This set of books, 54 volumes, is supposed to set forth the best of philosophical thought and writings throughout history. But one searches in vain to find a single woman represented! One is reasonably led to ask: Weren't there wise women, women of a philosophical bent of mind, as well as men during these past thousands of years? There must have been. Then why were they ignored? There are many reasons for this; some quite legitimate given the facts of our earliest beginnings as a species.

But few people consider that it wasn't until this century that women even began to have a legitimate voice of any kind in philosophy. Still, in spite of all the efforts on the part of women to be heard, that voice is a very small one and remains virtually ignored by men. Yet it should have been evident in the far, distant past that humanity could never solve the intransigent problems confronting all societies while excluding the voice of an entire half of humankind from the decision-making processes of societies and governments.

Unbelievably, this has been the case throughout history! I say unbelievably because such a thing is insane on the face of it! And as a result of men excluding women in the decision-making processes, by men denying women an equal voice, the history of the world has been one of unremitting hatreds, prejudices, war, and violence of every description.

This exclusion of women can best be stated in terms of men having never accepted women as of equal value to them. The result has been a history of resentment on the part of women, of competition and combativeness rather than fostering and encouraging what should be the compatibility of differences.

The hardness of men and the softness of women should be melded in order to produce an alloy of toughness, which is neither too hard nor too soft. But this can only be accomplished once the compatibility of differences, rather than competition and combativeness, is the norm, and the equal value of women to men is accomplished fact.

A large part of the work of the Bodfish Philosophical Society must be directed to the goal of educating men to the need of accepting and welcoming women as of equal value to themselves. But this begins with educating women to the facts of the history of their exclusion as of equal value, as well as the facts of our contemporary world in this respect. Once women truly understand these things, their efforts can be directed toward a solution, for it is well said that defining the problem is half of the solution.

Throughout all of history, men have depended on women being their own worst enemies. And this has proven to be the case. The failure of women to recognize and act on the problem has enabled unscrupulous men to continue in their exclusive dominance to the continuing conditions of war and violence.

But if women are to find their own voice in national and world affairs, if they are to represent themselves as equal in value to the wisdom of men, they must begin with a well-reasoned, comprehensive, cogent and intelligible philosophy of their own. Then the melding of the two halves of humankind, that of both men and women can be accomplished and world peace can become a reasonable goal.

It would seem obviously insane that we can expect peace in the world when men have always excluded women, half of the human race, from attempts at world peace. But this is, in fact, the case. It will take women of exceptional intelligence and sensitivity, women of determination and perseverance together with a willingness to commit themselves, to change things and develop their own philosophy. Men, of course, are counting on this never happening.

But it must be recognized that men have a vested interest in not allowing women an equal voice in decision-making. They see this as a threat to their dominance over women, a dominance, which has kept the world in conflict throughout all of history and is still on going with no end in sight.

Granted, a situation that has existed throughout history, and still exists, is not going to be easy to change. But if the world is ever to know peace and be a safe place for children, such a change is absolutely essential. The goal of the Bodfish Philosophical Society is, in part; that of the members committing themselves to the process that will lead to this needed change.

A very substantial part of the problem of women developing a philosophy is founded in the fact that it is only with the most supreme and difficult effort that philosophy can be divorced from theology. One of the reasons for this is exemplified by the intellectual schizophrenia associated with the dualism of theology, that of attempting to make God omniscient, omnipotent and omnipresent while at the same time not blaming Him for being responsible for evil.

I treat of this subject in depth and at length in my Hey, God! book. It is not an easy subject to resolve. It finally led Thomas Aquinas, one of the greatest of theologians, to proclaim at the end of his life: "All that I have done is nothing but straw!"

Dualism has been the bane of the great philosophers, and writers of the stature of Hawthorne and Melville. But all such were given to the idea that God had to be perfect by the definition of men, not that of God's Himself. And I began to believe that God is far more human than men and women give Him credit for being.

But a successful philosophy must be divorced from theology. It must accommodate the facts, knowledge, and not confuse belief for knowledge. There is a desperate need for an entirely new theology, which will accommodate itself to facts rather than myths and beliefs. But until such a theology is developed, the present theology based on myths and beliefs will continue to contaminate every philosophy that attempts to reconcile the two disciplines. That the two are supposed to be rooted in the ideal of seeking after truth should disabuse of the notion that they can be reconciled when theology makes assumptions which admit of no empirical facts whereas philosophy must begin with empirical facts. But once you drag God into any discussion of philosophy, all bets are off because the history of humanity has been one of nothing but hatreds and prejudices together with the killing and murdering of millions in the name of God. You cannot divorce a point of view from an institution to which you belong; particularly if that institution is a church.

I recently made the point to a friend and clergyman (surprisingly, I still have a few of these) that it is all well and good for the Baptists to denounce Clinton's pro-pervert stand, but as long as you wear a religious label the world sees a religious agenda rather than one of true morality. And while this is equally true of Catholics, Jews, Moslems and Hindus, one has to grant that the Baptists are an easy target when it comes to religiosity rather than a genuine and compassionate concern for humanity. The point being it still remains a truism that regardless of the label, and exceptions aside, people see your agenda as supporting your institutional beliefs rather than a genuine and selfless concern for all of humanity.

I receive many requests for support of various causes. Recently, I received a couple from The Rutherford Institute and The Heritage Foundation. I am in agreement with a lot of the work by these institutions. The fact that William J. Bennett, former U.S. Secretary of Education, is prominent in these institutions led to my early involvement in them. But these institutions led of good, well intentioned men like Dr. Bennett have a political agenda dominated by a religious point of view. And this is where they and I part company.

For example, what is the thinking when it comes to asking for a Constitutional Amendment that uses the word *desecrate* in respect to honoring our flag? You cannot desecrate something unless it is considered Holy! Are these people in Congress and elsewhere trying to make our flag an object of holy veneration? I vehemently object to such muddy politico/religious thinking! But does this attitude on my part mean I fail to honor our flag, that I fail in remembering all those who have died to insure our liberty and rights as Americans and for whom our flag is a symbol of this sacrifice? Of course not.

But this does point up the fact that intelligent, educated people are not immune to muddy, confused thinking and that such people can be caught up in the emotion of something that flies in the face of logic. One might call such thinking actually *stupid*! That's a very harsh term, especially when applied to educated people such as those in Congress. While the term is often applied to politicians in general, it is usually done so in anger and with full knowledge that these are not really stupid people.

But as I point out in my critique of To Kill A Mockingbird, when any group of people get together on an emotional issue, the group-think of such people often results in stupid decisions and actions. Just like a lynch mob; or in the specific case of our flag Congress itself.

The lesson should be implicit that if women are to develop their own philosophy, they must be very careful to avoid falling into such an emotional trap. Men, of course, will be quick to point out that women have not been able to develop a philosophy, that they have been excluded from The Great Conversation, just because of their being unable to avoid the emotional trap.

But if women are to be successful in developing a philosophy of their own which will complement that of men and bring the two halves of humanity into a partnership based on the compatibility of differences, they must avoid the emotional trap and it must begin with the ultimate statement of fact: Men and Women are of Equal Value!

With that statement of ultimate fact as a focus of direction and to keep them on course, I firmly believe women will be able to develop a philosophy of their own.

Women, as with men, have an enormous challenge when it comes to developing a sensible and workable philosophy. But men have had thousands of years to develop their philosophy. And women are going to have to run swiftly in order to catch up.

It must be admitted from the outset that the great majority of women will not participate in this effort. Like the apathetic American who does not vote because he or she tells himself or herself: "My one vote doesn't count," most women will tell themselves that they don't count in committing to the work of developing their philosophy.

Intellectual laziness is not the purview of men only; women are just as guilty of this. A further problem exists in the fact that women have had thousands of years of being trained, brain-washed, to believe they cannot contribute to philosophy, that they cannot have a legitimate, equal voice in national and world affairs.

Like the good person who is not a good citizen, who is too apathetic or too busy to be free, most women will continue in the defeatist attitude that nothing they do will make any difference. The obvious conclusion of such thinking is a self-fulfilling prophecy of nothing being done.

Men are depending on the great majority of women to be just like themselves in equal value to one thing: The desire to escape personal responsibility in confronting evil! Men are also depending on women to be just like themselves in avoiding getting involved, in avoiding taking any blame for the worsening conditions in the world, especially for children.

It has to be admitted that both men and women are equally guilty of not wanting to commit to a course of action that will change things for the better. They are all too busy, etc. The same excuses apply to both men and women; and the same guilt in proportion to these excuses.

I had a beautiful woman recently tell me that what was needed was on too great a scale for her to comprehend, too grand to have any hope of accomplishing. This is a natural reaction to what I am proposing. I know this. But if I, as a mere man, can envision such a thing, I know there are women who are just as capable of envisioning the same thing. All they have to do is stand up, come forth and be counted. And as proper leadership evolves from within the ranks of women who dedicate themselves to developing their philosophy, I know such a thing is possible for them. And as we all know, a revolution only requires a small number of such dedicated people.

And I also believe it is absolutely imperative that this small number of dedicated women come together and begin this revolution in developing their philosophy, and as quickly as possible, if the world is ever to know peace before men, lacking that equal voice of women, succeed in their present course of destroying the world!

I had a marvelous chat with a woman the other night. During our conversation, since confession is good for the soul (depending, of course, on to whom you confess) I found myself admitting that as a writer there is always the first person pronoun to confront, the big I as it were, and I (there it is) fight a continual battle with this. She was gracious enough to point out that in most cases, particularly in the kind of writing I do, it isn't always possible to overcome the necessity of this first person singular pronoun. In nothing did this become such a critical factor as in the critique of To Kill A Mockingbird.

Admittedly, writers would love to have their every word engraved in stone and, as a consequence, often find themselves in an adversarial relationship with editors. And, unfortunately, many have not allowed themselves the benefit of someone who approaches their work objectively, red pen in hand.

Still, of all people, writers should be the most sensitive to the need of those with the essential editing skills of editing and proofing. No writer can fail to profit from such. And writers, you would think, would know they are the worst critics of their own work. It is hard to believe that any writer would feel competent to judge his own writing without the aid of a good editor. But, alas, there are many such writers. Too many. Most become columnists. And if they can't write, they become talk show hosts. In defense of writers I do have to say that the ratio of critics to writers runs about a million to one. An old joke line ran: "Everyone's a critic!" And this is largely true.

I was having a good conversation with a very intelligent fellow the other day. He had some excellent points, but his biggest problem was his inability to articulate them properly. A not uncommon difficulty with many intelligent people though you would think such people would easily recognize this fact and not be guilty of such a thing. The root of the problem is the fact that so many people like this fellow, intelligent as they are, seem to believe that verbal expression is sufficient to make a point. It isn't.

As I told this man, unless you can give written expression to an idea it is of little or no value. In other words, anyone can carry on speaking at length, even ad nauseum, but unless you can put an idea on paper, you probably have not clarified it in your own mind and may not have anything of genuine substance to offer. Written expression provides an opportunity to examine an idea in far greater detail than is possible from merely belaboring it in speech, something even a fool can do. And often does since it is the purview of fools to identify themselves as such by their much speaking.

Too many people, and not all of them fools by any means, have the mistaken notion that their much speaking is sufficient to express their ideas and accomplish the desired purpose without first giving them written expression. But this is an error, and most often, the result of intellectual laziness. As a result, there are many speakers, as with critics, but very few writers.

I have also tried to impress the fact upon many people that they abuse their listeners if they have not given written expression to their ideas before they try to convince others verbally of a point of view. And it has to be admitted that there seems to be too many people that simply want an audience and love to hear themselves talk. Such people are the stuff of preachers and politicians.

If you are a person of ideas, if you are given to subtle turns of mind, you find yourself quite comfortable being alone with your thoughts. You can spend hours turning ideas over in your mind before committing them to words on paper. But like my good friend Henry Thoreau, I long ago discovered that in most cases pain was my reward for my labors as a writer. Most especially, that writing of a philosophical nature since most societies have an aversion to their philosophers. People in general do not want conventional wisdom put to the test; which, alas, is the vocation, the calling if you will, of the philosopher.

As to writing for profit, I early abhorred the thinking of Thoreau's Indian who thought it the obligation of others to buy his baskets on the basis of his having made them. Rather, like Henry, it seemed far more attractive to me to avoid the necessity of selling my baskets at all for as Henry pointed out: "The life which men praise and regard as successful is but one kind. Why should we exaggerate any one kind at the expense of the others?"

I often quote Henry Thoreau because despite his egotism over the years he has become a close and wise friend. And hardly a day, or moon- or star-lit night, passes that I am not reminded of Henry's observation: "What is nature to me if I have no one with whom to share it?" His wisdom shines in statements like: "It is never too late to give up our prejudices. No way of thinking or doing, however ancient, can be trusted without proof." But sadly, even tragically for humanity, petty and small minds are not subject to change.

As I delved ever deeper into the vaunted wisdom and often puissant writings of the ancients like Pliny, Suetonius, Livy and Catullus as well as the relative moderns like Kant, Kierkegaard and so many others, I came to personally discover the grounds of Thoreau's statement though he himself had missed it. And as a result, I went considerably further than my friend through the discovery of what he and all these others had missed; purposely or otherwise.

By excluding an entire half of humankind, women, by devaluing women and children, these ancients and their more recent counterparts had never attained to wisdom. And I came to believe, as Thoreau said: "One may almost doubt if the wisest man has learned anything of absolute value by living." Henry was absolutely correct in his dismal assessment. But he never discovered the why? of this. Apparently he and these others left the dirty work for me. Why do I call it dirty work? For several reasons.

First, it should be obvious that none of these men wanted to touch it. Second, men still don't. The resentment and antagonism of men toward the Amendment, as well as the continued and determined efforts by men to keep women in their place, is the proof of this. And third, it isn't the kind of work that exactly endears me to the world. In fact, because the job description requires I confront ignorance and prejudice on every hand, beginning with my own, it is a supremely lonely job and I have lost many friends in doing it. The letters, e-mails and calls consigning me to the outer reaches outnumber those of encouragement by about fifty-to-one.

But one of the most important things I learned from my own study of the ancient and modern philosophers was confirmed by Henry: "None can be an impartial or wise observer of human life but from the vantage ground of what we should call voluntary poverty."

To actually love and seek wisdom is to devote both mind and body to it. The superfluities of life readily evidence themselves in due course to such seeking people. But it would be a gross mistake to equate any kind of poverty, by whatever definition, with wisdom.

Most certainly the voluntary poverty of which Thoreau speaks is not the sour grapes of those lacking means or of those too lazy and shiftless to work. Neither is it the voluntary poverty of those who delude themselves that they somehow honor God through their poverty and resort to holy begging in His name. Far too many of these think God owes them a living, that having attained a seminary or university education for example, they have earned the right to become holy leaches. Or not so holy if they by-pass the churches and go into politics or become university professors.

And there have been many would-be philosophers throughout history who have believed their lofty thoughts removed them from the obligation of earning their daily bread. Most religious leaders (and politicians and university professors) fall into this category and, if successful, have removed themselves from poverty by any definition and like Tom Lehrer's "Old Dope Peddler" have done well by doing good. The opiate of religion usually serving as well as the real thing and has the added benefit of keeping the poor from killing the rich.

There are various definitions of poverty though the most common is usually understood as living in real want. But the voluntary poverty of which Thoreau and others have written is that poverty of being unencumbered by superfluities, not a lack of the necessaries of life. And for me, having those necessaries met, I find no need of encumbering myself with things that rob me of the liberty and freedom to pursue my thoughts; and most especially, to pursue them without deprivation or harm to others. As an aside, this desire to be free of encumbrances has been a very contentious point between me and most of the women with whom I have been intimately involved. It continues to be so.

However, this is not a criticism of such women. If anything, it is a valid criticism of me. After all, why should any woman in her right mind want a poet/philosopher as her close companion or life partner? In such a case, I have to bow to the correct judgment of the compatibility of differences. If it isn't there in my case, it is no valid criticism of women in general. But being such as I am, and alone, what should it be to me that I should be judged by the kind of vehicle I drive? Most certainly that I have a vehicle at all, that I can afford to maintain it, keep it registered and insured, etc. removes me from real poverty in this instance. That I own my home, regardless of how humble, clear of any mortgage certainly removes me from most definitions of poverty.

But the fault people may find with me on the basis of what kind of vehicle or home I own is a critical aspect of wisdom. Such fault-finding is evidence of the philosophical battleground of the failure of people to distinguish between what is truly respectable as opposed to what most people consider respectable influenced by, in too many cases, the false demands and requirements imposed by their respective cultures.

In Thoreau's time, it was a question of whether a man was judged by a patch on his clothing or whether he wore the latest fashions. In this respect, nothing has changed; only some of the materials, like a car, by which such faulty thinking on the part of far too many people continues to evidence it. As much as people would like to argue the point, it still too often comes down to: *He with the most toys when he dies wins.* This in spite of the fact that the majority throughout all of history says only what is done for others is of any real lasting value.

I have had the toys. And I don't flatter myself by choosing to do without them. Neither do I find fault with those who still choose the toys over the choice I have made to do without them. I do, however, find fault with those who hypocritically say they care about children and put the emphasis on the toys rather than the children.

This has become far too typical of American society in general. As I pointed out in the last issue of TAP as well as my critique of To Kill A Mockingbird, we have become a society that is indifferent to children. As with little Dill in Harper Lee's novel, we have bought our children the toys and then told them: "Now, go play with the toys and leave us alone!" Who dares call this wise, let alone an expression of love for children!

However, if the voluntary poverty of the true poet/philosopher is wise in the sense of Thoreau's statement, it is only a mechanism of liberty and freedom by which he or she can give that much more to others; though this must often be measured by the contribution of bringing ideas, hope and beauty into the lives of others; or, when circumstances demand it, the confronting of ignorance, bigotry, prejudice, and injustice.

But as I have pointed out, the weakness of philosophy throughout the ages has been that of excluding an entire one-half of humanity, women, from the Great Conversation, the failure of otherwise wise men to accept women as of equal value to men; and, most important of all, the failure of men to recognize the fact that unless children are made the absolute priority of their philosophy and thence of nations, real wisdom is unattainable.

Notwithstanding this obvious failure of philosophers, at times it is the odious and thankless task of the poet/philosopher to confront actual insanity on the part of a whole society or nation. America has not escaped this insanity which has evidenced itself from time to time (not to mention current events). One only has to consider the issue of slavery, the early laws concerning witchcraft and forced religious views by fiat of law, and Prohibition.

How, any reasonable person has to ask, could an entire nation be lead into such insanity as to prohibit the sale of alcohol? Just think of one of the most prominent leaders of such insanity: Billy Sunday. Like Cotton Mather of old, Billy was considered by many of the religious to be a marvelous man. Some still hold both men to be such. And to such an extent during this particular era of national insanity that America bowed to the preaching and definitions of morality of Billy Sunday and so many others like him, thereby leading the entire nation into the national insanity of trying to legislate morality on a massive, and totally irrational, scale through the Volstead Act!

In respect to Puritan Calvinistic Theology, Slavery and Prohibition, America was little different because of these in comparison to Tojo's Japan, Hitler's Germany or Stalin's Russia which are some of the most prominent recent historical examples of the insanity of entire nations. And to look at the world today, where have the ancient hatreds of bigotry, prejudice and religion been laid to rest?

But fearing the power of the pen, nations have always persecuted and banned their poet/philosophers. So it has ever been throughout history. And dare we broach the present insanity of harping on tobacco while excluding alcohol, which is so much more destructive to society? Let alone, the insanity of the legal sale and use of tobacco and alcohol while hypocritically excluding less harmful drugs like marijuana? Who dares speak to the issue of creating an entire criminal class, just as Prohibition did, of otherwise law-abiding citizens? But what a powerful club is placed in Caesar's hand by such insanity and perversion of law! But tobacco, as marijuana, was an easy target for unscrupulous and greedy lawyers; just as guns are in spite of all the warnings of the Founding Fathers and logical thinking to the contrary. Who dares say the bigoted and hypocritical insanity of the old Puritans exemplified by Cotton Mather's theology (and that of Billy Sunday's) is not still with us?

I have been thoroughly denounced because of my advocating the need of moral absolutes as essential for the survival and advancement of any society. My strong opposition to homosexuals as teachers in the classroom, society's approval of pornography and the encouraging of violence through so-called games and entertainment keeps me outside the pale of those calling themselves *liberal*. But so-called conservatives, especially those in the churches, are just as quick to denounce me for my position regarding things like marijuana, tobacco and alcohol. Imagine the vilification to which I subject myself from such people when I tell them of my advocating the legalization of prostitution!

As I said: It's dirty work; a dirty job I am doing. And I'm not properly grateful it fell to me. Just yesterday a lovely young lady told me she would hate to be in my place and asked me how I manage to keep doing such work? My answer, as always, was that it is a compulsion since no one in his or her right mind would purposely choose to take on the job. But having taken it on as a poet/philosopher, I can hardly blame anyone but myself for having done so or for my suffering the resulting consequences. But one of the necessities of the job, I quickly discovered, was to simplify as much of my life as possible; hence my regard for the advice of my friend Henry.

And the fact that a wise man or woman will choose to live simply is not to denigrate those who are not called to such a passion (and it must be a passion for it to be legitimate); not even those who find fault with those so called. A passionate love affair with wisdom is quite obviously mad to the majority; as is a passionate love affair between a man and a woman. But the seeming madness of these does not lessen one whit the reality of such passion; for even those who are mad in such a fashion have their reasons if not believed by others in possession of reason itself.

That my friend Henry missed obtaining the full wisdom he sought by failing to recognize the obvious which I discovered concerning women and children, that he missed so much which would have benefited him mightily because of his not marrying and having children, does not lessen the true wisdom he did obtain. But I can pity him as a friend for his having missed one of the fullest dimensions of life and living. And, thereby, having missed so much from which his own philosophical seekings would have profited to the comfort of his own mind and soul as well as those of others including myself.

In my critique of To Kill A Mockingbird, I make the statement that I have lived too long and I know too much. A lovely girl, having read the critique, called me and chastised me for this. She said I had too much to offer to say such a thing. Maybe she's right. Naturally I would like to believe this. But I really don't know. But I do know it is vitally important to let people like the girl with AIDS know they are loved and cared for in spite of this dread killer infecting their bodies.

I also know how important it was for me to hold her tightly, for me to caress her hair and kiss her cheek as we danced. I know how important it was for me to make her feel like the beautiful girl she is in spite of the disease. I know there is nothing wrong in wanting the flowers and praise before we die. And I know there is something definitely wrong with the people who withhold these things until it is too late.

Of course, the music and the dance end and the grim realities are still there. This girl hasn't been able to escape these in spite of the magic of the moment or in spite of the rose. This is reality. But the magic of the moment and the rose still live and has a unique reality of their own. It is that kind of magical reality which can sustain us in the face of ugly realities. It is the kind of magic which can keep us hopeful that not everything we confront is the ugliness in our lives. It is the kind of magic that costs virtually nothing but is of inestimable value, priceless, and we all too often fail to make real in one another's lives while we still have time in season to do so.

The other day, I came home to find a message on my answering device from a close acquaintance of many years. Because of the above story and my associating with people who have AIDS, this acquaintance of many years told me I was no longer welcome in his home. It was only then that I learned that this man's wife, a woman over fifty years of age, had never heard of HIV!

The pain of being cut off any longer from association with this man and his wife was superseded by the appalling ignorance and prejudice of both. It was then that I decided I had to do something about such appalling ignorance and prejudice and decided to come clean about Ronnie.

It has been nearly ten years since my brother Ronald died of AIDS. Ronnie and I were as close as any two brothers could possibly be. We loved each other deeply and I miss him more than I can ever say. After a particularly bitter divorce, he became what might rightly be called a woman-hater. Meeting another man with a similar background, the two became inseparable.

Eventually they moved to San Francisco and later to Walnut Creek where Ronnie died.

I watched helplessly as the disease wasted his body. Ten years ago, we were all really in the Dark Ages of AIDS awareness and treatment. Not that any treatment would have availed. All doctors could do was try to make Ronnie's death as painless as possible. But ten years ago, any mention of association with a person infected by this dread killer caused fear in most other people. Since that time, I have worked with and been very close to a number of people with the disease. And I have been enormously pleased that the disease has received the attention it has; that so many have dedicated themselves to finding a cure. But given such widespread attention, even internationally, how is it possible for people like this acquaintance of mine and his wife to be so abysmally ignorant and prejudiced concerning it?

No thinking or truly compassionate person can possibly understand or explain such ignorance and prejudice. But here it is, exemplified by these two people. And if supposedly educated and enlightened people can be so ignorant and prejudiced, it only proves how very far we have yet to go in the educative process. I have learned this: We cannot take it for granted, we cannot assume, that we are doing a successful job of education when such people remain so abysmally, even hurtfully, ignorant and prejudiced. And if I am construed as picking on religion, I believe I am fully justified in doing so. This ex-friend and his wife are far too typical of those who are led by their religious prejudices rather than reality and common sense, let alone love and compassion.

But, typically as well of such people, they resent being called religious. My ex-friend and his wife were always quick to denounce anyone who called them religious; just as I used to myself. After all, according to their bigoted and perverted view (and mine at the time), they are in possession of The Truth! And this being the case (as they choose to believe), they are not religious; they are Right!

Such people also choose (as I did) to ignore the fact that anyone is properly identified as religious who holds to a sectarian belief. And in spite of often vehement claims to the contrary by Christians, for example, there is no such thing as The Church (the ecclesia); one of the primary reasons such people hold on to their bigoted and superstitious prejudice of being the sole possessors of The Truth.

I love God as my Heavenly Father. But I also believe that as our Creator, God has made what I call in my Hey, God! book, errors of love. It only seems reasonable to me that if we are made in the image of God, that as His children, the same creativity with which we are endowed exhibits itself in our own creative efforts, including the mistakes and errors of love. No artist, creator, ever looks at the finished work and pronounces it perfect. It is a part of us as human beings, a divine part I believe, to set goals and strive to do better in building and creating.

No parent is free of the errors of love in raising children. We may try to do our best, but those errors always find themselves intruding; and often when we are the best intentioned. Just so, I believe our Heavenly Father has made such errors and learned from them as we ourselves. But as parents we live with the hope and expectation that our children will learn and do better than we. And I believe God has this expectation of us to learn and do better, to advance in knowledge and apply this knowledge in gaining wisdom.

I further believe it is our responsibility, not that of God's, to confront and overcome evil in the world. This is the sum of what is rightly called my religious beliefs. But because of my work on behalf of children, and especially because of the Amendment, religious people often attempt to Christianize my writing and me. I recently had a call from just such a man and became a little abrasive with him as he kept pressing the issue of how spiritual he was and how important it was that I make Jesus and the Bible prominent in my work.

I finally said to him: "Please spare me the sophistries and pious religious drivel and tell me what you are actually doing to make the world a better place for children! And I don't mean a better place for Christian (nor, of course, Jewish, Hindu or Moslem) children, I mean ALL children! And don't even try to tell me you are trying unless you are politically active! You aren't!"

And I most certainly didn't mean politically active in the cause of some religious or John Birch Society agenda. As I have often pointed out, I have had many people and organizations offer to help with the work for the Amendment if I would allow them to tie it to their cause and agenda. I have summarily refused all such offers. The Amendment is the right and wise thing to do. Good unprejudiced people will support it on this basis alone, not on the basis of some religious or political ideology or agenda. Further, can any call him- or herself good in this context if the only fault they can find with the Amendment is with its author?

It was a most pleasant surprise to hear that one of the would-be Popes of Protestantism, Pat Robertson, has lost the tax-exempt status for his hardly veiled, and now fully unmasked, PAC the Christian Coalition. That this has always been a rabidly fundamentalist charismatic organization designed to force a religious agenda of Robertson's persuasion has long been recognized. So much so that it has been a downright embarrassment to legitimate, charitable organizations as well as being a bigoted, religious rip-off in the name of God (naturally) to the taxpayers.

But let's face it. God has always been in dire straits, His clothes ragged and His hand out, even facing bankruptcy on a continuing basis; and in need of money according to Roberts, Robertson, Schuller, Kennedy, et al., and religion in general. Now of course, it isn't God who actually needs money these are quick to point out. Such people only make it look that way in order to support their religious empires. But if you don't pony up, go to hell! God certainly has it in for those who don't give snake-oil salesmen the money.

I recently received a typical holy begging letter from James Kennedy of Coral Ridge, one of many such Christian leaders including people like James Dobson who claim to be so concerned for children and who have never replied to the Amendment. Many of you know of this man and his influence in Christian circles (reminding me of gullible women. And men). The letter was a plea for funds to support Judge Roy Moore of Alabama who got in hot water for posting the Ten Commandments in his court and having a Protestant minister opening each session of the court with a Jesus prayer. Thereby telling Jews, Moslems, Hindus, agnostics, and deists that Moore's court was a little more considerate and inclined to the Jesus people rather than the motley crowd of plain old God's people.

Most certainly those like Franklin recognized the social benefits of religion, as well as the pitfalls, and he most certainly believed in God. And he recognized the need of the churches as a social necessity and moral teaching. All cultures have had taboos against the dishonoring of parents by children, taboos against adultery, lying, cheating, stealing, and murder. Notwithstanding the movies and books written by men, why give the Ten Commandments all the credit for some taboos which were in place long before their being given to Moses?

***

I wrote the following as an editorial for our local paper. But it contains some points of general importance, which I would like to share with all of my readers:

Most of us here in the Valley are fully (and in many cases, painfully) aware of the fact that we live in a very ecologically sensitive area, an area that has attracted the continued attention of many private conservation-minded groups as well as those of our friendly federal government. From the willow fly-catcher to various butterflies, rodents, plants and flowers to Indian burial grounds, our Valley is abundantly blessed with those elements which bring us the constant attention and oversight of experts and specialists who know how to protect endangered species and sacred sites from brutish and crass Valleyites who have little regard for such things and are so insensitive as to want to just be left alone and live as they wish in peace.

Now I wouldn't want the reader to think I am among those who believe that everything that moves in our Valley is meant by God to be used for target practice or plowed under for a new crop of marijuana. But when it comes to the intrusion of Big Brother into our lives for our benefit, I have to confess to an element of cynical doubt that has crept into my thinking as I begin to enter my dotage.

Those who know me well, knowing how shy and retiring, almost reclusive, I am, also know how reluctant I am to enter into any kind of controversy. Wishing to avoid conflict and confrontation, I am a most peaceable man who lives quietly to himself and usually tries to go along in order to get along.

But being a true red-blooded American, I don't countenance bullies and I know when my rights and those of others as Americans are being threatened. After all, it is the American way to stick up for the underdog, to confront injustice and fight for the right, to be the defenders of those who are threatened by tyrants and despots! It is at such times that I heed the clarion call to arms and come out of my shy, retiring, and afraid-of-women state and stand up to be counted.

A great and unrealized threat to an endangered species is occurring in the Valley, a threat that cannot continue to go unrecognized and unchallenged! And just what is this endangered species? you ask. Well, I'll tell you: It is unelegans bacchusdiptera, otherwise known as "The Common Barfly."

Most of my fellow citizens here in the Valley know how Alcoholic Beverage Control (ABC) agents ran amok during the recent Whisky Flat Days celebration. It was my good fortune to have been at Arlie's Club (one of the better establishments where clean Levi's and a T-shirt without holes aren't considered being over-dressed) when the arrests were made there. In fact, I had just been in conversation with two of the girls who were later arrested and was sitting with the daughter of one of our own local constables when the busts (no pun intended) came down (and I have to add that the dirty old man who had offered one of the girls twenty dollars to expose her breasts had already left).

The constable's daughter and I were enjoying the music provided by Oscar Whittington's band and saw the two agents enter the bar. The girl (a very lovely redhead, by the way) and I looked at each other and silently mouthed one word: Cops. They were so obvious they might as well as have been wearing badges and uniforms.

Now I am certain that if anyone at the club had been paranoid instead of simply having a good time, enjoying the music and dancing, enjoying the friendly atmosphere among friends, these agents wouldn't have found such easy pickings. But no one was suspicious, and welcomed the newcomers. Little did my friends realize they were to be prey to these vultures that had the Gestapo power of The State to arrest on the basis of Observation Only because of the Presumption of Guilt!

And those who tried to stick up for friends who were being arrested soon found themselves arrested as well!

I have written at length about the fact that far too many good people are not good citizens. This power of The State, the same as that of Totalitarian regimes, to arrest on the basis of observation only came as a shock to people. But far too many such people allowed this power of the State to come about because of their own apathy as citizens. They failed to know the issues and candidates; some don't even know the names of their government representatives and have never even written a letter to their local legislators. Some, I'm almost ashamed to say, don't even vote!

Well, since it isn't their ox that is being gored, most of the good people of the Valley, especially those of the churches which greatly outnumber the bars, seem to applaud the arrests and eagerly look forward to the extinction of *unelegans bacchusdiptera*. You don't smoke; stick it to those who do. You don't drink or go to a bar; stick it to those who do.

However, I would caution such good people that while no one of any reason wants drunks on our roads, while no one in their right mind advocates smoking, there is an essential point such good people seem to be missing in all of this. And it is a point that would seem so obvious as to be an insult to intelligence to even mention.

But here it is since it seems to need mention: If The State is intent on running the bars out of business, if the agents of The State can arrest on the basis of *Observation Only*, if good people of the Valley are encouraging the extinction of the common barfly, it is only a matter of time until agents wielding such power of The State will come for you as well! And then you may well find from painful, and humiliating, experience, how costly it can be to try to prove your innocence when the perversion of Due Process makes the presumption of guilt, rather than the presumption of innocence, the criteria by which you are judged.

And if tobacco is taxed out of existence by the bullying force of a short-sighted electorate, greedy lawyers and posturing politicians and forcing, as Prohibition did of alcohol, a black market and attendant crime, when will a loaf of bread be next? History is replete with such instances of the power of Caesar moving from sin taxes to taxing the necessaries of life. And since no people can reasonably expect to be both ignorant and free (and I would add, cannot expect to be free when not actively involved politically), I urge all of you to read David Hume's Pulitzer-winning book Mean Justice which targets Kern County and helps explain why the Valley is receiving so much attention from police agencies.

But, then, isn't it a commentary on the insanity of a people who are supposed to be self-governing and still allows laws that make it a crime for ordinary citizens to lie to government officials and elected representatives but not for them to lie to us? And a lot of such lying is exposed in Mean Justice.

It is said that a word to the wise is sufficient. But since it takes wisdom to appreciate how the extinction of the common barfly impacts on all of us, I would be less than human by failing to admit to a certain amount of pessimism regarding the final outcome. Still, there is this to be said for pessimism: It is easily delighted by being surprised.

***

Well, it's summer with a vengeance. The temperature has gone over one hundred degrees at times and the desert rat in me is responding accordingly. I luxuriate in the heat after the cruel cold of winter. And there is still the music, whether summer or winter.

I was doing some music with a local group when one of the members decided to talk to me during a break about my article on my friend Nelson, an alcoholic who committed suicide. This fellow is a business columnist and has a couple of books on economics in print. The music is his emotional outlet, just as it is mine.

"Sam," he said, "I have never told you this before but I just wanted you to know that your article in the paper about Nelson had me crying like I haven't done since I was a child. I had to tell you this and tell you how important your writing about such things as alcoholism is to people like me." Yes, this fellow is an alcoholic. And the booze is killing him. Like Nelson, he knows this. And he isn't going to quit any more than Nelson would. We both know this as well.

When I returned home and reflected on this fellow's comments, I thanked God once more that I don't fight the battle of such an addiction. But there is hardly a day that I don't thank God for this. I have lived in such an environment, worked with too many such people, for too many years; to take my lack of such an addiction for granted. I am, as one alcoholic friend told me, truly blessed in this regard.

But in the loneliness of this job for children, the loneliness of not having anyone to whom I can turn and say: "Sweetheart, what do you think about this?" the bottle has, at times, beckoned. And there has been the temptation, at times, to try to find some release by viewing things through the bottom of a glass. In other words, I can fully appreciate and understand why some people find the problems they confront too much to bear; especially the psychosis of grief that drives some to the bottle, other drugs or even suicide.

But so far I continue to be blessed. And, so far, I am still able to deal with my own pain and madness without resorting to chemical escape while being ever mindful that such can happen at any time, that I am only human and not immune to such a thing through any noble virtue of character I possess.

I recently had a beautiful woman visiting me. She has been through hell. And I wasn't going to contribute to that hell by taking advantage of her in her vulnerable state no matter how badly I need the inspiration of a woman in my life, in spite of the fact that such lack of inspiration prevents the best of my creative efforts though not that of simply doing my job.

Noble? I easily dispute that word when applied to me. Human? That I will accept; all too human in spite of my occasional lapses into some seeming acts of kindness or virtue. As to inspiration, nothing can inspire a man like a woman. And this is, as I believe, the way God intended things to be. But I am always careful to point out the difference between creativity and simply doing a job. Creativity requires inspiration. Doing your job does not. The job only requires the necessity of motivation. Like taking care of a family and keeping a roof over your head; or working for the Amendment.

But I'll continue to escape the siren call of chemical alternatives to the pain of loneliness and lack of inspiration in my life as long as there is the music, there are people who respond to my writing as my fellow musician did, as long as I can still give beautiful women the flowers they deserve and I have the children depending on me to be a man in the best sense of the term. Isn't this what being a man is supposed to be about?

CHAPTER TWELVE

This particular issue of TAP is composed of material from my book "Birds With Broken Wings" which many readers have requested.

In talking with the owner of one of the local bookstores recently, a lovely lady whose advice I take wholeheartedly, she asked why she or anyone should buy and read this book I was proposing to write: Birds With Broken Wings; a very legitimate and reasonable question.

I tried to answer her in this manner. I have been exposed to the Glory of Evil and the Dark Side of love and romance. Not only exposed, I began to undertake a purposeful investigation of these things that led where angels (and all good Baptists) fear to tread. For example, Barflies and prostitutes make their peculiar contributions to the book.

It was during this attempt at an explanation when the picture formed in my mind of addressing an auditorium full of women. My opening remark to them is:

Women hunger and thirst for romance. What is it that men want? The entire audience responds with a resounding chorus in unison with one word: SEX!

I then say: No, really ladies, what do men really want?

Again, with a single voice the chorus returns, loudly: SEX!

Seeing that I am getting no where fast I decide to try a new tack. I ask: Please, ladies, as a Romantic, a Poet, what do I, as a man, want?

Back it comes: SEX! There is a definite mind set at work here.

Okay, honestly, as a Romantic, a Poet, what do I want from a woman: SEX! Satisfied?

But now that I have admitted to being one of those, a man, my admission of common guilt is only true to a point; I want a great deal more from a woman because, like Thoreau, I don't think as other men.

Believe it or not, ladies, some men like myself want romance as much as you do. It is in searching for this elusive thing that I have discovered so much that betrays you ladies in the very areas you are supposed to excel in the romance department. I treat the causes and results of such betrayal in this book.

This betrayal is responsible to a great degree for so many *Birds With Broken Wings*. These are the many girls and women I have met under every conceivable circumstance of life who have suffered tragedies in their lives which have led them to despairing of finding a decent man, let alone romance.

There is much in the book which is, to say the least, controversial. But there is much that I hope men and women will take to heart in the search for this elusive thing called Romance.

And in my own defense of some of these controversial issues that I raise, I point out the fact that I love women. If I didn't, I wouldn't have married so many.

THE MISSING HALF OF HUMANKIND: WOMEN!

There is what I have come to call the Missing Half in the history of humankind. In my studies of history, philosophy, theology and political ideologies it finally dawned on me that women are conspicuous by their absence in all these things.

I had written much of the Birds book before I began to actively explore this phenomenon. The book was incomplete, this I knew. But what was missing? It was when I began to undertake this examination of the missing half of humankind in the philosophies of men that have guided the course of history that I wrote the book The Missing Half of Humankind: Women!

But it took the experiences of the Birds book to make me sensitive to the issues I explore in the Missing Half book. I sincerely hope you will read both books. And I hope men and women will respond to the questions and issues raised.

PROLOGUE

Why can't life be more like the music? I asked.

He replied: *Because people don't listen to the music anymore.*

I was in one of the dangerous parts of this city, visiting friends. Drive-by shootings, welfare and drugs were an endemic part of the culture in this community. But I was here largely because of the music.

It was late evening when I arrived. My friend's little girl met me at the door and asked if I had brought my guitar. I told her I had more than that. I then proceeded to unload both guitars, my clarinet, and tenor saxophone. Since it was fairly mild weather, I set the instruments up on the front porch of the house.

We sat together and using the acoustic guitar, I played and sang a simple song for the little girl. A couple of her little friends wandered over and sat on the grass listening.

I put the guitar in the little girl's lap and told her to try to pick out the notes to the song. Then I played a couple of melodies on the clarinet. But it was that big, beautiful tenor sax that had the attention of the children. More children and adults had gathered.

A tenor sax is a difficult instrument to mute. But the children were anxious to hear it. So I picked it up and began to play. The neighborhood could hear this. For many of my audience, this was the first time they had heard the kind of music that I had grown up playing and listening to, the music of Sammy Kaye, Russ Morgan, Guy Lombardo.

By the time I had played two songs, I had more than a dozen children and several adults in attendance. By now both guitars were in the hands of children and I had an impromptu audience of children and adults listening to music of a by-gone era, the big band and ballad music of the 30s and 40s which I had been playing and singing in a club down South.

Country Western is a large part of my life as well. I thoroughly enjoy much of this and my voice, nearly baritone, is well suited to this kind of music, especially the slow, romantic ballads. A lot of really good music has recently fled other fields and gone Country.

Unquestionably children readily respond to music. I wish every child could have music lessons and learn to play an instrument. But I have learned that only the music of a softer and gentler time, of an age of relative innocence that promised real love and romance, clean fun and hope of a future, works in the hearts and minds of children to their good.

The young men and women that had gathered, mostly teenagers, many in gang clothes and sporting identifying tattoos, were curiously silent as I played. There was no profanity, gang signals or chatter. They were caught up in a kind of music they had never heard live before. Most of them knew me but hadn't known of the music that was such a part of my life.

It was getting late and we had to go in the house. I hated to call an end to the magic of the music and it hurt to see the children leave. I knew what most of them were going home to. I knew the destructive noise of the kinds of so-called music they would hear in such homes, noise that accompanied violence, drugs and alcohol abuse. But thanks to the magic of a different kind of music, it would be a quieter night on this block and my friend's little girl didn't awaken screaming from her nightmares.

But the kind of music that both children and adults need in their lives is denied them. Few will ever have opportunity to learn to play a clarinet or saxophone and how many might have a better chance at life if such things could be made available to them?

I have made love to many women by singing and playing music to them, by writing them love letters, by nothing more than holding hands or dancing while beautiful music played in the background. These are the softer and gentler things of romance, of the real poetry of life, the things people say they hunger for but can't seem to find.

A very lovely lady who knows me well recently wrote and said I should spend my time writing of the evils of this world. She has read much of my writing that has been concentrated on the abuse of children, of the destruction of family and family values, of our nation's loss of its moral bearings and the corruption and chaos that seems endemic of the leadership of our government, schools, churches.

But sustained anger takes its toll. I needed to write a book like this in order to focus on the things that have real and eternal value, the love of family and children, the love between men and women. As the two halves of humanity, it is the relationship between men and women that predicts the future of a nation. Lacking understanding in this area, all else, children especially, suffers accordingly and the loss of hope among our young people, the loss of direction for our nation is the result.

This book deals with the loss of so much in our lives, the things that contributed to real love and romance the loss of which produced a generation of young women that I came to call: Birds With Broken Wings.

FATHERS AND DAUGHTERS
CHAPTER FOUR

I am, understandably, somewhat cautious in writing love letters. But I wrote one just recently and sent it to a very beautiful young lady. She is Kellie Martin, one of the stars of Life Goes On. This is going to take some explaining, of course, for those who know me and, most importantly, to not embarrass Kellie and my children.

I don't believe there is in the whole of Scripture a more heart-rending story than that of Nathan's confrontation of David's sin as described in the 12th chapter of II Samuel. It is made all the more significant because of the issues involved, love and romance versus lust. It is the significance of that poor man's little ewe lamb that is either pure or vile depending on the heart condition of those that read the story. If you are not familiar with the story, I hope you will read it; only then will you know what I mean as you read the following.

I have been a TV-basher for decades. I have not recanted my position but, thanks to Kellie, I have another perspective that was misplaced until I considered her and the show in which she stars. I am not given to mindless entertainment vis-a-vis TV. When it comes to TV series, I never got much beyond The Waltons and Little House. I read, travel, and write; I don't watch TV. But, by chance, I was switching channels one evening and a young lady's eyes stopped me in my tracks. I found myself riveted to the screen in a way I have never before experienced. It was crazy!

Discovering that the show was a series called "Life Goes On", I recalled skipping past the thing on a number of occasions without bothering to stop and check it out. That was before I saw Kellie's eyes. It happened that this occurred on the Family Channel and the segment I was watching was a re-run. I watched till the show was over, the uneasiest feeling clouding my mind. That little lady's eyes were haunting me and I didn't really know why. What was wrong with me?

I'm not usually so slow on the up-take. Finding out that the show, in re-runs, aired at 6pm weekdays, I tuned in again the following evening and watched the entire thing. I did this all week. Those eyes bewitched, enchanted, and haunted me together with the growing realization that this young lady was not just playing a part; she genuinely cared about people.

Maybe, I told myself, my love of young people, the thousands of teenagers I have worked with in the schools; maybe the answer to my uneasiness lay in that? No, that wasn't it. I know the tenderness evoked by the eyes of a baby; but it wasn't that either; although it was somehow vaguely close.

I didn't realize it at the time, but I had seen those eyes before and had succeeded in burying the memory so deeply that the pain of recalling them was more than I felt I could endure. It had taken years to overcome the pain of seeing the light of those eyes snuffed out and I struggled desperately, unconsciously, to keep the memory of them buried along with my eldest daughter, Diana.

Because of the inherent selfishness of adultery and divorce and the cruelties of judicial systems, I didn't have much of a chance to know Diana as a father longs to know a daughter. Before I realized it, she was a young woman and I hadn't even gotten to really know her as a child.

This was a very painful thing for me. I don't know why I thought it would make any difference, but I decided one evening to take Diana and her brother Daniel, my eldest son, to dinner in Redondo Beach, my old turf. I would risk telling them a story, which I hoped might make a difference. It went this way:

Not so very long after the divorce between their mother and me, I met a girl; nothing unusual in that, particularly not in the Camelot days of The South Bay. I was young and handsome, had a Cadillac convertible and a good job, loved music and knew a lot of people, had a lot of friends, especially in the theater arts. We were the young and beautiful people of the South Bay, living the lives others could only dream of or see in movies.

Life was gay and carefree, we were the true *Immortals* of the age and the world was our oyster. Then I met the girl who was to shape my life and destiny; irrevocably. Stunningly beautiful, even by extravagantly high South Bay standards, red hair, green eyes, slightly short of five-feet tall and a figure that defies description. But it was her voice, more than anything else that was the epitome of femininity. Her voice was that of a choir of angels, a divine music unparalleled in the universe.

Here, at last, was the very physical personification of all that the poets and artists had tried in vain to capture, the reason for slaying dragons and hewing out wilderness places, a reason to cheerfully face any obstacle, any danger, the reason which gave reason to the sun's rising and setting, gave intelligibility to life itself, definition to soul, to heart, to being! Here was love to exhaust the Poet's Thesaurus of words and phrases in its most raw and profoundly jealous and unforgiving essence, demanding virtually everything! This Pearl of Great Price! Only one thing was lacking, a lack for which I had no experiential frame of reference, a lack which was to doom my own heart's best efforts; she didn't have Kellie's eyes.

I gave it everything I had to offer. I lived, really lived, for months, in that heavenly aerie where only those that really love ever dwell. But I was the innocent in such affairs of the heart. I didn't know how to guard against the enemies of such a thing, I didn't know the hatred such beauty could engender in the hearts of others. Tragically, my love for this beautiful girl was betrayed and I nearly died for the loss. I drank heavily for a while but found no relief from the pain and grief in that and soon gave it up. And though I wouldn't die, neither was I ever to fully recover either. While her eyes had not been Kellie's and I had not, at the time, any basis of comparison, when I last saw her as a woman fully grown and having gone through several men, her eyes had become hard and brittle, cynical and suspicious. I grieved more for that than almost anything else. It was then that I learned what was to become too common in my experience over the years. This beautiful girl had an ugly father, but as with many such fathers, he had been able to hide his ugliness.

Redondo, Hermosa, Manhattan Beach, Malibu and Venice were a fairyland, filled with magic and beauty. The Albatross in Malibu, with its dining area built out over the surf, the quaint, picturesque little place up Trancas Canyon and the beautiful drive up to it, clean, uncrowded beaches; my friends in the various theater groups and the music (oh, the music! I sang, played clarinet and tenor sax). There was more than enough magic in which to seek the love I had found and lost. But I was never to find it again, not even in such a rare environment.

A most peculiar thing; none of my friends and acquaintances of the time seemed to understand what it was, exactly, that I had lost and I was looking for? As one girl told me at the time, "You don't have any trouble getting any girl you want. What's the problem?" I couldn't give her a satisfactory answer. There was no way, at the time, that I could even explain it to myself. There have been a number of women since the girl, their warmth and softness filling the needed role that exists in all men's lives. But never again was I to find that real romance that I had once known.

As we sat there, the father telling his teenage children that he had once known what real love was, had in fact experienced it in all its grand and bitter facets, had drunk its cup from brim to lees, and had never betrayed its memory, a hush, almost church-like in its reverential aura, seemed to surround us. I realized that I had, after the years had done their task of giving me the words, been able to make what I had, and had lost, real to my daughter. I had emptied my very soul to her in the hope of giving her something of real value. I had been able, after all these years, to tell her that her father had experienced the very thing that the poets and great artists, the great composers and their music, try to explain. I was trying to tell her not to ever lose hope of real love, never to settle for second best, but to find that man to whom she would be the poetry of his very existence; she was of far too great value to settle for less and would spend her life feeling cheated if she settled for anything less, that it would be a constant empty, aching yearning until it was satisfied.

Almost as though it were cued, we got up silently from our table. I paid the check and we walked out into the summer evening. I drove the children back in silence. I had to return to Lancaster but it was hard to tell them goodbye. As we got out of my car, Diana walked around to me and, putting her arms around my neck and looking directly into my eyes said almost in a whisper: "Dad, I really do love you." Then she kissed me. She was crying softly but I could see Kellie's eyes through the tears for the first time in my life and my very heart and soul melted within me. There would be no turning back from this, the most profound truth in the universe, the purest expression of love between a man and a woman that can possibly exist! And it was the look in a daughter's eyes for her father!

Far beyond any physical thing, far beyond any attempt at definition, pure beyond any understanding this side of heaven and eternity; innocent beyond innocence, Trust beyond trust, a totality of the giving, in sacredness far beyond anything the churches claim knowledge of, the utterly selfless giving of the very being of the person in absolute trust and understanding! Deathless! Immortal!

For many years, I have tried, vainly, to find that look in the eyes of other women. Invariably, it has worked out in continued betrayal of love where those eyes didn't exist and, through loneliness and desperation, I took the risk anyhow.

TV Guide lists Life Goes On as #1 among the 10 top shows recommended for Teens. Quote: Parents who struggle, kids who cope, and believable love. And it is Kellie, largely, who makes it believable. But such believability is only achieved through the vulnerability of genuinely caring about others; no matter how masterful the actor or actress, this is not something that can be learned as a craft; it is either there or it is not.

And, so, I fear for Kellie, as I do for Karrie, my remaining little angel, as someone who has that rare and precious gift of really caring. And because of this, they are vulnerable to the evil that men do and those eyes betray their love to those who would take advantage as well as to those who would return that love in kind.

People have often asked why I don't write fiction rather than the hard and thankless task of history, philosophy and politics. It wasn't until, after all these years of keeping the memory buried, only to have it reawakened by Kellie, that I have a proper answer. No man, knowing what I do, can deal with a fictitious romance. Oh, I tried a few, only to cheat others as well as myself in the process; I have conned myself into believing many things that were not so in order to assuage the pain of loneliness. Who of us has not?

But to attempt to describe the indescribable; I cannot. I can place flowers on the nightstand of my Lady, I can try, with all my powers, to describe my feelings to her, I can do the thankless and grimy tasks of day-to-day living and punching a clock as expressions of my love, but if those eyes of innocent trust and wonder and unreserved giving are missing, I soon realize, as it continues to play itself out, it is all in vain.

Damned by an age which despises Cooper and Thoreau, the art of language, hopes, dreams and ideals of true love and true romance, our young people have been cheated of the most precious thing of all: the ability to give and receive pure, unselfish love, this having been betrayed and traded for unbridled lust where our young girls are the predominant victims, an age where we are learning, more and more, that our young girls are preyed upon by even those of their own families! How willing I would be to put the rope around the neck of any that would betray the trust of a child in such a fashion! These maimers and cripplers of innocence cannot be human beings! They are beasts; devouring, unclean, predatory, satanic destroying animals and should be treated as such!

As I began to face up to what Kellie had opened in my own soul which I thought had been successfully buried, the question was what to do about it? For several days I struggled with the question. So it was that I determined to write the love letter.

I know nothing and everything about Kellie Martin. It's what I know of genuine love and romance, what I know from her eyes that truly counts about Kellie, that makes me fearful for her and all the Kellies she represents. So it was that the letter was one I might very well have written to one of my own daughters or a thousand Kellies. Certainly my girls have been the recipients of the thoughts of their father. But, how many times did I fail to warn those thousands of teenagers I was entrusted with in the schools? Now, having seen Diana's eyes once again in Kellie, I had to at least try to do something about it.

Not long after the incident I have described my little girl was killed in a motorcycle accident after having been married just less than a year. She lay in a coma for several days. Danny and I would sit by her side, reading the Bible and praying, hoping against hope that she would come out of it. But it wasn't to be. She slipped quietly away from us without ever regaining consciousness.

Would telling any of this to Kellie be of any meaning or help to her? The heart continues to have its reasons of which Reason knows nothing so I felt I had to make the attempt. Those eyes are far too rare and precious not to try!

Sure, I can tell myself that true love and romance were not in the curriculum guide when I was a teacher. And, to be fair to myself, I did my utmost to make my young charges aware of my own feelings in such matters. But I could, should, have done more!

Kellie's eyes are those of my daughter Karen's as well. But Karen has been hurt and betrayed so much in her young life, seeking love and fulfillment that she is beginning to lose the open, wonder-filled, pure, honest, trusting elements of these wells and windows of the soul. People who care as much as Karen and Kellie can never hide what they really feel, their eyes betray them. I grieve to see in Karen's eyes the increasing knowledge of an evil world of selfish, using and abusing, people.

Are we now a society for which genuine love and romance are anachronistic, a harking back to simpler times where the search for such a Holy Grail was not an exercise in quixotic futility? I will not have it so! Not as long as there are girls like Kellie, not as long as there are daughters like Diana and Karen who can truly love their fathers and evoke the purest love in the universe in those father's hearts!

I'll never forget the time I took Karen out for our very first grown-up dinner together. She was only seventeen but she was breathtakingly beautiful. I had difficulty believing that this beautiful little woman was my own daughter, the little girl I use to tumble with, cuddle, tease and tickle.

I had made reservations for the dinner at one of the finest restaurants in the area. Every eye in the place was on us. I was bursting with pride that my little girl was pleased to let her daddy show her off and show her off I did. Now you just can't do this with your sons. A father has an altogether different relationship with sons. As they grow up, they become men in their own right; but those little angels? Never! They will never become women; they will always be Daddy's Little Girl!

Karrie (she will never be Karen to her dad) couldn't possibly have known the turmoil of my own thoughts as we sat in this fashionable restaurant and I savored every moment of this precious time together. I wanted to capture it forever, indelibly, on my heart and soul, to have it there for recall when the shadows of life began to lengthen, when she would move into her own sphere of living her own life and dad would recede.

What kind of men are the "Daddies" of all these girls who sell out their dreams of a good man so cheaply? And all these young men who treat girls so shabbily, what are their fathers teaching them? What redeeming note can be sounded for a culture which treats its children in such a fashion, leaving them without their right to dream and hope?

I have a hard-earned reputation for never betraying a confidence. Powerful men and women have chosen me as a confidante on this basis because, curiously, they find it very difficult to find people they can trust, and yet this doesn't lessen their need, as human beings, for someone they can talk to.

About a year ago, a CEO who heads a large organization covering 22 states called me about a personal problem he was having. In the course of the conversation I asked him: "J-, don't you have anybody you can trust?" His reply stunned me: "No one." At the most human level imaginable, here was a man who commanded legions, whose most basic need, someone he could simply talk to and share with, was denied him.

It's a pity I haven't been in closer contact with those in show business, especially young people. I have been remiss in not keeping in touch with so many over the years. There is probably no other business where loneliness is so rampant. The entertainment business being by its very nature so fiercely competitive, betrayal is a commonplace. As I mentioned in a previous chapter, there are two broad classes of people who never know who their real friends are: One, the wealthy and powerful; two, beautiful women.

But now, thanks in large part to a little lady with wondrous eyes, Kellie, I am going to try to reach out to a group of people who, while as actors and actresses, attempt to portray love too often fail to find even one person they can trust, let alone love without reservation.

It is a truism that it is, indeed, lonely at the top. Too many times, in seeking gratification of the ego in reaching success, we let the things of real value fall victim. Hence, too many times, as I have discovered, *Rosebud* becomes the preoccupation of later life and the dying word on the lips of the powerful.

It was one of the greatest experts on love who ever lived who said that even though love were betrayed seventy times seven, the heart of the real lover never stops forgiving and seeking, never fails of the hope that next time it will be found.

My critical remarks concerning women in general over the past few years have led some to the distortion that I don't like women. Nothing could be further from the truth. I candidly admit that I'm not sure that I will ever be able to trust another one. The very idea terrifies me at times. But I'm more than willing to try.

Further, these critical comments have most often been directed at a system which has victimized both men and women, too often casting them in an adversarial and competitive relationship rather than one in which each looks and works for the best for the other.

Perhaps it is the purview of a man who still finds meaning in the music of the great musicals of the theater, who still finds the barking squirrel and the call of a quail or the chirp of a cricket more important than so many other things which demand of our time, to find some sense in all the madness of this age. I do admit saying, at one time, that I had discovered that while women loved poetry, I hadn't found one yet who could live with the poet. But though I admit, as stated, that the idea terrifies me, I haven't given up hope of finding such a one.

Because of Kellie, I have opened a host of old wounds that might defy healing otherwise. As I draw them into the light, I see more closely the stars, the trees, rocks, mountains and streams of my sauntering, the things I have sought refuge in so that I might have the courage of my convictions and write and speak as I have these past years.

When I have written of the evil that men do, nowhere is such evil more apparent than in its destructiveness in the lives of our young people. When I speak out about the abuses of children in our schools and society, when I agonize at the loss of their hopes and dreams of a future and my anger flames against their betrayers, I realize that the righteous wrath that inflames my soul has its source in what I, personally, know of real hopes, dreams, love and romance because of the fact that I have never given up, never betrayed, the best part of the child within myself.

Maybe this is because my earliest lessons in the subject were taught by my great-grandmother and my grandparents who were so very transparent in their love for my brother and me and for one another. Maybe it's because I was raised reading Cooper, Hawthorne, Thackery and so many others who held on to the dream. Maybe it was my earliest experiences as a child in the wilderness of the forest fastness where I could actually live the romance and adventure of which men like Cooper wrote. Or, maybe, it really took hold when I moved to Redondo Beach and discovered girls at Mira Costa High School.

The tragedy of my life seems to have been my unwillingness to compromise the ideals of real love and romance as so eloquently expressed in our best literature, our best music and art. I could never involve myself with one of these beautiful girls with the thought of ever betraying them by unfaithfulness and, unreasonably as it seemed to turn out, I actually believed that my own faithfulness would be returned in kind, thinking they felt as I did about the matter. To me, it was a simple, basic thing: One man, one woman. If you had one, you had your limit!

I have been born to the wrong generation. That's not to tell God His business but, as some of my detractors have pointed out, any man who says that God has made mistakes must surely endure the mark of Ichabod over his brow mustn't he?

As I got on in the business of making a living over the years, particularly in the schools, I came into increasing contact with the government agencies like CPS and the Juvenile Justice System. I began to know the probation officer better than the parent. The horror of what was happening to our children and young people became a living nightmare for me. I witnessed the loss of moral absolutes and moral leadership for the children. The decimation of the 60s continues to do its dirty work in the schools and homes of America.

As I would, increasingly, become exposed to the burgeoning Social Service answer to our betrayal of our children, my heart would sicken at the growing number of children having babies, the increasing number of such very young girls, children themselves, actually, with one or more babies, sitting in welfare offices waiting to go on the dole or trying to find a sympathetic ear for their hopelessness. I would wonder where the men were? Where were the fathers of these babies, the husbands of these child-brides?

I was born to the wrong generation; obviously. Imagine having the mind-set that no real man worthy of the name would be able to bear the shame of abandoning his responsibility to these girls and these children!

And so it was that a litany of sorrows was beginning to be formulated in my mind and would lead to my work of the last few years. A challenge to the evil that men do, a challenge to the tyranny of Caesar and his minions who would lead the betrayal of our young people and their hopes and dreams.

I have written so much on this theme in the political context that it would be unfair to my readers to rehash it here. What I have failed to do until now is to give vent to my own heart's anguish as I watch these girls with babies trying to cope with a system of evil not of their making. Sure I blame women for not leading where they are the most effective; I blame them for their part in allowing their sex to become a commercial commodity to be bartered, for lending themselves to the system of pornography to satisfy the unholy lust of evil men. But they can never be blamed for the evil that so-called *men* do; the evil of the double standard where the girl was to be pure and chaste but it was acceptable for the boy to be experienced! Just who, exactly, were the purveyors of this invidious, twisted, distorted lie from the very bottom of the pit of Hades!

It will take a book of many pages, a huge data base, to make sense of the immensely complex issues, twists and turns of history, that have led to what children and young people face today. Evil men and seducers have a long and black history. But there was a time in this nation when we cherished our young, when we planned for our posterity, when we knew and practiced the truth of that implacable and immutable imperative of history: *A nation which does not cherish its young has no future as a nation.*

It's cold now here in the mountains and we're expecting a snowstorm. We have a new county complex in our small community. It will facilitate dealing with the increased welfare cases which are, more and more, being referred from Bakersfield because the cost of housing is cheaper here than there. I see more and more young girls, often pushing a stroller with a baby and a toddler at their side, heading up the road to the welfare office in the cold.

I'm reminded of the young lady who told me things were better for her now compared to when she was in Flagstaff and had to pull her little girl in a wagon through the deep snow to go to the store a great distance away. The husband was in jail. Things were much better for her now.

The curse of beauty. So many of these girls are pretty but their attractiveness proves to be their tragedy when they are led to believe that boys will commit and provide for them. Where is the mature leadership of family, of a society, which should be able to teach them better, should set the examples of morality and good judgment which these girls so desperately need? Who is going to tell them the truth of the fact that boys only want one thing from them and when that is given so freely, it has little value! Why aren't they being taught to wait for a real man in their lives, why are they being encouraged to squander the preciousness of their youth on snot-nosed brats who have neither the ability nor intention of providing for them as a real man would? So it is that I was either born to the wrong generation or I have simply lived too long. I am an anachronistic dinosaur who refuses to accept the bludgeoning of such evils as terminal. I don't seem to be able to accept my fate and just let go.

Hollywood, as well as the schools, churches and families, must give an account. And our leaders in government? Dear God in Heaven, what they have to account for!

It was in another life that I sat with my arm about a sweet scented girl in my convertible by the beach in Palos Verdes and watched the sun set; the waves wash the shore and listened to Ebb Tide on the car radio. With that beautiful, warm, soft girl in my arms in such a setting, the world was a kind place and understood the needs of lovers.

I could spend an evening with my girl at the Ambassador Hotel's Coconut Grove for a marvelous dinner, dancing and live entertainment; we could cruise Sunset with the top down and never worry about other people. Just as we could do going to Malibu or driving Pacific Coast Highway from Manhattan Beach to San Diego. We did indeed live the lives of Lotus-Eaters.

Beauty is always in danger and at the risk of envy. That is the reason for so much that is ugly being whitewashed and thereby christened equal to beauty. When I visit the scenes of my youthful Camelot, it is hard to believe the devastation, the wholesale destruction of so much that was once a source of such beauty and joy of living.

I don't know, yet, how long Life Goes On has been airing. The new episodes have Kellie caring for a boy with AIDS. With the objectivity of a new viewer, I look at Kellie in the old re-runs and Kellie in the new episodes. She is growing up. I'm watching her with a father's compassion. It might be Karrie on the screen and I find myself wishing I could offer her my own counsel, could help her through the pain of growing up and deal with the unfairness and injustice all about. A flashback to Marilyn Monroe reminds me of the desperate loneliness of so many show business personalities and the Mansons and their type who through their own ugliness would try to destroy beauty. There are a lot of sick and evil people out there who would hurt those whom they envy.

There are a few who remind me, occasionally, to take a look over my shoulder once in a while; this, primarily, because of my political essays. But I doubt that there are any in our society who have more legitimate fear of Kooks and Cranks than those who are in show business. This has to, together with the multitude of those who would try to use successful people, make for limited friendships.

Curious, isn't it, that the industry, Hollywood in particular, which gives us the illusion of love would be so desperate for it itself? Notwithstanding all the sex and violence, this is an industry filled with lonely people who are largely trying to find the very things, love and trust, commitment and fidelity that they sell so effectively as fairytales, playing the parts that elude them in real life.

Are the majority of us any different? I think not. The only real difference is that most of us aren't making our living by acting out our fantasies. We will accept the placebos and do our vicarious living through the personalities we view on screen. It wouldn't help our own fantasies much to wonder about the loneliness, hurt and disappointments of our beautiful people. It wouldn't help us to know the tragedies of their own lives in their failures to find the things of real value we all need and seek.

As I watch Kellie in her role of Rebecca dealing with the boy with AIDS, as I compare her eyes with the early episodes of her girlhood, I find a change, the change I watched in my own daughters' eyes as they became young women. And I hurt. Do they have to grow up in such a fashion that what was so sweet and innocent has to change to suspicion and distrust through having to face too many hard choices while they are children? What can we say of a society that no longer encourages innocence and wonder that steals our children's rights to a childhood?

I have told my girls that no matter what they do in their lives, they will always be my little angels; they will never become women but will always be my daughters. But not the most loving father will ever be able to protect his little girls from discovering, for themselves, the tragic fact that the majority of boys and men will take advantage of them if they allow it. More and more, I am hearing girls of the age of Karrie and Kellie telling me there are no good men their own age. There is too much truth in what they are saying. The welfare offices testify to the ugly truth of their condemnation.

Would it do any good to point to the high divorce rate and call attention to the fact that so many girls are molested by a stepfather or one of his relatives? And, further, that this is because the mother usually has the custody of the children and often doesn't waste much time filling the missing father's side of the bed?

Would it do any good to point out the fact that our schools, entertainment media and society seems to shove our boys and girls together in relationships for which neither are prepared, that teaches there are no consequences for the lack of personal responsibility? Would it help to call attention to the fact that young people, especially our girls who because of indifference are so desperate for someone to love them that they are easy prey to anyone who shows them a little kindness and consideration, seek out someone who seems to have some time for them and cares for them?

I can't see the world from Karrie and Kellie's eyes but I can see their eyes as only a father can. Regardless of their experiences with other men in their lives, Karrie and Kellie will always be the kind of girls who will need their fathers (as, I have to suppose, all girls do). A father should be the man who never fails them. If they should find good husbands, these men should never fail them either.

If I were to ever get behind another pulpit, I would preach on South Pacific. But that is because I know the Bible and the heart of God well enough to do so. For example, "This Nearly Was Mine" is not a romantic cliche in my life; I lived it.

South Pacific is one of our all-time great musicals. Richard Rogers and Oscar Hammerstein II really outdid themselves on this one. With a Broadway cast led by Ezio Pinza and Mary Martin, the unsurpassed music lives in the hearts of multiplied millions. Michener would never have believed his Tales of the South Pacific could have resulted in such a romance of brilliance.

The great musicals of American art still speak to all those who refuse to give up the dream that men and women can still find love; those who don't seek it out or give up are the much poorer for it. Such people cheat themselves of the haunting truth of Some Enchanted Evening and Bali Ha'i for fear, perhaps, of not being able to endure the pain of This Nearly Was Mine. Such cowards will never understand Carefully Taught.

I was only beginning to learn to play the clarinet and saxophone from the great music teacher of old Kernville, Williard Swadburg, when the music of South Pacific came onto the airwaves. But I added the songs as quickly as possible to my, then, slim repertoire. Music became such a passion of mine in high school that I joined with another boy, Russell, as the only two boys in a class of girls for Music Appreciation. Now that was truly heroic!

As a man, in spite of my fears I still hold on to the dream of finding the warmth and love, the inspiration that only a woman can provide. I am still that Cockeyed Optimist: "I hear the human race, is falling on its face, and hasn't very far to go. But every Whippoorwill, is selling me a bill, and telling me it just ain't so! ...

But I'm stuck like a dope, with a thing called hope and I can't get it out of my heart!"

One of the nicest compliments I have received recently was from a woman who said she enjoyed reading my writing because it was down to earth. I will forego the high-sounding rhetoric, no matter how erudite, and the jarring of literary critics that the lyrics of such music as that of South Pacific doesn't qualify as poetic art. Let me bear the brunt of those who are so callous as to not recognize the merits of such things while I pity them as they remain outside the pale of romance.

If a man or woman can relate to This Nearly Was Mine, who has felt the pain of Paradise Lost without it destroying them, without making them give up the dream of Paradise Regained, they are really alive. Those of us whose hearts are moved to look into the distance and give ourselves to the haunting melancholy of Bali Ha'i are not without hope of that love that will fulfill our purpose and destiny as human beings. Our critics never give themselves to understanding and confronting the lessons of hatred (Carefully Taught) simply because other people are different.

In spite of the pain of the continual betrayal of love, the music remains in my own heart but I have been robbed of the memories. I can recall the warmth and softness of the women I have known, but their betrayal of love by their infidelity has stolen their faces from memory, stolen the secrets of lovers, and stolen the special, precious memories of the sharing of lives, the meeting of the challenges of life together for the benefit of one another and family; so much loss, huge chunks of life itself buried deeply in the subconscious as callous protection from the pain and grief of tragedy. It's not unlike my delight in placing a fresh flower on the nightstand of my Lady. She is gone now, betraying my love for her for the cares and concerns of this world, the easy seduction by so-called men who prey on silly women who are easily flattered and go for the better deal, betraying the flowers and the things of real value for those things that will only perish in the using and the sins of the flesh.

I can't help but wonder if the churches will ever get beyond the dusty, musty stories of past glories and battles won; the rudimentary fundamentals of the faith and recognize the longing of hearts, the need for the gentle strength of faith that builds on the present rather than the constant recitation of the past. A far more powerful sermon could be preached on the themes of South Pacific than the tired cliches of Moses in the bulrushes, the dusty tales re-hashed endlessly. To teach the young the grand old stories is considered necessary. But when the pabulum is simply supplied a garnish and expected to sustain the adult, something is missing; the meat! But the churches are no more heedful of this missing ingredient, confusing it with theology, than they are of the necessity of hearts which seek meaning in meaningless ceremonies and, consequently, find those needs only hollowly met.

If I were back in the pulpit, I would preach on South Pacific. I would quote Corny as Kansas in August and ask the relevant question: Who made such feelings corny? I would reach out to hearts with God's own love in Some Enchanted Evening and Bali Ha'i. I would address the reasonable questions of Carefully Taught and ask, further, what happened to our music which used to be fun (Phil Harris and Spike Jones), romantic (Rudolf Friml, Rogers and Hammerstein) inspiring (Sousa), lilting, spirited and just plain good to listen to (the Big Bands)? And the same could be said of our literature.

Among my theological writings, there is my treatment of the loss of innocence in The Garden. As long as Adam and Eve were true to love, they shared each other's innocence; when a third party, Satan, was allowed to intrude, innocence was blasted. When a young man and woman come together, each for the first time, there is the sharing of innocence all over again, *The two become one.* Allow a third party to intrude, and innocence is blasted once again. As with virginity; once betrayed, it is never to be regained. It is a tragedy of monstrous proportions that purity and chastity are held to be and treated of such slight value in our contemporary society.

We have invited the wholesale blasting of purity, chastity and innocence in our society and are reaping a whirlwind of hopelessness. We now live in an age where the things I have boldly put into print regarding my daughters and Kellie call up the most vicious thoughts of things like "Something About Amelia", and, most recently, "Not In My Family", of the perversions of bestial men who prey upon the innocents.

It was still possible, when I was a freshman teacher, to give a girl or boy in one of my classes an encouraging hug of genuine affection. No longer. We now live with an evil connotation attaching to virtually all male/female relationships.

I think Marilyn vos Savant is a remarkably clear-thinking woman. When asked which she considered the most powerful, love or reason, she replied: "I think love is more important, but human reason is more powerful. Love may give us some great intentions, but reason is what actually gets the job done." Not the most romantic phraseology but she is certainly accurate in her assessment.

If that girl thinks that boy really loves her, why won't she give reason a chance? Reason dictates that real love seeks to please the object of that love, not make demands to satisfy itself.

Having sons as well as daughters, I have much to say on that subject as well but the message, while the same in its most profound similarities, is different in many respects. It is essentially different in respect to the responsibilities that attach to the relationships between fathers and daughters as compared to fathers and sons.

As a man, I want my sons to be able to meet certain demands as men that I do not expect of my daughters. Not that I don't have high expectations for the girls, but I know men have the ultimate responsibility for leadership. No man can ever blame a woman for his failure as a man. I want them to be the kind of men that deserve the respect of women like Karrie and Kellie. This is not easy in our society.

The lesson of the 60s was that without moral restraints a society is bound to drift into moral anarchy. But I have learned the lessons of a tender heart because of my daughters and girls like Kellie. I have learned that they need the genuine love of a man, they need the music, poetry and flowers and unfailing, gentle strength.

I remember a time when it was enough to sit by the hour and listen to Nat King Cole with that soft, warm girl in my arms. Now our young people seem to think sex is the most significant expression of love and lose that which is of far greater value in the process.

In my solitude as I walk among the pines, rocks and hills of the forest, my attention is drawn ever more to the plight of our young people. Who really speaks to and for them? What is my generation really doing of any consequence which offers them hope of anything changing for the better?

Long after my years at Cal State Long Beach and other schools, after teaching in Watts and East San Jose, I realize that things have not gotten better for those whose frustrations led to the '65 riots, Woodstock, Selma and Kent State. I know the answers are in my clear mountain stream and the call of the quail. I know they are in those classrooms where teachers have a chance to make a difference to those young people if teachers really care. I know the answers are in the way parents respond in love to the needs of their children.

But we now have a society which does not love children, that warehouses them and expects them to by-pass childhood, and punishes them for having dreams and hopes of a future. The problems and answers are national in scope and require a hugely complex database. An understanding of the function of chaos is essential to coming up with solutions. Human behavior is complex in the extreme. We don't even understand the mechanisms of the relationship between the father and the daughter and the husband and the wife. I do know there is a difference in the innocence and purity of each, a difference in what would be evil in the one case and holy in the other. But how that distinction is made without any effort of will or mind in some and not in others I don't know. I just know it is the basest, most destructive evil imaginable when the distinction fails.

Because of the evil that men do, we seem not to be able to deal with the questions with the required honesty. But in the case of real love and romance, if men like me are to spare our own feelings, if we are more concerned with embarrassing ourselves than trying to reach out to our young people with hope and understanding, they will continue to be left with the purveyors of lust as their teachers.

If you can relate to my own heart's concern for young people, you will understand my trying to bring the issue of the exploitation of young girls and women, especially, by the entertainment industry out into the open. I am gratified to see people like Shelly Winters finally speaking openly about it.

No other industry has been so deadly in regard to the exploitation of women, especially the attractive ones. I know how odd it seems to the general readership that I would be defending those who seem to have it made. But, in my own experience, this is not the case. Very few of even the most beautiful girls and women make it successfully in this industry. It doesn't help their cause that so many willingly give themselves to exploitation.

In my case, I know that if I didn't have beautiful daughters whom I love more than my own life, I probably wouldn't give it much thought. But it takes fathers worthy of the name to concern themselves in this matter. Further, we all know the impact the industry has on our young people. Shows like Clarissa, Degrassi High, Class of 96, Beverly Hills 90210, etc. have an incalculable effect on the direction our young people take in making decisions that will have life-long implications.

Since TV has such an inordinate impact on the lives of young people, the media has an enormous responsibility. Kellie and Life Goes On is one of the most promising aspects of dealing with this responsibility in a positive fashion. I will be expecting to hear from you, my readers, as to your own thoughts on the subject.

Life is, at best, a bittersweet waltz. Life does, indeed, go on. But how wonderful it would be if all those fathers who are blessed with Little Angels would consider just how precious little time is given us to make the difference in their lives that will give them the chance for growing up with the sense of their true value.

If our little girls had such a sense of worth, how different so many things would be. I was fortunate. I was given one more chance and I took it. If I hadn't...! But, thank God, I did take it! And I won a reprieve from what would have become my worst nightmare.

Parents are not supposed to bury their children. There is something terribly unfair, terribly wrong, about this! But it happens. Diana's eyes are now a blessing, not the curse they might have been if I hadn't risked what I did. Diana, like my remaining little angel Karen, is the best part of me because I was honest with her. By opening the deepest part of my own heart and soul to her, letting her know how very human her father was and how very precious she was to me, she is with me in a way that gained something of such eternal value even death must bow in homage to it.

If I can help fathers and daughters realize how important it is to be honest with each other, to understand each other, what a difference that would make in our world. Sadly, you can't make people care. But for those that do, it is a different world where there are no tired cliches of love, where the music continues to live in our hearts and hope never fails. And if I have made a fool of myself in sharing these things with you, I sincerely apologize. Most of all, I desperately hope I have not embarrassed Karrie or Kellie. Perhaps it will accomplish some good in the telling; for their sakes I hope so.

Hopefully, having said these things, I may be able to get on with the business of dealing with the ordinary things that comprise so much of our lives of quiet desperation. If, as Thoreau said, If life is only a waiting, so be it should prove to be the case, I would despair. But, I somehow doubt that such is the case. I don't believe he thought so either. Life is making choices and setting events into action. It will always be better to choose to love than hate, to give than receive, to live for others rather than selfishly, to take the risk of betrayal rather than shelter ourselves in reclusive seclusion from caring.

Will my sons understand? Not until they have Little Angels of their own; how could they? But I pray they will come to understanding in their own relationships with the daughters of other fathers. Only then can they expect any real happiness in their own lives and be able to come to a knowledge of their own value as men. I am not ignoring the role mothers play in all this. But I can't presume to speak for them. I'm having a difficult enough time trying to sort through dad's role.

It would certainly be far easier to fictionalize the things I have said; to put the events and words in the form of characters rather than exposing myself. But the most sensitive among you will realize the loss this would represent. So I am taking the risk of personalizing things of such intimacy that the enemies of those things that are pure, honest and of good report may try to use them against me.

The Poet and Philosopher have too often been dismissed to some hazy area of gauzy scenes, ephemeral and ethereal sidelines of non-importance far removed from the place of action where the real work is going on. In truth, there is too much justification for this condemnation. Too many times have poets and philosophers played it safe by sidelining themselves and not intruding into areas of life where they might suffer some hurt by speaking out.

This is the safe position of the liberal academic. Having done battle in the universities in just this arena, I carry the scars of the maverick that would not be whipped into shape and bull-headedly keeps carrying a standard for individual liberty with corresponding responsibility. This kept me in trouble throughout my academic career. But in too many cases, it has been the well-intentioned conservative who, without the required qualifications and credentials, has become my enemy because he lacked those essentials of understanding and substituted ignorance and prejudice for them.

I can only say, in my defense, that if people would respond to those things of real value, those things represented by Diana, Karrie and Kellie, our little ewe lambs, there wouldn't be terrorist bombs, Kooks in Texas, riots in our cities and inner city hopelessness, the wholesale destruction of young people, especially our girls, by Hollywood and society in general, failure in our schools and homes, in the leadership of our nation.

I have to confess my natural affinity for the theater, for the performing arts. In having to deal with so much reality of day-to-day living and ugliness, there is a natural attraction for those like myself to a different world where make-believe is preferable to the evil that abounds. My success with young people in the classroom was my being able to involve myself in their world, with the extremes of emotions to which they were so susceptible, and understand those extremes rather than condemn them.

Where else is the actual poetry of life so evident as in our young people with their dreams and hopes? They haven't yet been taught or learned what is impossible. We are desperately in need for the right kind of leadership that will encourage them in their dreams rather than a continued pounding into them the gloom of the real world. Prepare them; by all means; but not at the cost of their ability to dream and hope.

There is no other age that is so altruistic and so easily led in hope as the adolescent. All things are possible at this age. I have often said I could move mountains if I were able to exercise the authority to lead young people in the right direction. But our society and schools are the enemies of such direction and dreams.

When you are standing before such a class of young people and you are truthful with them, when they find you believable in caring about them, they are the most open people in the world. They will share their hopes and dreams in an atmosphere of possibilities. It is a wonderful experience to listen to them and encourage them in the sharing.

The idealism of youth is a thing precious in itself, something to encourage and build on. This is the age where the arts, literature, music, the theater and plays should be the basis for life. The very extremes of emotions which attract our young people to the ideals of love and romance should be encouraged in purity of those ideals rather than the utter casting aside of those moral absolutes which would temper those extremes of emotion by necessary reason.

Role models; here is where it fails. The teachers, families, society, have to provide the basis of the ideals of real love and romance, of the possibilities of the realization of hopes and dreams. Young people reach out in desperation for the realities of those ideals in our society. Hollywood provides the opportunity of expression that should be found in the school environment. Unhappily, Hollywood is grounded in the profit motive whereas the schools should be motivated by the human product of young people who are not only equipped for real life, but able to find their hopes and dreams encouraged during this very brief span of transition from childhood to adulthood.

But such leadership in the schools should be of the kind of people who have not betrayed the best of the child within themselves, who are able to relate, in kind, to the hopes and dreams of the child/adult. The best of such teachers and leaders will still have some of the wonder of Kellie's eyes.

Where does this gray-hair get the notion that speaking of such things in this manner can accomplish anything of substantive value? Because I have never given up the same hopes and dreams. *The Play is the Thing*! still rings in my own heart and soul. The tragedy I see in so many my age is the loss of these things in their own lives; even worse, those who don't even know what I am talking about!

Diana, Karrie and Kellie know. Millions of our young people know. They are the risk-takers who know, in their hearts, that: all things are possible to them that believe. How is it that my generation gave up the dream and betrayed it for our young people? I know this: until my generation does the things necessary to restore the dream, we risk losing the only thing that makes it all worthwhile, the very meaning of our existence, our children!

As long as it is my part to make every attempt to try to move people to respond in love and kindness to the needs of our children and young people, I will continue to risk it all as a man with nothing to lose. And also because I believe this is the normal and reasonably expected thing to do by those who consider themselves men in the best sense of the word. A man is a man for that.

CHAPTER THIRTEEN

PRETTY WOMAN

As to religion for example, here is a fact: We'll never reach the stars as long as Christians, Jews, Moslems, Hindus, etc. think they speak for God and God can't speak for Himself. I think it odd that those who belong to these religions say they believe God is all-powerful but needs their religion to think and speak for Him. Of course, it might be easier to give credence to these religions if they made any sense and didn't promote hypocrisy, divisiveness, ignorance, superstitions, prejudice, bigotry, cruelty, and hatred.

How much better, in my opinion, if those who would be missionaries would follow the example of Albert Schweitzer who gave himself in the name of God and humanity alone with no sectarian, religious distinction; but, for the most part, the smaller hypocrisies in our lives go unnoticed, by ourselves, at least; which always reminds me of chickens.

My grandfather never tired of telling the story about a relative who believed so strongly in the myth of the Biblical Sabbath that he would do no work of any kind on a Sunday (I won't go into the confusion and controversy that reigns among the religious about this issue of Lord's Day vs. Sabbath).

Since this fellow raised chickens and they required feeding every day, on Saturday nights he would place a pan of feed on the gatepost to the chicken pen. Then every Sunday morning, he would accidentally bump into this post spilling the feed into the chicken yard. True story.

Well, we laugh of course. But I don't think God saw the humor in this, only the hypocrisy. And when I think of the story and hypocrisy, I think of politicians and Hollywood as well as religious people. Still, Hollywood at least gives us something of real value ever once in a while. And one of these things of real value was the film "Pretty Woman." Pretty Woman with Julia Roberts (much like Cannery Row with Debra Winger) is one of my all-time favorite Cinderella stories.

A part of the charm of living is comparing the view coming in with the view looking back. That is, if you have the good fortune to live long enough to do so and your life has had anything charming about it. A great part of the pleasure I take from watching the film is derived from the fourteen years I spent living in places like Redondo, Hermosa and Manhattan Beach, the time spent in Hollywood and Malibu, driving through areas like Beverly Hills and up and down Rodeo Drive watching the beautiful people and feeling a part of it all.

Young and with a Cadillac convertible, I would cruise these areas and others like Sunset Strip with a date (as opposed to looking for one). We could park on the beaches with the top of the car down and watch the surf roll in while listening to beautiful music on the radio (with reverb), or LP changer. I was one of the first, and one of the very few, to have such a marvelous device in a car. Dinner and entertainment at places like the Ambassador Hotel's Coconut Grove and Malibu's Albatross which had the dining area built out over the beach were magic; my former life.

So I watch Pretty Woman with a very real sense of the locale in which it was filmed. And I've attended the opera in San Francisco where I've lived as well. And climate-wise, I'll still take the South Bay in SoCal. I never think about this without recalling Sam Clemens remarking that the coldest winter he ever spent was a summer in San Francisco.

"When I was a little girl" is the theme I have heard so often from so many women. Little boys have their fantasies as well. How often I preface some of my remarks with the words, "When I was a little boy."

Well, there should be princesses to rescue and knights to rescue them. The story is the same for both boys and girls and each knows the role they want to play. When I was a little boy, I dreamed of being heroic just like Tom Sawyer. I dreamed of princesses and damsels in distress I would rescue from all kinds of dangers.

Julia Roberts brought an amazing talent, as well as her extraordinary natural beauty, to her role as the hooker Vivian Ward. In the end, she wanted more; she wanted fairy tales. And in grand Hollywood fairy tale fashion, she got more. And we all applauded; a good-hearted girl, with a tragic past, won in the end. I don't always agree with Siskel and Ebert but Pretty Woman was one film about which we agreed. It's no wonder Julia Roberts was an academy nominee for her role as Vivian. She was superb.

It is a mistake to call the film a comedy or even a romantic comedy. While there are many comedic scenes, lines, and dialogues, while you can't help laughing during scenes like the snail shooting out of the tongs during the dinner, I remember the tears forming in my eyes when I first saw the film.

I hadn't yet written the Birds book at that time. But when I wrote it Vivian Ward wasn't far from my mind. By then, I had a lot of stories that had been told me by the Vivians I had known. But none had her happy ending. More typical were the girls who would show me the scars from needles, beatings, and the slashes on their wrists from attempted suicide. In fact, when confronted with the question, Vivian's girl friend and roommate could only name one girl for whom the fairy tale had come true: Cinder----rella.

I knew a barmaid once who told me she was waiting for some guy to come in, sweep her off her feet and take her away from it all. The *all* was a tragic childhood, giving birth at fifteen, having several children by different men, drugs and alcohol, welfare, being beaten up, in short, the things that happen to so many women who start life on the wrong path.

She was a beautiful woman but just how realistic was it to expect some guy of any worth to come into the bar and sweep her off her feet? And take care of her and her children? Not very. Cinderella is a beautiful fairy tale. But it's still a fairy tale.

Realistic is the fact expressed to me by another beautiful girl in similar circumstances who said, "What have I got to offer anyone?" She knew it took more than beauty. There had to be a person there as well, a person of accomplishment besides the ability to have children by multiple fathers and thorough-going experience with vulgar language, drugs, alcohol, and the systems of welfare and Child Protective Services.

Vivian had something going for her besides her natural beauty that most girls in her position don't: Like Cinderella, she didn't have any children. Many girls would have a much better chance at life, at accomplishment, if they hadn't been molested. Molestation not only steals a child's innocence and childhood; it steals the sense of self-worth. Many girls would have a better chance at life if they didn't think they could begin having children at fifteen and there would always be someone to help them pay for them and care for them. Life isn't that way, they discover too late. You would think girls would have learned by now that our society does not require boys be responsible for the babies they father like rutting animals.

I love Pretty Woman because injustice is confronted, overcome, and things are made right in the end. The bullies have been punished by the success of a woman who discovers her self-worth with the help of a good man. But as Vivian points out in the end, after the knight rescues the princess, she rescues him right back. It took both to rescue and save each other. But keep in mind, Vivian didn't have children.

Unmarried, she had been bright enough, she had enough genuine virtue and character, not to fall into that trap where the babies, the children, always pay the price for selfish individuals doing things their way with no thought of the consequences for children. But it takes the cooperation of a whole society to teach, encourage, and support this kind of morality and just plain good sense.

Throughout the film there are those like the hotel manager Barney, so well played by Hector Elizondo, who recognize the value of Vivian as a person. But they see her as a person only when her guard is down, when she doesn't have to be hard and detached. She wants to be a good person but life hasn't rewarded her wanting to be a good person. Life is very real that way; it rewards effort rather than wishful thinking. There is always a price to be paid for doing things our way rather than doing the disciplined, difficult, and practical things. Like abstaining from sex or scrupulously practicing birth control until you are ready to care for the resulting babies.

Education is one of those disciplined, difficult, and practical things. And our children are increasingly being defrauded of an education. Even worse, they are being defrauded of seeing education as something of value. Too many children are being taught that they can do things their way and still have it their way in the end. There aren't many jobs available for those proficient in Nintendo or riding a motorcycle; and very few openings for those with skill with a football or basketball.

There simply isn't much of a future for those whose only skills are quoting sports statistics, drinking beer, smoking pot, having babies or riding a Harley. Do it your way and become successful is a myth ever as much as Cinderella; unless you are Frank Sinatra or Julia Roberts, the very, very, rare exceptions to the rule. And this in no wise is meant to imply they didn't pay their dues on the way to success.

Too many beautiful girls have thought their beauty would never fade, that beauty could stand alone. I believe Julia Roberts would be the first to disabuse of such a notion for as the German proverb states: "Beauty fades. Virtue remains." It is virtue that pursues, among other things, the self-discipline that leads to personal excellence, an education and making something of value of your life, of having something to offer that is a constant companion and reminder that you are of value as a person.

If you notice, Vivian wanted more, she wanted fairy tales because Edward had shown her fairy tales. She was introduced to a society that included the magic of opera, for example. And as Edward rightly pointed out, it was something you loved or hated and your response to it often spoke volumes of your actual character.

Edward has introduced Vivian to a society where good breeding, good manners, are essentials and rightly expected. He is trying to help her accommodate herself to this society and fit in. For Edward, the extraordinary beauty of Vivian, her genuine character, deserve to be tutored in the things that compliment her beauty and character. Virtually no one wants to see a beautiful rose left alone to grow in a vacant dirt lot. It deserves to be in a beautiful garden and carefully tended.

There is the scene, for example, where Edward is teaching Vivian to play chess. He teaches her to stop fidgeting, to overcome the visible nervousness that betrays a lack of self-confidence. Vivian, like Susie in Cannery Row, is a quick study and is showing a thirst for knowledge and civilized, correct behavior. She wants to be a lady. She wants this badly enough and has enough good sense to have the hotel manager instruct her in correct table manners before a formal dinner in a fine restaurant.

Edward, like Doc in Cannery Row, is increasingly seeing that Vivian has the indispensable virtue that he needs in a woman: She has real character. She wants to make something of herself and is willing to pay the price. As with Susie, there is a very real and valuable person behind the facade of coarseness that has been thrust upon Vivian by her circumstances of birth.

Vivian isn't using her dreadful childhood as an excuse for not doing something with her life. And Edward is giving her the chance for this by providing the paradigm for doing so. But it is still the genuine character of Vivian that assumes personal responsibility for taking full advantage of the opportunity Edward has offered her.

It is a tragic myth, among young people especially, that you will be rewarded for your undiscovered talents and genius. Few things are as common as unrewarded talent and genius. Pretty Woman, like Cannery Row, is a fairy tale, a Cinderella story. It doesn't happen in real life. But it remains a beautiful story regardless, a story that does have a certain kind of reality when it deals with those things of real value in a person, those things that will reach the hearts of others who are equally real persons with those same values and the genuine virtue and character to exercise personal self-discipline and responsibility.

I used to tell my pupils: Get an education. It is one thing that no one can ever take away from you. But it should go without saying that getting the education is one thing and putting it to good use is another. I have had many women with Vivian's background tell me they would like to stop using vulgar language, for example. They recognize the fact that language, like your personal friends and associations, speaks volumes about the character of the individual.

The academic environment of the classroom is one place where the emphasis on correct language should be made prominently important. I'll never forget a woman telling me one time that while my own speech was correct and I used an above average vocabulary, somehow it seemed to fit with me. While uneducated herself, she recognized me as an educated man who did not affect being better than anyone else by using language as an affectation. It was a natural result of a good education and good reading habits, good associations, something she realized she wanted for herself. When you are able to make something like this of value to others, you have done well. And one of the responsibilities of parenthood is to make such a thing desirable to your children. Being able to speak well and properly, the encouraging of associating with good and mannerly people is just as easy to teach children as teaching them to be vulgar and uncivilized by your example.

Like it or not, first impressions are all-important. And in spite of the old saw about not judging a book by its cover, first impressions are proven to be accurate most of the time. Correct speech, good manners and dress, all part of a good education, are most often the determining factors for success. And they certainly speak of the person's sense of confidence and self-worth.

There was no excuse for those salesladies treating Vivian as they did. But you can certainly understand their attitude toward her. She was out of place and it was only natural for the salesladies to want her out of their establishment (of course, we couldn't help but applaud Vivian going back later for some payback. Such a thing is just too deliciously normal and human, too precious to ignore or fail to take advantage).

Still, you can't make a silk purse of a sow's ear and Vivian had to have the genuine character that removed her from being such or no amount of fine apparel could have made her a lady. She had to possess the virtue of genuinely wanting to be a lady before such a thing could be possible.

It is true, as Eliza pointed out in "My Fair Lady," another of the truly great Cinderella stories with an emphasis on the extreme importance of proper speech and manners, that if you treat a flower girl like a duchess, she will respond like a duchess. This goes a long way toward making a lady of the flower girl. But the virtue of character must be there to begin with. And Eliza, Susie, and Vivian as Cinderellas had that kind of virtue.

If the girl wants nothing better than to remain a flower girl or prostitute, nothing will change that. If she wants to remain a sweat hog and run with bikers (a well-recognized stereotypical characterization, not a personal assessment or attack) and associate with ignorant losers, if she loves to use foul language and pass herself off from man-to-man, you don't have a Cinderella. Such a girl will not likely attend an opera nor appreciate one.

No, Cinderella had virtue going for her; something not emphasized, and that too few little girls are learning, in our society. Not to mention little boys. Vivian, as Cinderella, possessed virtue and was willing to pay the price for doing better. She had learned she had potential and was prepared to get a legitimate job and finish high school; she was determined to make something of herself. She even got this message across to her friend and roommate Kit at the end of the story.

But it took the good person in Edward to accomplish this change in Vivian. Both had touched the good person in each other, the person of real virtue. They had, in fact, rescued each other. How many times it takes just this, the chance encounter with a good person, with good persons, to bring this to pass.

Barney first establishes the proper relationship and has the proper attitude toward Vivian. She can play Edward's niece as long as there will be no other *uncles* for her to visit when he leaves. Barney shows real class and good breeding in his handling of the situation. Then, when confronted with the real person in Vivian when she drops her guard, he does all he can to help her.

Bridgette is another person of real class. She helps Vivian prepare herself with the proper attire for the forthcoming dinner. She does this in spite of Vivian's admission that Edward is not her uncle. As Bridgette replies to this honesty on the part of Vivian with the remark "They never are, dear," she joins Barney in genuine compassion for the good person they recognize in Vivian.

While Edward realized from Vivian's reaction to the beauty and power of the opera they attend that she is, indeed, a person of real, genuine sensitivity, value, and character, it takes Barney confronting him in inimitable good taste and civilized behavior to bring him to the right decision.

Looking at the ruby and diamond necklace and earrings as Edward is checking out of the hotel, Barney's simple but elegantly phrased, discreet yet genuinely caring and purposely directed statement: "It must be difficult to let go of something so beautiful", brings Edward to his senses. Edward knows the manager isn't talking about a necklace or just the physical beauty of Vivian. Then, Barney's ingenuous parting thrust that by the way the chauffeur took Vivian home the previous day.

Barney stands out as a man of real refinement with a true appreciation of beauty. He never looks at Vivian with lechery, but as a man who genuinely loves and appreciates beauty and refinement. His acknowledgment of Vivian's true beauty of virtue by kissing her hand rather than shaking it, his heartfelt "It has been a pleasure knowing you," these are things, like Vivian's obvious genuine love of the opera, even the best families and schools cannot guarantee a person. This requires virtue. The virtue must be there for such things to be genuine and without affectation.

Edward and Vivian had a lot of help from others like Barney and Bridgette, people possessing genuine virtue, to make the fairy tale come true. And to give Edward his due, when Vivian tells him the clerks at the store had been mean to her, he takes immediate and appropriate action. You have to have spent some time on Rodeo Drive to savor the full import of what transpires.

The fun begins with Edward telling Vivian as they are walking on Rodeo Drive that people aren't looking at her, they are looking at him. And I laugh every time at the scene when he tells her to get rid of her gum and she spits it out right on the sidewalk of that fantasy strip of fairy tale stores flaunting signs of Gucci, Louis Vuitton, Chanel, and Diamonds on Rodeo. I really begin to crack up when Edward says almost sotto voce: "I don't believe you did that."

Sucking up. When Edward informs the manager of the store they go into that they are prepared to spend an obscene amount of money and it will require some major sucking up, the manager is just absolutely marvelous: "Sir, if I may say so, you're certainly in the right store, and the right city, for that kind of thing."

And those of us acquainted with Beverly Hills and such stores can't help laughing uproariously at the manager's intentionally obsequious but direct question: "Sir, when you said an obscene amount of money, just how obscene are we talking about, profane or reeelly offensive?" No matter how many times I watch the film, I still totally crack up every time when Edward replies *reeelly offensive* and the manager turns away with the deeply intoned, heartfelt remark made in a prayerfully reverential voice: "I like it." Folks, if you're going to worship, *reeelly* worship!

But regardless of the fact that Vivian, in the words of her roommate *cleaned up real nice*, it was Vivian's virtue that was essential for the fairy tale to come true. It is her real virtue, not a display of hypocrisy, which is hurt and outraged at the cruelty of Edward telling Stuckey about her being a hooker.

It is the virtue of Edward that comes to their rescue when he acknowledges his cruelty, genuinely repents of it and tries to make restitution. But his clumsy attempt at restitution makes Vivian feel he has treated her as a prostitute though Edward has not recognized it as such. It takes Barney to finally cut through the blindness of Edward and save the day.

Still, had it not been for the virtue of Vivian expressed in her love, understanding, and forgiveness of Edward, it could never have happened; rather than an accident of life, rather than a fairy tale, how much better to increase the odds of happiness by instilling virtue in our children, by encouraging them by our example, by encouraging education in their lives. But sadly and tragically, even the best parents have the deck stacked against them attempting to do so in our contemporary society.

I used to tell my pupils I didn't have any answers to life for them on a mass basis; that the answers were only there on an individual basis. I emphasized to them the necessity of their getting an education rather than an education being given them. In other words, there was no royal path to knowledge.

And there is no royal path to becoming a lady or a gentleman. In my own experience I have met so many girls who had no desire to become ladies. But for those I have met who wanted to become ladies, the hardest thing in the world for me to do is admit there is little or nothing I can do for them. As with education, I would have to tell them to get an education; don't expect someone to give them an education. That is not a fine distinction; there is a world of difference between the two.

Vivian faced up to what was required of her to become a lady, to become a person of value to herself and for herself. She was prepared to start a new life, a hard life of self-discipline that required her disassociating herself from her former lifestyle and finally accepting personal responsibility for making something of herself. She stopped blaming others and the circumstances that had led her into prostitution, and took control of her life. The Edward Lewis Scholarship Fund; that was no joke. Edward had shown her another way, a better way. And Vivian shared this with her friend.

But, tragically, there aren't enough Edwards to go around, or Barneys or Bridgettes. They are vastly outnumbered by the bums. Vivian had been accused by her mother of being a bum magnet. I have known many beautiful girls who fit this description. But unlike Vivian, most began life with too many strikes against them. Not only do they lack education; there are the children. And those children doom most of these girls. And the children are doomed in turn.

I was sitting in a coffee shop with a very beautiful young woman. I had asked her out and we were getting acquainted. She shared something with me that I will never forget. "Sam, when men find out I have a child their reaction is always 'Oh, you got a kid.' And that's the last I hear from them."

I couldn't bring myself to tell her: Well, what do you expect? Isn't that a normal reaction (I might not hold such a thing against her but neither am I naive about it)?

Most of these girls will settle for some man moving in with them for sex. More children result from this. But the so-called men don't take responsibility for these children. And sadly the girls never seem to learn the lesson. I feel like saying to them: Get real! How can you expect a man to take on the responsibility for your irresponsibility and mistakes, to take on the responsibility for another man's children? Men will use you but they won't marry you. And one day, that beautiful girl will look in the mirror and realize, too late, that it's all over. Lacking virtue, she has nothing left to offer.

Vivian told Edward that when people tell you you're a bum and put you down often enough, you begin to believe it. And that's true. But, once more, let's get real. When you start having the babies at fifteen and unmarried, when you have no education or job skills, your enemy, time, is just waiting down the road and suddenly you wake up one morning and you're no longer young. It's all over.

The curse of beauty in our society is producing girls who lack the maturity to handle the attention of boys. They too often confront a society that encourages teen sex with no responsibility attaching. There is no real value attached to education and the laws are so perverted that society will reward irresponsible, ignorant, uneducated, unmarried teens having children. Knowing what is right has never been a preventative or guarantee of not doing what is wrong. Selfishness will rule where real virtue and character are missing.

I'm a writer. I was born to write. But it took the discipline of the academic learning of the subject in order for me to write well. I know the power of the pen when I bring tears of sorrow or joy and laughter to the eyes of others. There is power in words both written and spoken. As I was talking about children to a woman the other day, she began to cry as I described the beauty of the love of the two children in my novel. Taking her hand in mine, I said to her: Now, if the words I write are as effective in bringing tears to the reader, the story I'm trying to tell on behalf of children will be successful in accomplishing its mission.

But this requires not only inspiration, but motivation as well. And that is what made Edward and Vivian a successful Cinderella story. Both the inspiration and the motivation were there for them. Lacking these, they would have been doomed. Lacking these, I know I'll never succeed; that I will be doomed.

As I've said so often, how much I would rather devote my life to writing of the softer and gentler things, of butterflies and rainbows, love and romance; but the need for the hard things that need attention won't go away and that hound of heaven dogs my heels; so, to get on with it.

Pursuing my Mad Man Hypothesis as per Tolstoi, Dostoevsky, and Harper Lee, I know the New Way for humanity by the path of the Amendment requires moving both hearts and minds to take concentrated and determined action by good people against the evil that is destroying children and threatens the future of all humanity.

Since the history of our species has been one of continuing and unremitting violence, there has never been any question that a new way is needed, something that has never before been done. The great philosophers and men like Napoleon, Emerson and Thoreau dreamed of such a revolution for humanity that did not require musket and cannon to effect.

What most do not seem to realize is that this new way requires such a new way of thinking it has escaped the best thinkers. It has also escaped these worthies that such a new way is bound to alienate all spectrums of humanity; the left, middle, and the right, religiously and politically. Just where do people have their brains that fail to see this? Changing the world, changing the course of humanity, obviously requires such a new way of thinking, such a departure from the past that the very foreignness of it is bound to antagonize, alienate, and invite censure. It is very naive at best to believe such a thing could result in any other reaction.

Enter the mad man hypothesis. A way that is contrary to the prevailing sanity of the world is needed. The madness of not involving the entire half of humankind that has been studiously ignored by philosophy, religion and politics, women, in the process of finding a solution to the problem of violence should be obvious. The further madness of failing to make children the priority of the world should be equally obvious.

This is the madness of the Amendment. It is a madness that opens the door to calling humanity to account and making these mad things I am suggesting, acts of sanity. But it is my contention that it is the world that is insane by ignoring the necessity of taking this new way for humanity. Once this step is taken, I believe humankind will recognize its former insanity.

In Jewish folklore, the Golem is an image endowed with life, an avenging or protecting angel. In medieval legends, the church applied this to wooden images given life by saints. But there was no Golem to protect those two little girls, Melissa and Julie, in Belgium; and no saints or angels of any kind. They died horribly of thirst alone in that black dungeon screaming out for God to help them until their throats were so dry they couldn't even whisper a prayer for death to deliver them since not even God could help them. But it wasn't God's place to do so, it was ours. It was our responsibility as human beings to see that these little ones should never have been in harm's way to begin with! And I say: To hell with any system of religion or politics that would excuse our responsibility for the monsters we allow in our midst that abuse and murder children!

But as long as humankind continues to allow beasts in the form of humans like Marc Dutroux and his wife Michelle Martin and others to roam among civilized people, so long will children pay the price for our failure to act. Then religious people of all persuasions worldwide have the unmitigated, hypocritical gall to tell us it's God's will that children die at the hands of monsters!

To compound the gall and hypocrisy such people will preach how much God loves children! But, of course, He only loves them in the name of their peculiar religion or belief system. We love singing, for example, Jesus loves the little children of the world, but where do we see the churches placing the proper emphasis on children, all children, as the future of humanity? Or making women of equal value to men in the process? We don't; any more than we see such an emphasis in the religions of Judaism, Moslemism, or any other-ism including government-ism. People profane God Himself by this kind of hypocrisy. And I ask myself: Where is the collective conscience of humanity when confronted by the fact that we, not God, are responsible for the Melissas and Julies?

Having said all this, I invite the good people of America to take a positive step toward national virtue and character by the Amendment, a step which all good people can agree is needed on behalf of children and, if you will, for our own national redemption. A large part of the path I have taken in the pursuit of knowledge has to do with particle physics. Why? Because I believe it is the area of science in which so many of the answers to human behavior will be found. And human behavior will determine the course of the Amendment.

A better understanding of God and His creation will also be found, I believe, in particle physics research. I've mentioned tachyons and the important role they are playing in this understanding. I've also mentioned the discovery that neutrinos may have mass and if so will reshape our understanding of how atoms work, and explain the mass of the universe and why it is expanding so slowly.

One of the most important reasons I am given to the phrase *I don't know* can be understood from a recent discovery of a puzzling phenomenon called sonoluminescence, the transformation of sound into light, a heretofore-unknown reaction. How can sound produce light?

A small bubble of air in a column of water is hit with ultrasound. A tremendous expansion of this bubble results. The higher, instantaneous pressure causes the bubble to collapse and compress, reaching a temperature greater than the surface of the sun.

Of the greatest interest to me is that when this happens, a blue light is produced which has a cyclic rate of 30,000 times a second. This, to our human eyes, appears as a constant light, of course. Far from being just a scientific curiosity, the potential for such a new source of heat and light is truly mind-boggling!

But like cosmic particles that bombard us constantly, once in a while one may hit the brain just right to elicit a response. This is one of the problems we confront with new generations of electronics, satellites, and virtual intelligence given machines that do not rely on mechanical connections but might, in some manner, react to what we currently call telepathy.

The advances in telekinesis show promise of realizing ideas from science fiction. Do these advances in science and physics threaten religion? You bet they do! Back to the Scopes Trial; will those who think they speak for God by way of human invented and manufactured religions feel threatened by this kind of knowledge? You bet they will!

But I still believe God can speak for Himself. And I further believe that knowledge that helps us better understand God and His creation is good knowledge. But how far removed are we, really, from those who would censure

Galileo and Copernicus, from those who burned heretics and witches at the stake? Not that far, I fear.

The letters and calls I receive consigning me to the outer reaches and perdition from those who purport to uphold the honor of God haven't changed. They might as well have been written during the medieval times of the Dark Ages.

I continue to maintain that children are the closest thing to the heart of God Himself. I further maintain it is the Devil's work to try to get people to focus on religion and politics in order to get our eyes off God's priority, the children.

Don't try to tell me that a Moslem or Jewish parent loves his child any less than a Christian! How I wish those who preach such a damnable doctrine could be of the heart and mind of Albert Schweitzer; but how to get the peoples of the world to focus on children rather than their peculiar systems of religion and politics? That, folks, is the real challenge of the Amendment; that, folks, has been the conundrum of humanity since the very beginning of our time on earth.

I believe there is a Devil. I believe it would be to his purpose to keep the focus of humanity on everything but children. If he exists, he has been enormously successful throughout history in doing precisely this. Divide and conquer is a familiar tactic. If the Devil and his wicked servants existed, they would continue to keep people fighting about systems of religion and politics to enable the wicked to continue to be successful and the good will never overcome the evil. But there has never been the need of a Devil to accomplish this. It only requires good people fighting among themselves and failing to cooperate.

Good people fight the battle on many fronts. Some fight against pornography and abortion. These are good things to fight against. Good people fight for many good causes. But ask yourself why good people have never yet prevailed? Why is evil always in the ascendancy? That's an honest and legitimate question.

I maintain it is because good people are so fragmented and divisive over their beliefs that they can never get their act together. If just once good people could agree on a single cause, they could move mountains. I offer the Amendment as that cause. But will good people come together in this cause?

CHAPTER FOURTEEN

The Donald and Oprah? Only in America! And it goes without saying, only for two of the richest people in America. But as the pundits are pointing out, it does make for some comic relief in the electioneering.

While I have long advocated the absolute necessity for a woman vice-president, I have also pointed out that it must be a viable choice of the Republican or Democrat parties in order to be taken with the necessary seriousness. And no matter the thinking it is only a matter of time, and by force of circumstances the time could be this next presidential election, though I hold faint hope of this proving the case

Either the Republican or Democrat Party better get wise to this; and in a hurry so it won't appear a gimmick or afterthought. As I pointed out to George Bush, the party which makes this decision will be the party which will go into the history books as the one which stands for the equality of women, the other half of humanity. The political value of such a decision, devoid of the ideals of simply just being fair and doing the right thing, is beyond calculation.

For some reason I can never mention politics without thinking of Sam Clemens' remark about Judas Iscariot only being a premature congressman; and pork. By now everyone has heard that the Fat Award goes to Philadelphia. It seems Philly has the greatest population of obese people in America. Right On Philadelphia! Oink, Oink.

A business division of Weedpatch University Macabre Toys had a big commercial hit as usual for Xmas in Freddie the Frog. This is the little fellow who is so realistic that when he is squeezed his six-inches-long tongue shoots out of his mouth with an agonized croak and he oozes a mucus-like substance and actually pees on you. A real favorite with little boys who have sisters or a teacher they want to impress.

As to the continued efforts on the part of Weedpatch University and myself to stamp out discrimination against our little green friends I ask: Have you hugged or kissed a frog today? Any interested parties are invited to join the pickets in front of Green Frog Markets in Bakersfield until these places either change the name or start hiring frogs.

***

Peggy Lee should never have sung Ghost Riders and Frank Sinatra should never have attempted Old Man River. In Frank's case, it is thoroughly embarrassing to listen to him struggling to do the song. Peggy Lee is out of place as a woman trying to sing such a totally man's song as Ghost Riders. As gifted as these two singers are and in spite of their not doing the songs badly, Ghost Riders belongs to Vaughn Monroe and Old Man River belongs to Paul Robeson. The advice of common sense: Once something is done perfectly, don't try to improve on it. Or, in the popular equivalent: If it ain't broke, don't try to fix it. As I shared recently with a beautiful woman, it wouldn't occur to me to try to improve the model (of women, that is). I think God got it right.

I'm not sure why this reminds me of it, but it seems every time I sing at the Club, two standards have become Cool Water and Drinkin' Champagne. But I am certain that this is not the reason one beautiful girl told me in phraseology distinctive to demure, polite, and civilized young ladies of outstanding manners, breeding and refinement: "I think I'll just sit here and get pukin' drunk." I tried not to take this as a criticism. She had other things on her mind, like a boyfriend who was hitting on another girl. And as further proof that she was not criticizing the music, she insisted on showing me a butterfly tattoo on her right breast. It was really a very beautiful and genuinely exquisite work of art. The butterfly was nice also.

I have often said that if I had the patent on sex I would be as rich as the guy who invented air-conditioning. Well, at least the swamp cooler. Would you believe the electric oscillating room fan? A Popsicle stick and a six-inch square of cardboard cut from a cereal box stapled to it?

In an on-going discussion with a lovely lady psychologist concerning "Men are from Mars, Women are from Venus", I suggested that if this is the case, shouldn't there be some kind of embassy where the two could meet on neutral ground? Makes sense to me. But only if you accept the premise that men and women are really alien to each other. And in spite of my view as a boy that little girls were truly an alien species, I believe the honoring of the compatibility of differences and of the equal value of women to men is the answer, not an embassy.

In a sudden burst of good housekeeping in preparation for company, I started by getting rid of dust bunnies the size of jackrabbits. Wherever do these things come from? Then, to relieve me from my housekeeping duties that included getting the weedeater out of my bathroom and the cobwebs off my kitchen sink and stove, the unthinkable occurred.

Well, it's happened to all of us who are heavily involved with computers and maintaining web sites. My system crashed big time! And not even the boot disk or restart would avail. I know enough about computers to be dangerous. In other words, I can create problems with them that defy the ordinary. But I swear this wasn't my fault.

It all started with the system telling me in the customary user-friendly hieroglyphics intelligible only to savants, Atlanteans, Fox Mulder and space aliens that I had a problem with Outlook Express, my email program. But the system continued to work for a while. Then I began to get error messages of different kinds. Not the ubiquitous Error 404, which would mean I hadn't done anything wrong, but the system wouldn't admit what it did wrong and always refuses to accept any guilt or responsibility, but things like Hi Mem error. At which point the system would fail to boot. Bill Gates refusing to return my calls, it was time to call in the Marines.

The first fellow I called tried to comfort me with the news that a particularly wicked virus was going around and I may have been a victim of it. Seems this one eats your hard drive and nothing will avail but replacing the drive. Not good. But since I never, but never, download anything from anyone I don't know, let alone save it to my drive, I didn't think this was the case.

Some years ago before his fall from grace (and, like my computer, refusing to acknowledge any real wrong-doing) Jimmy Swaggart told in his book "There Is A River" about his needing a valve job on his car. Since this was in his salad days before hitting the big time of TV evangelism and the sheep began to support him in the usual style of TV evangelists requiring millions of dollars for peddling their various and deviant gospels, he said he couldn't afford to have the necessary repairs made on the car and just drove it until it quit on him.

Depending only on God, he anoints the hood of the car with olive oil, lays hands on it and beseeches the Almighty to intervene for the sake of his most humble and obedient servant. Bingo (no pun intended against Catholics)! Instant valve job and the now miraculously healed car runs perfectly thereafter. God is Great, God is Good! All glory to God! Hallelujah! Praise Jesus!, etc. When all else fails and an honest job requiring honest work isn't your thing, blame it on God and call it prayer, the forte of religion.

Now apart from my extensive treatise about Holy Liars and religious charlatans, why this particular story crossed my mind when my computer failed I'm not sure. But the idea of pouring olive oil on the infernal device, laying my hands on it and chanting BE HEALED! did come to mind. Now the average person may not have thought of this. But then mine has not been the ordinary life and education. So I possess much knowledge and know many useful things of which the average person is woefully (blessedly and blissfully?) ignorant and deficient and this got me to thinking about olive oil. See, what did I tell you?

But was the olive oil good ol' Jimmy used from Italy or Israel? Did I have the right olive oil that God was obligated to honor and bless? And how to choose which was the right olive oil to begin with? This decision I knew, because of my extensive and exhaustive theological training and experience, would require a great deal of study in order to arrive at the correct olive oil to use. Why, people have persecuted and even killed other people in the name of God over issues of even lesser import! You can't be too careful in the religious arena.

Now if I had been raised with a belief in Catholic holy water or the equally miraculous curative power of the Jordan or Ganges, the difficulty wouldn't have been there to confront. But I needed my computer now and didn't have time to do the necessary research on olive oil. Besides which, according to a few friends, I had already angered the Deity by sharing my heretical idea that Father God might presume a Mother God as well. So I knew I had to exercise a great deal of caution before entertaining the anointing of oil and laying on of hands to heal my computer. Now these kinds of questions do not come readily to the average mind; which only proves my point about my own.

My grandfather firmly believed in the efficacy of the pouring of olive oil on his congregants before the laying on of hands and prayer for the sick as per the instructions found in the epistle of James. But danged if I could remember whether grandad's olive oil came from Italy or Israel? And what if I chose wrong and a bolt of lightning came down from above to consume both the computer and me? The story of Elijah and the false prophets was there to warn of any presumptuousness on my part. And I had no hankering to be consumed by fire from on high no matter the explanation of the boat captain quoted by Sam Clemens that Elijah had gasoline and matches at the ready and gave God a little help.

But what a story I would have if it worked; not that it wouldn't make a really great story if it didn't. All I would have to do is join the ranks of all these other holy liars like the really Big Bugs in religion such as Tammy Faye, Kenneth Copeland, Pat Robertson, Robert Schuller and the Pope! Why, raising a computer from the dead would be just like..., but I digress.

Besides, since grandad had passed on and neither Jimmy nor the pope was readily available to advise me, I decided the olive oil with laying on of hands was probably not a good idea in this case. And I really didn't have time for the necessary research such a profound theological question regarding the correct oil demanded.

Being somewhat of a character myself (according to some uncharitable souls), I have a couple of really wacko friends who know a great deal about computers. In fact, that is all they seem to know or care about. One idea of hell is to be locked in a room with only these guys for company; unless, of course, you live and breathe computers.

Well, life is more than computers for me, but these fellows are useful in cases such as I was facing. And they owe me big time for bailing them out so often about other things, like fiascoes involving the government, the law, the IRS, etc., of which they steadfastly remain ignorant. So, I bit the bullet and called on one.

After putting in four hours of working on the problem, his diagnosis was the memory chips or the motherboard was at fault. If you are diagnosed with a terminal disease, you get a second opinion; or even a third and fourth. And when you face such a diagnosis on your computer, you better do the same thing.

So, on to my friendly wacko number two. In his case, he has become so grossly obese due to eating enough to feed a starving village that he is on disability and confined to his apartment. Not as a stipulation for disability, but due to the fact that he can't wear anything like normal clothes and waddles when he tries, infrequently, to walk. When the idea that gluttony is a vice was first formed, they must have had my porcine buddy in mind. The first picture to come to mind when seeing him is of an enormous white slug, or that he could be the poster boy for Moby Dick and you begin looking for a harpoon.

And before anyone condemns me for talking about him this way, I say it to his face and he is equally free in his compliments about me. After all, what are friends for? Only the fact that we are both certifiable and working on postal and terminal madness keeps the relationship intact. And as a matter of fact I did suggest he move to Philadelphia. He declined, pointing out that Philadelphia is not a place people move to, but rather move from, at any opportunity.

He lost his last hi-tech job after three DUIs and three accidents in three months; might be a record of some kind. Kind of like his eight (or nine, he can't seem to remember) marriages. The further fact that he could only function with a daily and steady intake of drugs and alcohol might have contributed to his dismissal (and rather heterodox marriage habits).

But like many mad scientists, he has a certain genius for some things besides enormous food intake and specializing in phone sex since even Viagra doesn't benefit him. His wizardry with electronics had kept him employed until his dietary and driving habits overcame even his employer's need of his genius. And while he lacks certain human characteristics, like a conscience for example, we do engage in some exchanges of ideas such as his work designing the guidance system for smart bombs and the night vision for stealth fighters so successful in Desert Storm.

As a point of strictly academic interest, he wonders what his contribution was in killing people with more accuracy and efficiency. We have a lot of fun tossing this around, his Malthusian orientation quite properly devoid of any silly or quaint vestiges of humanitarianism keeping the topic on track.

I pack up the computer and take it over to him. But before I left, I gutted the machine and made sure every cable contact was thoroughly clean, and applied dielectric to each one before reassembly. By doing this, the machine did boot and came up running; which proved my other expert friend was wrong about the memory chips and motherboard. But people like this friend get so caught up in the esoterica of the machines and programs, they often overlook the obvious such as the need of taking the machines apart occasionally and doing the needed mechanical service.

But there were still a number of error messages and since I did want the upgrades for some programs, I decided to enlist the aid of Moby Dick who keeps track of such things. It took three days and nights to do the entire job. People are very naive who believe you can do such things by just installing a few disks or running so-called fix-it programs. There is no magic bullet for fixing computers.

In this case, it meant three days and nights with my fat psycho buddy during which time that anointing with olive oil, laying on of hands and prayer did intrude into my mind more than once. I think I did, at one point, threaten my buddy with hauling out the olive oil. But at least this hell with my psycho friend, unlike that of the Bible and Dante, was one I knew had a door out. But had Dante known of TV and computers...

Though my job was primarily that of hauling out his trash, cooking and doing dishes, and my buddy not having TV due to his failure to pay his cable bill, finding myself repeatedly watching True Lies and Medicine Man (the only tapes available besides an extensive library of porno films), during the interminable downloads of needed programs and updates, the final results were worth the effort.

And in spite of the fact that it will take literally weeks of fine-tuning and working out bugs, as I told another friend later the machine has been reincarnated as the fastest cockroach on the block (yeah, I know. But it's still a great line that only proves TV does have some redeeming qualities of refinement and culture to offer).

***

My friend and soul brother Henry Thoreau wrote: "Every man is the Lord of a realm beside which the earthly empire of the Czar is but a petty state, a hummock left by the ice."

Henry addressed an issue close to my own heart and mind, and that mind is the empire of which he speaks, an empire largely ignored by most. Of course, in keeping with the history of the human race, Henry uses the word man rather than person, which would include women. And history does not allow of women being in possession of such an empire of the mind; which accounts for their being excluded by men from the King of all disciplines, the world of philosophy, which is the world of the mind.

I have some very rewarding conversations with my beautiful daughter Karen. She has been witness to many of the changes of my mind in regard to many things, not the least of these being religious views I once held and taught my own children. One of the most difficult tasks I've ever had was in letting my children know that some of the things I had taught them were wrong and due to my own prejudices. But my children have been marvelous in forgiving me and have been willing to let me explain the causes of my changes of mind in respect to these things.

Our most recent conversation had to do with this frontier of the mind. Karen knows that as a woman she has been limited in many respects and she appreciates what I am trying to do to bring justice and fairness to women, she understands this distinction of equal rights as opposed to equal value. But as I explain to Karen, if I had not had daughters like her and her sister Diana, as a man I would have cared less about these things. It was her and her sister who taught me to care about such things.

Because Karen is exceptionally intelligent as well as beautiful, I feel very keenly the need to get women such as herself to understand the vital necessity of addressing the issue of equal value by their taking the initiative for exploring this frontier of the mind which is the purview of philosophy, the discipline from which women have always been excluded by men. Karen is quick to pick up on points of a discussion and carry them to further areas. One of especial interest to both of us is brain function.

In science we are confronting the fact that computers which will be able to emulate actual brain function are in our very near future. This, together with accomplished facts of genetic engineering, is forcing changes and choices that will require great wisdom to handle appropriately. Microprocessors are being wired into the optic nerve to give sight to the blind. Some will be small enough to course through our veins and give instant feedback about health conditions.

I can't help but be reminded of that classic old SciFi flick of 1956 "Forbidden Planet". You may recall that the machines which were guided by the minds of the Krell, machines which were designed to relieve the Krell of all work so they would be able to dedicate themselves to pure thought and philosophy, did not take into account the Monster of the Id., the totally and mindlessly selfish primitive beast that lurks in our hearts.

But as long as women are excluded by men as being of lesser value, as long as women are excluded from the very philosophies which will dictate the decisions made by men, there is no hope of wisdom prevailing and overcoming the monster either in the sciences or governments, and the Beast will continue to prevail to our own destruction. I often ask myself: Are we up against terminal and invincible ignorance and prejudice in this respect? Or will women eventually get their act together and form their own philosophy as I have said they must do in order to ever be accepted by men as of equal value?

I had given a copy of the flyer for the Bodfish Philosophical Society to a lovely woman sitting next to me at the bar. Instead of taking it home with her as I suggested, she started reading it immediately. At a couple of points as she read, she exclaimed: "This is right on!" Then she reached the end, saw my name and gave a gasp! "You mean you wrote this? A man actually wrote this? I thought it was a woman!"

Well, as you can easily imagine, that touched off quite a conversation during which several of the other patrons at the bar got involved. But my point is why hadn't a woman written what I did? Why should a man be doing what women should be doing for themselves? And not just for themselves but for the sake of all humanity? Then, perhaps it is the responsibility of a man to point this out to women? Ironic? No, simple justice, perhaps; even the fulfilling of my responsibility as a man.

I will state unequivocally that as a man the only real joy and happiness I have experienced in my own life, the motivation to write, sing and make music of the softer and gentler things, the things of real beauty and romance, the things of eternal value, have come to me from women and children. When Thoreau wrote, for example, that as the spider in a garret, he could be happy in a prison as long as he had his thoughts to sustain him, he was wrong. HDT, as Soren Kierkegaard and so many others, placed too much emphasis on the meditative, contemplative aspect of intellectualism. And, lacking that all-important dimension of a complete life experience, wife and children, such men were blind to the joy and happiness, the understanding and compassion these bring to a man.

As a writer and poet, I know, as these men would freely admit, that Truth can only be found through the experiences of life, not academic disciplines and empirical facts alone. As philosophers both of these men, and so many like them, failed miserably in many of their attempts at addressing the real issues of life, the things of eternal value. They never were able to present the full picture of life and living. These worthy thinkers would never say they knew

301

what it was like to be pregnant or give birth. Only a man-fool would do so. But there has never been any deficiency of numbers in this genre.

It is in their philosophies, philosophies which fail so miserably to account for the real basis of strife in humanity, that such men too often fall into the camp of those fools who would tell us they know, as men, what it feels like to give birth. Ladies of the world, your fight is against incomplete philosophies of men that fail to consider or cannot understand you as the other half of the human equation!

Now I would be the last to decry the poetic glorification of God's most beautiful, if often inconvenient, Creation. The stars, a sunrise or sunset, the trees and grass washed and scented by a recent rain, the enchantment of a wild, native trout stream, the grandeur of the Tetons and Rockies, so much to excite the artistic exultation of the artist and poet! But even Thoreau admitted: "What is Nature to me if I have no one with whom to share it?" He spoke better than he knew.

The greatest intrigue and mystery of a man's life should be that other half of humanity, a woman. In contemplation of that compatibility of differences I mention so often, I find whole worlds to explore. A woman at her best is all the intrigue and excitement the best of pioneers and explorers could wish for. I never tire of talking with these mysterious creatures, of learning the differences in their thought processes from my own as a man.

But in most cases, the great thinkers of civilization have done solos when the music required a duet with a woman. My hope in addressing this problem is to get men and women together in making real music. The purest poetry is rightly defined as an actual recounting of life, of real lives of ordinary people. A part of the poetry of real life is the literature of a culture.

As television and videos began to supplant books, I witnessed the decline of literature and the consequent loss to our young people of virtue and romantic ideals and a plunge into illiteracy and ignorance of our heritage. This, together with the widening gap between haves and have-nots, has cheated our children of the American Dream. As a teacher of many years' experience, I realized the truth of Robert M. Hutchins' warning that the failure to propagate the heritage of Western Civilization through the great literature of the past would lead to the situation we face today.

Hutchins, Editor-in-Chief for The Great Books of the Western World, made the valid point in 1951 that unless the ideas expressed in the best of our literature of the past was taught to our children, the results would be catastrophic! He was right. Another point of Hutchins is one I take to heart in my own writing. This has to do with the failure of our schools to blend science and the arts, which has led to over-specialization. Dante's Divine Comedy and Newton's Principia should be studied together. But I have to wonder if Hutchins was alive today and I confronted him with the fact that not a single woman was allowed a contribution to that 54-volume set of books purporting to represent the best of human wisdom, whether he would be ashamed? I hope he would be.

You will find that I intrude mathematics in my writing. Far from being out of place, bridging the gap between the hard sciences and the arts and social sciences is essential to real learning. This need has resulted in my sprinkling anecdotes throughout my writings, stories that relate to the reality of life. But it is a truism that the difference between reality and fiction is that fiction has to make sense. And while the phrase of Henry James that life is mostly a splendid waste ring often true, I contend life needn't be.

A butterfly is a thing of beauty. But part of the charm of the butterfly is its seeming erratic flight. Far from being erratic, that butterfly knows exactly what it is doing. While I would never make such an outrageous claim of always knowing exactly what I am doing, my writing often takes on the flight pattern of the butterfly, combining diverse elements like poetry and mathematics. But this is in the tradition of poetry and philosophy, of those writers of the past who saw life as multi-dimensional rather than a narrow specific.

The reader will find the essentials of love, music and laughter incorporated in most of my writing. The solutions to the problems of humanity must include these elements. And as with the reality of life itself, these things have a seemingly erratic flight path. My book "The Missing Half of Humankind: Women!" incorporates many diverse elements to make a point; the point being that women have been excluded from the philosophies of men, philosophies that have determined the destiny of nations. By excluding an entire one-half of the human race, the history of humankind has been a history of conflict without resolution.

Much as I admire the great thinkers and writers of the past, much as they need to be studied, I have come to accept the fact that the exclusion of women in The Great Conversation, as Hutchins called it, has resulted in much harm to humanity. The Missing Half book is not intended to be definitive. It is intended to call attention to the problem and seek a forum where women will be listened to by men; a most uncommon thing. One point alone, a point made by me, a man, should be of great interest to women: There can be no hope of world peace and harmony unless the problem of the historical conflict between men and women is resolved!

As proof of the point, I have several women in positions of power such as columnists and politicians who have asked to be placed on my email list. The following was a recent communication I shared with these women, and shows the very diversity of the subject:

BODFISH PHILOSOPHICAL SOCIETY

Miss Cathy, do you have a headache? No. Well let me give you one. What do you think about Mr. and Mrs. God? (It is at times like these that I desperately need to be able to turn to that significant other and say: Sweetheart, what do you think about this? But failing such a one in my life so it would be her headache, I chose to pick on Cathy).

Philosophy must be divorced from theology! Without dispute religion and its resulting theologies, have been some of the most successful inventions of men to maintain their dominance over women. And it is imperative that women understand this and confront it before they can devise a meaningful philosophy of their own which must begin with the ultimate statement of fact: Men and Women are of equal value!

But what about a New Theology that considers Mr. and Mrs. God? Samuel and Samantha Heath. But just the name Heath does not specify gender. Does the name God (Elohim) specify gender? No. The Adam of the Bible does not specify gender either. God (Elohim, plural and not gender specific) says in Genesis: "Let US make man (the Adam, again plural and not gender-specific) in OUR image."

If there is any credence to the story in Genesis, and I give a lot of credence to it, the US and OUR in the beginning may well have been a Mr. and Mrs. God. It seems reasonable that God (the plural US and OUR) may well have created male and female in their image. Thus such a union of the creator(s) of humankind would anticipate the pattern of man and wife, of equal value, having children seems reasonable.

That US appears in the casting out of Adam and Eve but the later narrative of the Bible, except for the confounding of language where that US appears for the last time, has been totally masculanized.

The origin of the story of Creation and the Garden as given in the Bible cannot possibly be determined. But if it has any basis in fact whatsoever, and I believe it does, how did it happen that what begins with that US comes to be a Masculine God Only in the rest of the Bible?

A father and mother are necessary to life. Why should it have been any different in the original Creation? The early chapters of Genesis lend themselves to the view of a Father and Mother God in the act of the original creation.

We do not know if further material on this theme was lost or destroyed. But we do know there are some very important differences, conflicts and contradictions, in the Creation story in the first chapters of Genesis, which at least indicate this to be the case. The question is a nagging one of why the US was retained in those very first chapters and discounted throughout the rest of the Bible (keeping in mind that chapters of the Bible were of a much later invention and the original books were not divided into either verses or chapters)?

If the He of He created them male and female is understood as generic of the plural, just as we use it in English, as it should be since the He had decided to make the Adam in Our image and after Our likeness, it makes it all the more plausible that a Father and Mother God were involved, or perhaps a council of gods since the Bible does credit there being sons of God before the creation of Adam.

The use of the words Man and Mankind as with He is generic of both genders and has a history; and that history is one of male dominance, as in both philosophy and theology, to the exclusion of considering women as of equal value to men. The Biblical history of male dominance is clear. But there is a fracture, if you will, in the retention of the US in the beginning of Genesis. Inexplicable as this is, there it is nevertheless.

But it is logical to assume that the Biblical story of the creation of humanity had a history long before it was given in a written narrative, writing itself being of comparatively very recent invention and very, very far removed from the actual events cited. And much is ignored or not cited.

In fact, it is known that early hominids, long before Homo sapiens appeared, buried their dead with ceremony indicating a belief in an afterlife. What did they worship and how was it that they had such a belief? Did the oral history of creation retain the story of a Father and Mother God and did this oral tradition find its way into the early account of the US in Genesis?

The attempt by theologians to force an explanation for the use of US and OUR in Genesis by use of the imperial WE or supposed trinity fails miserably on the basis of the historical origin philologically as well as within the context of the use of the plural terms in Genesis.

One of the most intractable problems, even a fatal flaw, of theories of evolution has been the lack of fossil evidence for the demarcation between sexes. When and how did life become male and female, particularly in the higher vertebrate life forms? Given the theory of evolution, such fossil evidence should be enormously abundant. But it doesn't exist. And while I have no fault to find concerning certain facts of evolution, this missing fossil link alone gives some credence to a special creation by God of some kind.

But since true philosophy has to be divorced from myths and legends and deal with pragmatic facts, it has always been impossible to arrive at a true philosophy when beliefs rather than facts contaminate all such attempts. Further, it is my contention that no true philosophy can be had which excludes a full half of humanity: Women.

It is the position of the Bodfish Philosophical Society that conflict has been the history of the human race because women have never been accepted as of equal value to men. Because of this, women have been denied access to philosophy and the result has been the continued failure of women to have a legitimate voice in the decision-making processes of men thereby having no legitimate voice in world affairs. That women must form a philosophy of their own is absolutely essential to gaining such a voice. But a large part of doing this must consider the argument presented in Mr. and Mrs. God.

Therefore, a New Theology, which I have advocated for years, should be evaluated on the basis that men have controlled both philosophy and theology for the whole of human history; the result being the continued domination of women by men and the exclusion of women from these two most essential things in world affairs. That both men and women must find a way to honor the compatibility of differences in such a way as to value one another equally is an absolute essential of world peace. It is my further contention that this must begin by women presenting men a philosophy of their own which will harmonize with the need of men for such a thing. If both are done correctly devoid of competition and combativeness, the philosophies of both men and women should meld forming a perfect union and thereby making world peace achievable.

Women cannot accomplish the purpose by getting in men's faces. And it isn't women are equal to men, it isn't women are of equal value to men, it is men and women are of equal value period! Women cannot make their point, let alone win the battle, by getting confrontational with men. Their philosophy must speak for them through logic and empirical facts. Men of good character will then have no choice but to respond in like manner. Once this is accomplished, real dialogue about the actual issues can be enjoined.

There are too many women who believe they must get in the faces of men, that they must make demands and make up in volume and ferocity what they lack in logic and proper, civilized behavior in addressing the facts. Most certainly women have every right to be angry and frustrated. But when did a temper tantrum ever gain the right end and make a reasoned and logical point?

***

For the benefit of new readers, once in a while I have to include repeats of certain items in TAP. My pedigree as a theologian is one of these items.

Having been immersed as a child in both fundamentalist Protestantism and Catholicism, I bring a lot of experience of the religion of Christianity to bear in my writing. I started my college career with the specific intention of becoming a minister and was eventually ordained to the ministry and served as pastor in several churches.

My spiritual mentor in college was Dr. Charles Lee Feinberg, Ph.D., Th.D. who was the Dean of Talbot Theological Seminary. Dr. Feinberg was head of the translating committee for the New American Standard Bible. I still have an autographed pilot edition of this Bible.

Uncle Charles, as he insisted I call him, was also the reviser for the New Scofield Reference Bible and wrote many books of commentary on the Old Testament especially since his background was in Semitic languages.

Dr. Feinberg represented the best of theological scholarship and Christianity to me. I miss him sorely. Because of his influence as a scholar, I eventually amassed a theological library of some 5,000 volumes of the very best of Biblical scholarship, one of the finest to be found outside of a seminary's library. For years I immersed myself in Biblical studies, following in the footsteps of Uncle Charles. As a result, I became expert myself in Biblical studies and the history of the church. I memorized thousands of Bible verses, many Psalms and even whole chapters of the Bible.

Most would agree that it is a very petty and small mind that is not subject to change when confronted by facts that jar with ignorance and prejudice based on opinion and beliefs only. And most would agree that one of the most difficult things we face as human beings is being able to divorce what we believe from what we know. And sadly, even tragically, most people are unwilling, even unable, to do this.

Recently, three Christian women fled Pakistan under the threat of death because that nation is a Moslem nation. In many nations religious persecution is still a fact of life. But no one who really knows the history of Christianity can point a finger at Pakistan. The historical facts of religious persecution in the name of Jesus are just as real as persecution in the name of Yahweh and Mohammed.

America was founded on certain ideals among which were both freedom of religion and freedom from religion. The founding fathers wisely precluded a religion of the state such as those of Pakistan's and Israel's. But even in America today we do not lack in people who would force their religious views on others, even those who would, if they could, force their views of Christianity on others even to the extent of making it a state religion. Imagine if you will, a strictly Baptist America with it being against the law to practice any other form of Protestantism; or any other religion?

It is a historical fact that some of the greatest crimes against humanity have been perpetrated in the name of God. Even Stalin and Hitler, according to them, had God on their side. I am not thanked by most people for asking them to try to separate what they believe from what they know, I am not thanked by most for pointing out that their own beliefs are largely born of opinion, ignorance and prejudice. I don't make a lot of friends by attacking such ignorance and prejudice, of teachings by others which individuals fail to examine and question for themselves.

But it was in confronting my own ignorance and prejudices, in spite of all the scholarship that had gone into supporting my ignorance and prejudices, that brought me to the place where I recognized that the pain and suffering inflicted on so many millions of people in the name of God was an affront to God Himself.

As a Christian, it seemed I had to believe that God was going to send Albert Schweitzer to hell for rejecting Jesus and Livingston was going to heaven. But both men had sacrificed themselves for the benefit of others. No, you couldn't have it both ways. If you believed the teaching of Christianity in some of its forms, but not all, Schweitzer had to go to hell and Livingston was going to heaven.

The basis of the amendment for children is that of beginning a dialogue about the future of humanity devoid of any religious or political beliefs. My position is that children are the closest thing to the heart of God Himself. And if people could get past their religious prejudices, they would recognize the truth of this and concentrate their efforts on the benefit of children. As Jesus pointed out, unless one becomes as a little child they cannot enter into the kingdom of heaven; and I believe Jesus knew what he was talking about.

Logically, all parents want the same things for their children regardless of their religious or political differences. So why do people insist that only their own religious or political beliefs are the way to accomplish the best for children; because of ignorant prejudices based solely on their beliefs, not factual knowledge.

Do you think that if you had the power to do so, you could make the world a perfect world if you could make it a Christian one? The first thing you confront is the fact that someone would have to decide which kind of Christian it would be? I don't see Pat Robertson and the Pope agreeing on this. For that matter, you couldn't get the churches in your own community agreeing on this; and if God is not the author of confusion then whence the confusion in the Christian religion; because of sectarianism.

Certainly there are few subjects about which people get so irrational as that of religious beliefs; been there myself. So I understand why people get so angry with me when I point out facts that jar with their beliefs. As human beings we all want a belief system that will offer us some peace of mind, some comfort in the face of so much evil. But the responsibility of knowledge is there to confront as well. If I know something is wrong, I have the responsibility to confront it and overcome it no matter what warm and fuzzy things I have to sacrifice for the sake of that knowledge.

And knowledge dictates that anything that causes people to separate, even hate, torture and murder in the name of any deity is wrong. So, I came to the point of concentrating on the children. A child is innocent of hatred and bigotry based on religion or politics or race. Children have to be taught of adults to hate others based on such things. Put a group of children of all persuasions and background together to play and they will be children. There will be no distinctions among them until they are taught of adults to make such distinctions.

I am certain that if people would only stop to think about it, the point of Harper Lee's Pulitzer-winning novel To Kill A Mockingbird would be taken wholeheartedly. The fact that the innocent wisdom of childhood is eventually sacrificed to the often-brutal prejudices of adulthood was the focus of my critique of the book on behalf of children.

One of the reasons I am dedicated to putting the child molester out of our society is that this crime against humanity destroys that wonderful wisdom of innocence in a child. And that molested child often goes on to molest others. The amendment will break this chain of molestation.

But what are the other causes of the betrayal of the innocent wisdom of childhood, an innocent wisdom in which there are no distinctions of race, religion or politics? They are the adult prejudices that teach children to hate those who are different because of race, religion and politics. You would think the logic of such a thing would convince most people. But it doesn't; which only proves how very difficult it is for people to separate what they believe from what they know.

I've lost many friends over the years because of what they construe as my criticism of religion. But these friends have yet to offer any legitimate basis for their complaints against me. Their own unwillingness to sacrifice their beliefs to the facts and logic make my point of the very divisiveness of religious beliefs.

If God is to be truly loved and honored, truly worshiped, can this be done at the same time you are willing to hate those who don't agree with your beliefs? I don't think so. And if we are indeed the children of God, should the members of the family hate and separate from one another on the basis of beliefs rather than the basis of facts? Shouldn't we rather grow up and be the responsible and sensible adults, living together in harmony, as God must surely have intended? The question should be a rhetorical one. But ignorance and prejudice raise their ugly heads and do the job they have been doing since the dawn of the human race proving that we have never attained to wisdom. And while logic dictates that as long as racial, religious and political hatreds exist the world can never know peace, are you yourself willing to examine your own beliefs in the face of this logic?

In my paper for the Bodfish Philosophical Society in this issue of TAP I bring up the question of the use of the Hebrew words for God and Man in the first chapters of Genesis. But doing so, I know will alienate people who are willing to cling to their prejudices in spite of the facts. Still it remains for those of us who know better to do better. Even at the risk of alienating friends and loved ones.

And it was this willingness to cling to my own prejudices, more than anything else, that prevented me for many years from confronting them. People who genuinely loved me, including people like Uncle Charles had taught me these prejudices. It was almost like I was betraying these loving people who certainly intended me no harm by teaching me things that were contrary even to fact and reason.

Yet in retrospect I now realize that I sometimes served the purpose of evil while believing I was serving God. And so it goes with a great many good people who follow in this same pathway of error. I am well experienced in how blind to facts and reason prejudice can make us as human beings. Even knowing as I did the legitimate arguments against such prejudices that those who loved me had taught me, I followed such a blind path for years.

But having finally confronted my own blind prejudices, I know the difficulties in doing so. And had not children become the focus of my life, I would still be following in the footsteps of the same blind and unquestioning prejudices that ruled in my life for so many years. So it is that I have become convinced that only by making God's priority of the children our priority devoid of any racial, religious or political ideologies will we have any future as a species.

Another area of confrontation with prejudice involves homosexuality. I make the point that perversion has never been the proud monument of any nation. And if the homosexual lobby is successful with the aid of the universities and Hollywood in promoting perversion, it cannot but have a detrimental effect on children. That is a fact.

But like pointing to the high incidence of molestation in welfare communities and this being the cause of the early puberty of the children in such communities which are disproportionately Negro, I am not thanked for dealing with the facts. Certainly men like Jesse Jackson and Alan Keyes do not want to deal with these facts and neither does the CDC. As a result of dealing with facts, I am often accused of being homophobic and racist. But calling me names won't change the facts. And neither will calling me names because I stomp on some toes in my pursuit of truth and present facts that get in the way of religious prejudices.

I will never forget a professor of Biology I had in college who told me with tears in his eyes that he wished he had never learned facts that got in the way of his religious beliefs. But he was honest enough to let the facts, not his beliefs and emotions, rule in his life. Overcoming our prejudices is not an easy task. And people don't always line up to congratulate us for doing so.

But I ask for the umpteenth time, is God so hampered that He cannot speak for Himself; that He needs the religious inventions of men and women to do His talking for Him? I think not. But when will reasonable voices be raised in His behalf devoid of religious bigotries and hatreds? Not as long as that good Catholic, Protestant, Jew, Hindu or Moslem continues to believe and teach that he or she is right and all others wrong. And especially wrong to the point of attempting to justify what God would clearly be against: Bigotry and hatreds in His name!

***

Elmer Gantry isn't required reading in the schools. But it should be. I have known all the characters in the novel; I was raised among such people. So when those ugly men take the fellow out and horsewhip him to the glory and honor of God, I know very well the thinking of such people; even as I understand the thinking of those God-fearing, Bible-believing, Jesus-loving people in that mob who were going to lynch Tom Robinson in Harper Lee's novel.

Those men who whip this other man nearly to death for the honor of God and Jesus are quite sincere when they tell him: "By God, we may not be very good Christians but we aren't going to let some blasphemer go around lying and disrespecting the Bible!"

You see, the most despicable and low-down kind of people can commit virtual atrocities in the name of God and Jesus, in the names of Yahweh, Muhammad and Buddha, and justify themselves by saying it is all done for the glory of God. We may not be very good Christians but we're willing to horsewhip you to death if you don't see things our way! There will never be that bloodless revolution leading to world peace, the dream of Emerson, Thoreau, even Napoleon, as long as such lies hold sway in the minds of people in the name of God!

***

I have to ask - If God could not help by leading someone to save those little girls, Melissa and Julie in Belgium, honesty demands we examine this. If God could not save those little girls because it is our responsibility to confront and overcome evil, not that of God, then how shall we proceed?

Ideas. Perhaps God can give us ideas. This is how, I believe, the idea of the amendment as a place to start in the process of overcoming evil came to me. And the idea of the equation k+w=p, and that women must be accepted as of equal value to men before we will ever attain to wisdom and peace in the world.

As to ideas for example, I can suggest things and put these things in the minds of others. But it remains for others to act or not to act on these suggestions or ideas. People choose what they want to believe; they make choices concerning their actions or inactions on what they choose to believe. By the use of propaganda, Hitler said he could make people believe white was black and black was white. To the greater extent, he was correct.

I have my best conversations with God as I lie in bed at night hoping I will be able to sleep. Sleep has been a very big problem for me the past few years since the nightmares started and I undertook the work for the amendment. So I escape to God and talk to Him. There is much to commend this to me; and so the ideas continue to come to me, whether of God or not.

***

I don't think there is anything of courage in being compelled to explore, of being endowed with a pioneer instinct that draws one into uncharted territory. But few are compelled in this fashion. And it is not a criticism of those who are not. While I have always had an affinity for wilderness places, it was the frontier of the mind that drew me like the moth to the flame. I knew that this kind of exploration could lead to exploring the stars.

The great theologian Aquinas admitted three months before he died that all he had done was nothing but straw. Aquinas was not a pioneer; he was not an explorer. He stayed on the dead end path trampled and beaten to rubble by countless millions of hopeless shuffling feet throughout history, that path of religious dualism that attempts to excuse God for evil while at the same time making Him responsible for everything; an impossibility which leads, invariably, to intellectual schizophrenia, hypocrisy, and even intellectual prostitution.

I am an avid student of philosophy among other things. I came to realize that a problem of thousands of years' duration, the historical problem of hatred, prejudice, warfare and violence of every description, must remain intractable only if another way has been missed. So I veered off the historical, dead-end pathway and entered into an entirely new world of exploration, the frontier of the mind, dedicating myself to the ideal of philosophy which is a seeking for truth no matter where it should lead me. Now many have claimed to do this. But their proclaimed discoveries have never led the world out of conflict and into peace. So, one has to ask as I did of myself: What's wrong with this picture?

Melville may have missed the mark by as wide a margin as Aquinas but at least he was honest enough to credit room for originality, he could admit that there was the possibility of something new under the sun though he never discovered it himself. But neither Aquinas nor Melville discovered the secret of humankind needing to accept the responsibility of confronting and overcoming evil rather than believing it was God's responsibility. And neither could see the necessity of accepting women as of equal value to men. Small wonder to me that Aquinas died knowing he had missed the mark.

So this new way by the frontier of the mind, the ultimate *terra incognito*, suggested itself to me, a frontier which once penetrated would open the way to entirely new worlds and the stars themselves, this new way by making children the priority of the human race and thereby prepare humankind to reach the stars.

It is a popular misconception that the poet involves himself with matters far removed from reality, in ethereal ideas and gauzy scenes. Nothing could be further from the truth for a real poet knows both the diabolical and the divine and can separate them based on actual experience. Far from being some kind of wimp, the real poet is the toughest individual, man or woman, you will ever come up against. And should he turn his gift toward the glory of evil, you have the consummate con artist who actually believes in his own righteousness. And for the best success, the con is made with humor since the best of humor does indeed have a moral basis.

I have to confess in all due modesty that there has been a rare few humorists of my stature, those like Sam Clemens, Charles Schultz, Bill Watterson, Stalin, and the Marquis de Sade. All the while heeding the maxim: Laugh, and the world wonders what you are up to?

It is for this reason that I occasionally venture into humor in all humility, and in spite of my shy, retiring, and afraid of women personality and ways, I pull myself up to my full just a fraction of an inch short of six feet, manfully square my shoulders and reach out with both hands and seize Life by the throat.

Suffering the flu, my fevered mind refused to quit and let me rest so I decided to give way to the delirium under which I often find inspiration for some of my finest work. Faulkner had his laudanum, I get the flu. It was to blame for the realization that men had it right. Why can't a woman be more like a man?

In My Fair Lady you have the ultimate distillation of wisdom in Professor Henry Higgins' soliloquy set to music as he presents this philosophy of the purest genius, in phrases more precious than the fabled rhinestones of Kohinoor:

Why can't a woman be more like a man?

Women are irrational, that's all there is to that
Men are so honest, so thoroughly square
Historically noble, historically fair
When you win, he'll always give your back a pat
Why can't a woman be like that?
Men are so pleasant, so easy to please
Whenever you're with them, you're always at ease
Instead of growing up to be like their mothers,
why don't women become like their fathers instead?
Why can't a woman learn to use her head?
Why is thinking something women never do?
Why is logic never even tried?
Fixing up their hair is all they ever do
Why don't they straighten up the mess that's inside?
Men are so friendly, good natured and kind,
why a better companion, you never will find
Men are so decent, such regular chaps
There to help you through any mishaps
To buck you up when you're feeling so glum
Why can't a woman be a chum?
Why one man in a million may shout a bit
One in a thousand you may distrust a bit
But by and large, we are a marvelous sex.

Now, to the reality; Eliza will prove the equal of Higgins. And he finally accepts that. But the wounded male still cries out Mother! Mother! when Eliza leaves. Now they are equal in value to each other. And each needs the other. Higgins is haunted as he returns to his now sterile environment, an environment turned sterile by Eliza's absence. He has Become Accustomed to Her Face. She almost makes the day begin. I'm so grateful she's a woman and so easy to forget, almost like a habit one can always break ... and yet? Accustomed to her face.

Ah, this is an entirely different thing than the kind of equality Higgins had accorded Eliza just a short time previously. Now he faces the real value of Eliza as an equality of value, something he had never bargained for; as the woman without the man is not a total person, so the man without the woman. And though it may be argued successfully and with full justification that not all women need a man and not all men need a woman, what would the world be without the love between a man and a woman? And what would the world be when that love is born and nourished by each being truly accepted of equal value to the other?

***

Returning to that favorite topic of mine, the frontier of the mind, I have written a great deal about the hope of particle physics explaining much of what is presently thought of as supernatural or Psi, the paranormal. Particle research studies have given us a view of how things like precognition, prescience, telekinesis, and other like phenomena may actually work.

That *Sea of Consciousness* that people like Doyle and Edison and so many poets have written of may actually exist. *The Universal Lyre* of poetry and philosophy may indeed have a basis in fact. Particle research is the basis of understanding brain function and the possibility of computers that will emulate brain function. Particle physics is the basis of all genetic engineering and the basis of solving the physical problems confronting us in space exploration.

It seems we are born with a sense of immortality. When we look to the stars there it is, a seemingly universal truth of our immortality, of our being created and born to inherit and reach the stars, born with a desire to claim our inheritance of the stars.

But I continue to emphasize the need of wisdom before it will be possible for us to claim our inheritance. The choice comes down to, it would certainly seem, our mutually assured destruction as a species, or coming together on the basis of the amendment and prioritizing children as the future of the human race and acting accordingly.

As I explain to people: the amendment is not the answer, it is the first logical step to the answer. Once it becomes the law of the land, other things begin to fall into place.

Not the least of these things is proving to our children that we are not indifferent to them, an indifference which has led to children killing children, which is a direct accusation against Americans that we do not, as a society, give children the priority they must become for any hope of a future as a nation. Like little Dill in TKM, as a society we have bought our children the toys and then with the most utterly selfish of motives told them: "Now, go play with the toys and leave us alone!"

By directly addressing the problem of this indifference through the amendment at the most fundamental level of all human rights, the right of a child to a lawfully protected innocent childhood, we will have taken that first all-important step toward an answer, and a future, for the human race.

I am often asked about the status of the amendment. As most of you know, every governor, every U.S. Senator and many Representatives, the President and many influential media and Hollywood personalities know of the amendment.

The replies I have received over the past three years have been most revealing of the thoughts of these influential people. Many are waiting, for good reason, to see where the amendment is going before they commit themselves. And I understand the realities of this wait and see attitude.

These people depend on my never betraying their trust; they depend on my respecting their understandable need of confidentially. And while there are many times I would like to tell all of you that this or that national or international figure supports the amendment, I know you will understand why I will not do it. But these people will step forward to be counted when that flash point of history will ignite the fuse of the bomb of the amendment; just as Uncle Tom's Cabin did in causing the Civil War.

So, be patient. Remember that while I live with the constant nightmare of children being tortured and murdered because the amendment is not yet the law of the land, I am also fully aware of what the amendment demands of society. And it is not a demand to be taken lightly. The amendment is of such profound complexity legally and sociologically, something never before done by any nation in history, the very fact of this is not lost on these powerful and influential figures that know of it. Nor is it lost on me. I struggle with it daily and nightly just as I do with the nightmares.

About the Author

Samuel D. G. Heath, Ph. D.

Other books in print by the author:

BIRDS WITH BROKEN WINGS
DONNIE AND JEAN, an angel's story
TO KILL A MOCKINGBIRD, a critique on behalf of children
HEY, GOD! What went wrong and when are You going to fix it?
THE AMERICAN POET WEEDPATCH GAZETTE for 2008
THE AMERICAN POET WEEDPATCH GAZETTE for 2007
THE AMERICAN POET WEEDPATCH GAZETTE for 2006
THE AMERICAN POET WEEDPATCH GAZETTE for 2005
THE AMERICAN POET WEEDPATCH GAZETTE for 2004
THE AMERICAN POET WEEDPATCH GAZETTE for 2003
THE AMERICAN POET WEEDPATCH GAZETTE for 2002
THE AMERICAN POET WEEDPATCH GAZETTE for 2001
THE AMERICAN POET WEEDPATCH GAZETTE for 2000

Presently out of print:
IT SHOULDN'T HURT TO BE A CHILD!
WOMEN, BACHELORS, IGUANA RANCHING, AND RELIGION
THE MISSING HALF OF HUMANKIND: WOMEN!
THE MISSING HALF OF PHILOSOPHY: WOMEN!
THE LORD AND THE WEEDPATCHER
CONFESSIONS AND REFLECTIONS OF AN OKIE INTELLECTUAL
or Where the heck is Weedpatch?
MORE CONFESSIONS AND REFLECTIONS OF AN OKIE
INTELLECTUAL

Dr. Heath was born in Weedpatch, California. He has worked as a manual laborer, mechanic, machinist, peace officer, engineer, pastor, builder and developer, educator, social services practitioner (CPS), professional musician and singer. He is also a private pilot and a columnist.
Awarded American Legion Scholarship and is an award winning author.

He has two surviving children: Daniel and Michael. His daughters Diana and Karen have passed away.

Academic Degrees:
Ph. D. – U.S.I.U., San Diego, CA.
M. A. – Chapman University, Orange, CA.
M. S. (Eqv.) — U.C. Extension at UCLA. Los Angeles, CA.
B. V. E. – C.S. University. Long Beach, CA.
A. A. – Cerritos College. Cerritos, CA.

Other Colleges and Universities attended:
Santa Monica Technical College, Biola University, and C.S. University, Northridge.

Dr. Heath holds life credentials in the following areas:
Psychology, Professional Education, Library Science, English, German, History, Administration (K-12), Administration and Supervision of Vocational Education and Vocational Education-Trade and Industry.

In addition to his work in public education, Dr. Heath started three private schools, K-12, two in California and one in Colorado. His teaching and administrative experience covers every grade level and graduate school.

Comments by some who have read the author's works

Your writing is very important. You are having an impact on lives! Never lose your precious gift of humor. V. T.

You raise a number of issues in your material ... The Church has languished at times under leaders whose theology was more historically systematic than Biblical ... (But) The questions you raise serve as very dangerous doctrines.
John MacArthur, a contemporary of the author at Biola/Talbot and pastor of Grace Community Church in Sun Valley.

You have my eternal gratitude for relieving me from the tyranny of religion. D. R.

Before reading your wonderful writings, I had given up hope. Now I believe and anticipate that just maybe things can change for the better. J. D.

I started reading your book, The Lord and the Weedpatcher, and found I couldn't put it down. Uproariously funny, I laughed the whole way through. Thank you so much for lighting up my life! M.G.

Doctor Heath, every man with daughters owes you a debt of gratitude! I have had all three of my girls read your Birds With Broken Wings book. D. W.

I am truly moved by your art! While reading your writing I found a true treasure: Clarity! I felt as if I was truly on fire with the inspiration you invoked! L. B.

You really love women! Thank you for the most precious gift of all, the gift of love. Keep on being you! D. B.

Your writing complements coffee-cup-and-music. I've gotten a sense of your values, as well as a provocativeness that suggests a man both distinguished and truly sensual. Do keep up such vibrant work! E. R.

Some men are merely handsome. You are a beautiful man! One of these days some wise, discerning, smart woman is going to snag you. Make sure she is truly worthy of you. Desirable men like you (very rare indeed) who write so sensitively, compellingly and beautifully are sitting ducks for every designing woman! M. G.

Now, poet, musician, teacher, philosopher, friend, counselor and whatever else you have done in your life, I am finally realizing all the things you say people don't understand about a poet. They see, feel, write and talk differently than the rest of the world. Their glasses seem to be rose colored at times and other times they are blue. There seems to be no black or white in the things they see only soft pastel hues. Others see things as darker colors, but these are not the romantic poets you speak of. C. M.

You are the only man I have ever met who truly understands women! B. J.

Dr. Heath;
You are one of the best writers I've had the privilege to run across. You have been specially gifted for putting your thoughts, ideas, and inspirations to paper (or keyboard), no matter the topic.
Even when in dire straits, your words are strong and true. I look forward to reading many more of your unique writings. T. S.